wrangling with senators as fascinating as his river expeditions. . . . If you've ever used a topographic map, thank Powell. His legacy deserves more attention, and Ross's biography stands to correct this."
                                    —*Library Journal* (starred review)

"Ross makes vivid Powell's adventures, drawing on journals and contemporary accounts, even capturing the drama of vicious battles among scientists vying for federal funds, including Powell's clashes with senators and bureaucrats, in this fascinating portrait."   —*Booklist*

"This enthralling tale by adventure writer Ross focuses on the life of John Wesley Powell, an explorer, geologist, and early proponent of environmental sustainability. . . . Ross displays a flair for adventure writing as he recounts Powell's service with the Union Army during the Civil War (which cost him half an arm) and subsequent work on geological surveys of the West, and he renders Powell's 1869 expedition of the Colorado River and the Grand Canyon in breathtaking detail. . . . Ross demonstrates a facility for both human history and natural history, clearly showing why Powell's ideas matter today." —*Publishers Weekly*

"John Wesley Powell was not just a great explorer—he was the great prophet of the arid West whose vision is now coming true in a dusty era of drought and wildfire. This book reminds us to pay attention to savvy people, not to our preferred dreams and delusions—in that sense it couldn't be more timely."   —Bill McKibben, author of *The End of Nature*

"Powell was famous in his day as the first Anglo explorer to travel the length of the Colorado River. . . . His voyages down that wild watercourse are the stuff of legend. . . . Ross's view through the lens of the unfolding [climate change] crisis lends Powell and his arguments new relevance."   —*Kirkus Reviews*

"A long overdue look at the meaning of the American West and the critical environmental partnership between land and people. John Ross has enriched our understanding of Powell's explorations and our turbulent legacy to protect what remains."
                —Linda Lear, author of *Rachel Carson: Witness for Nature*

"John Ross offers a stunning re-creation of John Wesley Powell's heroic journey down the Colorado River. It's an epic adventure that forever transformed the American West."
                —Douglas Brinkley, author of *The Wilderness Warrior*

PENGUIN BOOKS

THE PROMISE OF THE GRAND CANYON

John F. Ross is a historian, writer, and a former editor of *American Heritage* and *Smithsonian* magazines. His two most recent books are *Enduring Courage: Ace Pilot Eddie Rickenbacker and the Dawn of the Age of Speed* and *War on the Run: The Epic Story of Robert Rogers and the Conquest of America's First Frontier*, which won the Fort Ticonderoga Award for Contributions to American History.

THE PROMISE OF THE
GRAND CANYON

John Wesley Powell's Perilous Journey
and His Vision for the American West

JOHN F. ROSS

PENGUIN BOOKS

PENGUIN BOOKS
An imprint of Penguin Random House LLC
penguinrandomhouse.com

First published in the United States of America by Viking,
an imprint of Penguin Random House LLC, 2018
Published in Penguin Books 2019

ISBN 9780525429876 (hardcover)
ISBN 9780143128953 (paperback)
ISBN 9780698409989 (ebook)

Printed in the United States of America

Map illustrations by Jeffrey L. Ward

Set in New Century Schoolbook LT Pro
Designed by Nancy Resnick

To Timothy Dickinson

Contents

Acknowledgments

No single experience put me closer to John Wesley Powell than a raft and dory trip down the Colorado River through the Grand Canyon. I'm indebted to the Arizona Raft Adventure river guides, who did so much more than conduct my family and me safely down the river. Second-generation river guide Bruce Quayle not only shared his stories of the river in 1983, meeting Ed Abbey, and how to negotiate immense standing waves, but also read from his father Amil's cowboy poetry. "Tater, the Invincible Dachshund" tells the hilarious, but trenchant life of a dog that gets half eaten by coyotes, run over by a Datsun pickup, chewed up by German shepherds, and stolen by Mexican bandits, yet still manages to survive and does so cheerfully. Could be a parable for writing books, if not living one's life. Thank you to trip leader Derik Spice, and guides Aaron Cavagnolo, Larry Vermeern, Phil Sgamma, and Natalie Zollinger for sharing their personal journeys, insights about life on the river, and theories about Powell's 1869 river expedition. And a warm thanks to Ann Crittenden for setting up the trip. Experiencing the Grand Canyon, especially on the river itself, is a gift—and the guides are the purveyors of the stories that keep alive the history of the Grand Canyon and its great river, tales of fortitude and exploration, of geology and the extraordinary richness of Native American cultures, of the Kolb brothers, and the eccentricities of Georgie White. Thanks to all my paddling buddies with whom I've shared enjoyable river time in the Canadian Arctic and Siberia, on the Yak, the Potomac, and Kennebec.

One of the great joys of writing a book is engaging with passionate scholars and independent historians. The topic of John Wesley Powell has spawned a particularly robust—and opinionated!—group. Among them are the inveterate river rats who have meticulously traced Powell's river trips and seize every opportunity they can to grab a paddle and get wet, the geologists who have examined the rock strata along the Green and Colorado, the boat builders who have re-created Powell's rowboats from scratch, and the historians who have spent years digging for clues and theorizing about Powell and the expedition members on that famous trip just about 150 years ago. This book draws on their work and taps into their passion for history and discovery. I thank Wayne Ranney, Richard Quarteroli, Brad Dimock, Earle Spammer, and Michael Ghiglieri for generously sharing their insights. Don Lago, who has done quality work sleuthing Powell's documents that relate to the 1869 river trip and has offered multiple fascinating theories, never failed to respond thoughtfully to my myriad questions. I would particularly like to thank Ray Sumner, a descendent of Jack Sumner, who opened up so many new doors for me with his assiduous research and penetrating questions. His enthusiasm reminds me of why I write history.

This book would not have been possible without the fine work of dozens upon dozens of archivists, librarians, and historians, only a few of them that I can personally thank here. They include Lizeth Zepeda, the Arizona Historical Society; Stephen J. Pyne, Arizona State University; Scott House, Cape Girardeau, MO; John F. Underwood, Christ United Methodist Church, Jackson, OH; Sarah Gilmor, Stephen H. Hart Library & Research Center, History Colorado; Kevin Cummings and Jeremy Tiemann, Illinois Natural History Survey; April Karlene Anderson, Dr. Jo Ann Rayfield Archives, Illinois State University; Meg Miner and Tony Heaton, the Ames Library, Illinois Wesleyan University; Mike Stroth, Jackson (OH) Historical Society; Cynthia Nelson, Kenosha

History Center; William Kemp, McLean County (Illinois) Museum of History; Louisa Hoffman, Oberlin College Archives; Scott Tutti Jackson, Ohio History Connection; Carol Holliger, Archives of Ohio United Methodism, Ohio Wesleyan University; Heather Henson, Shiloh National Military Park; Marc Rothenberg and Kathy Dorman, The Joseph Henry Papers, Smithsonian; Tad Bennicoff, Mary Markey, Heidi Stover, Smithsonian Institution Archives; William Fitzhugh, Senior Scientist, National Museum of Natural History; Art Molella, Lemelson Center for the Study of Invention and Innovation, Smithsonian; Mark Shenise, General Commission on Archives and History, the United Methodist Church; Gregory M. Walz, Research Center of the Utah State Archives & Utah State History; David Slay, Vicksburg National Military Park; Ann Wake, The Wake Kendall Group; Lee Grady, Wisconsin Historical Society; Terry Hogg; and Justin Solonick.

I would also like to thank the descendants of Emma Powell, William and Wendy Krag, who generously shared their portrait of Emma with me. Thanks to the always engaging members of the Literary Society of Washington, which Powell himself once belonged to, who were always ready to challenge me and support this project. And thanks to the history committee of the Cosmos Club for their committed effort to celebrate Powell's work and encourage mine.

I extend my deep thanks and appreciation for those who read all or parts of my manuscript: Sam Holt, Joseph Meany, Albert J. Beveridge III, Donald Ritchey, Kirk Johnson, Richard Quarteroli, Wayne Ranney, and Peter Cozzens. A special thanks goes to my researcher, the incomparable Marcia Thomas, who steered me through the maze of Powell's primary material and historiography with particular deftness. Her ability to wrest obscure documents from institutions was exceeded only by her sage guidance when my interpretations veered too close to the edge. Her good cheer was always a tonic. Any mistakes I've made, of course, are all mine.

I extend my deep gratitude to Timothy Dickinson, to whom this book is dedicated. Our frequent spirited conversations and debates at the Lisner-Louise-Dickson-Hurt Home in Friendship Heights, Washington, D.C., resulted in an abundance of important insights about Powell and his times. Over the years, no one has taught me more about the beauty and the extraordinary precision of the English language. I am deeply honored to call him my friend.

To my editor at Viking, Wendy Wolf, I take a deep bow. Her enthusiasm about this project, her excellent editing, rapier wit, and sound judgment, made this a far better book—and a more enjoyable experience along the way. And the editorial suggestions made by her assistant editor Georgia Bodnar on the manuscript hit the mark. And thanks to Terezia Cicel, who has carefully and patiently guided the book process, designer Nancy Resnick, cartographer Jeffrey Ward, indexer Stephen Callahan, production editor Eric Wechter, managing editors Tricia Conley and Tess Espinoza, jacket designer Elizabeth Yaffe, and senior publicist Tony Forde.

Not enough can be said about my first-class agent, Stuart Krichevsky, whose counsel, sagacity, humor, and patience I have come to rely on. And thanks also to his assistants Laura Usselman, Aemilia Phillips, and Hannah Schwartz.

My friend Larry O'Reilly was always ready to share a laugh, listen to my new discoveries, and cheer me on when the mountain sometimes seemed too difficult to climb. Thanks as well to my fellow writer Daniel Stashower—our walks around Wyngate became a forum for hashing out writing issues. Thanks to Cindy Scudder for her spot-on design and picture advice and Adam Gibbons for his web savviness. Thanks to my friend, the author, painter, and photographer Scott Warren, who is more knowledgeable about hiking the American Southwest than anyone I know. Our hiking and backpacking trips have always been a source of inspiration. And thanks to Sari Ateek for just always being there.

A round of applause for my parents and brother, Jim, who are always a great source of support. And thanks to my son, Forrister, tossed off a boat in Granite Rapid by a giant wave, for the adventures we have shared that have provided such sustenance to me. And to my daughter, Grace, a literary fiction agent and kayaking buddy who was a frequent sounding board on matters of writing and whose enthusiasm for this project and my work was unflagging.

But above all, no thanks can adequately express my love and deep appreciation for my wife, Diana Ingraham, who has stood beside me through thick and thin, and whose counsel is 24-karat gold.

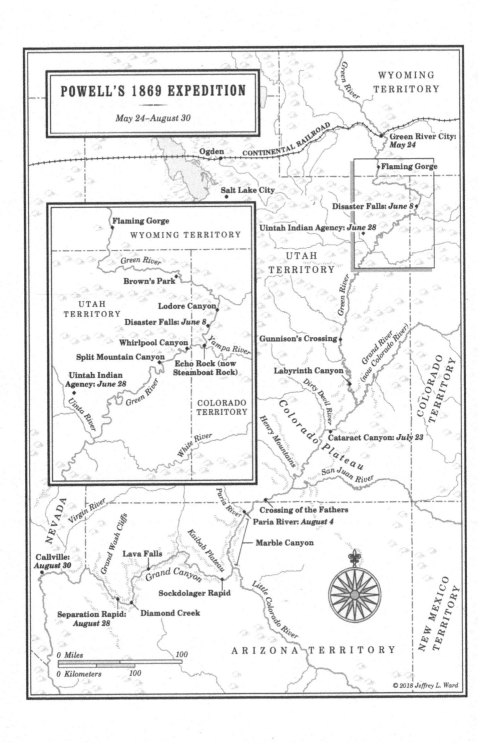

POWELL'S 1869 EXPEDITION

May 24–August 30

WYOMING TERRITORY

Green River

Green River City:
May 24

Ogden   CONTINENTAL RAILROAD

Flaming Gorge

Salt Lake City

Disaster Falls: June 8

Uintah Indian Agency: June 28

UTAH TERRITORY

Flaming Gorge
WYOMING TERRITORY

Green River

Brown's Park

Green River

Lodore Canyon

UTAH
TERRITORY

Disaster Falls: June 8

Whirlpool Canyon

Yampa River

Split Mountain Canyon

Echo Rock (now
Steamboat Rock)

Uintah Indian
Agency: June 28

Green River

Uinta River

COLORADO
TERRITORY

White River

Gunnison's Crossing

Labyrinth Canyon

Grand River (now Colorado River)

Dirty Devil River

COLORADO
TERRITORY

Cataract Canyon: July 23

Colorado Plateau

San Juan River

Henry Mountains

Crossing of the Fathers

Paria River: August 4

Paria River

Marble Canyon

Virgin River

Grand Wash Cliffs

Lava Falls

Kaibab Plateau

Grand Canyon

NEVADA

Callville:
August 30

Sockdolager Rapid

Little Colorado River

Separation Rapid:
August 28

Diamond Creek

ARIZONA   TERRITORY

NEW MEXICO
TERRITORY

0 Miles   100

0 Kilometers   100

© 2018 Jeffrey L. Ward

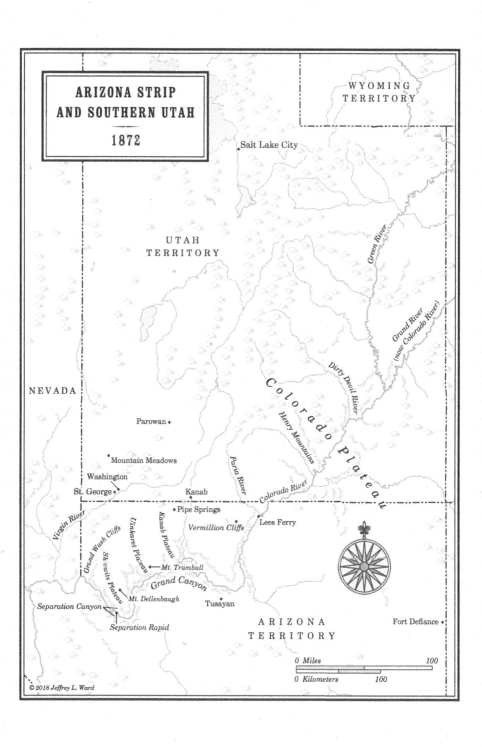

ARIZONA STRIP
AND SOUTHERN UTAH

1872

WYOMING
TERRITORY

Salt Lake City

UTAH
TERRITORY

Green River

*Grand River
(now Colorado River)*

Dirty Devil River

C o l o r a d o   P l a t e a u

NEVADA

Parowan ♦

Henry Mountains

Mountain Meadows

Washington
St. George ♦

Kanab

Paria River

Colorado River

Lees Ferry

♦ Pipe Springs

Vermillion Cliffs

Virgin River

Grand Wash Cliffs

Uinkaret Plateau

Kanab Plateau

Sh⁚wits Plateau

Mt. Trumbull

Grand Canyon

Separation Canyon

Mt. Dellenbaugh

Tusayan

ARIZONA
TERRITORY

Fort Defiance ♦

Separation Rapid

0 *Miles*   100

0 *Kilometers*   100

© 2018 Jeffrey L. Ward

Introduction

On January 17, 1890, John Wesley Powell strode into a Senate committee room in Washington to testify. He was hard to miss, one contemporary comparing him to a sturdy oak, gnarled and seamed from the blasts of many winters. Clear gray eyes stared out from a deeply lined face, mostly covered by a shaggy bird's nest of gray beard, flecked with cigar ash. No one would call the fifty-six-year-old veteran and explorer handsome, but one knew immediately when he entered a room. Only five feet six inches tall, he spoke rather slowly, but forcefully, with a fearless independence of mind. When he expressed himself emphatically, the stump of his right arm would bob and weave as if boxing with the ghosts of the war that had maimed him; every once in a while, Powell would reach around his back with his left hand and forcibly subdue it—a movement that invariably silenced a room. It was not often comfortable to watch him, but most always mesmerizing. The authority he radiated even in a room crowded with titanic personalities was palpable.

Only a few years after losing his forearm to a minié ball at the battle of Shiloh, he had organized the most daring exploration in American history. Ten men had climbed aboard puny wooden rowboats and pulled out into the Southwest's Green and Colorado rivers, then spent three months flying, crashing, and bounding through the terrible unknown cataracts of the canyonlands, and, finally, through the Grand Canyon itself, not knowing whether a falls or killing rapid lay around the next bend. Six men came out at the other end, barely alive, half naked, with only a few pounds of moldy flour between them. The experience had deeply changed Powell—and he had become a great American hero. Now, two decades later, Powell had come to testify not as a hero or explorer, but as one of America's foremost scientists, the head of the U.S. Geological Survey (USGS), and an architect of federal science. He had something deeply important to communicate about America's future.

The Senate Select Committee on Irrigation and Reclamation of Arid Lands was the gatekeeper of an issue pivotal to the development of the nation—through them the federal government could bring water to the western deserts and thus open great new lands to new generations of pioneers. The committee was composed mostly of senators from western states devoted to fulfilling their constituents' dreams of a home and ever-increasing affluence. They wanted to hear from Powell—arguably the most comprehensively knowledgeable person about those still-little-understood western lands. They craved to hear that irrigation works would bring an Eden to the West, vouchsafing the vision of Manifest Destiny—the divinely conferred right of Americans to push across the continent with wealth and industry bringing to blossom whatever they touched. But Powell would not tell them what they wanted to hear. He told them all too rightly that the West offered not enough water to reclaim by irrigation more than a tiny fraction of its land. Their dreams of a verdant West needed to be tempered and shaped to reality. Powell might as well have told them the Earth was flat. The senators were outraged.

He had brought a map to explain—one of the profoundest such documents ever created in American history. The "Arid Region of the United States" features the western half of the United States, the territory carved up in a jigsaw-puzzle riot of color. Shapes of various sizes, some half the size of states, are colored in oranges, greens, blues, reds, yellows, and pinks. It's a visually stunning, beautiful map. At first glance, one is captivated purely by its aesthetic. But the power of a well-designed map—as this one certainly is—comes from the powerful perspective it imparts, the intersection of geography and imagination: Contained within such maps lie entire worldviews, reams of fact, conclusions, and assumptions, which can often persuade its viewers into confronting new, sometimes revolutionary, ways of taking in the world.

Powell's map, assembled under his direction by USGS cartographers, revealed the western half of America separated into watersheds, the natural land basins through which water flows. Each patch represents a watershed—a hydrographic basin—wherein all entering raindrops or snowflakes drain into a common outlet. Where a raindrop fell, on one side of a mountain ridgeline or the other, for instance, the two points separated only by a matter of inches, would determine which stream or creek it fell into to be raced into larger rivers and finally into the sea. Drops hitting one edge of the Continental Divide, which runs along the crest of the Rockies, eventually reach the Pacific, while drops on the other edge will flow into the Atlantic or Arctic oceans.

This marked the first time that a map had been used to visualize a complex intersection of geographical factors—integrating water and land into a nuanced understanding of the Earth's surface. It was the Earth's first ecological map, building on, but pushing far beyond, Alexander von Humboldt's efforts earlier that century. Previous maps had mostly defined the nation by political boundaries or topographic features. Powell's map forces the viewer to imagine the West as defined by water and its natural movement. For its time, Powell's map was as stunning as NASA's photographs of Earth from space in the 1960s. The orderly drawing of Jeffersonian grids and political lines—Powell implicitly argued through this map—did not apply in the West; other, more complicated, natural phenomena were at play and must be taken very seriously.

Powell would use this map to unfold an argument that America should move cautiously as it plumbed its natural resources and developed the land—and to introduce the idea of sustainability and stewardship of the Earth. In that Senate room, the immensely powerful William Stewart from Nevada listened to Powell, and the more he heard, the more it grated against everything he stood for. In that gilded age, riches were there for the taking, enshrined as a divine promise to America. Powell would proffer a wholly new outlook by claiming that Americans needed to listen not only to their hearts, pocketbooks, and deep aspirations, but to what the land itself and the climate would tell them.

Stewart and Powell would lock into a titanic struggle over the very soul of America—the future of the American West and the shape of the nation's democracy. America's story had always closely aligned with that of Exodus—the tale of a people who left behind an oppressive Old World to enter a wilderness and ultimately build a divinely inspired, promised land. How would that promise look? Powell singlehandedly tried to change the American narrative.

This is the story of the most practical of American visionaries who arose in the vast midlands of a brand-new continent—at least from the perspective of its European newcomers—and was forged by the vise of a bitter dispute over slavery, then given new edges honed in the American West. From the perils of these experiences, his imagination enlarged and primed, he would launch a new vision for America, a bold challenge to the status quo. It is a particularly national story that profoundly shapes the country to this day.

This one-armed scientist-explorer threw down a gauntlet that remains essential and important for the time we live in. Not only for the drought and water shortage now afflicting the West, but for the larger world of climate change. While cautionary, it also offers a clear way forward.

CHAPTER 1

Into the Cauldron

I n 1838, four-year-old Wes rode next to his father, Joseph Powell, on the last leg of their journey south to Jackson from Chillicothe, their horse-drawn cart rolling easily down the unusually wide dirt road that wound through the rugged Appalachian foothills of southeastern Ohio. They may have felt like pioneers, but that same hard-beaten path had carried multifarious travelers since the last Ice Age, all drawn by the region's salt licks—the deposits of natural saltwater springs—so thick as to permanently frost the banks of local creeks.

First had come the mastodons and shaggy mammoths of the Pleistocene, later followed by herds of bison—and then the first human beings to leave a mark on the land, the mysterious mound-building peoples of a mere two millennia before. In historic times, the Shawnee had padded silently on moccasined feet, and just three decades earlier, the first European settlers had crossed the Appalachians to settle. Six age-old "salt roads" converged like the spokes of a wagon wheel upon what had only very recently become the town of Jackson.

The Powells' cart pulled up the steep escarpment to the rutted main street of Jackson, which crested the fifty-foot ridgeline, commanding views of a rugged hilly land harrowed by ridges, deep ravines, and creeks. Mean-looking wooden houses did duty for the town's main street, every bit as tough as its namesake, Andrew Jackson, Indian killer and hard-handed populist president. Eden it was not, but elements of civilization had reached there, most notably Presbyterian, Methodist, and Baptist churches. Jackson also boasted a post office, hotel, and six shops, including Mrs. Sylvester's, which sold ginger cakes. The town hall faced French's Tavern, Jackson's most thriving establishment.

The thirty-four-year-old Methodist preacher had brought his young family here from western New York State at the suggestion of a fellow Welsh minister. They had agreed that too few souls were left to save in the New York panhandle, a region roiled by evangelical Christian revivals. The Reverend Benjamin Chidlaw knew of several largely Welsh communities that thrived twenty miles outside Jackson, whose men worked blast furnaces that turned rich local veins of iron ore into pig iron, which the burgeoning railroads were already consuming in great quantities. Childlaw figured that these devout Calvinistic Methodists might profit from some ministering. That was all Joseph had needed to uproot his wife, Mary, two daughters, and Wes, to journey some five hundred miles southwest.

Joseph likely did not know that his destination lay in a veritable war zone. Only fifty miles separated Jackson from the Ohio River, which divided the free state of Ohio from slaveholding Kentucky. The lands bordering this "magic line"—as Harriet Tubman famously called it—rippled and bucked in disorder as southern bounty hunters pursued slaves escaping northward, often clashing with those who did not recognize human beings as chattel. In Ohio particularly, an outspoken breed of take-no-prisoners abolitionism had arisen, met with equally strident resistance from a merchant class desperate to preserve commerce with the cotton-rich South. And a hundred and twenty miles west of Jackson, in Cincinnati, the harrowing story of a mother's winter passage over the frozen Ohio to freedom, clutching her baby to her breast, would inspire Harriet Beecher Stowe to write the antislavery polemic

Uncle Tom's Cabin, which next to the Bible would become the most-read book of the nineteenth century and hasten the nation toward terrible civil war.

Joseph's immersion in this fraught borderland would force him down an unanticipated path. Unlike the vast majority of evangelical Methodists, most of whom condoned slavery—either owning slaves themselves or trusting in the Peculiar Institution to fade in time—Joseph would find that his faith called upon him to reject human bondage outright. He would become a radical, one among only a handful of white abolitionists making up a fringe movement whose members Ralph Waldo Emerson dismissed as "angry bigots." No one, certainly not the Sage of Concord, liked even the hint of getting their noses rubbed in the moral contradictions upon which the Founders had built the republic. Joseph's newly awakened beliefs would bring violence to his family's very door; his son would feel the repercussions of his father's radicalized passions most keenly. A flare of violence would imprint itself on the boy for life, shaping—more than any other experience over seven decades—how he would bring himself to face this treacherous world.

Joseph Powell's most symbolic act in America had come four years earlier as he held his newborn eldest surviving male child for the first time. Staring into the infant's blinking eyes, he named him John Wesley; not simply John or Wesley, but the full name of Methodism's great founder. The Welsh immigrant had first felt Methodism's powerful urgings in the Old World, but it would be in the New that they would fully flower. By so naming his son, Joseph had solemnly pledged the infant Wes to carry on the work of the Lord to which he himself had so ardently committed. Joseph would see to it that his son memorize the Gospels and shout out the hymns.

From an early age, Wes felt his father's expectations weigh

heavily upon his small shoulders. His father would leave for a month at a time to preach across the wilderness: Armed with a Bible, a volume of John Wesley's sermons, and a hymnbook without musical notations, Joseph would saddle up the family horse and ride forth on a twelve-stop circuit that would take him away for an eternity—or so it must have seemed to a family that ultimately swelled to eight children. Young Wes increasingly took on the duties of helping his siblings read their Bible lessons and sing their hymns. In these long absences his mother, Mary, tempered the rough edges of zeal that Joseph left behind, providing emotional support for her often-overburdened eldest son.

Wes had to grow up fast in a nation spreading ever faster before his feet and those of hundreds of thousands of other new Americans. No one had anticipated the speed with which the newly arrived Europeans, along with their enslaved Africans and West Indians, would settle the continent. Thomas Jefferson thought it might take a thousand years to reach the far Pacific, when in fact it took only a long lifetime. The frontier of 1800, running along the crest of the Appalachian Mountains, would jump beyond the Ohio Valley in just nine years, then surge across the length of the Mississippi by 1850. In 1890, the U.S. Census would declare the frontier gone.

In the first few decades of the nineteenth century, the flood of immigrants poured into the vast "trans-Appalachian" West—defined as the area west of the Appalachians, but east of the Mississippi—which contained more square miles than Great Britain, Germany, Italy, the Netherlands, and Belgium combined. They came from England, Germany, Switzerland, Scotland, Ireland, Belgium, France, Wales, the West Indies, and West Africa, borne by flatboat up the Ohio, on wagon or foot along ancient Indian trails, or later—like the Powells—upon the Erie Canal. Many of these newcomers could not speak English, and many were semiliterate at best; few had any idea what America—scarcely more than a name on the wind—offered aside from raw opportunity. This overwhelming tide brought about one of the most explosive population increases in history.

The center of American gravity—its politics, its institutional loyalties—was shifting inexorably west and south. With the federal government weak, as Andrew Jackson had willed it, at least by European standards, and no state religion to clarify doctrines of morality and conduct, the trans-Appalachian West lay in a ferment of new ideas and institutions. Evangelical Protestantism took hold tenaciously: Few other periods of sectarian growth in the history of Christianity rival its wildfire spread across America's heartland. Revivalist, evangelical Protestantism overshadowed the Anglican and Congregational traditions of the East Coast within a generation of the opening of the Erie Canal. New denominational energies, such as those of the Methodists, Baptists, and even entirely new churches—the Shakers, Disciples of Christ, Millerites—flourished, but none rose and spread so quickly as Methodism, which had outpaced all other American denominations by 1850.

Joseph lent his considerable energies to an inspired Methodist strategy to bring the Word to this huge moving frontier. He and some four thousand other circuit-riding preachers set out to reach remote settlements on horseback and foot. Often not even ordained, yet licensed to preach, many circuit riders came from among the ranks of artisans and shopkeepers who could support themselves and their families without depending on meager central church stipends. When not riding the appalling roads, Joseph worked long hours in the front room of their small house on Jackson's Main Street, stitching coats, shirts, and jackets late into the night by the flicker of a single candle. Better to wear out than to rust out, as the Founder liked to say.

In a land yet to see a national newspaper or electric telegraph, in which information traveled at the speed of a man on horseback and the post office was viewed with suspicion as an arm of intrusive government, the circuit riders stepped in as newsbearers and moral purveyors, arbiters of good manners and proper dress, the critical dispensers of knowledge and propriety to the young republic. For a generation or more, the cultural cohesion of trans-Appalachia was largely shaped and energized by the dedicated flock of exhausted, saddle-sore men pushing their horses from settlement to settlement. The peculiarly American figure of the itinerant preacher evoked the popular midwesterners' response to bad weather: "There's nothing out today but crows and Methodist preachers." The 1784 Book of Discipline, which laid down the principles and doctrine of the Church, contained words rewritten for an America suddenly embracing a continental vision: "To reform the continent, and to spread scriptural holiness over these lands." Methodism formed the bedrock of the American South's and Midwest's blend of apolitical anti-elitism and social conservatism.

The circuit rider depended on families to shelter and feed him. In return, he passed on news of his earlier stops—of who had died and who had been born, the by no means infrequent roster of appalling accidents or outbreaks of disease that haunted the frontier—sold the books he carried with him, both religious and secular, and handed out dated newspapers. The task routinely included passing on information not just about the next town, but about the rather ill-defined world at large, and how to live better in their own. Ordained or not, he might perform a marriage, funeral, or baptism. At midday, wherever he was, he would set up at a crossroads, perhaps, in front of a homestead, or quite frequently, in a mere field or barn—and set to preaching. Without notes, he would sermonize in homespun prose, Bible in hand, outlining how living John Wesley's "methodical" life meant forgoing cursing, drinking spirits, committing adultery, fornicating, and dressing provocatively or ostentatiously. "Cleanliness is next to godliness," he might tell them, citing one of Wesley's innumerable and often memorable axioms. Methodist preachers were advised themselves to "Beware of clownishness, [either in speech or dress. Wear no slouched hat.] *Be courteous to all*." He would lead them in a few hymns, perhaps "Amazing Grace" or "Come, Sinner, to the Gospel Feast."

The riders offered the men, women, and children of this New World the intoxicating chance to wipe away their sins right there and then on that patch of meadow, dusty road, or porch front—but only if they repented and took Jesus Christ as their personal savior. For a young republic of immigrants on the move, Joseph and his circuit-riding brethren brought nourishment that no bread or riches could provide, the chance to unload sins and embrace the opportunities of living a God-fearing, productive life in a land full of uncertainties. For Wes, the message rang clear that through self-discipline and constant industry, human beings could overcome evil and the challenges of a new land.

Joseph soon encountered firsthand the bizarre perversities of the slave order on his rounds. Should an enslaved person manage to cross the Ohio River, he or she entered a land that did not permit its citizens to hold slaves. Yet because these individuals were regarded as chattel, not human beings, bounty hunters and slave catchers could pursue them northward legally and forcibly retrieve such "property." In 1839, the year that Joseph built a Federal-style house on Main Street, the Ohio legislature passed a statewide fugitive slave law, eleven years before Congress would adopt a similarly severe piece of national legislation. The 1839 law compelled Ohio constabularies to retrieve escaped slaves, stipulating fines and jail sentences for those who facilitated the flight of the enslaved. Joseph would soon find himself forced to decide between obeying the laws of Ohio or those of his God. The Methodist founder had made his opinion clear: After a shocking visit to an eighteenth-century slave auction in Savannah, Georgia, the then Anglican cleric had written a treatise "On Slavery," which clearly voiced his moral and spiritual revulsion for the institution.

Joseph found a kindred spirit in George Crookham, a middle-aged man of Falstaffian proportions, a 350-pound "great hill of flesh" on whose 480-acre farm a few miles northwest of Jackson the Powells had camped when they first arrived in town. A polymath, "Big George" enjoyed wowing the locals by reading the newspaper upside down and out loud, performing complicated mathematical problems in his head, and identifying plants and birds brought before him—a veritable Samuel Johnson, noted one historian a century ago, "but a plant of the weeds and not of the town." Most notably, he had become Jackson's first open abolitionist. In the Powell kitchen, he shared news from abolitionist newspapers about the rash of violence as Kentucky slave catchers forced their way into Ohio homes and stole men and women, some of them even freedmen, and marched them south. Big George may have told Joseph about the Cincinnati Riots of 1836, during which a white mob had stormed the offices of James Birney, who published the antislavery *Cincinnati Weekly and Abolitionist*. The rabble had thrown Birney's printing press into the Ohio, butchered some African Americans, and burned some others from their homes. Ohio's fugitive law three years later had stemmed from the merchant class's determination to silence the few, but increasingly strident, voices of southern Ohio's abolitionists. The Methodist Church also hastened to quiet abolitionists within its own ranks lest their words ignite a wildfire. The Church's leadership forbade such antislavery crusaders from publishing in church journals, blocked their ordination, and quickly disciplined any who spoke out. The General Conference of 1836 even passed a comprehensive guide on how to curtail antislavery activity within the Church. Soon this would drive a schism into the ranks of American Methodism. But no pronouncements from the mainline Methodist leadership could dim Joseph's growing abhorrence for the corrupting institution of human bondage.

Ohio's prohibition of slavery did not mean that the majority of Jackson's townspeople even remotely believed that African Americans should be automatically endowed with the rights of Caucasians. The mostly Scots-Irish transplants from the Appalachian foothills of Virginia and Tennessee might well hold that chattel slavery had no place in a civilized society, but that did not mean that all races were created equal. Abolitionists aroused such harsh—and frequently violent—responses, not merely because they wanted to end slavery, but for their advocacy of a perspective that could soon enough give African American men the right to vote and represent themselves in court, perhaps even let them marry white women. That promised to overturn the hard established order of things in white America, a terrifying prospect for the Scots-Irish in Jackson.

To Joseph, and a growing number of evangelical Christians, the wickedness of human bondage demanded immediate eradication. A policy of waiting for slavery to die eventually smacked of cowardice. Through Big George, Joseph found a way to act on his beliefs. Jackson served as a stop on the Underground Railroad, the secret network of free blacks and committed whites who helped runaways move north, which had recently sprung to life in Ohio. Stations on the figuratively named "Railroad" offered food, a reasonably safe place to sleep, support, and directions or transport to the next station. Two Ohio River crossings funneled escaped fugitives through to Jackson's environs. Crookham had hidden black families on his farm and in the caves lining the banks of Salt Creek. Frequently mounting trips to study geology and collect plants and animals, Crookham traveled the countryside without raising suspicion—and could deliver the kind of information upon which the Railroad relied, such as news from Poke Patch, a black community to the south. His vocation also imposing frequent travel, Joseph was also well positioned to pass along information and warnings.

The biggest reason for Jackson's importance as a station lay in its proximity to Berlin X-Roads, a thriving black community then nearly as large as Jackson just six miles to its north, off the salt road. Standard histories of the region fail to mention Berlin X-Roads, and not a single physical trace of it exists today, the town having been razed during the Civil War. Yet when the Powells lived in Ohio, Berlin X-Roads cast a hard, oversized shadow on the residents of Jackson. Its very presence inflamed even further the tensions between Big George's and Joseph's abolitionism and the deep-rooted racism of almost all of the rest of Jackson's white residents.

Berlin X-Roads came into being in 1829 or 1830, when the former slave Thomas Woodson, who had bought his own and his family's freedom, purchased a two-hundred-acre homestead. He claimed to be the son of Thomas Jefferson and Sally Hemings. By the early 1840s, the community included 161 residents in two dozen families, most of them former slaves from Virginia. The poet Langston Hughes's grandfather Charles Henry Langston passed through the town, much of his family electing to remain.

Woodson and his wife alone owned 150 hogs, 400 head of cattle, and grew corn and wheat. Although the community paid public-school taxes, its children could not legally attend, and so it built a schoolhouse, which would predate Jackson's first dedicated school building. They also raised a church. The existence of such ongoing affluence and self-government in a black community directly challenged the brutal rationalization of Jackson's majority that black people were fundamentally inferior. Continued rumors of Woodson's assistance to escaped slaves added to the hostility that many of the townspeople must have felt toward Berlin X-Roads.

Big George almost certainly visited the outlying town and knew Woodson and his eldest sons, who had become prominent abolitionists in their own right. Crookham family lore maintains that Big George's son Jefferson drove carts full of concealed fugitives north, no doubt in concert with Woodson. It's likely that Joseph also made visits there, quite possibly with Wesley. Big George and Joseph may well have brought other abolitionists to Berlin X-Roads to visit the Woodsons. Tiny Jackson frequently hosted other white abolitionists, who sometimes stayed at the Powells'.

Among them included Charles Finney, an Oberlin professor who published the abolitionist *Oberlin Evangelist,* to which Joseph subscribed, and Salmon Chase, the future secretary of the treasury and chief justice, who would argue unsuccessfully against the constitutionality of fugitive slave laws before the Supreme Court in 1847. Joshua Giddings, who was censured by the House of Representatives for violating the rule against discussing slavery in 1842, also passed through. Young Wesley watched—and listened— as the most outspoken antislavery agitators visited his small town. He saw firsthand how these forceful thinkers were challenging, re-creating, and attempting to reform their troubled nation.

Joseph set to translating faith into action, handing out copies of Wesley's antislavery tract to the townspeople. On one occasion, Joseph, Crookham, and a visiting abolitionist professor took to Jackson's courthouse steps to exhort passersby about the evils of slavery. In no time, men emboldened by cheap whiskey poured angrily out of French's Tavern. They loudly heckled the dissenters. As the small crowd surged forward, taunts became jeers, then erupted into threats. The trio ducked into the nearby house of a friendly physician, where they spent the night, waiting for tempers to cool.

Soon Wes's classmates at the town's one-room school on Ford's Hill heard their fathers decry the senior Powell. Things became more difficult for him. The log cabin with benches along the walls housed a single class of widely varying ages, taught by a single schoolmaster, who summoned students by sounding a large metal horn. Attendance was irregular, large swaths of the school year taken up when the children needed to help their families harvest crops, hunt, and fulfill the other myriad demands of frontier life. A few of the boys were much older than Wesley, their voices already those of men, their fists already hardened from use.

One afternoon when Wes was ten, a knot of boys confronted

him after school. They taunted him, calling his father a nigger lover. Their jeers soon boiled beyond commonplace bullying. If he and his family liked blacks so much, they shouted, then why not go to live with them at Berlin X-Roads? With cold alarm Wes saw hands reaching into pockets stuffed with rocks. It all happened so quickly.

Stones started flying, several of them finding their bruising marks. Wes flew home pell-mell. When his mother opened the door, she found her son panting and wild-eyed, tears clouding his gray eyes. Wes had been bullied before, but the malevolence of this particular attack, with its Old Testament overtones, was something new and deeply troubling. His shame at being mobbed stung far more than the bruises themselves. As a northerner, Wes was already an outsider, but this act severed any possibility that he might fit in. The memories of those hailing stones and faces distorted in rage would linger on the edges of Wes's consciousness for the rest of his life.

His parents sensibly pulled him out of school. They turned to their friend Big George, who operated an informal classroom on his property, which he had started originally to educate his sixteen children, but had grown to take in the odd student interested in an education more robust than the locality's meager offerings. He had built a schoolhouse, connected by a dogtrot to a museum in which he stored his library and large collection of natural history specimens. Crookham fondly called it his Jack Oak College after the boards used to build it. John Wesley Powell, who became Crookham's temporary ward, would prove to be his most engaging student.

One of Jackson's earliest pioneers, Crookham had come from Pennsylvania as a twenty-year-old in 1799—not long after a settlement with the Shawnees had made southeastern Ohio tolerably safe for whites—to labor at a saltworks, the state's first industry. Jackson, then known as Purgatory, was a ramshackle huddle of shacks, overrun by tough young men who performed the hard, hot work of boiling down brine into piles of the darkly streaked salt crystals necessary to cure and preserve food. All along the sandstone banks of Salt Lick Creek lay holes or salt pans, dug by Native Americans. When these holes filled with salt-rich brine from saltwater springs, or licks, the Indians procured the mineral by using fire-heated rocks to steam off the water. In Purgatory, the pioneer men poured brine into long lines of twelve- to fifteen-gallon iron kettles, which bubbled over wood fires twenty-four hours a day.

From these old Indian wells, the young Crookham pulled out—much to his surprise—the oversized bones of what are now called megafauna: the huge, curious, and long-extinct animals that had roamed the land more than ten thousand years ago. The magical discoveries of tusks and breadloaf-sized mammoth molars, along with the superpredatory curves of saber-toothed cats, opened up its own well of cosmic questions in the teenaged Crookham. While some learned men had contemplated the possibility that species might become extinct, the idea was yet to be accepted, let alone understood. Dinosaurs had yet to be named or described. In the future lay the knowledge that more than 99.99 percent of all Earth-born life had already gone extinct. To the other salt boilers, such bones were simply obstacles, but in George Crookham, they ignited a fiercely burning curiosity in natural history that would last him a lifetime. The forests and creeks around Jackson would become his almost exclusive collecting area.

In Crookham's museum, Wes could touch the cool ivory of a nearly eleven-foot-long mammoth tusk, which Big George had wrestled out of the bank of Salt Lick Creek. At that time, few people had the opportunity to examine such an exotic fossil so closely. Imagining what kind of huge creature could support a pair of these tusks thrilled the boy. The darkened room held other treasures: the prodigious length of an eastern rattlesnake skin and a menagerie of skulls and pinned beetles, mounted birds, and glittering cave crystals. That room became a sanctuary from the chore-driven responsibilities of home and those taunting school-boys. Big George, in turn, found an able disciple.

The hulking man and slip of a boy mounted frequent expeditions, seeking blue-flag irises that fringed beaver ponds, or the pink ladyslipper orchids blossoming in the shadows of the hardwood forests to the east. Some five hundred ancient earthworks lay within the vicinity of the salt licks, lost witness to a long-vanished indigenous culture now known as the Mound Builders. The pair explored one complex known as the "fort," a rectangular earthen enclosure measuring about 100 by 110 feet, just northwest of town. It was easy enough for Wes to fill his pocket with arrowheads. His guide to this ancient world was a man far bigger than life, not only in his sheer immensity that would shake almost violently with laughter, but in his passionate long view of the connections between so many things visible to the naked eye. With Big George there was room to ask questions that Wes would not dare to put to his father.

Crookham taught Wes how to read a landscape: Far from a trackless wilderness, the land around Jackson revealed surprising secrets to those with patience and an inquisitive eye. The inexplicable fossil bones and the great earthen mounds spoke of a world shaped by others than the present immigrants. To Wes, the natural world was coming to be visibly governed by an intrinsic logic and unfolding clarity that his father's faith could not match. Big George provided a trellis onto which Wes's wonder could grow.

Of all the expeditions they took together, none thrilled him more than when William Mather joined them. Descended from the firebrand Puritan preachers Cotton and Increase, this was a quieter, gentler soul, whose dedication to the new science of geology had led him to organize Ohio's first geological survey. The former West Pointer had bought up part of the Pigeon Roost north of Jackson, a patch of forest into which passenger pigeons not long before had flocked to by the millions. There Mather had built a house, which Wes loved to visit so he could examine the geologist's extensive mineral collection, which counted twenty-six thousand items by the time of his death in 1859. Wes could not take his eyes off this mentor's maimed hand, a finger lost to snakebite. When the surgeon had been unable to sever the swollen digit with one blow of mallet and chisel, the unanesthetized Mather had calmly directed him to finish the job. Heavyset, with a thick thatch of dark hair set off by light eyes, Mather was manly and self-reliant, yet also admitted to an abounding curiosity in the so little discovered natural world.

Most often, the threesome would head out just beyond the licks, where Salt Creek suddenly angles northward and dashes through a several-mile-long gorge, revealing layer upon layer of Earth's history. Big George and Mather would debate why fossil shells could be found in the fine-grained sandstone, but not in the shale. The science of geology was only just beginning to open up the world's wonders. For most mid-nineteenth-century Americans, explanations of their physical world and of Earth itself remained locked up in biblical exegesis, from which many scholars had deduced or accepted an age of six thousand years. Christians viewed the formation of the world through the lens of a long string of catastrophic events, such as Noah's flood. Yet for Mather, Crookham, and the growing number of people reading the new textbooks pouring in from Europe, their understanding of Earth's formation was fast washing away. The myth-bending cutting edge of early nineteenth-century science was geology, especially as presented in three volumes published by the Englishman Charles Lyell between 1830 and 1833. *Principles of Geology* may have promised a summation of the latest in that science, but Lyell actually devoted the entire opus to a single line of argument, which on its surface appeared rather prosaic, but whose implications proved as revolutionary as the works of Galileo. Drawing on the work of an obscure Scotsman, Lyell argued that all forces that had shaped Earth's surface remained visible today. A journalist would christen this idea with the cumbrous name uniformitarianism, which in its very consonance reflected the gradual, slow-acting but cumulative processes that were shaping the Earth.

Lyell's argument cut to the core of how Christians construed Genesis. Believers in a world thrown together with violence and cataclysm were known as "catastrophists." Lyell's theory quietly overturned all it came into contact with. If catastrophic change had not formed the Earth, but gradual wearing had, then the Earth's age would stretch far, far further back than ever before imagined. More than a century later, the writer John McPhee would aptly label this "deep time" and offer a metaphor: If the span of Earth's history is reduced to the length from a king's nose to the end of the fingertip of his outstretched arm—the original definition of the English "yard"—then all human history could be erased with the single swipe of a nail file on the nail of the middle finger. Scientists of Powell's age did not know, as McPhee's contemporaries did, that Earth had existed for more than four billion years but did grasp that its age ran for many millions, not just a few thousand.

Similar to Copernicus's revelation that the sun did not revolve around the Earth, the idea of geologic time further distanced humanity from the center of things. A thoughtful gentleman scientist named Charles Darwin took Lyell's book on his long voyage aboard HMS *Beagle*. Freed from having to imagine a world only created in fire and flood, but one that stretched for eons and bore the accumulation of many gradual changes, Darwin began fleshing out his ideas about natural selection, which would rock humanity's inflated conception of itself and its place in the universe.

Mather and Crookham, with the curious boy in tow, were keenly feeling—and contributing to—seismic changes that would shift America in less than a century inexorably from a nation of faith-based explanations into one rooted in secular science. By mid-century, as Powell matured, geology had become not only fashionable and popular but vital to the economic expansion of the American West. The book most framing Wes's emerging worldview would not be the stately King James Bible but rather Lyell's dynamic *Principles*.

In the fall of 1846, Joseph was ordained in the Wesleyan Methodist Church, a recently seceded Methodist denomination more in line with his abolitionist views. As a result, he ended his circuit riding. His full-time presence now became even more unpleasant to the townspeople. One morning sometime that fall, the Powell family awoke to find its horse without its tail, its flanks splashed with paint, some of which had bespattered the walls of their house. The always-close siblings pulled together even tighter. In September, dark forces closed upon Berlin X-Roads when the badly beaten body of one of Thomas Woodson's sons was found by the roadside, a bounty hunter's devilry. Either he had been discovered with escaped slaves or had refused to divulge the whereabouts of those he was helping. Woodson had already lost another son to those seeking to derail the Underground Railroad.

The final blow for Joseph came when the Powells opened their door early one morning to find a shaken Big George. A mob had torched Jack Oak College the night before. Up in flames had gone all his notes and work on the history of Jackson, a book he would now never finish. A magnificent lifetime's collection of plant and animal specimens lay in ashes.

Joseph understood that his vulnerable family lay only a heartbeat away from bloody massacre. His wife had just given birth to their eighth and final child, Julietta. This radicalized preacher had arrived at a moment of hard reckoning. Until then, the spiritual uplift of outspoken abolitionism had outweighed its mostly social disadvantages. The risk calculus now needed recalculation.

Joseph brought his affairs together, selling his house and some other parcels of land he had acquired. He secured appointment to a Wisconsin parish. It would take the Powells well to the north, away from border violence.

They never looked back. Wes would not mention Jackson in all his voluminous writings, nor would he ever return. But some wounds would never heal, although they helped to inflame a new passion within him. Wes clutched a book or two that Crookham had given him, and tucked away a growing treasury of arrowheads and freshwater mollusk shells. In the rough layering of stone and earth, in the splendid variety of knapped arrowheads, in the rainbow-colored spectrum of beetle species, he had glimpsed a bright new world, cosmically larger and more fascinating than that found in the *Methodist Book of Discipline*. His faith would embrace a natural theology every bit as strong as his father's Methodism. He would find his god manifest in the magnificence of the natural and physical world—his reverence for which would never die, and would impart radiance and meaning to all his future work.

Hardship and opportunity had conspired to blaze a path that led away from Joseph's plans for him. But it would take all that Wes had to resist his powerful father: the growing boy would learn to keep his own counsel, to choose his movements quietly and wisely, and always to avoid direct confrontation, except when his own emerging sense of righteousness demanded it. Although he might ultimately reject his father's strict doctrine, it yet bequeathed him a militantly evangelical approach to life, along with an implacable commitment to human freedom. Wesley's firsthand experience of the freedmen of Berlin X-Roads and the fugitives on the Underground Railroad led him to listen empathetically even to those most different from him, a cast of mind that would evolve into an unusual thoughtfulness toward the Native Americans and Mormons he would encounter later. The ordeal on Ford's Hill had seared into Wes his outsider status; and with that came the outsider's gift of seeing the world differently. His father's evange-lism had forced upon him the belief that the world must be remade—and awoke in him a prophetic obligation to bring light to the people. One's beliefs had to be worth fighting for—and so his life would become a series of willed battles.

The challenges would begin right away.

CHAPTER 2

Osage Oranges and Pink Muckets

As the Powells journeyed north into Indiana in 1846 and on to the Great Lakes, then turned west and north again, the living land changed underfoot, craggy southern Ohio giving way to smooth, rolling prairies, any rough edges crushed under the press of a once mile-thick glacier and now scarred by the wagon-wheel ruts of the westward movement. The tracks they would travel on hardly resembled roads at all—little more than paths, crude trails carved through wooded lands or corduroyed with logs over long marshy stretches. The U.S. military had cut some roads the Powells would take, but lack of maintenance left them little better than mere cart paths, their beds turning into seas of wheel-sucking mud for much of the spring and summer. Even the Powells' Devon oxen could not negotiate such mires after a heavy rain. That year, the first plank road companies formed, but the toll highways of oak had not been built when the Powells traveled. "It was jirk and jolt, this way and that," wrote a pioneer girl who traveled their same trail.

They were not the only Americans on the move—much of the country was that year, as hundreds of wagon trains started off from Independence, Missouri, on a grueling 2,200-mile ordeal to the Pacific Northwest, while yet others headed southwest on the

Santa Fe Trail from Franklin, Missouri. That year the remarkably enterprising, self-taught carpenter, and devout leader of the Latter-day Saints, Brigham Young, drew thousands of Mormon pioneers across the plains and on to establish a new republic the following year on the desolate shores of the Great Salt Lake. At the same time, the Erie Canal and Ohio River bore a westward advance of expectant migrants while steamboats were beginning to ply the Mississippi between St. Louis and New Orleans. For this restless nation, 1846 marked one of the high points of America's movement to the far West. "I have often perplexed myself to divine the various motives that give impulse to this migration," wrote the historian Francis Parkman about a trip he took on the Oregon Trail.

Whereas opportunity certainly moved many Americans to spill across the continent, a mounting sense of the nation's conquering birthright gave further agency and authority to this impulse, which a journalist had termed "Manifest Destiny" the year before. While John O'Sullivan's column in the *New York Morning News* was directed toward the bristling conflict between Great Britain's and America's claims to ownership over the Pacific Northwest, his invocation of the phrase locked in a continental vision of the country's great expectations: "And that claim is by the right of our manifest destiny to overspread and to possess the whole of the continent which Providence has given us for the development of the great experiment of liberty and federated self-government entrusted to us." When Horace Greeley issued the famous command "Go West, young man," it was bound with iron-ribbed assumptions of an almost-divine sense of national self-discovery and superiority, a birthright of conquest so exalted as to often blind Americans to the consequences of their actions.

In the mid-1840s, much of the North American continent still lay up for grabs to white arrivals: While America and Britain contested the vast northwestern region of today's Oregon and

Washington states, and the British emphasized their possession of Canada, all other lands west of Texas and the Continental Divide were foreign territories over whose indigenous communities and land Mexico and Russia made rather vague legal claims. The lands of the future state of Alaska were indubitably part of the Russian empire. But James Polk, the ruthless, phenomenally shrewd son of a North Carolina farmer would give new heft to the manifest-ness of destiny and west-going when he rode a populistic expansionist wave into the presidency in 1845. The dark-horse Democrat was determined to redraw the political map of North America once and for all.

Whereas Jefferson had played the negotiation for the Louisiana Purchase cleverly against a Bonaparte preoccupied with Europe, there was nothing subtle about Polk's rapacious grab for the Southwest and Pacific territories. After provoking a war with Mexico, he sent troops across the international border and then claimed the territory encompassing the modern-day states of Arizona, Nevada, Colorado, and Utah. Meanwhile an independent Texas had just voted to join the United States. Polk negotiated the Oregon Treaty of 1846 with the British, which extended the American domain west of the Rockies and north of California by 285,000 square miles, stopping only to leave what would become western Canada to the British. That same year, U.S. warships sailed into California's Monterey Bay and raised the flag over the customs house, ending the short-lived, homegrown California Republic. In a single term, Polk had nearly doubled the nation's land area, all of it lying well west of the Mississippi.

Neither Mr. Polk nor the most vociferous advocates of manifest destiny, however, were prepared for what such continental scope might bring, even though Emerson had an inkling, writing that "the nervous, rocky west is intruding a new and continental element into the national mind, and we shall yet have an American genius." The nation came to its continental understanding only slowly and unsteadily, although the vague but red-hot beliefs engendered in manifest destiny and the later notions of the frontier would give the white man's conquest of North America extraordinary dimension. In that year of decision, young Wesley Powell, sitting with reins in hand atop one of the family's two wagons, would feel his own strong part in his nation's restless need to move west. More perhaps than anyone else, he would shape the newly emerging American West and, in so doing, help cast the national identity.

With the money from selling his holdings in Jackson, Joseph bought a 120-acre farm for $1,200 cash down in an area soon to be called South Grove in southeastern Wisconsin's Walworth County. The parcel, already bearing a tidy frame house and barn, soon swelled to 140 acres, of which 55 were improved. A stream ran through the property, teeming with pickerel; nut-laden trees delivered bagloads of hazelnuts, hickory nuts, and butternuts every fall. Frequent prairie and forest fires would often light the horizon while winter brought glimpses of the aurora borealis, the dancing lights of the northern sky, and the tracks of gray wolves coming near the Powells' increasingly crowded livestock pens. Of some reassurance to Joseph, the county derived its name from a former president of the New York Temperance League. Sober industry meshed perfectly with his plans for the future.

In a surprising, but nevertheless quite common, example of simple American pioneering optimism, Joseph had determined that his family's fortunes lay in farming, despite his near-complete ignorance of planting cycles, crop pests, varieties of weather, animal husbandry, or any other of the myriad skills and knowledge sets demanded by the farming life. Yet that optimism was not ill founded: The earliest hardscrabble European-American pioneers had discovered that wheat and other small grains thrived without fertilization in the Wisconsin Territory's loamy soil, producing ten to fifteen or even more bushels per acre. The Territory's grain production would swell from little more than two hundred thousand bushels in 1839 to more than four million only nine years later, when soaring population brought statehood.

Not that Joseph planned on doing the farming himself. He pressed these onerous responsibilities onto the shoulders of twelve-year-old Wesley and his eight-year-old brother, Bram. After purchasing a cow, chickens, and a pig, Joseph turned his attentions to ministering a nearby Methodist community populated by Welshmen who had landed at Southport harbor in July 1842. Once more he would mount up and ride off, leaving all farm responsibilities to children not yet in their teens. When Wes cracked his ox-whip and drove the breaking plow through the sod, he would be on his own, engaging far-older farm laborers to plant and harvest the twice-annual wheat crop, besides growing barley for the swine, Irish potatoes for general family use, and oats, hay, and buckwheat for the stock. There was so much to learn. Venomous massasauga rattlesnakes occasionally emerged from the wetlands or tall prairie grass and had to be killed. The Powells would raise eighteen pigs—and young Wes would oversee the killing and butchering.

In 1849, a band of Winnebago Indians crossed onto the Powell property and camped without permission on the creek bank. Wes remembered them as "footsore and disconsolate," sinking down to camp in shoddy canvas tents, while their horses drank thirstily from the creek. They returned weeks later in better shape, the Indian agents in Chicago having showered them with calico dresses, blankets, and shoes. They camped again, this time for a week of feasting and celebration, not seeming to mind the presence of Wes, his mother, his brother, and two older sisters. From one of them who spoke passable English, Mary discovered that the newly acquired goods came in payment for their agreement to hand over their ancestral lands, some of which the Powells now occupied.

Their forefathers had camped here for as long as they could remember, particularly on the north side of the creek amid the burr oaks. "The strip of land on which we had planted our apple orchard," recalled Wes, "had been their rabbit preserve." Wes joined them at the campfire inside their circle of tents, fascinated by the colors of dress, the strange tongue, and the subtle flow of the dancers. He had never encountered Indians before—and this experience would spark a lifelong fascination with them and their cultures.

Such moments of reflection, however, remained rare. There was always something to do. The conservationist John Muir, only four years Wes's junior, had also grown up on a Wisconsin farm, not seventy miles from Southport. He vividly remembered that even during heavy rains or snowstorms, the whole family worked in the barn "shelling corn, fanning wheat, thrashing with the flail, making ax-handles or ox-yokes, mending things, or sprouting and sorting potatoes in the cellar." Muir's Presbyterian father also piled onerous responsibility on his son, John taking on the brunt of farm work at age eleven. Such responsibility imposed at an early age was nothing out of the ordinary, whether in agricultural communities or in the factories springing up in New England.

While the Powells might sell their wheat locally, far better profit lay in delivering it to the port towns of Southport or Racine on Lake Michigan. No hired hand could be trusted to take so valuable a cargo, nor buy or barter the items necessary to keep up the farm, so that ordeal fell on Wes, too. In the autumn when the muddy roads dried, he took the five- to six-day roundtrip journey half a dozen times a year or more. As an early teenager, Wes would stow a small sack of flour or cornmeal under his seat and join a line of farmers' carts heading east. He buried himself in Bunyan's *Pilgrim's Progress,* that compelling religious allegory tracing the journey of its workaday protagonist, Christian, in flight from his hometown—the "City of Destruction"—to the "Celestial City." Along the way, he becomes mired in the "Slough of Despond," an awful swamp that plays upon his doubts and fears, an experience that Wes could all too readily empathize with. Young Powell also had to overcome the travails of the broken roads, repeatedly mending the ox yoke, shivering through rain and snowstorms. He joined rowdy gatherings of other farmers, most far older than he, hearing probably much-distorted tales of the wider world and learning to draw deeply upon his own bank of fortitude. He had no choice: His family depended on it. But for the young boy on the brink of manhood, the time away from the constant farm chores and the kerfuffle of family life became something he enjoyed, and a time to flex his newfound independence. Bunyan's words resonated deeply. Christian did not merely grind mechanically through life but was instead energized and directed by a quest for the truth. Wes would come to define his life in these terms.

Most often he headed to Southport; although Racine boasted a new plank road that proved more negotiable in wet weather, it cost two cents a mile to use. When Wes reached Southport, soon to be rechristened Kenosha, he crossed Pike Creek over a queens truss bridge at Main and Church streets, entering a thriving lakeside town of several hundred oak-and-black-walnut frame houses, boasting a blacksmith forge and funeral home, as well as shops to mend and buy harnesses, saddles, carriages, wagons, and cabinets. Visitors could find refreshment in a sprinkling of taverns and hotels. In 1845, the Territory's first free public school had opened here. He would sell his load of wheat either at the Durkee or C. I. Hutchinson & Co. warehouses for as much as a dollar a bushel in those first years.

Mr. C. I. Hutchinson was the brightest example of entrepreneurial success in this lakeside timber boomtown. Wes would have been likely to catch sight or sound of "the General" at his warehouse or around town. Before turning up in Southport in 1841, this Connecticut Yankee had run a Georgia textile mill. The still-sleepy Southport had never seen anything like him, a man who in short order would build not only an immense grain storehouse and the longest pier that had ever graced Lake Michigan but also a large steam mill and two modern vessels efficiently designed to carry maximum grain cargoes to Chicago.

The grain boom times had been generous. But then a series of droughts, savage storms, and pestilences beset the area. The overleveraged Hutchinson took a bad hit when a storm sank his schooner *Samuel Hale,* ruining eleven thousand bushels of wheat. Hutchinson's enterprises teetered on the edge of solvency. During the fall of 1849, desperately short of cash, he offered farmers IOUs for the grain they delivered, redeemable in the spring, when the ice would break and open the lake to navigation. Whether the Powells took Hutchinson's paper is unknown, but even had they not the events of the next several weeks would certainly have hit them inescapably hard, as it did every other farmer in the region.

When the ice broke on April 6, 1850, Southport's dock grew lively with workers loading ships with grain from Hutchinson's warehouse. When the farmers showed up, however, and presented their IOUs, Hutchinson could not be found. Word soon came that he and his wife had left early that spring for California. In short order, more than two hundred angry farmers massed in front of the warehouse, the crowd soon doubling, many now wielding clubs, pitchforks, and axes. There being no police force, only the interdiction of the brave mayor prevented the mob from turning violent. His honor gave word that no more grain would leave until matters sorted themselves out.

Before skipping town, Hutchinson had sold most of the wheat to an Ohio merchant, who was probably unaware of the IOUs issued, and certainly wholly uninterested in covering them. The following day, a deputy U.S. marshal attempted to enforce a writ of replevin permitting the gentleman from Ohio to ship the grain. But the surging crowd prevented it from being removed to the brig

Buffalo at dock. Later that day, a farmer broke into the warehouse and started taking back the grain, soon joined by others. "Riot in Southport!" screamed the headlines in the *Milwaukee Sentinel,* as even more farmers streamed into town. "Walking with hickory canes has been customary for a day or two past," Colonel M. Frank wrote in his journal. Two companies of Milwaukee militia arrived to enforce the federal writ. The small farmers, already running narrow margins, had been "egregiously swindled," as one U.S. congressman observed. The ill feeling would last for years. Hutchinson escaped unscathed to become a successful mayor of Sacramento, whose obituary in the *Daily Union* read: "Having died with his harness on. A man with many friends, few enemies and a fame free from scandal or misdeed. His example is a legacy to the commonwealth."

In the fall of 1850, the wheat market fell again, opening the "red-eye years," so named from the tear-stained faces of so many farm families. Wes had seen up close how benign conditions could reign one year, only to be reversed the following summer season, as pests, bad weather, or a fluctuating market dropped the bottom out. Tack on a systematic lack of credit, crippling mortgage indebtedness, and sky-high interest rates, and farmers had narrow room indeed left to maneuver. But perhaps most vividly, Wes saw how powerful interests could abuse the farmers without their having any legal recourse. Such an experience might well have soured Wes on agriculture, as it did with Muir, who came to regard farmers as aliens who "toiled and sweated and grubbed themselves into their graves years before their natural dying days, in getting a living on a quarter-section of land and vaguely trying to get rich." But for Wes, his Wisconsin days engendered a far warmer regard for the small farmer and his way of life—more in line with Jefferson's idea of the natural nobility of the American yeoman. The work was hard but honest. The small farmer and local entrepreneur made America strong and great, just as long as their efforts upon the land were smartly planned and unimpeded by duplicitous individuals.

The Hutchinson debacle convinced Joseph of the need to move. Before 1850 ended, he had sold the property and taken the family to northern Illinois. At that moment, Wes turned sixteen, the legal age of majority, which meant that he could guide his own future more firmly. He then began a long, frustrating pursuit of an education. That winter, he trudged twenty miles to the one-room schoolhouse of Janesville, Wisconsin. It turned out to be a bitter disappointment. The schoolmaster proved little better educated than he. A farm family gave him room and board, delighting in the enthusiastic young man with a strong tenor voice, who knew how to attend to their infant, rocking it to sleep in the evenings as he studied in front of the fire. The following summer, Wes returned home to a parcel of unimproved but promising land in Bonus Prairie, Boone County, Illinois, to help break sod for his father.

Despite the setbacks that plagued many farmers, each move had improved Joseph and Mary's financial situation, which now grew secure. Joseph took to sponsoring Wesleyan Methodist camp meetings in warmer weather. But farming never lay close to his heart, and in the matter of little more than a year, he once more sold his fields, this time set on helping to found a Wesleyan Methodist college in Wheaton, Illinois, thirty miles west of Chicago. This new school would follow the liberal tenets of Oberlin, accepting any qualified candidate whether black or white, male or female, so long as they followed a strict body of rules. Joseph would become a trustee. The five-acre lot on East Jefferson Street would be the last place that Wes's father and mother lived.

Joseph battled to guide his son's future into the ministry with his purse strings. Wes's passion for natural science had only grown more pronounced. He often raised eyebrows in Wheaton when he returned from his frequent collecting expeditions, his mother's glass preserve jars filled with creatures, including, on one occasion, a large eastern rattlesnake. Bringing home one of God's unholiest creatures most certainly must have set Joseph's teeth on edge, but it did not shake his conviction that Wes would someday spread the word of God. Joseph gladly paid for Wes's enrollment at colleges that taught theology but would not support tuition at schools that boasted offerings in natural history and science. Wes could enroll in his father's new Illinois Institute, but it did not offer a single class in science, logic, or more than basic mathematics. Over the next six years, Wes tested wills with his father and attempted to get an education on his own terms; he would find himself seesawing between brief fits of college study and spells teaching school after his tuition money invariably ran out. To make money he would teach in Jefferson Prairie, Decatur, and Clinton. He would enroll in three colleges: Illinois College, Illinois Institute (later Wheaton), and Oberlin, but drop out of each, bored with the limited coursework in the sciences. His education would come through other channels.

In the fall of 1854, Wesley, now twenty years old, moved just east of Decatur, Illinois, to live with his older sister's family. Martha had married John Davis, a progressively minded farmer, and now oversaw a busy household of ten children. Wes took to teaching the sons and daughters of farmers at the Cherry Point schoolhouse for $24 a month. This short, energetic, already charismatic young man, now sporting a fashionable pair of bushy sideburns, discovered a new talent: teaching his geography lessons by singing. Not uncommon in midwestern classrooms, teachers singing not only made lessons more memorable but also cut through the boredom of a culture more concerned with the plow than the book. Wes's singing class proved so popular that he offered one in the evening, open to the townspeople. Hundreds flocked to sing, each carrying a candle. Wes led them in singing at the top of their voices the names of the states, their capitals, rivers and their lengths, capes, bays, and mountain peaks, an exuberant celebration of their American heritage. Wes discovered that he had a knack for drawing people together in common, excited purpose.

Although he enjoyed the teaching and the joyful noise of his young nephews and nieces, Wes yearned for a wider world. His brother-in-law belonged to a movement of agricultural populists rolling over the midwestern prairies before the Civil War, devoted to raising the standards of the farmer and reworking the agricultural way of life. Davis wrote occasional pieces on his prairie-spun philosophy for the *Dewitt Courier,* waxing warmly about the growing mechanization of the prairie that was raising a new American prosperity. When Davis broached the idea of starting a fruit-tree nursery, Wes eagerly jumped aboard, borrowing the considerable sum of several hundred dollars to make up his share. But Wes's entrepreneurial experiment came to an abrupt end when his father wrote curtly from Wheaton that "the borrowing of money to make money is not one whit better than highway robbery." Reluctantly Wes heeded the commandment, withdrawing his investment as fast as he could and repaying his lenders. The incident no doubt marked the beginning of his practical distancing from his father. His parents' offer still stood to pay for his attendance at the Illinois Institute or Oberlin, but Wes again turned down an education confined largely to religious instruction.

His brother-in-law suggested to Wes that he might consider enrolling at Davis's alma mater, Illinois College in Jacksonville, if he could come up with the $30 tuition. The school would accept Davis's promise that Wes would be good for the further hundred dollars required for living expenses. Wes passed the entrance examination after cramming for five weeks with the help of a local tutor, who lent him books on mathematics, science, Latin, and

Greek—no insignificant feat for a young man whose formal education was spotty at best.

So, in October 1855, Wes enrolled in Illinois College's three-year agricultural science program. Although required to attend daily chapel, he had at least landed in a college that taught science, if only the applied kind that would benefit a farmer. His marks proved excellent. He joined a literary society and debated the question of whether phrenology deserved the rank of a serious discipline. Most important of all, he met a former professor who remained a large presence in the college town. Jonathan B. Turner had mentored John Davis in developing a progressive western agrarian outlook at college in the late 1840s. The outspoken Turner, a Yale-educated Congregationalist minister, had since been forced to resign his professorship, another casualty of the mounting sectional animosities: His abolitionism and liberal religious doctrines had grated too harshly on the ears of many southerners attending the Presbyterian school, and so Turner had retired to his house on college hill. Clutching a letter of introduction from his brother-in-law, Wes had called upon Turner, who gave him a tour of his experimental seventeen-and-a-half-acre lot of flower and vegetable gardens and hedged fields.

Turner had been one of several eastern elite academics who had come to the prairie west in the 1830s, bent on helping the Illinois farmer profit from the new scientific age. While John Davis's description of Jacksonville as the "Athens of Illinois" might have been a little grandiose, it indicated how deeply Turner and his fellow professors believed that the slowly forming western lands harbored the right conditions for a new era in American history. Turner had noticed that western farmers tended to build their farms near copses of trees, the only source of the critical fencing material necessary to contain and protect livestock and crops in the days before barbed wire. Because these stands remained widely scattered and separated by miles of prairie, many farmers lived far from central locations that would make possible democratic- and society-building institutions, such as public schools and churches. Turner set out to find a cheap solution to fencing in the form of a fast-growing hedge—"horse-high, bull-strong, and pig-tight"—freeing farmers from their dependence on woodlands. He experimented with barberry, box, and hawthorn, even sending away to England for seeds, but had little success until a circuit-riding preacher gave him some Osage orange, so named from its bumpy, grapefruit-sized, somewhat-citrus-smelling seedpod. If pruned and its tendrils woven just right, it grew rapidly in straight lines so dense that not even small birds could pass through it. Soon Osage hedgerows stretched across thousands of miles of the Midwest, contributing to the rise of town life and civic engagement.

Wes loved this quick-minded radical thinker, who expanded as easily on growing plants and inventing agricultural machines as on his cosmic theories about humankind. Turner believed that three great races—yellow, white, and black—had each been created with separate and equal characteristics to push humanity toward greater perfection. All would have their day, and none could be judged as inherently superior. Even if deterministic and simple, Turner's thought possessed a utopian grandeur, the wide-open prairie lands quickly welcoming and spreading a genuine intellectual content to the western movement. He was seeking to turn farmers into "thinking laborers," as distinct from the more urban professions that consisted of "laborious thinkers." The latest findings in science should be easily available to all farmers, freeing them from always having to move on once the soil was depleted.

Turner would prove instrumental in bringing about the Morrill Act, which Lincoln signed into law on July 2, 1862, that directed the federal government to provide land grants for the states to finance institutions devoted to teaching agricultural and industrial workers. This most important education law in American history would anticipate—and indeed initiate—the system of state universities, but even more important it would enshrine the idea that every male citizen should have access to government-supported collegiate education in those practical subjects for which the young nation thirsted.

Money problems forced Wes out after a semester, but he was back the following fall after a stint teaching, although he would have to quit again soon. But Turner had stirred up Wes's ideas, energizing forward-looking thoughts rooted in prairie optimism, but, as it proved, of even far greater scope.

Over the summers Wes underwent his real education—certainly out in the fields and wild forests, but now especially in far more ambitious forays on the nation's river courses. He would experience firsthand one of America's most astounding geographical realities: that it boasts more miles of navigable inland waterways than all the rest of the world combined, creating a veinlike matrix in which one river falls into another to yet another again until their combined waters empty out into the sea. The rivers' connectivity provided exceptional freedom of movement. And along with this came an interaction of new ideas and older traditions—sometimes comical, but often enough explosive, collisions of people from innumerable backgrounds, castes, and inheritances. In the Midwest, a new America was being consolidated to the creak of the oar and the rhythmic slap of the paddlewheel. Upon the muddy waters of the Mississippi took place one of the most colorful, violent, and productive experiments in American history. More than any other single factor, river-transportation improvements had brought about the antebellum transformation of the Midwest from a little-settled backwater to the nation's breadbasket.

For young men of the early- to mid-nineteenth-century Midwest, before railroads and later highways, the rivers of the heartland—the Mississippi, Ohio, Missouri, and the great streams feeding them—beckoned with intoxicating appeal. While upperclass easterners took the Grand Tour of Europe, or like Richard

Henry Dana, Jr., signed on for an ocean voyage such as he chronicled in *Two Years Before the Mast,* midwesterners and curious easterners rode flatboats and jumped, or booked passage, on steamboats. While Mark Twain certainly became Old Man River's most famous champion, watercourses attracted many teenagers, such as nineteen-year-old Abraham Lincoln, who signed on as a bow-hand on a flatboat floating to New Orleans in 1828. Testing themselves against strong currents became a rite of passage. "The instance of a young man of enterprize and standing, as a merchant, trader, planter, or even farmer, who has not made at least one trip to New Orleans, is uncommon," wrote the missionary Timothy C. Flint in 1828. The long trip, he added, was more perilous than a voyage across the Atlantic.

In the summer of 1856, when Wes rowed his flat-bottomed skiff into the Mississippi current at St. Anthony Falls near Minneapolis, he was not only participating in a grand American tradition, but pushing into the messy, democratizing turmoil of the great American river. That summer he would take the river all the way to New Orleans. The following year he rowed from Pittsburgh to the mouth of the Ohio. In 1858, he rowed down the Illinois River from Ottawa to its mouth, then up the Des Moines.

Along the way, he encountered the entire range of American enterprise as the waterborne pageant laden with lumber, pork, cheese, butter, flour, corn, and whiskey floated past him. Boats descending the Ohio to its junction with the Mississippi bore cloth, tools, agricultural implements, ammunition, and, again, whiskey. Great creaking flatboats, or "broadhorns," often stretching one hundred feet, carried their cargo, large families, their crews, and livestock. After completing a single trip downriver, boatmen typically chopped up these makeshift craft for fuel and lumber.

"I remember the annual processions of mighty rafts that used to glide by Hannibal when I was a boy—an acre or so of white, sweet-smelling boards in each raft, a crew of two dozen men or

more," recalled Twain. Prostitutes primped deckside aboard floating brothels, sometimes sliding provocatively by chapel-boats
manned by exhorting ministers. Other vessels shipped entertain-
ers or sometimes printers with their print shops while hucksters
sold snake oil from smaller vessels. For a mostly agricultural people so often desperately bored, diversion came in bouts of heavy
drinking and endless hands of cards. Hundreds of boats rafted
together by night, not only for protection from roving bands of
river pirates but for companionship; a curious camaraderie developed among the constantly churning mix of people they would
never meet again. Preachers vied for people's souls while pickpock-
ets, card sharks, and wily con men emptied pockets.

On the river, steamboats had become king, gaudily painted cre-
ations belching steam from towering stacks, their sternwheels
furiously churning and moving them up to twelve knots an hour,
faster than the fastest sailing ships on the ocean. On the river,
steamboat designs may have appeared the epitome of ingenuity, but
everywhere Wes looked there were formidable competitors, such as
Henry Miller Shreve's snag boat, whose steam-powered windlass
enabled its crew to clear a 150-mile logjam from where the Red
River joined the Mississippi. Two years before, a steamship toiling
day and night had set the transit record, traveling between New
Orleans and Louisville in four days, nine hours, and thirty minutes. In 1815, when Wes's father was a teenager, that same trip had
taken twenty-five days.

Wes learned to keep a weather eye out for the sight or sound of
steamboats, their captains paying no heed to craft the size of his
skiff. When fog descended, dodging the river's myriad snags, drifting trees, sandbars, wreck heaps, and small islands became yet
more hazardous. The river claimed lives as a matter of course.

A typical skiff was pointed at the bow, blunt at the stern, and
flat bottomed, measuring on the order of fifteen feet long, three
and a half feet wide, and fourteen inches deep. Skiffs had become
the ubiquitous small boats on the river, as ferries across streams,

as tenders for larger vessels, and as fishing craft. Each steamboat carried a "yawl" skiff, which not only brought passengers aboard but scouted the main channel and took off cargo to lighten the load should the mother ship catch on a sandbar, or even, if necessary, to function as a lifeboat. The slightest change in the lines of a skiff—for instance, a wider stern—enabled it to take on more weight and gain more balance, but sacrifice speed and ease of turning. Wes would watch the French bateaux with pointed bow and stern, dugouts, pirogues, and "covered sleds" or "ferry-flats," silently gauging their maneuverability and functionality.

But this particular skiff would give Wes ample freedom to prosecute the next serious stage of his self-education: assembling a first-class collection of freshwater shells. North America boasts the world's largest diversity of freshwater mussels, some 350 varieties known in Powell's day, the richest concentration lying in the Ohio and western stretches of the Mississippi, ranging from the 1.5-inch Lilliputian to the dinner-plate-sized white heel splitter and five-pound washboard, some living for up to a hundred years. Their vernacular names caught the rough poetry of pioneer life: lady's dagger, elephant ear, deer toe, pimpleback, pink mucket, fawn's foot. Wes liked to beach his skiff on the shoals that appeared at riverbends to poke among the rocks for shells dropped by muskrat or raccoon, as the iridescent white, pink, and purple interiors struck his eye. The trash piles, or middens, of early riparian Indians also proved rich hunting grounds.

He found bivalves in the gravelly bottoms of streams and rivers, detecting their rough contours with his bare feet. Colorful markings defined the butterfly and the rainbow. In bankside outcroppings, Wes pulled fossil mollusks, their shells heavier and grainier, lacking the chalkiness of living species. After several weeks on the river, the skiff rattled and grumbled from the shifting bags of shells. Wes not only discerned the telling similarities and differences between species, but also how much individuals within a single species might vary. He could also detect the relations between shells and where they grew. In fast water, he knew he would find the monkey face, its knobby protuberances preventing the swiftest current from washing it away. In lakes or on slower-moving streams, he would dig out yellow sand shells or shiny-rayed pocketbooks, their smooth shells enabling them to ride effortlessly through mud and sand.

Wes was beginning to weave together strands of the bright web that connects the teeming natural world. Although science knew little yet of glaciology—let alone how the Wisconsin Glaciation more than ten thousand years earlier had scraped, abraded, and gouged much of North America under a mile-high mass of ice—he became conversant with what would soon be termed "glacial wash," the pebbles, clay, sand, and cobbles that the great sheets had dumped upon the emerging landscape as they receded. He began to tell how soil and vegetation altered with changes in the drift. The intimate relation between surface geology and agriculture made itself inescapably clear.

Victorian naturalists had begun to collect marine invertebrates seriously, believing them a key to unlocking the secrets of life. Darwin had driven himself to distraction—and deeper ill health—systemetizing the world's largest barnacle collection over eight years. Collecting invertebrates caught fire in America as well, Edgar Allan Poe lending his name to promote *The Conchologist's First Book* in 1839. As American naturalists ranged across a new continent, they still collected with something of a chip on their shoulders, laboring under the European disdain embodied in the unfounded assumption that America's fauna and flora, like its indigenous peoples, were somehow degenerate. The great French naturalist Georges-Louis Leclerc, comte de Buffon, whose six-thousand-page *Histoire Naturelle* had been consulted by most educated men on both sides of the Atlantic, claimed that the New World's cold and wet climate had withered its fauna. "In America, therefore," opined Leclerc in his fifth volume, "animated Nature is weaker, less active, and more circumscribed in the variety of her productions." The count's theory of North American degeneracy rang pleasantly in the ears of social scientists and politicians intent on proving that European civilization remained—and could remain—superior to that of the raw New World. Many American naturalists, Wes included, readily saw that the collections of their continent's natural gifts were fuel for a mounting nationalism.

For Wes, any casual assumption of nature's permanence began to dissolve. Rivers jumped their courses, mussel species simply died out—the world existed in endless flux. What could he be sure of that was permanent?

January 1859 found the twenty-four-year-old teaching in Hennepin, a small northern Illinois farming town perched on bluffs carved by the Illinois River as it broke south from its westward course. His on-again, off-again sampling of higher education was over. Financial difficulties and boredom had ended his brief matriculations at Illinois College, Illinois Institute, and Oberlin, leaving him with no degree to show for his efforts. Yet he found that he had been born with a talent for teaching and administration, which soon carried him to become principal of the Hennepin School system for $100 a month. More important, he had discovered that fieldwork satisfied his ever-burning curiosity far more than the classroom. Teaching furnished him with the long breaks necessary to explore.

Outside Hennepin, he found rich hunting grounds for fossils in the slag heaps of coal mines, then chased up Senachiwine and Crow creeks and other tributaries of the Illinois. His forays collecting mollusks by now not only reached along the Mississippi, but also the Ohio, Des Moines, Wabash, and Illinois rivers. He had searched the small interior waters of Wisconsin and Illinois, got up to the Great Lakes, and lingered so long prospecting for minerals in the Iron Mountains south of St. Louis that he had to pawn his watch to get home. His mollusk collection had grown into one of North America's finest, which he carefully housed in sturdy wooden boxes he built himself. Anyone can pick up something and stick it in their pocket. But when a collector moves beyond the desire to own only the finest, most unusual specimens and settles in to collect a wide diversity of examples, then new insights become available, detail upon detail that beget new questions. "Facts fall from the poetic observer as ripe seeds," wrote Thoreau upon discovering the beauty of keeping precise records of the seasons and climate around Walden Pond.

In 1860, the twenty-six-year-old got the professional break he so desperately craved: His impressive collection, along with a good word from Professor Turner, earned him membership in the Natural History Society of Illinois, and his mollusks drew second prize at the Illinois Agricultural Society fair in Jacksonville. Then, again with Turner's warm endorsement, he joined the Natural History Society's committee on conchology, eagerly becoming its secretary. The 1860 census listed Wesley not as a teacher or farmer, but as a "naturalist." In truth, this designation remained a stretch—he was still only a very talented amateur, his collection representing more sweat and passion than knowledge and expertise; many of the specimens he identified only by locality. College credentials might have evaded him, but his mollusks now landed him among serious scientists, whom he soon impressed with his drive and intense curiosity. His emerging abilities, it became apparent, lay not in careful, detailed descriptions, but in discerning wider patterns—a general field of inquiry that would later be termed as ecology.

And, even better, he was in love.

Her name was Emma, the daughter of his maternal half-uncle and his wife, Joseph and Harriet Dean. In 1855, his mother had received a startling letter that the Deans had actually come to America a half dozen years earlier and were living in Detroit. Joseph and Harriet Dean had agreed to travel with Mary and Joseph from England in 1829, but never showed up at the ship. Now here they belatedly were, Joseph working as a hatmaker and doing well. Mary set off at once to see them. On one of Wes's many collecting trips, he passed through Detroit and met his cousin Emma, a year and a half his junior. Just topping five feet, she had flashing blue eyes that lit up an oval face, her dark brown hair swept back into an elaborate braid. The quick and curious Emma delighted in her first cousin's stories.

When Wes's parents could see that the romance was more than a passing fancy, they grew alarmed at the closeness of kinship, even though Mary's brother and she had different mothers. Joseph put his foot down hard, forbidding any marriage. But Wes, in a decision that declared and finally defined his independence, ignored his father's command.

They got engaged. But before they could get married, the nation convulsed into war.

CHAPTER 3

Thinking Bayonets

O n April 15, 1861, the day following the fall of Fort Sumter, Lincoln called upon the state governors to raise seventy-five thousand volunteers for a three-month commitment to put down "combinations too powerful to be suppressed by the ordinary course of judicial proceedings," which pushed Arkansas, North Carolina, Tennessee, and Virginia to secede in short order. Just a fortnight later, the quickly mounting tensions forced Lincoln's hand further. He called for more volunteers, this time for a wartime commitment of three years. The conflict that he had worked so hard to prevent was coming to pass.

Five days after this latest call, the thickly bewhiskered twenty-seven-year-old John Wesley Powell, along with nine others from Hennepin, took the train six miles east to Granville, where they enlisted in the 20th Illinois Volunteer Infantry Regiment. The newly minted private looked upon going to war as the ultimate patriotic act: "It was a great thing to destroy slavery," he would write, his father's sentiments now an organic part of his outlook, "but the integrity of the Union was of no less importance . . ." Like a family torn asunder by a deadly feud, the Union needed a firm hand to pull it back together. Powell steadfastly believed that Lincoln was strong and wise enough to do it.

The Rock Island Railroad deposited the party in Joliet around

4 p.m. They marched to the fairgrounds, where they found sheds scattered with straw for their pallets. After a slim meal of sour-bread, a slice of bacon apiece, and coffee in tin cups, the new soldiers retired to the floors without overcoats or blankets, and shivered the night away. Soon they were issued blankets and .58 caliber Springfield muskets. Days of drilling followed. The men voted Powell sergeant of Company H, as much in recognition of his college training and position as principal of Hennepin as for his yet-to-be-unveiled soldierly talents. But he had no intention of merely teaching boys fresh from the plow how to march and mark time.

To Powell, so well acquainted with Midwest river systems, the outgoing Union general-in-chief Winfield Scott's proposed Ana-conda Plan would have made eminent sense: Starve Southern ports with naval blockades, then fight down the Mississippi to New Orleans, and split the rebel states in two. A sustained Union offensive would require much expertise not only at overrunning defensive works but in building them as well. The fresh-faced in-fantryman decided his immediate future lay in becoming an ex-pert in the science of fortification. The method in Methodism had seen to it that he knew how to study—or more accurately, in his case—how to cram. With little in the way of formal education, he had willed himself into a naturalist, then conchologist, and, after that, into an apparently gifted teacher. Now he turned to military engineering and the science of war. He secured leave to travel sixty miles by rail to Chicago, ostensibly to buy a uniform, but with the real purpose of obtaining copies of Dennis Hart Mahan's *Treatise on Field Fortifications* and another volume by Sébastien Le Prestre de Vauban, the seventeenth-century master of fortress building. He also bought a slim book on tactics and army regula-tions and managed a quick side trip to visit Emma in Detroit.

Back in Joliet, Powell pored over these manuals, musing on the "uses of counterscarp galleries" and the "relation between the terre-plein and interior crest of the square redoubt." For a mind untutored in engineering, the task of mastering such concepts proved daunting indeed, but he found a willing helper in his commanding officer, Lieutenant Colonel C. Caroll Marsh.

On June 13, 1861, the 20th Illinois was formally mustered into service, Marsh promoting Powell to second lieutenant to fill a vacancy. The regiment traveled by train to Alton, then on to St. Louis, where the townspeople turned out to cheer their 961 saviors. St. Louis's armory furnished Enfield rifles and handsome new blue uniforms. "We now had a very extravagant opinion of ourselves," recalled a veteran of the outfit years later. On July 6, they chugged down the Mississippi to Cape Girardeau in southeastern Missouri aboard the steamer *Illinois*. The town reminded one army surgeon of a French village, consisting of basically one long, narrow, deeply rutted street leading up from the river between low houses with projecting eaves. For all its modest demeanor, however, Cape Girardeau occupied a strategic position—the first high ground commanding the Mississippi north of its confluence with the Ohio at Cairo. The ability to deploy artillery at Cape Girardeau would prevent Confederate warships from sailing north to raid St. Louis. The ten companies set up their Sibley tents just to the north in an open area near the bank.

Marsh ordered Powell to survey the ground with an eye toward fortifying the headland. Powell set to work, breaking only for a five-day expedition with Companies H, E, and G to pursue guerillas into the interior. Bushwhackers were known to lie in roadside swamps, wrote an embittered infantryman, and would "murder Jesus Christ if they thought he was a Union man." The expedition came home unbloodied.

Within two weeks of the 20th Illinois's arrival, the newly appointed commander of the Department of the West, Major General John C. Frémont, appeared with a large retinue of foreigners, including illegally commissioned Hungarian and Italian veterans bedecked with feathers and gold loops. When the forty-eight-year-old general asked Marsh whether he had given thought to fortifying the town, the colonel turned to Powell. For someone who had been a village schoolmaster only weeks before, the chance to meet the Pathfinder must have been electrifying. Frémont was as colorful a character as the young republic would bring forth—charismatic, outspoken, always in a web of quarrels and intrigues. The illegitimate son of a Richmond socialite, he had been court-martialed for mutiny in the Mexican War, served as a U.S. senator, and run in 1856 as the first Republican candidate for president. But perhaps most impressive to Powell was Frémont's reputation as the greatest western explorer since Lewis and Clark, having mounted five expeditions into the still-unknown western vastness. His first, in 1842, a five-month journey at the head of twenty-five men, including Kit Carson, made him a national hero, his report excerpted in newspapers across the nation. "Frémont has touched my imagination," wrote Henry Wadsworth Longfellow, and he no doubt touched Powell's as well. With strong government backing, Frémont ground out a plethora of reports and maps that would not only bring him his sobriquet, but guide thousands west to Oregon, direct the '49ers to California, and inspire Brigham Young to seek out Utah.

Lincoln had tasked Frémont with the tall order of keeping the turbulent border state of Missouri from seceding while maintaining the adjacent stretch of the Mississippi as a wedge into the heart of the Confederacy. Although professing neutrality, Missouri lay deeply divided. Depredations and brutalities were visited upon civilians of both sympathies. Cape Girardeau proved to be one of the few Unionist havens in southeastern Missouri. "Quite a number of beautiful girls here," commented one soldier, the consequence of many Union-sympathizing fathers sending their daughters there for protection.

Frémont, whose dark ringlets fell over a handsome brow, sized up the young lieutenant. This seasoned explorer had learned something about judging men. Powell succinctly outlined his ideas for a series of four strongpoints forming a square around the town—two on the river bluffs and two inland overlooking the major road approaches. Frémont liked what he heard. The following day, he ordered immediate construction to begin, directing Captain Henry Flad of the Engineer Regiment of the West to supervise the overall design. Colonel Marsh assigned Powell to oversee work on the critically placed Fort D, the position with the best river vantage. Powell set the loyalist Missouri militia to work. He paid escaped slaves to join in.

No attack came. Frémont lasted only three months in command, but still made the war-changing decision to elevate a binge-drinking former Illinois shopkeeper to brigadier general above John Pope, his highly competent and most senior officer of that rank. Ulysses S. Grant combined the unassuming character, dogged persistence, and iron will that the Union so desperately needed to command its raw new armies.

Grant's first action in command of southeast Missouri and the southern tip of Illinois was to inspect Cape Girardeau on August 30, where he met Powell and heard about the ambitious plans under way. The neophyte general confidently elaborated on ideas about defending this small town, exhibiting skills he would later demonstrate again and again, to U.S. senators and presidents, to railroadmen, fur trappers, and Indians—a quiet, no-nonsense, sustained competence undiminished by grandstanding. Powell could not only pick up skills at lightning speed, but also at once put them effectively to work.

In October Grant detached the "acting engineer" from the 20th Illinois and authorized him to independently raise an artillery battery and manage Cape Girardeau's siege guns, a rare action for a general to take toward so junior an officer, even in the feverish expansion of Union forces. A deep vote of confidence, indeed. Powell undertook to raise a company of 132 men in two days, a task that proved surprisingly easy. Many men displaced from their homesteads by partisan violence were eager to sign up for Battery F of the Second Light Artillery, 20th Illinois Volunteers. A lot were skilled, liberal-leaning German immigrants who had come to America after the failed 1848 German revolts. Mostly in their twenties and thirties, they represented a broad spectrum of common occupations, from baker, house painter, and druggist, to farmer, carpenter, and "segar maker." At twenty-seven, Powell was only a little older than the median age of his recruits.

The still-green soldier once more showed himself a quick study. Managing an artillery battery has always been a complicated task. Powell now commanded more than a hundred men who operated six cannons, each hitched to a limber pulled by six horses. In support of each artillery piece, another six horses drew yet another limber, which itself dragged a caisson, a two-wheeled carriage bearing ammunition chests and an extra wheel. A battery also included a forge, ambulance, and battery wagon, requiring in all about 125 horses. Each time a cannon was discharged, a team of men underwent "the cannoneer's hop," a precise sequence of cleaning the barrel, priming, ramming the charge, aiming, and firing. In battle, the entire process often had to be performed under heavy fire and war's irregular conditions. Training—and more training—was essential.

When Grant returned to the Cape in late November, he and Powell spent three hours inspecting the fortifications. Their horseback tour might easily have taken a quarter of the time, but the general enjoyed the younger man's company. Grant extended an invitation for dinner aboard his steamboat, where their bond grew even stronger. Of the two leaders graven in his mind, Powell felt drawn to Grant in a way he had not been to Frémont. Unlike Frémont, Grant usually traveled with the smallest possible command staff, which left Powell free to talk to and observe his commander up close. Grant wore a private's uniform with stars sewn on it and an unassuming slouch hat; a surgeon described him as a man with "gentle" eyes who did "nothing carelessly." His one nod to sartorial splendor was a longish square-cut beard. "One of my superstitions," Grant would write about his childhood, "had always been when I started to go anywhere or do anything, not to run back or to stop until the thing was accomplished." The new commander would become a model of leadership for the newly coined engineer—humble yet fiercely willful, and never a quitter.

Grant gave Powell leave on November 28 to travel to Detroit to marry Emma. Sharp in his blue uniform—very much the "efficient officer," as Grant described him—Powell arrived at 6 p.m. One local newspaper would recall the bride as "a very beautiful young woman." They were immediately married in the parlor of her father's house. Powell's parents were several hundred miles away. By 8 p.m. that night, the couple had boarded a train back to Cape Girardeau. Like many officers' wives, Emma would follow her husband on campaign, embracing the opportunity to escape her childhood home.

By early December, Powell's battery had still not been formally mustered in, leaving him to reassure the men that their pay would soon come. Only after Grant himself fired off a rather irritated dispatch to headquarters, "respectfully" asking for the incorporation of Battery F, did it officially come into being, Powell as its captain.

In the early winter of 1862, Grant began his southward thrust into Tennessee by overwhelming Forts Henry and Donelson and forcing the enemy to regroup at Corinth, a strategic railroad hub in northern Mississippi. The Union's western commander, Major General Henry Halleck, ordered Grant to assemble his forces at a rural steamboat dock on the Tennessee River just 22 miles from Corinth. He ordered Grant to await reinforcement by Major General Don Carlos Buell's 35,000-man army, which lay 120 miles away, and by Halleck's own. Only at full strength did the cautious Halleck want Grant to attack the Confederates at Corinth. But tiny Pittsburg Landing, only envisioned as a way station, would soon etch itself into the divided nation's consciousness, its name to be eclipsed by Shiloh, a small neighboring church.

On March 14, Battery F steamed southward from Cape Girardeau to join Grant's forces at the Landing. Powell left Emma in
Savannah, a riverside hamlet nine miles downstream from the
Landing. When the battery arrived, white Sibley tents were scattered thickly over the rough plateau on the high western bluffs
that overlooked a broken landscape of heavy forests, small fields,
orchards, and steep ravines. Five major farm roads transected the
area, notably the Corinth Road that ran southwestward. The battery found a place to camp. Light drilling duties left men time to
play cards and roll dice, pitch horseshoes, or write letters. Pink
blossoms hung heavily on the branches of peach trees, and Johnny-
jump-ups carpeted the fields. Neither Grant nor his friend and
division commander, Brigadier General William Tecumseh Sherman, saw any reason to raise defensive works, not imagining that
the Confederates would ever dream of leaving their Corinth
stronghold.

But General Albert Sidney Johnston, the Confederacy's commander at Corinth and its most senior field officer, had no intention of letting the Union army swell to full strength. He ordered a
surprise attack on the Union position at Pittsburg Landing. His
40,000 men marched for two days through wretched weather, coming within a mile of Union pickets on Saturday night. Scouts
alerted Sherman to unusual amounts of hostile activity, only to be
stood down by the general, who was convinced that nighttime and
their imaginations had taken the better of them.

At 7:30 a.m., the rattle of musketry and the roar of artillery
startled Powell awake in his tent. General P. G. T. Beauregard
staggered four Confederate corps one right behind the other, with
the design of piercing enemy defenses. The plan worked: The Confederates drove right into the Union line so fast that they overran
groggy bluecoats drinking coffee around their breakfast fires.
Many Union soldiers did not stop running until they hit the river.

Battery F lay encamped well back from the front line. Powell
ordered its horses harnessed and artillery limbered. The men

gulped down their breakfasts and stood by their guns. And then they waited. The din of drum and bugle grew loud, the thunder of artillery louder still. Powell found himself in an awkward position. Recently arrived, his was one of five Illinois batteries not yet assigned to an infantry division. As the men eyed one another nervously, Powell awaited orders. A rabble, many shouting that all was lost, passed by. Then in stumbled the walking wounded. Still no orders.

While the Union forces fell back in disarray, many Confederates, famished from their forced march, paused to finish the hastily abandoned Union breakfasts and to loot possessions, affording the Union army a precious hour to re-form its shattered center. The battle now degenerated into what one historian has called "a disorganized, murderous fistfight." The attack had nearly dissolved Grant's Sixth Division under Brigadier General Benjamin Prentiss, which had begun the day with 5,400 men, but by 9:45 a.m. could muster only about 500.

By 9 a.m., Powell had made up his mind that—with or without orders—he would take his guns into action. The day before he had learned that the battery might be attached to General John Mc-Clernand's division, which lay down the Corinth Road and to the left of Sherman's division. Moving the battery forward over the worn thoroughfare, now choked with the wounded, proved nearly impossible for the six-horse teams to negotiate, particularly at its two bridges. The less than mile-and-a-half move to the front took ninety agonizing minutes. The broken spirit of stragglers and wounded alike declared everything they needed to know about the desperate struggle ahead.

As it swung west, the Corinth Road cut through Duncan Field, in the center of which stood a farmhouse and some small outbuildings. Its gunners striding briskly beside their pieces, Powell's battery approached the farm to support McClernand's foundering left. The timing could not have been worse: Just as Powell's men rolled forward, the center Union front collapsed. Battery F came up directly against Confederate regiments from Mississippi and Tennessee. A volley dropped the horse of the sergeant riding next to Powell, badly injuring its rider. The screams of the battery's wounded horses rent the air; another man fell. Powell looked to see where he might unlimber his guns and make a stand but, at that very moment, hundreds of demoralized Union men broke to run back behind the Duncan house, then crossed the field in head-long flight.

Battery F now lay terribly exposed. Powell ordered it to fall back. Unhitching the dead and dying horses, the cannoneers swung their cumbersome guns around under unremitting fire. All their training threatened to disintegrate in one shrill instant in the hysteria inflamed by the screams of horses and men and the hiss of minié balls. But Powell rode up and down and kept his head, and the men struggled on. They abandoned one cannon, its horses substituting for the disabled animals on the other guns and caisson wagons—a black mark indeed for an artillery unit—but Powell counted it lucky to escape with the other five pieces.

Battery F pulled back four hundred yards behind the original line, then moved a few hundred more feet south down Eastern Corinth Road before pulling in behind Minnesota and Missouri batteries. Powell galloped off, quickly encountering his fellow Il-linoisan Brigadier General W. H. L. Wallace, who agreed to incorporate Battery F into his division.

Spurring back to the guns as his men unlimbered them, Powell examined the patch of woods in front of them, which ran a ragged half mile along the rutted secondary road. Soon some eleven thousand men would jam these woods, a spot that became known as the Hornet's Nest. Powell had landed himself and his battery in one of the war's fiercest actions, the epicenter of a battle in which more men died in two days than in all previous American military encounters combined. The cannon sounded like "the roaring of a great herd of lions," noted Confederate private Henry Morton Stanley, who would famously go on to meet Livingston in the

African jungle. Battery F lay seventy-five to one hundred yards immediately behind the Hornet's Nest front line.

Around midday, Grant rode up, instructing his divisional generals to hold the position at all costs. Over the course of the early afternoon, men from fourteen of the sixteen Confederate brigades hammered the Hornet's Nest in eight furious charges. "Men fell around us as leaves from the trees," recalled a terrified private. The men of one Ohio battery simply abandoned everything and fled the scene.

Powell held firm. His five guns methodically poured fire over and through slight gaps in the trees. Confederates came within sixty paces of the Union infantry before steady fire forced them back. The scream of cannons and the cries of the wounded rent the smoky air. Grant's division commanders had taken his orders to heart, continuing to hold the line at the Hornet's Nest even as their flanks began to cave in. They now manned a bulge, or salient, deeply vulnerable to being cut off. Wallace ordered Battery F to support the collapsing left flank in a peach orchard. Powell leaped off his horse as his men readied the cannon, directing them to aim at the enemy right where Confederate soldiers had taken cover behind a fence. He ordered the men to load solid shot so as to knock the railings down. He raised his right arm to signal his gunners to commence firing.

A musket ball from some two hundred yards away struck Powell just above the wrist, the soft lead shattering hard bone, flattening, and then plowing down his forearm. In the chaos of the battle, he barely noticed the wound, realizing its severity only when he tried to mount his horse. Under a nearby tree, now bereft of most branches, he examined his crushed hand, but the sight of more Union soldiers running from the field drew his attention. A terrible anger boiled within him at their apparent cowardice. Only then did he see three Confederate brigades in hasty pursuit. The Union left center now teetered on the edge of collapse.

Light-headed with shock, Powell did not shake off a medical officer who rushed to cut away his sleeve. But before the medic could finish, General Wallace galloped up, dismounted, and in one fluid motion swung Powell onto the saddle of a nearby horse, barking at a sergeant to accompany Powell back to the Landing. Powell could do little more than weakly nod his thanks. Just minutes later, an enemy ball would smash into the back of Wallace's head and exit his eye. He would fall to the ground, apparently dead. The Confederates pressing in, his men left him.

The sergeant led Powell through the gauntlet formed now by the two Confederate wings pressing pincerlike on the flanks of the ragged Union salient, rounds flying all around them. They made the Landing just in time. At 5:45 p.m., the Confederates cut off the Hornet's Nest, leaving 2,250 soldiers prisoner. But the Union's stubborn resistance had given Grant sufficient time to assemble a formidable defensive line along the bluff commanding the Landing. Without their captain, Battery F had hastily retreated and now took up their position there.

The Confederates suffered their own crippling loss that day when their talented commander General Johnston took a ball to his left calf and bled to death. Southern assaults continued, but they were poorly coordinated and ultimately collapsed under the fire from the guns amassed above the Landing. After this long, bloody day, the Confederates had little will or energy left to sustain the offensive. Johnston's successor, General P. G. T. Beauregard, called off the attack as night fell, telegraphing Richmond that his army had won a "complete victory."

At the Landing, Powell watched dazedly as wagons delivered load after load of wounded to an old warehouse, now a temporary hospital, where a ghastly heap of amputated arms and legs steadily grew. The river below the bluff was crowded with dozens of requisitioned boats of every size and shape, each inch jammed with the stricken. Powell squeezed aboard a craft, which steamed off to Savannah. Emma met her delirious husband on the bankside. "Now, now," gasped Powell in response to Emma's tears. "Everything is going to be all right."

The army had turned nearly every structure into makeshift hospitals, Powell winding up in a bed on the second floor of the town hall. The American continent had never seen such a concentration of catastrophically wounded soldiers. The medical staff was simply overwhelmed. Of the eleven thousand nominal surgeons attached to the entire Union forces, only five hundred had performed operations in civilian life. That day, many became surgeons on the job by trial and, too often, error. "Amputations were abundant," wrote a federal surgeon, "and, as usual in very many cases in the upper extremities, entirely unnecessary." Yet a decision to amputate was less capricious than it might have seemed. Unlike a high-velocity rifle bullet, a relatively slow-moving, yet heavy and soft lead minié ball crashes into the human body, flattening and deforming upon impact. It did not just break bone, but splintered it, not only puncturing the tissue but shredding it, driving dirt and sweaty scraps of clothing into the opening it created.

Doctors often probed wounds with unwashed fingers to find the lead, moving along the line of shrieking patients, reusing sponges from previous procedures. Under these Dantesque conditions and well before the development of antibiotics, wounds were invaded by every form of microorganism; sepsis alone killed more than 90 percent of those it afflicted. Without the time, the tools, or the most basic skills to attempt reconstructive surgery, the medical staff correctly saw amputation as the most effective means to stave off death.

Surgeon William H. Medcalfe of the 49th Illinois Volunteers attended the delirious Powell, with Emma at his side. Powell was lucky: The forty-year-old University of Pennsylvania Medical School graduate boasted more surgical experience than most of his peers. During his civilian practice in Olney, Illinois, he had performed, among other operations, the complicated facial reconstruction of a girl shot by accident. Medcalfe cleaned Powell's wound, then extracted the spent round and bandaged the mangled hand and wrist. Samuel Gross's then standard on the subject, *A Manual of Military Surgery,* which Medcalfe carried with him, recommended against amputation until the patient could bear the shock and loss of blood. Powell's complexion remained deadly pale, his pulse small and threading. Medcalfe gave him laudanum and instructed Emma to force tea into him. All Saturday night she attended to her husband of only four months, amid the groans and cries of the wounded.

The evening turned chilly and a heavy rain set in, amplifying the unimaginable misery of the wounded left on the field of battle. All of Grant's divisional commanders, even the indomitable Sherman, felt that the day had been lost, urging their leader to put the river between them and the victorious enemy. When Major General James B. McPherson articulated plans for pulling back, Grant exploded. "Retreat? No. I propose to attack at daylight and whip them." With Major General Lew Wallace's division now arrived, plus some elements of Buell's Army of the Ohio, Grant could bring reinforcements onto the still confused battlefield.

The ensuing Union assault that Monday morning caught the exhausted Confederates completely off guard. While their lines did not break, they fell back. Just after 2 p.m., a staff officer asked Beauregard: "General, do you not think our troops are in the condition of a lump of sugar thoroughly soaked with water, but yet preserving its original shape, though ready to dissolve?" Beauregard agreed. Pessimistic about the offensive in the first place, he ordered his worn-out army back to Corinth.

"I wanted to pursue," wrote Grant, "but had not the heart to order the men who had fought desperately for two days." On the battlefield, soldiers retrieved the soaked, shivering, and bloody Brigadier General W. H. L. Wallace, who had lifted the wounded Powell onto a horse the day before. Somehow he had survived through the night. Wallace ended up under his wife's care in Grant's headquarters at Savannah but died in her arms several days later.

Surgeon Medcalfe waited through Monday, regularly stumbling in to check on Powell, but must have had many more terribly critical cases to contend with. Powell's wound was not so frightful as to make amputation absolutely necessary right away. Indeed Emma may herself have urged delay. Even so, Medcalfe was risking much by waiting. Amputations performed within forty-eight hours offered a 25 percent likelihood of mortality, but rose to 50 percent subsequently.

Finally, on Tuesday, April 8, just as forty-eight hours had elapsed since Powell took the bullet, Medcalfe prepared him for surgery, pouring chloroform onto a sponge that he placed over the shallowly breathing face. The anesthetic proved a lifesaver, not only dulling the pain but giving, as one fellow amputee testified, the sensation of a "vessel sailing through the air." Medcalfe deployed his bone saw with speed, finishing the procedure in the fewest possible minutes to minimize shock and blood loss. During a similar amputation, General "Stonewall" Jackson—Lee's most effective lieutenant—remembered hearing the most beautiful violin music, only to wake up and realize that the sound had been that of a saw on the bone of his left arm. He died of pneumonia nine days later.

Medcalfe tied off the arteries with threads, then rasped and scraped the bone edges, pulled a flap of skin over the stump below the elbow, and sewed it closed. He did little to the nerve ends. Neuralgic pain would haunt Powell for the rest of his life. But he was alive.

The Union's remarkable turnaround at Shiloh dealt the Confederates a hard blow in the western theater. At first, Northern newspapers hailed Grant as a hero, Congress suspending business and Lincoln declaring a national day of thanksgiving. But rejoicing soon turned to shock as the horrifying enormity of the butcher's bill emerged. Any smug certainty that an overall Union victory must come soon also died in the aftermath of that grim battle. Scrutiny turned upon Grant, particularly on his neglecting to build defensive positions at Pittsburg Landing. Rumors of his drinking at Shiloh swept north.

One evening at the White House, a group of advisers and friends pressed Lincoln to fire the beset general. The president listened with characteristic care, then stood and simply replied, "I can't spare this man; he fights."

As soon as he was able, Powell scrawled a letter with his remaining hand to his mother back in Illinois. The script may have been boyish and straggly, but it displayed indomitable spirit in its simple acknowledgment that liberty comes at a price. People from all over town dropped in to witness this inspiring document with their own eyes.

Powell had come of age that bloody week. Emma did her best to buoy his spirits, keeping a sharp eye out for those tiny dark spots that marked the first sign of gangrene. No longer could he wash his own hand or button his shirt. Emma faithfully attended to these prosaic transactions: keeping the wound clean, washing his clothes, and generally serving as his lost right hand. Powell later credited her continued presence, fortitude, and unwearied devotion with keeping him alive.

Four months later, Powell reported to Springfield with orders to keep a more active convalescence as a recruiting officer—of course, accompanied by Emma. Here he worked on writing legibly with his left hand. Even though a committed, even ardent, recruiter, the sight of a still-pale amputee must have engendered some misgivings among possible recruits. But Powell longed to get back to the action. By March 1863, he and Emma had rejoined his men at Lake Providence, Louisiana, where Grant's forces were mobilizing to assault Vicksburg, the "Gibraltar of the South."

Sitting on a hairpin bend of the Mississippi, forty miles west of the state's capital, Jackson, its mansions perched on high, steep bluffs, the town served as "the nailhead that held the South's two halves together," Jefferson Davis had explained. Its fall would cripple the Confederacy, perhaps fatally. But taking this citadel remained no easy task. Treacherous wetlands bogged down anyone who approached by land. The formidable heights gave its batteries a deadly vantage against gunboats.

Grant moved most of his army to Milliken's Bend and Young's Point, small Louisiana towns on the west bank to the northeast of Vicksburg. In his first action for nearly a year with Battery F, Powell took the company from Lake Providence to Milliken's Bend in late March. Several Union attempts on Vicksburg had failed badly already, so Grant devised a brilliant plan that would yield one of the fastest, most successful, and unorthodox campaigns of the war. Wetlands prevented an approach from the north, so Grant's most effective gambit was to send the Union army south along the west bank of the Mississippi to well below Vicksburg. There they would cross the river, then work their way back north to attack. This massive logistical undertaking would rely on his moving the Union ships down past the fortress to the ferry point. Otherwise he could not move his men across the river.

In mid-April the Union forces began their march south, working their way along Walnut Bayou Road, which ran atop the natural levees skirting Roundaway Bayou between Richmond, Louisiana, and New Carthage. The heat had already risen, and sweat quickly soaked the men's wool uniforms. The spring rains were heavy that year, creating vast lakes out of swamps and bayous. Ground travel proved possible only along the tops of narrow levees, but these were thick with deep mud and periodically riven by great, flood-torn cuts. "I look upon the Whole thing as one of the most hazardous & desperate moves of this or any war," wrote Sherman to his wife. The troops lit bales of cotton to drive away the clouds of gnats. The coughing, exhausted men kept a sharp lookout for water snakes and the occasional alligator.

Powell and his command were constantly forced to improvise methods for moving their heavy guns along these awful tracks, often assembling corduroy roads—lines of felled trees packed side by side—to secure footing for their animals and the wagon wheels. The road ran through an interminable bog, intersected by numerous half-flooded bayous. They threw up bridges of lumber they cut themselves, jury-rigging and gerrymandering their way over the broken landscape. They reassembled their gun carriages and mustered whatever they could to pull their big pieces out of the muddy pits. Powell closely monitored the condition of the exhausted horses and kept his men focused.

While his army wearily marched toward the obscure Bruinsburg Landing, Grant persuaded the acting rear admiral David D. Porter, his equal in rank and commander of the gunboats, to take the squadron by night on a hair-raising dash past Vicksburg's batteries. Porter brought off the maneuver brilliantly, escaping with far fewer casualties than anticipated. Several days later, an armada of leased army steamboats again rushed southward past the guns to fulfill Grant's ambitious plans.

Six days after breaking camp, after seventy miles of marching, Powell brought Battery F to the designated river crossing. On April 30, the ramshackle flotilla ferried 24,000 men and sixty guns across the Mississippi, the nation's largest amphibious operation until Normandy in World War II. A vast river to their back and the stronghold of Vicksburg across their land route now separated the Union army from its base of supplies, but at least they had found dry land. After months of repulses, Grant's men now had the mighty citadel in their sights.

A direct drive north upon Vicksburg was ruled out by the absence of roads and the need to cross at least four major waterways to knock aside the garrisons of the forward Confederate positions. Instead, Grant decided to push west toward Jackson and cut off the railway that carried critical supplies to his objective. In doing so, he would brook conventional military wisdom, forgoing the traditional supply chain, which supported an advancing army. Without the cumbersome wagon train, the army could move fast, but now faced the chance of being cut off by Lieutenant General John C. Pemberton's Confederate Army of Mississippi. Powell and Battery F, who depended on more than a hundred horses to move their guns and powder, now found themselves foraging for the two dozen pounds of grain and hay that each animal required daily. When the soldiers butchered more meat than they could eat, they impaled what remained on their bayonets, shouldered their rifles, and marched off.

During the first seventeen days of May, the Army of the Tennessee would cover more than one hundred miles, fight five actions—Port Gibson, Raymond, Jackson, Champion Hill, and Big Black River Bridge—sever the Southern Railroad of Mississippi, take the state's capital, and press Pemberton's Confederates into Vicksburg. Battery F fought at the two final battles, Champion Hill and Big Black River Bridge. Three months of hard travel had driven into Powell critical lessons in the business of war—particularly the necessity for being flexible—but perhaps most important, the centrality of logistics. While Grant would receive most of his kudos from the civilian Northern press for his battlefield mastery, it was his logistical acumen, over a gallery of different landscapes, that would win the war, illustrating the axiom that amateur soldiers talk about tactics, while professionals study logistics. Powell could see what it took to live off a hostile countryside, which would figure prominently in his struggle against a more impersonal, ferocious enemy than the Rebels—the Colorado River.

Thousands upon thousands of Confederate infantrymen now retreated into the citadel. They blocked approaches with felled trees, threw up military emplacements, and reinforced the twisting seven-mile line of defense, which clung to tangled clumps of irregular hills, bluffs, and narrow ridges. Some twenty-eight thousand Confederates now manned the elaborate landward defenses, while several thousand more covered the river batteries.

On May 19, and then on the 22nd, Grant threw headlong assaults at the fortifications, only to see both repulsed with telling casualties. Grant's only choice now remained to besiege this key stronghold. The day after the last fruitless repulse, Grant ordered the construction of thirteen "approaches," zones wherein tunnelers and trench diggers could work their way up to or under Confederate salients. Battery F took position at Ransom's Approach—named after Brigadier General Thomas E. G. Ransom—on the northeastern outskirts of the city, into which they lobbed shells by day. Shaken by the realization that no structure, including their homes, offered sufficient protection, the town's five thousand civilians began digging caves into the yellowish loess topsoil of the broad hillside. The besiegers snickered at this "Prairie Dog Village" but would have been startled to learn that some caves had grown sumptuous with carpets and furniture, even including doors and separate rooms.

Powell found himself at the heart of the action. The paucity of trained engineers, made particularly acute by the sheer length of the siege lines, gave him ample opportunities to take an active leadership role. The sappers worked hardest and most effectively under cover of night as they laid out the works and dug trenches. Sap rollers—large protective structures made of intricately woven baskets packed with earth—protected their slow but steady work. As they dug, so the rollers advanced. Powell's battery continued to direct heavy covering fire into the city. They made fascines, bundles of cane bound together with telegraph wire that offered additional protection. Although the usual rumors flew that Grant was off drinking, he regularly visited Ransom's Approach to draw upon Powell's opinion.

On June 15, ground was broken at Ransom's Approach, about

two hundred yards from the Confederate lines. In ten days, the sap—some five feet deep and seven or eight feet wide, a series of half-parallels and winding *boyaux*—had crept to within seventy-five yards of the enemy rifle pits. Ransom ordered Powell to bring up two of his twelve-pounders to establish a dangerous, but brutally effective, battery position. The steepness of the sap forced the battery to unlimber the guns and drag the 1,230-pound brass cannon by hand and rope—grueling work in the heat of the Mississippi spring. Two days later, the Confederates, suddenly realizing that something was afoot, directed two Parrott twenty-pounders to rake Ransom's Approach. Powell worked his men day and night in shifts, widening and reinforcing a small area that could hold two pieces, creating an earthen parapet with embrasures for the gun muzzles. In this confined space, the men remounted the guns, then brought up powder and shot.

They came so close to the enemy that the men needed to build mantelets, thick boards to cover the embrasures when not in use. When Battery F was ready, the gun crew slammed open their mantelet and opened fire. In that brief moment, a storm of rifle balls poured through. A gunner jumped on his smoking piece and yelled at the enemy, "Too late!"

Covered by Powell's now ferocious close-range fire, the sappers pressed to within a few yards of the Rebel line by June 28, the day that nearby Logan's Approach detonated a mine that collapsed part of the Confederate position. The Unionists prepared for an all-out assault on the fourth of July.

Union artillery and snipers, the destruction wrought by the mine explosions, and the terrible privations extracted by the dwindling supplies convinced Confederate commander lieutenant general John C. Pemberton that Vicksburg could no longer be defended. On July 3, he raised a flag of truce and met with Grant to discuss terms of surrender. That day Major General George Meade's Army of the Potomac had defeated Lee's Army of Northern Virginia at

Gettysburg. While not finished, the now-split Confederacy was clearly on the ropes.

While his comrades crawled into the caves dug by the towns-people, Powell explored the former no-man's-land, particularly searching the waterfall and ledges at Mint Springs Bayou for bi-valve fossils. But the six weeks of work in the saps had exhausted him, even if it had kept his mind off his throbbing stump. Simply unable to continue with his unit, he requested leave to go with Emma to Detroit, where his arm underwent a resection to deaden some of the incessant pain. In two months, he rejoined Battery F, but elected to stay behind when it joined Sherman on his march to Atlanta. His younger brother Walter marched on with the guns.

At Vicksburg, Powell assumed command of one of the newly formed U.S. Colored Infantry regiments, many of whose volun-teers consisted of entire male family teams from particular plan-tations. Company B contained five Birdlong men from a plantation in Marksville, Louisiana—two men in their forties and three of their sons, all listed as eighteen, although they could well have been younger. The regiment also contained a contraband named General Jackson. Former slaves who had never known freedom underwent a culture shock in the Union camps, finding that their white comrades spoke in accents hard to understand and ate food alien to them. When Powell began training his five companies in weapon handling and garrison duty, it proved a frustrating expe-rience. Few of his charges were literate. And these black men just tasting freedom were exchanging slavery for a new net of tight restrictions.

Powell worked through these problems with characteristic pa-tience. What brought things to a crisis point—and one even he could do little about—was the ravages of disease. The white soldiers had already passed through a "seasoning" period, during which they either acquired various immunities or died. The newly freed inductees, until recently imprisoned on isolated plantations, had no exposures. They died in appalling numbers, leaving brief and heart-rending military records. Of the 463 men under Powell's command, more than a third died within months. It was a dispiriting task to set out to train these all-too-eager recruits who fell so quickly in front of him.

In late July, Battery F sustained heavy casualties at the Battle of Atlanta, in which Major General James B. McPherson, Powell's overall commanding officer at Vicksburg and Grant's best friend, was killed. The Confederates captured Powell's brother Walter among a number of his fellow gunners, packing them off to prisoner-of-war camps. Powell could learn nothing of their whereabouts, which only fed a deepening shadow of guilt that he had somehow let his unit down.

By September, no doubt partly moved by this guilt, even if undeserved, Powell turned down a promotion to lieutenant colonel in the U.S. Colored Troops and asked to be returned to his old unit in Atlanta. General O. O. Howard, now commanding the Army of the Tennessee—Grant having assumed the post of general in chief—appointed Powell to command all artillery units not presently accompanying Howard's march. He took a promotion to major. Powell, noted his superior, was "a straightforward and attentive officer," just the man to combine dispersed units.

Now in charge of sixteen batteries and their thousand men, Powell was ordered to move them to Savannah, Georgia, and join Sherman on his march north into the Carolinas. Getting his guns and men there entailed a long, circuitous journey through Nashville, where Union general George H. Thomas was preparing to annihilate John Bell Hood's Army of the Tennessee. Arriving at Nashville in the first week of December, Thomas pressed Powell into service, who, with two other majors, would oversee the construction of entrenchments around the city. When Thomas launched his final attack on Hood in mid-December, Powell rode by his side, coordinating the bombardment of Nashville's defenses.

The resulting conclusive Union victory proved to be the last full-scale battle in the western theater.

Two weeks later, Powell mustered out of the service. Four months after that, the war reached its endgame for all intents and purposes at Appomattox Court House in Virginia.

Powell came home to good news. Walter had been released from a prison camp in Columbia, South Carolina. But his appearance shocked the major. The five-foot-ten youthful man with thick arms and a strong back had been reduced to a barely recognizable husk of the quiet schoolteacher he had so recently been. The Powells could give thanks that he had returned from the Confederate Camp Sorghum, but it had been a close thing. Conditions there resembled those at Andersonville, a name synonymous with mistreatment and want, prisoners living amid squalor, rampant disease, starvation, and brutal treatment by guards. There was little shade against the burning sun, and the imprisoned men lived in their own filth, which brought about frequent outbreaks of dysentery. Whether because of sunstroke, dehydration, or terrible stress, Walter had simply snapped. A fellow Illinois soldier recalled seeing him walk into the deadly no-man's-land separating prisoners and guards, hands held aloft and praying in a loud voice "as mad as he could be." He would suffer from bouts of anger, moodiness, and depression for the rest of his life.

Of the ten men who had left Hennepin to enlist with a song in their hearts, two had died, two were crippled for life, and one had deserted.

Powell himself had changed indeed. The war had proven a master class in how to solve problems on the fly and lead small units through unimaginably harrowing conditions. "The Western volunteer became on occasion a pack mule, a fighting machine, an intelligent thinker and talker upon the tactics of armies, logistics, and the policy of the Government generally," wrote Lucian B. Crooker, whose 55th Illinois saw combat along with Powell at

Shiloh and Vicksburg. They had built bridges, fixed railroads, stormed forts, besieged cities, foraged profitably off the land, and seen so many of their friends die. Powell could feel justifiably proud that he had paid a terrible but magnificent price for saving the Union.

Now, as the soldiers from both sides came home, Americans would turn back to the fitting business of a growing nation—a big part of which lay in developing the still-little-known West.

CHAPTER 4

First Thoughts West

At war's end, a flood of the maimed returned home from the armies, the thirty-one-year-old Powell among more than twenty thousand Union soldiers missing a limb. He returned to a Victorian society with clear ideas about disability. "Formerly, a cripple was a cripple," wrote journalist William H. Rideing, "and hobbled through the world an object of pity to sympathetic elders, and of derision of wicked youngsters." Even after serving their country, the limbless soldiers would often be dismissed as "deformed," bundled together with the blind, the mentally deficient, and orphaned children, as in one way or another not whole—and therefore unable to contribute seriously to society. For Victorian Americans, physical deformities suggested the presence of mental deficiencies. Views would begin to change—albeit slowly—in part by the sheer presence of so many disfigured vets.

Right after the Confederate capitulation, William Oland Bourne, a magazine editor with hard experience as a chaplain in a Civil War hospital, tried to invigorate Union veterans who had lost their right arms by offering cash prizes in a left-hand writing contest. He assembled an eminent board, including the first Theodore Roosevelt—father of the future president—to judge submissions. Good penmanship, Bourne believed rather patronizingly, would be a means for crippled veterans to find a middle-class job and reassert their manliness. Hundreds of entries poured in.

While some contestants rather predictably copied out the Emancipation Proclamation or the Gettysburg Address in child-like scrawl, others wrote heartbreakingly of their experiences. Many felt themselves victimized by an evil fate that no amount of restitution could offset. Now their country no longer needed them. "To be compelled just in the prime of life (when teeming with anticipation of future prosperity and pleasure) to consent to be a permanent cripple for life," wrote John Thompson, "and to depend entirely on others for assistance is a matter of no small moment." He felt that he had lost his place in society. Others, however, viewed their disabilities as a sign of bravery in freedom's cause and hard-won manhood. One disabled corporal offered himself and fellow amputees as "living monuments of the late cruel and bloody Rebellion"; another that their conspicuous disabilities embodied "the price of liberty and Union, and are richer ornaments than the purest gold." Ezra Hilts wrote that while the war "cost rivers of blood," this sacrifice would "cement our Union more strongly and strengthen the whole framework of our government." There appeared a wide no-man's-land between those apparently condemned to a life of fatalism and those who remain charged with unbounded American optimism.

Powell showed no intention of retiring to a rocking chair on the porch of a general store to bore customers with war stories. His spilled blood and shattered bone had sealed a sacred compact tying him even more deeply and imaginatively to the cause of the Union. As to the physical nature of his loss, Powell rarely if ever called attention to it, let alone begged special consideration, although it had become an inescapable part of his functioning adult makeup. Indeed, he viewed his disability not just as a badge of honor but as a focus of endless purpose to bear him throughout his life. The Powell who emerged from the crucible of war seemed possessed by an unstoppable consuming energy, the restlessness and frustrations of his earlier days transformed now into a consistent driving power.

Powell's achievements over the next few years give the overriding impression of a man burdened with something he must prove and make whole. Such a force would often be mistaken for pure ambition—as if this was the only thing that could surely convey such drive—but his iron will toward self-healing along with other deep currents were pressing him with far greater urgency and energies. He would need to prove himself over and over—both intellectually and physically. He faced a lifetime of people patting him on his shoulder with a pitying look in their eyes.

While other amputees would rise to positions of great influence—for instance, the left-arm amputees Lucius Fairchild and Francis R. T. Nichols, who went on to become governors, respectively, of Wisconsin and Louisiana—none would come close to matching Powell's pervasive influence over the advancement of the nation. In four years' time, the man now known as the Major—no longer "Professor"—could persuade others against all evidence that he was equipped not just in character but in intellectual grasp and leadership skills to confront and conquer one of the most onerous physical challenges attempted in American history. His presence often made able-bodied men uncomfortable, sometimes feeling inadequate, and indeed would stir feelings of resentment, sometimes to the point of anger. But it would also forge him into a yet more formidable leader, taking him beyond the courageous crippled gunner commanding Battle F under heavy fire at Ransom's Approach.

When Powell returned to visit his parents in Wheaton, Joseph told him to settle down to teaching and get "this nonsense of science and adventure out of your mind." He listened with only half an ear. He turned down a nomination for a lucrative clerkship of

DuPage County on the Republican ticket, instead taking a professorship of geology at Bloomington's Illinois Wesleyan University for far less money in the fall of 1865. While besieging Vicksburg, he had received an honorary master's degree from Illinois Wesleyan, which, two years later, gave him the minimum credentials to assume the job.

The small prairie college had indeed hired itself an unorthodox professor, whose classrooms buzzed with rare excitement. "Textbooks went to the winds with Major Powell," his then student J. B. Taylor recalled thirty-five years later, evoking a third-floor classroom as clear in memory as if he had just rushed in to catch a class. For Taylor, the "artillerist, true to his artillery instinct, [was] firing his batteries all the while at the entrenched enemies," which appeared to have been the sluggish orthodoxies being shipped out from Yale and Princeton. His classes followed him into the woods to collect plant and animal specimens, filled notebooks with observations, pressed flowers, leaves, and grasses. "He made us feel that we had conquered the commonplace, broken our way through the accepted, and come into the heritage of free thinkers."

In March 1866, Powell delivered a lecture in Bloomington's popular Sunday Lyceum series titled "Perpetual Motion," in which he refuted the notion to an audience of students and townspeople. But the phrase also describes his almost manic activities on campus. Powell teamed with a mathematics professor to restructure the curriculum and rethink faculty responsibilities; he then drew up plans for a central building consolidating the fast-growing campus, designed a college seal, and coined the motto "Scientia et Sapientia" ("knowledge and wisdom"), all of which the university enthusiastically embraced. Still juggling a prodigious teaching load, he found time to establish a local chapter of the state natural history society, as well as a small museum, of which he named himself curator. But not even that could put his expectations to sleep. Having exhausted every opportunity at Illinois Wesleyan, he lobbied the nearby Illinois State Normal University for a faculty position. Normal boasted a much more substantial natural history museum, run by the Illinois Natural History Society.

At the Society's ninth annual meeting in late June 1866, Powell argued that the organization's museum, which included his own mollusk collection, deserved recognition as a state treasure—and therefore should receive public funding. At first, his listeners found this amusing, but gradually became enthusiastic. He introduced a motion that would direct three professors, himself not included, to approach the state board of education to explore any such possibility. The motion passed. The delegation met with the board, which endorsed their going down to Springfield to meet with state legislators. It seemed obvious to all involved that Powell should be the one to make the case.

Therefore early in 1867, Powell appeared three times before the general assembly, revealing for the first time his ability to put legislators under his powerful, imaginative spell. He analogized his natural history organization to the Royal Societies of London, Russia, Belgium, and Sweden, and to the Smithsonian in Washington. "All civilized nations," he proclaimed, "deem it wise to foster such institutions." Republican Illinois should take its rightful place. He laid his plan before them: a general commissioner and curator to be hired to oversee research and collections, and take charge of the museum. Those assembled agreed, appropriating $1,500 for the Society to pay a curator's salary, plus $1,000 for books, apparatus, and supplies. In the meantime, Powell had convinced Normal to make him a professor of geology, with teaching responsibilities limited to winter months only.

The Society applauded Powell's success, then promptly voted him the curatorship. The minutes-old museum director then pulled from his pocket a prepared speech, which contained the astounding proposal that the Society put its newly bestowed discretionary funds toward a collecting trip out west, himself in charge.

Ordinarily, so nakedly ambitious a proposition would have provoked a spirited resistance, but Powell adroitly steered the discussion away from himself toward the vision of a glorious future at the
Society's very fingertips: He was merely proposing to be the agent
who would heap greater glory on this still slightly known institution and its patrons—to be embodied in grizzly bearskins, boxfuls
of pressed columbines, and curious insects from the sparsely examined lands beyond. The truth was that the Midwest had no more to
offer him. He had trolled all the state's rivers for mollusks, had
studied what was accessible of this flatland's geology. The West—
and the nation's future—beckoned over the low Illinois skyline.

The Society authorized Powell to spend half of his expense
money on one of the nation's first college field trips out west. At
this meeting, it also voted to have the curator print up and conspicuously display in the museum a passage from St. Paul's letter
to the Romans: "The visible things of God from the creation of the
world are clearly seen, being understood by the things that are
made." Powell obliged, then planned his trip.

The Society's $500 certainly could not underwrite such an ambi-
tious undertaking, but he leveraged it to raise more, drawing a
matching grant from the new Illinois Industrial University in Urbana (today's University of Illinois), then raising $100 more from
the Chicago Academy of Sciences, which also agreed to pitch in
tools and supplies. Powell promised in return a rich bounty of
natural history specimens. He needed still more support, so in
April the audacious young curator boarded a train for Washington
to beseech his former commander—now general of the United
States Army—for assistance. Ulysses S. Grant already knew Powell as a resourceful man of his word, but even the usually impas-
sive general grew openly enthusiastic about the plan laid before
him. If Grant had reservations about the propriety of putting

federal resources toward a state venture, they soon dissolved before Powell's extraordinarily persuasive depiction of Grant's adopted home state winning the further glories it deserved. Write
me a letter, Grant told the Major, with a formal request.

In Washington, Powell arranged to meet Joseph Henry, the
first secretary of the newly established Smithsonian Institution.
The two got along well, marking the beginning of a long, rich col-
laboration that would prove as critical—perhaps more so in the
long run—than Grant's genuine goodwill. On the spot Henry
wrote a letter of introduction to Secretary of War Edwin Stanton.
Six days later, Powell delivered a clever request to Grant not for
outright cash but "that the officers of the Commissary Department, on the route traveled by the party, may be instructed to sell
supplies to it at government rates."

Powell had indeed stirred Grant up. "A party of Naturalists,
under the auspices of the State Normal University of Illinois will
visit the Mauvaises Terres [Bad Lands] of Southwestern Dakotah
for the purpose of making a more thorough geological survey of
that region," read the general's glowing letter of endorsement.
"From thence the party will proceed to explore the 'Parks' in the
Rocky Mountains." The letter further authorized the U.S. Commissary Department to furnish Powell with supplies at low-cost
government rates for an expedition a dozen strong and directed
U.S. troops to escort the party from Fort Laramie through the
Badlands.

Now winged with meaningful federal support, Powell elicited
passes worth $1,700 from four major railway lines. American Ex-
press and Wells, Fargo & Co. also agreed to help, waiving shipping
costs for the voluminous mass of artifacts and specimens that
Powell confidently planned to ship back to the Midwest. Joseph
Henry loaned the shoestring operation expensive barometers and
thermometers on the condition that Powell would submit the collected readings to the Smithsonian upon his return. With summer

quickly approaching, Powell raced home to fill his ranks from among his friends, family, and students. Emma signed up first. Each participant would contribute the not-insignificant amount of $300. His sister Nellie's husband, Almon Thompson, would come along as an entomologist, along with a Rock Island minister and several high-spirited undergraduates. With money from his own pocket, Powell now believed he would break even, if just barely. Still, throughout the expedition, he would need to borrow, cajole, and negotiate to keep it going.

Late that May of 1867, Powell and his wife headed west to Council Bluffs, Iowa, ahead of the rest of the team to buy wagons, draft animals, and supplies. The Chicago and North Western Railway had arrived only a little earlier that year, in the westernmost advance of the long eastern railroads. The small town, perched on either side of the Missouri north of the infall of the Platte River, had earned its name reputedly from an 1804 powwow between Lewis and Clark and the Otoe Indians. It thrived, soon becoming a busy steamship port and point of departure for the great wagon trains heading into the Missouri Territory and the Mormon exodus to the Utah Territory in the 1840s and 1850s. The Oregon and California trails struck off here also, funneling a mass of fortune seekers toward the 1849 and 1859 gold rushes in the California and Colorado territories. Powell chanced to meet Lieutenant General William T. Sherman, whom he had known during the war and was now commanding the sprawling Military Division of the Missouri, devoted to uniting nearly all western military organizations under a single command. Sherman shared his latest intelligence about the Dakota Badlands, in which the Lakota Sioux, the tribe of Red Cloud and Sitting Bull, had taken up arms in reaction to the postwar increase in white encroachment. Too dangerous to go there, Sherman advised, even under military escort. Powell knew Sherman as a man who rarely exaggerated, so took this warning to heart, a decision that would change history. Instead, the expedition would head directly to Denver City, the jumping-off spot for collecting in the Rocky Mountains, specifically in the three "parks," vast mountain valleys on the western slope of the Front Range.

For forty days, the small party drove their mule-drawn wagons along a clear trail paralleling the Platte over the plains from Council Bluffs to Denver City. Nighttime found them circling the wagons and building fires. This was by no means a virgin route: Stagecoach stations appeared every dozen or so miles, stores and military outposts less frequently. But the voyagers examined with great trepidation an abandoned wagon with a blood- and hair-smeared wheel. They found a victim of Indian retaliation shoveled into a shallow grave nearby. On July 6, 1867, they arrived in Denver City, finding a dusty, windblown town of fewer than five thousand people at the confluence of the South Platte and Cherry Creek. The stunning backdrop of snow-covered Rockies somewhat mitigated the dirt-road approach and the newborn city's down-in-the-mouth appearance, even though it had just become the territorial capital that year. "You seem to be walking in a city of demons," wrote the Englishman William Hepworth Dixon of the dozen hot and dirty streets, which boasted a total of two hotels, a bank, a theater, half a dozen chapels, fifty gambling houses, and a hundred grog shops. "Every fifth house appears to be a bar, a whisky-shop, a lager-beer saloon," he continued. "Every tenth house appears to be either a brothel or a gaming-house. . . . In these horrible dens a man's life is of no more worth than a dog's." With little access to wood, brick had become the primary building material. Another visitor noted that the aspiring city looked as if it "had been dropped out of the clouds accidentally, by some one who meant to carry it further on, but got tired, and let it fall anywhere."

Gold fever had slammed Denver City on the map eight years earlier, when nearby Cherry Creek yielded shiny pieces of the precious metal, creating an overnight boomtown with a gambler's black heart. Its finest citizens reputedly engaged in epic poker games staking city lots as chips, blocks of the city changing hands in a single round. By the time the expedition arrived, the bluster had generally worn thin as the strike petered out—the town now surviving by catering to the area's fledgling mining industries of silver ore, lead, and zinc. But Denver City no longer felt like a destination, just a stop on the way to somewhere else.

Here Powell would meet another man who would turn out to be critical to his developing plans, which far exceeded leading a pack of greenhorns on a collecting trip. William Byers, the square-cut, handsome owner of the *Rocky Mountain News,* always had a strong opinion. He was a big personality in a town that bred colorful characters. Byers's expansive boosterism could indeed take on the plain fanciful, a prime example being his publication of a *Shipping News* column. He set out to convince others that the Platte River, referred to jocularly by some as "mile wide and inch deep," would soon become a major steamboat highway, a ludicrous bit of wishful thinking. Part huckster, part showman, Byers was nonetheless a shrewd businessman.

As had so many others, Byers came to this outpost with high hopes of reinventing himself and making a fortune. The discovery of gold just before the war had brought a torrent of '59ers into the area, he among them. But instead of arriving pick in hand, he had come out with his brothers-in-law at the head of two wagons in March 1859, one bearing the heavy, flat stone slabs upon which printers then laid out type, along with a press, paper, and font, bought from a defunct Nebraska printing business. He had no journalistic experience whatsoever, but figured that starting a paper was a far better bet than prospecting. Not knowing where he would land, he had named his new paper the *Rocky Mountain News,* selling ad space to Omaha merchants eager to attract business out west. He had laid out the first two pages before leaving, filled with by-now stock stories such as that of Commodore Perry's opening up Japan five years before.

After arriving at the junction of Cherry Creek and the Platte, he found the two competing communities of Denver City and Aurora facing one another across the big river. Hearing that another press was setting type for its first edition, Byers leaped into action, rented a room over a saloon, and set to work. His brothers-in-law pitched in by erecting a tarp against the wet winter snow that poured torrents of water through the unshingled roof. Early the next morning, clutching copies of his first smudged edition, Byers hit the dirt streets, beating out his competitor by twenty minutes. His defeated adversary sold Byers his press and type for $30.

Byers would serve as a guide in the Rockies, taking Albert Bierstadt to Mount Evans from Idaho Springs, during which time the painter sketched a scene he would later immortalize in oils as "Storm in the Rocky Mountains." Byers relished the chance to rub shoulders with the now-aging mountain men Kit Carson, Jim Beckworth, and Jim Baker, who frequented his table. Within a few years, he was claiming to know more about the Colorado Territory than any man alive. He had thoughts, too, about the development of the West, ideas that Powell would listen to. Four years before they met, Byers wrote that "more than one half of the total area of the United States cannot produce crops of grain or vegetables with certainty except by irrigation." Therefore, he argued, "every drop of water that emerges from the great mountain chains of the west, in their thousands of streams, should be made useful." When Powell met Byers a day or two after reaching Denver City, they would have much to talk about. The two different, but very savvy men fit together well. Powell had found just the local patron he needed.

Snow blocked Berthould Pass, preventing the expedition from getting up into the Rockies and beginning their collecting activities, so Byers suggested that Powell climb what would later become known as Pikes Peak, a 14,000-foot mountain visible from Denver City—which the Major did on July 27 with several others of the expedition and, quite unusually, Emma, who rode a white-eyed Indian pony. They believed that she, outfitted in a felt hat, green veil, and long dress, was the first woman to attain the summit. She was not, having been beaten out nine years earlier, but her participation brought her acclaim for her courage and endurance. Powell simply stated that she "could ride all day on horseback like a veteran."

Atop the peak, Powell cast his eyes westward to the Rockies, imagining what lay beyond. He had come out to Colorado not simply to collect, teach, and break in a new generation of young men or to plant the Illinois flag. All this had been merely a fistful of rationalizations for beginning a far, far larger quest: Quite simply, he hungered to finish what Lewis and Clark had commenced more than sixty years before, when they set out on their legendary expedition to explore the continent. Since then, the Dakota Badlands, Death Valley, the inhospitable salt flats of Utah, the rugged mountain country of the Grand Tetons—indeed all but one part of the continental nation—had been visited and described. The lone exception was an enigmatic tract of high mountain desert and canyonland, lying within a 100-by-300-mile rectangle covering southern Utah and northern Arizona. That land, 250 miles directly west of where Powell now stood, embraced some of the most hostile but extraordinarily scenic territory in the world. Therein lay America's most improbably iconic land forms: the Grand, Zion, and Bryce canyons, all yet to bear European names, and today's Canyonlands and Capitol Reef, an area that many decades later would boast one of the densest concentrations of national parks and monuments in America.

That landscape had defied the most robust attempts to cross it in a straight line, its steep vertical interruptions both downward and skyward all combining to taunt its visitors with an inscrutable maze of mazes. Some of the most formidable explorers of that age had sought to conquer it. As the 32nd Congress drew to an end in early 1853, it appropriated funds for surveying different routes for a transcontinental railroad, including a central passage championed by Senator Thomas Hart Benton. The following year, Captain John Williams Gunnison led an expedition north across the 38th parallel, overcoming the Rockies on its way into northern Utah, to the Green River and on to Sevier Lake. The trip's surgeon and de facto geologist, James Schiel, wrote that "if one considers the fantastic formations on the other side of the river, the churches, temples, houses, and towers, one cannot avoid the impression that at one time evil spirits had lived here and had found death in a struggle of extermination." At the Green River ford, Gunnison split his party in two. Not long afterward, a band of Pahvant Utes surprised Gunnison's own group, the captain dying when an arrow struck him as he knelt to wash his face in a stream. Seven of his men perished also.

During 1853 and 1854, the great Pathfinder himself, John C. Frémont, sought a railroad-worthy tract along the 38th parallel just north of the Grand Canyon, but could not negotiate those eerie chasms. Their supplies dwindling, Frémont's party camped on the banks of the Green River, their leader forcing them to foreswear cannibalism. They lived off shoe leather and officers' scabbards instead. Remarkably, only one man died. Frémont beat a hasty retreat from these threatening lands, abandoning all but his party's most necessary supplies to stumble to the nearest Mormon outpost.

Most recently, in 1858, Lieutenant Joseph Ives of the U.S. Army topographical engineers had reached the floor of the Grand Canyon itself near Diamond Creek. Ives had begun late the previous autumn from the Colorado River's mouth on the shore of the Gulf of California, under instructions to steam upstream to establish a water route to the Great Basin. Just before embarking, news of the

Utah War, pitting Mormon colonists against the U.S. Army, reached them—and the mission took on greater import as federal commanders demanded information about the river's navigability for strategic purposes. Ives had commissioned a Philadelphia shipyard to build a crude 54-foot iron steamboat; crated in sections, the USS *Explorer* was shipped to California by way of Panama. Ives invited the geologist John Strong Newberry, the topographer F. W. von Egloffstein, and the artist Balduin Möllhausen to accompany his armed exploration.

At first, Ives seemed enamored of his surroundings as the party made its way easily north upriver past Fort Yuma along most of today's western Arizona. But things changed. In early January 1858, the *Explorer* steamed into the Grand Canyon's first large chasm, Black Canyon, today submerged under the waters of Hoover Dam. "We were shooting swiftly past the entrance, eagerly gazing into the mysterious depths beyond," recorded Ives, "when the Explorer, with a stunning crash, brought up abruptly and instantaneously against a sunken rock. . . . The concussion was so violent that the men near the bow were thrown overboard. . . . [T]he fireman, who was pitching a log into the fire, went half-way in with it; the boiler was thrown out of place; the steam pipe doubled up; the wheel-house torn away; and it was expected that the boat would fill and sink instantly by all." Inspection revealed no breach in the hull or damage beyond repair; Ives, however, had had enough, declaring the river once and for all unnavigable.

Nonetheless Ives pressed on by mule, along with Newberry, von Egloffstein, Möllhausen, twenty soldiers, and two Hualapai guides, who led them to Diamond Creek, this perhaps making them the first Europeans to tread the floor of the Grand Canyon. Even though he did write some admiring sections about the Big Cañon, as he called it, Ives famously concluded in his 1861 *Report Upon the Colorado River of the West* that "it can be approached only from the south, and after entering it there is nothing to do but leave.

Ours has been the first, and will doubtless be the last, party of whites to visit this profitless locality. It seems intended by nature that the Colorado river, along the greater portion of its lonely and majestic way, shall be forever unvisited and undisturbed."

In stark contrast, Newberry, the physician-turned-geologist, reported that he had drawn a significantly different experience from his surveys of the rocky chasms. Although the same thirst swelled his tongue just as it had Ives's, Newberry was clearly enchanted: "Though valueless to the agriculturalist," he wrote, "dreaded and shunned by the emigrant, the miner, and even the adventurous trapper, the Colorado Plateau is to the geologist a paradise. Nowhere on the surface of the earth, as far as we know, are the secrets of its structure so fully revealed as here."

Newberry would return the next year with another topographical engineer, Captain John N. Macomb, pressing nearly to the confluence of the Green and Grand rivers during another ordeal of an expedition. Macomb expressed the same disgust for the grueling landscape that Pike, Long, Frémont, and Ives had all shared. "I cannot conceive of a more worthless and impractical region than the one we now found ourselves in," he wrote. "I doubt not there are repetitions and *varieties* of it for hundreds of miles down the great Colorado."

They were neither the first nor the last who were simply confounded by this extreme country. They included the religious, the gold-and-empire seekers, the railroad surveyors, the men of commerce, and the suppliers of fur. It had killed, parched, or merely scared the wits out of all those nonnatives who had ventured within, as though some mighty curse fell upon all who had entered. It remained unknowable, inscrutable, and inescapably harsh. Frémont, indeed no stranger to extremity, shook his head when the prospect of running the Colorado and Green rivers raised its head. "No trappers have been found bold enough to undertake a voyage which has so certain a prospect for a fatal termination."

No one else standing on Pikes Peak that summer's day, even the Major's wife, Emma, knew yet the depth of Powell's bold ambition, nor the radical plan taking shape in his mind. He had now determined to go down the Green and the Colorado into the Grand Canyon. No one could now sway him from that task.

After a difficult passage into the Rockies, Powell's party came to Middle Park. A broad plain opened in front of them, flanked by distant peaks, the Grand River running through a green meadow in the shadows of an abrupt gray mountain wall. Faint mist and steam indicated the presence of hot springs. Near the springs, as Byers had told them, they came upon a two-room log cabin with low ceilings and a flat roof. A hitching post stood out front near a flagpole. Twenty-seven-year-old Jack Sumner, the slight, boyish-faced younger brother of Byers's wife, strode out to greet them.

Sumner had been too young to join his brothers in helping Byers drag the printing press to Denver City eight years before, but had come out west anyway the previous year. Byers had a job waiting for him: to occupy the sulfur springs and land around it, which Byers had picked up in a shady land deal that blatantly ignored Indian claims. Sumner had raised a trading post for trappers and Utes, buying furs and selling flour at a quarter a pound. The back room served as a "regular hunter's abode," observed one visitor—sporting a wooden bunk, large fireplace, and cupboard and table, with piles of skins and bags of sugar sitting on the floor. A veritable arsenal hung on the walls. Byers had sent Powell here with a letter of introduction—and this meeting, too, would have a profound influence on Powell's upcoming plans.

In many ways a pocket edition of Kit Carson, as his nephew would recall, Sumner delighted in rolling up his left sleeve to show off the scar from an arrow wound. One of eight children, he had grown up on a farm near Muscatine, a bluffside town on the Mississippi in eastern Iowa. Sumner's grandfather had served both as governor of Ohio and the Iowa Territory. But his father's farm held little charm for Jack, who—like Powell—escaped to the rivers and fields to hunt, explore, and trap. He would inherit considerable real estate upon his mother's death. As a corporal in the 32nd Iowa Volunteer Infantry, he had spent two weeks at Vicksburg during the siege, then fought at Nashville, earning some renown as a sharpshooter. He was a voracious reader. That summer and the next, Sumner would guide Powell's collecting efforts.

In front of the cabin raced the Grand River, running southwest from Sulphur Springs through Colorado and into Utah, where it joined the Green River to become the Colorado. From there, the river worked its way south through southern Utah, then cut west through the mighty canyons of northern Arizona, finally passing on into Mexico and draining into the Bay of California. The river pierced the very heart of these canyonlands. The trappers congregating at the trading post had spoken about building boats and descending the Grand to trap beaver in the waters beyond, but this had never risen beyond mere campfire talk. But now such discussion linked Powell and Sumner as they sat in the post's back room.

As Sumner remembered it decades later, Powell had asked whether he would join him on a geological exploration of the Badlands the following summer. Sumner claimed to have declined, suggesting instead an exploration of the Colorado "from the junction of the Green and Grand rivers to the Gulf of Mexico." In this version, Powell scoffed at the idea as foolhardy and impossible, but "after several windy fights around the camp fire, I finally outwinded him, and it was agreed that he should come out the following spring and we would make the attempt." Sumner would also, just as improbably, claim to have designed the expedition's boats.

But these were an old man's memories, torqued to recover his faded importance. Powell already had the idea well in hand. But now he had the man who would help bring it off. He could not have made a better choice in the here and now than Jack Sumner.

As the summer of 1867 ended, Powell stopped in Denver City for a few days, delivering a talk on "Peaks, Parks, and Plains" to an eager audience at the YMCA in the Methodist church. With only one summer of experience in the West, Powell had the audacity to tell residents of Denver about their own backyard. But they crowded in to hear this man who spoke with a "pleasing and persuasive" talking style, as the *Colorado Daily Tribune* noted. Few, if any, in the audience had heard such cosmic explanations of the mountains under whose shadows they lived. Powell called upon them to imagine the familiar ranges as reefs encompassed by an ancient torrid sea, which lapped upon shores green with tropical blooms, and through which strange predators stalked. Great forests had grown, then fallen and decayed, ultimately transforming into coal beds, while streams of liquid rock poured forth across the future parks and plains: heady stuff for these Bible-reading pioneers. The newspaper correspondent stopped taking notes in mid-lecture—whether because his fingers cramped or his mind filled to overflowing with exotic imagery—then just settled in to listen to this mesmerizing scientific storyteller.

Byers's *Rocky Mountain News* reported in early November that Powell planned to return the following spring to descend the Green River to where it met the Grand to create the Colorado.

Back east that fall, Powell keenly fell to distributing "over two thousand pounds of choice minerals, six thousand plants, and a large 'assortment' of beasts, birds, and reptiles, and Indian curiosities," the haul of the expedition as recorded by one participant. Each member had brought home a human scalp bartered from the

Indians. In December, when Powell presented his report before the Illinois State Board of Education, they expressed their pleasure, noting that he had been "successful beyond expectations." Into his report Powell had unobtrusively tucked mention of his intention to return to the Grand River the following summer to explore the headwaters of the Colorado, although he still made no mention of running the river through its Grand Canyon. He then delivered an avalanche of lectures on the West in Chicago, Urbana, and Bloomington, then returned to the Normal museum to label, catalogue, and arrange specimens drawn from the expedition's large boxes. He made sure to let others know what he was doing. "Too much credit cannot be given to Prof. Powell," gushed the Bloomington paper. "He works sixteen hours a day, and pays his assistants out of his own meager salary." As he unpacked boxes, he was already in full-scale planning mode for the following summer and beyond.

Powell's next venture would be yet another field trip to collect more specimens in the summer of 1868—but he clearly saw this as only a warm-up. This became most visibly evident on April 2, 1868, when he wrote Grant and put his cards on the table. He now requested that the army freely provision both an exploratory trip and a surveying expedition down the Green and Colorado through the yet-to-be navigated Grand Canyon. This "general scientific survey" would enlarge knowledge of their still insufficiently explored nation, because the Grand Canyon would "give the best geological section of the continent." Such a topographical inquiry could not wait, he continued, but should be immediately undertaken as "powerful tribes of Indians . . . will doubtless become hostile as the prospector and the pioneer encroach upon their hunting grounds." He ended his argument with a cunning pitch to the pocketbook of a nation still smarting from the costs of war: "The aid asked of the Government is trivial in comparison with what such expeditions have usually cost it."

Grant wrote back that he supported the endeavor because of the work's "national interest." But he then ran into problems with the commissary general, A. B. Eaton, who declared that the government could not supply rations to men not employed or in federal service. Powell's request landed at a tumultuous time in the nation's capital. Lincoln's successor, Andrew Johnson, had increasingly clashed with Republican lawmakers over Reconstruction policies for the vanquished South. When Johnson attempted to fire Secretary of War Edwin Stanton, who opposed the president's lenient policies toward the former Confederate states, Stanton locked himself into his Washington office. Johnson had twisted Grant's arm to take over the position, but the general had declined. The legality of Johnson's decision to remove Stanton featured prominently in the House's decision to impeach the president in late February on eleven articles that outlined his various "high crimes and misdemeanors."

The matter then fell into the Senate's lap. Finding themselves one vote shy of conviction, senators set on removing Johnson declared a ten-day hiatus in mid-May, buying them time to persuade at least one senator to change his mind. Powell's request could easily have gotten lost in the high drama, but the Major had asked the Smithsonian's Joseph Henry to write a note to Representative James Garfield of Ohio, a highly promising politician who had been a college president in his twenties, a major general in his early thirties, and retained a strong interest in matters of the mind. The "expedition is purely one of science and has no relation to personal or pecuniary interest," wrote Henry. The secretary added specifically that the "professor intends to give special attention to the hydrology of the mountain system in its relation to agriculture." Powell's instinct to bring Garfield into the ring would prove spot on—the Ohio congressman's political career would end up in the White House in 1881—and Garfield made sure that Powell's request got to the Senate.

On the last day before the Senate would vote on the impeach-
ment, Senator Henry Wilson of Massachusetts laid a resolution of
both houses before the Senate, requesting that it ratify the expedition's funding. In his third term, the Republican legislator was an
experienced hand, who would become Grant's second-term vice
president five years later. Wilson shrewdly waited to introduce the
bill when more than twenty senators out of fifty-four were absent.
Even so, the bill provoked bitter debate. Illinois senator Lyman
Trumbull claimed that Powell's venture would obtain scientific
information that the government should have and get it cheaper
than any other way. But that flinty Vermonter George Edmunds
called it a backdoor way of organizing expeditions for this government and questioned the propriety of the American taxpayer un-
derwriting a private expedition. After all, plenty of army officers
were available. Senator Lot Morrill of Maine found it "a very novel
proceeding that the Government shall be called upon to support
an expedition over which it has no control." Indeed, such an unprecedented request contrasted starkly with the government's tradition of military-led exploration, most often conducted by West
Point graduates well trained in engineering and survey techniques.
Furthermore most senators had never heard of this obscure, crippled professor from Illinois.

But Powell had not asked for direct funding; such a request
would have been doomed. Most important, he wrapped his submission in the flag, delicately reminding the congressional leadership
of the embarrassment invited by a nation that left its very own
territory unmapped and undescribed. Knowing his colleagues
well, Wilson called the discussion to a close with a compromise
amendment limiting the allocation to only twenty-five naturalists
and giving the army the right to refuse Powell rations should it
prove "detrimental to the interests of the military service." The
bill carried 25 to 7 on the shoulders of a Republican-dominated
Congress soon to nominate Grant. Even so, it is astounding that

Powell's measure sailed through a government still wrestling with such staggering war debt.

On June 29, eighteen days after Congress passed the appropriation, the Colorado River Exploring Expedition left Chicago on the Chicago & Western with its twenty-three members, which included one minister who had quit his flock to join, and another cleric who brought along his twelve-year-old son, Henry, largely because Emma Powell was fond of the boy. Eagerness easily trumped experience among the college students who made up most of the party, but Powell needed as many enthusiastic hands as possible to fulfill his ambitious promises to many institutions for natural history specimens. Young Henry joined Emma in the ornithological section, which was tasked to secure sixty-seven pairs of every kind of bird in the country to barter with other museums and give to the Smithsonian. Powell's brother, Walter, still suffering the consequences of his imprisonment during the war, joined the group as well.

Since the previous year, the railroad had leaped five hundred miles west from Council Bluffs, Iowa, to Cheyenne, Wyoming—creating yet one more "Hell on Wheels" riddled with prostitution, gambling, and the consumption of as much whiskey as the railroad could ship west. Gone was the long, tedious, and difficult wagon ride over the plains. Powell bought a herd of wild ponies in Cheyenne to make possible the hundred-mile ride south to Denver City. He watched as his young charges sought to break in the horses with predictably disastrous results, most getting thrown and some breaking limbs, although that did not stop any from continuing. "We knew nothing about mountaineering," wrote one member, "and could hardly cinch a saddle." Thundering rains pummeled their short journey, made even more wretched by Powell's cost-saving decision to forego tents.

Powell and his wife traveled ahead by stagecoach to Denver City. Byers had already whipped up the public's expectations, but now pleaded: "No more artists, artisans or laborers wanted for the 'Powell Colorado Expedition' until further notice." By July 14, the day before the others arrived, Byers published a summary of Powell's plans, which included the summer's exploration of the Grand and possibly Green rivers. "Then, next spring or summer, the railroad meanwhile having reached Green River, new supplies and boats will be obtained thence and the great cañon of the Colorado will be descended and explored. The Professor contemplates thorough work, even if it takes two or three years."

Byers and Powell had discussed the possibility of climbing the still-unsummited Longs Peak. If Pikes Peak was a benign, easily accessible mountain, then its brother could only be described as dangerous and aloof, its approaches fortified by sheer granite cliffs and deep snows for all but a handful of weeks in the summer. Byers himself had tried and failed to climb it in 1864. His small party, which included several scientists, had encountered a stupendous chasm running against the vertical face of the main peak—and been stopped cold. Explaining that they had surveyed almost all around that peak, Byers concluded that they were "quite sure that no living creature, unless it had wings to fly, was ever upon the summit" and predicted sourly that no man would ever reach the top.

Powell convinced Byers to try again, this time with the Major leading the way. They agreed to tackle the mountain in August, with Sumner and a few others. In late July, Powell took his crew to Middle Park to begin collecting. Sumner glanced over Powell's young men and declared them about as fit for outdoor work as "I would be behind a dry-goods counter." As Reverend W. C. Wood and Henry approached the Grand for the first time, they saw a prospector drive his wagon halfway across the river, when the dangerous currents, hidden by the sparkling waters, ripped a wheel away. When Wood rode in to retrieve it, he quickly found the river so powerful and deep that he jumped with alarm from his saddle. A mountain man watching from the bank turned to action, braving the river, mounting the frightened horse, and dragging the wagon's party to safety. The hero of the moment introduced himself as Oramel Howland, a part-time printer for Byers, who worked for Sumner in the warm months.

The newcomers would also meet another of Sumner's friends, a thirty-year-old backwoods trapper named Bill Dunn, sporting dark hair that cascaded over a buckskin of dark, oleaginous luster, "doubtless due to the fact that he has lived on fat venison and killed many beavers since he first donned his uniform years ago," noted Powell. At the outset, these mountain men had little truck with Powell, Wood reporting that "it seems to be the general opinion of the mountaineers that [Powell] doesn't get along much." These men relied on spontaneous improvisation; after all, their lives would repeatedly depend on it. So alien a figure as Powell, who brooded about supplies and logistics, kept talking about geology and collecting flowers and birds, must have seemed a pantywaist indeed. When the mountain men and students passed the whiskey bottle around the bonfire in the evenings, the tall tales grew ever more raucous and outlandish. Powell made little contribution to the noise. A good preacher's son, he did not join in with the constant whiskey drinking and frequent cussing that the mountain men enjoyed so much. Casually tossed insults did not warrant even a guffaw or good-natured retort. To these free spirits, he seemed uptight, self-righteous, and probably not what he said he was. But perhaps worst of all, his aloofness smacked of the judgmental and its dangerous corollary—the conviction that he held himself somehow better than they. But it would be these mountain-hardened men, not the passionate young undergraduates, upon whom the Major would call for his dangerous river trip.

Powell's young men spread out over Middle Park, eventually collecting more than two hundred bird species. That summer,

Sumner killed three grizzlies, two mountain lions, and a large host of elk, deer, sheep, wolves, and beavers. "All think it a hard life," wrote young Allen Durley in his journal, although Lewis Keplinger, who had marched with Sherman through Georgia and completed his studies at Illinois Wesleyan that spring, exulted in the raspberries and gooseberries they found. Powell had some of his charges transcribe an elementary Ute vocabulary, not a universally popular task. "'Tis most stupid work these children of the mountains have little or no idea of the eternal fitness of things," wrote one. Powell alone welcomed the Indians when they came begging at dinnertime, and he continued to buy objects and clothing.

On Friday, August 21, a group of dignitaries descended on Middle Park, intent on fishing for trout, collecting a few agates, and meeting Indians. Schuyler Colfax, presently speaker of the house and previously a journalist, was stumping as Grant's vice president designate. He had spent the past week in Denver City, Central City, and Georgetown, rousing patriotic sentiment and denigrating the entire Democratic Party as war-opposing Copperheads. Samuel Bowles, the influential publisher of the *Springfield (Mass.) Republican,* Alexander Hunt, governor of the Colorado Territory, and John Bross, the lieutenant governor of Illinois, accompanied Colfax. Bowles praised the generous hospitality of Major Powell and his assistant W. L. Byers (as Bowles saw fit to characterize the newspaperman) and their wives. The group hooked string upon string of speckled mountain trout; on Saturday afternoon, Powell led them to the crest of a narrow ridge immediately above the springs, for views of Middle Park and the miles of snow-capped peaks that spread in either direction. He pointed to the imposing outline of Longs Peak, announcing that he and Byers would leave on the morrow to climb it, an impressive declaration even for those influential men of action. Powell, who knew how to elicit grandeur and stateliness at such moments, went on to hold forth on how the mountains had formed—still a new and surprising subject. Byers found no reason to speak up; it was Powell's show. The

Major's audience could now plainly see that his interest centered not so much on the conquest of one more summit, but in furthering science and adding to the understanding of how geographic features took shape. The mountains were certainly a grand sight, but as seen through Powell's eyes, they became something even more marvelous: the key to unlocking nature's deepest secrets and a reflection of the enormous possibility of human will and courage.

Later that evening, the party gathered outside Sumner's cabin, conversation stretching far into the night about the future of these swiftly opening western lands, leaving Powell with a powerful memory he would call into service a decade later as he formulated his radical assessment of the development of the American West. While virtually all agreed that mining would define this vast expanse of mountain and wilderness, Powell submitted that agriculture and manufacturing would soon develop on a mammoth scale, calling attention to the rewards that irrigation had conferred on the arid regions of Egypt, Persia, India, and China. "In a very few decades all the water of the arid region of the United States would be used in irrigation," predicted Powell.

When Powell laid out his plans for the next year's expedition—to explore the headwaters of the Colorado, and then begin a descent through the unknown canyonland—all shook their heads that the federal government had left so important a responsibility to a private enterprise; but all agreed that Powell was the man to do it. For Powell, a passage down the Colorado would not be merely a high-adventure river trip, the bold effort of a team of men fighting unheralded obstacles to get from one point to another. Instead, he would be inserting the final—and strangest—piece in the American jigsaw puzzle left by nearly a century of continental American exploration. What Lewis and Clark had begun more than sixty years ago, he would complete by fitting into place this last difficult patch of terra incognita. So when Bowles rhetorically wrote, "Is any other nation so ignorant of itself?," one can hear the echoes of Powell's own words.

"We should be out of the Park before this time," wrote Bowles. "But the Utes and Prof Powell are so interesting that I have lingered long, and must stop." Darkly handsome, with what his friend Emily Dickinson described as "that Arabian presence," Bowles was well known for his sharp tongue and keen intelligence, but also for his penchant for the romantic. In his book about that western trip, he remained entranced by the vision that Powell had evoked. "The whole field of observation and inquiry which Professor Powell has undertaken is more interesting and important than any which lies before our men of science. . . . Here are the central forces that formed the Continent; here more striking studies in physical geography, geology, and natural history, than are proffered anywhere else." Equally was Bowles enamored of the Major: "Professor Powell is well educated, an enthusiast, resolute, a gallant leader . . . He is every way the soul, as he is the purse of the expedition; he leads the way in all danger and difficulty . . ."

On Sunday morning, as the Colfax group departed for Denver City, Powell gathered the team.

There's nothing easy about Longs Peak. When mere talk of climbing it had come up, "[t]he old mountaineers had fun at our expense," wrote Keplinger. "The idea of a bunch of tenderfeet coming out and trying to do a thing like that was ridiculous!" Longs rises dramatically, nine thousand feet above the Great Plain, boulders and loose rock crowding its steep slopes, which are punctuated with sheer granite faces. Few animals but marmots can survive its often unrelenting winds, unpredictable storms, and frequent lightning strikes. To negotiate a path to its summit necessitates threading often narrow, frequently snow- or ice-covered ledges. A modern guide has likened an assault on Longs as attacking "a citadel . . . a castle with defenses."

On August 20, Powell set out on horseback with his brother Walter, the ever-enthusiastic Keplinger, Byers, Sam Garman,

Jack Sumner, and Ned Farrell, one of the Sulphur Springs mountain men. A pack mule known as Grizzly bore ten days of supplies. Each man wore a pistol and packed a rifle. The party carried two sets of barometers and thermometers, courtesy of the Smithsonian. Powell would take a difficult, circuitous four-day route to reach his object.

The party rode up the Grand River to Grand Lake. They then followed a promising ridgeline east, albeit through an exacting tangle of rocks and tree blow-downs that tripped the horses and even the mule. Grizzly indeed pitched off the trail, falling forty feet end over end. It sprang up with a look of astonishment on its face, and the expedition continued.

They soon passed above the timber line to spend their first night near Ptarmigan Mountain. They climbed 13,310-foot Mount. Alice—probably the first white men to do so—braving its biting winds and subarctic cold. Catching their breath, they gazed toward Longs, now looming defiantly about five miles distant. They carefully wound their way down a precipitous northern ridge, then up again to the summit of Chiefs Head Peak, probably another first ascent. They followed a path along one more ridge toward Longs, a route that quickly narrowed to a knife's edge.

Keplinger came upon Jack Sumner sitting, evidently discouraged by the prospect of negotiating a steeply rising ridgeline only eighteen inches wide. Now the cocky greenhorn poked fun at the mountain man. "Hello, Jack, what's the matter?" and Keplinger confidently moved ahead, Sumner yelling after him that he could go anywhere Keplinger could. But that young man was left recalling with pleasure that Sumner got down on his haunches and "cooned it." Shortly afterward, the party reluctantly turned back. On their descent, they saw a gully running down the southern flank of the mountain well above them, crowned by a feature now known as the Notch. They would find out the hard way that only one passage offers a nontechnical approach to the summit. The so-called Keyhole Route requires that climbers snake their way

270 degrees around the mountain and then pass through a small opening in the rocks to get to the summit.

At 2 p.m., the group camped back at timberline and built a fire. Although they had climbed two thirteen-thousand-foot peaks that day, the irrepressible Keplinger asked Powell whether he might reconnoiter up the gully. Powell assented. When night fell with no sign of "Kep," he sent Sumner after him with bundles of dry sticks for signal fires. Sumner's shouts, and the fires, helped Kep get down a harrowing descent. He reported that he had neared the top—and now thought he knew how to approach the summit, even though his shaken countenance suggested otherwise. The narrow ledges, pocketed with ice and snow, had exacted everything he had; the unrelentingly strong winds had nearly pitched him off the mountain several times. That night the small group crowded behind a large leaning rock, which protected them somewhat from stiff gusts of wind and scattered rains as they shivered through a cheerless night.

The next morning brought an unexpectedly fair day. At 6 a.m., the seven began up the steep, boulder-clogged gully, negotiating several treacherous snow drifts. A hundred yards or so below the Notch, they took Keplinger's recommendation to cut west and up to the top of the gully, reaching a boulder field that was mounted by the Keyhole. After climbing through it, they cut sharply to the left, making a dangerous traverse of what is now known as the Ledges, up a broad gully (the present Trough), and across the Narrows, a thin-lipped ledge clinging to a sheer face. When they approached the Homestretch, a 275-foot, near-vertical polished slab, their hearts must have sunk—the peak, so close, appeared unassailable.

But once again Keplinger found a way through a break in the wall, snaking upward on both hands and feet. The rest followed without major mishap, and at 10 a.m., Powell heaved himself onto the summit with a cry of "Glory to God!" They spent three hours on top, a level area several football fields in extent, from which they could make out Denver City across to the east, Pikes Peak to the south, Hot Sulphur Springs and a crescent of ranges to the south, west, and north. The men deposited a slip of paper bearing their names, along with barometric readings, into an empty baking soda can to leave behind. Giddy from his outsized role, Kep dropped a biscuit into the can with an additional note christening it as "an everlasting memento of Major Powell's skill in bread making." Earlier Powell had insisted on taking his turn at baking, but one-handed kneading had left the biscuits dense and unappetizing, although Keplinger acknowledged that his were no better. The Major told him to remove both items, feeling it did not honor the dignity of the occasion, then took off his hat and spoke a few solemn words: "We have reached the summit of Longs, accomplishing what others thought impossible." Yet this effort would be but a warm-up for yet greater achievements.

How Powell had managed to lead such a difficult first ascent defies comprehension: the rock slippery, his boots offering insufficient traction, the wind blowing savagely. By perpetually shifting his weight and balancing carefully—and aided by the others—he had persevered, his ferocious refusal to quit keeping the others going. Fall he did, at one point badly bruising his stump, but the others fell, too, Byers's tumble breaking a barometer.

Indeed, Powell had not merely come through but conclusively proved to Byers and Sumner that he indeed was no pantywaist but a man who could not only outface towering physical challenges with one arm but could also lead men on a daunting challenge. Again, he had needed to prove his fitness, but this climb was a crucial test. He required Sumner's unwavering faith in him to prosecute the unimaginable challenges that lay ahead.

As summer wound down, most of the expedition traveled to Denver City and back to school, but a handful remained with Powell, who intended to overwinter and continue the reconnaissance along the Green River that lay far to the west in present-day northeastern Utah. On September 9, he had his brother Walter lead a pack train west some two dozen miles across Middle Park to Gore Pass, following an often indistinct trail marked by famed guide Jim Bridger in 1861. Powell instructed Walter to trace the Yampa River up to the White River watershed, then to follow that river, which intersects the Green. The going proved more difficult than anyone anticipated, frequent rains and hailstorms battering them. One of Walter's team spent a month hopelessly lost, before miraculously appearing in camp. Another man—a mountain man, to boot—decided that he had had enough, loading as much of the supplies as a mule could carry before skulking off. Some of the team pursued him, only to scurry back when the thief fired upon them.

Overwintering on the Green appeared too ambitious, so Powell determined to stop over on the banks of the White River, not far from present-day Meeker, Colorado. They would build cabins near the winter camps of several bands of Utes, among whom Powell would spend much of his time. Before settling in, he took a number of the expedition northwest to Green River City, just over the present-day Wyoming line, a nine-day journey on horseback. The continental railroad, heading toward Promontory and its completion, had just come to this small town perched on the river's banks. Powell had realized what an extraordinary opportunity this offered him: No longer would he be confined to building boats in the southwest, but could have them built virtually anywhere else and shipped by rail to river's edge. From Green River City, he would initiate the river journey the following summer. He knew that others would also recognize the same opportunity, so he had no time to waste.

Winter conditions did not deter him from making several exploratory excursions—down the White to the Green, northward to the Yampa, and around the Uinta Mountains. Emma prepared and identified the 175 species of birds that the expedition had collected. The Major labored over his Ute dictionary, which began to take robust form. That winter he wrote to the president of Illinois Normal University that they had enjoyed a mild season: "I have explored the canyon of the Green where it cuts through the foot of the Uintah Mountains, and find that boats can be taken down. So that the prospects for making the passage of the 'Grand Canyon' of the Colorado is still brighter. The Canyon of the Green was said to be impassable." A few months later, the Bloomington *Daily Pantagraph* reported that "with Powell, to think was to dare. The impulse to make the terrific descent was irresistible. Those who know him and his battle experience, will recognize this feature of his character. That which seemed impossible to others, grew to him to be an imperative necessity."

That winter, Powell's river team started to coalesce. Traveling with the greenhorns the past two years had convinced him of the need for hard-weathered men, not just the young, however eager they were. Jack Sumner would serve well as his deputy. Sumner's friend Oramel Howland agreed to come and would bring along his quiet, younger half-brother Seneca. The trapper Bill Dunn seemed to have toughness aplenty, so he, too, was recruited. Sumner no doubt secured their participation with assurances that Powell indeed could pull off this expedition. The Major also signed on a frequent customer of Sumner's trading post, the twenty-year-old Billy Hawkins, "an athlete and a jovial good fellow," as Powell described him, to serve as cook at $1.50 per day. A scrappy orphan, Hawkins had lied about his age and entered a Missouri cavalry regiment at fifteen and rode in a major cavalry charge against a Confederate force twice as large. Byers himself toyed with joining the expedition, but eventually backed out. With his contributions toward equipment and groceries, along with some outright loans, Byers became Powell's largest financial benefactor, exceeding the Illinois Board of Education's $600.

On February 25, Powell drew up a contract with Sumner, Oramel Howland, and Bill Dunn, which stipulated that Sumner would take sextant readings while Dunn would take barometric recordings. Howland would make topographical drawings of the river's course. The men would help do the work necessary to get the boats safely downriver and save specimens for stuffing. In turn, the men would have time to prospect, receiving $25 per month and a commission on each skin procured—$0.50 for a porcupine, $3.50 for an otter, and $10.00 for a grown grizzly. This was how a private expedition financed itself.

With a hard core of personnel committed to the coming summer's undertaking, Powell turned to figuring out what kind of boats he would need. No one had designed craft for even remotely so rigorous a whitewater challenge. On the Mississippi and the Great Lakes, he had seen boats that handled chop well, even while loaded with freight. And he knew the perfect man in Chicago to build them.

And so, in the spring, the Powells headed back east by way of the Windy City.

CHAPTER 5

Descent

As Powell pulled together logistics for the river trip, he still knew precious little about what lay before him. He had researched the region as best he could during the winter of 1868, scrambling down to the banks of the Green River to peer into its rapids and muddy waters. He had interviewed Indians and trappers, studied the terrain from atop more high peaks than anyone else had ever climbed in the Rockies, and started to make sense of parts of the area's geology. Such vast, inscrutable landscapes give rise to great tall tales, and Powell had heard many. One man told him how he had laid out a city at the confluence of the Green and Grand rivers before Indians chased him out. Others fed him disturbing accounts of how the river plunged underground, only to emerge miles later. The Canyon elicited the wildest flights of fancy.

He knew only the general outlines of the river's descent: The Green coursed south out of Wyoming into the Utah Territory, where, despite a brief swing into western Colorado, it moved south on its way to join the Grand River in southeastern Utah to form the Colorado, located in today's Canyonlands National Park. From there, the great new river flowed into the Arizona Territory and roared west through the Grand Canyon on its way to the Gulf of California. The expedition would traverse the entire Colorado Plateau, the human-heart-shaped, 130,000-square-mile desert province that straddles the Four Corners, the juncture of the present-day states of Utah, Arizona, Colorado, and New Mexico. Averaging about 6,000 feet—second in height only to the Tibetan Plateau—this is a remote, difficult land of mesas, cliffs, escarpments, and endless canyons. This family of rivers cut like coronary arteries from the north-northeast of the plateau to its southwestern edge, where the united river attains its most magnificent expression as it drops precipitously through the Grand Canyon, and off the plateau.

Powell knew precious little else, except that the party's put-in at Green River City in southwestern Wyoming lay at 6,115 feet above sea level. When the Colorado races out of the Grand Canyon, it has nearly reached sea level. Without knowing how long the combined Green and Colorado flowed—whether they meandered and snaked or ran straight as an arrow—he could only guess at the average or most extreme drop per mile. Even had he known the exact mileage, he still could not determine the nature of the elevation loss, whether the river fell gradually or was punctuated by significant, large-scale drops in the form of great falls. The Yellowstone tumbled over two formidable waterfalls, one of them 300 feet tall, nearly twice the height of Niagara Falls. A far more modest undetected plunge could doom the expedition in seconds if the steep walls hemming them in afforded them no chance to pull off the river in time. Even if they could get ashore, a great falls could well trap the expedition. Unable to go downstream or upstream, they would have to abandon their boats and head overland. Even if they could scale the formidable cliffs overhanging the river, they still would need to cross some of the nation's most inhospitable desert country.

Such uncertainties face all those who head off into the unknown. The smartest of them carefully figure out exigencies. Powell calculated that they would need ten months to reach their destination, including time to overwinter as he figured that ice would clog the river, yet another tribute to how little the land was known. Each of the expedition's three freight boats would carry a ton of supplies: the axes, hammers, saws, augers, nails, and screws necessary to raise a cabin against the cold, plus two or three dozen traps and a large quantity of ammunition. Their soldierly provisions would consist of flour, bacon, dried apples, coffee, beans, sugar, and baking powder. To document and collect the data necessary for a map, they would take two sextants, four chronometers, and four barometers, as well as thermometers and compasses.

Powell had asked an old Paiute man if anyone had gone right down the river. Yes, came the answer. A fellow tribesman had attempted to run the Canyon in a canoe with his wife and little boy. "The rocks," the Indian said, holding his hands vertically above his head, and looking between them to the heavens, "the rocks h-e-a-p h-e-a-p high! The water hoo-woogh, hoo-woogh, hoo-woogh! Water pony [the canoe] heap buck! Water ketch 'em No see 'em Ingin any more! No see 'em papoose any more!" The Indians indeed, despite periodic visits to their sacred places, otherwise kept clear of this ominous Canyon.

The strangest story from this strange land came from reports of a nobody prospector, James White. At 3 p.m. on September 7, 1867, at the Mormon outpost of Callville on the Colorado just downstream of the Canyon, a startled resident dragged White's emaciated, bruised, and ragged form from the shallows. His skin sunburned to leather, the delirious man clung tightly to a makeshift raft cobbled from driftwood. He could neither talk nor stand. The entire tiny population of Callville—a handful of Mormon missionaries, U.S. soldiers, and barge workers—had reached this desolate outpost aboard a steam-driven paddlewheeler traveling upstream from the Gulf of California. None had arrived from the north or east—sixty miles directly upstream of the settlement lay ferocious rapids choked with bone-crunching rocks. Above that lay an even more formidable basin of the great Canyon, untraversed by even the most intrepid, much less navigated by boat or raft. But when White came to his senses, he babbled a fabulous tale. He claimed to have made his way nearly 500 miles through that monstrous Canyon in only two weeks. Too fabulous a story indeed, yet here he was.

White asserted that he and two companions had been prospecting near the San Juan River, several hundred miles from Callville as the crow flies, when an Indian attack—White never specified which tribe—left one dead and the two survivors fleeing for their lives. White and his companion hurriedly built a raft and pushed off into the Colorado River. Not long after, White's companion, who had not tied himself to the raft, disappeared into a rapid. White appeared hazy about most major details of his alleged journey, but perhaps understandably did not seem to care in the sheer joy of being alive. He remembered trading his gun for the cooked hindquarters of a dog with some Indians who appeared on the bank.

A physician who had accompanied William Byers on his thwarted attempt on Longs Peak interviewed White, but interjected many of his own speculations in the account he wrote, getting the geography all wrong. Many years later, an engineer and river runner, Robert Brewster Stanton, interviewed White again, but he also overlaid his own assumptions on a narrative difficult enough in itself, blurring all distinction between the interview and his preformed conclusions. Stanton believed that White had started his trip below the Grand Canyon, floating only some sixty miles. A century and a half later, the story still remains shrouded in mystery, one that has an ending, but no clear beginning.

White lived until ninety, never appearing to care much whether people believed him or not. Why did he not bypass the Canyon on land? What about the great eddies that can tie up rafters in hours-consuming circles—if they are lucky? For the most part, river runners do not believe that anyone without a life jacket could have survived the Canyon's notorious rapids. Adventurers have tried to replicate White's alleged run, some drowning in the process, but some more recent ones have succeeded, although none at anything approaching White's speed through the Canyon. The river was high, so it is not absolutely impossible that he could have made it, the human will to live being what it is. Yet even extraordinary fortitude could not protect an increasingly exhausted man from the repeated, maiming blows of rock against his flesh and bones. Perhaps the most persuasive argument for White's having done what he claimed is the yet greater improbability of the alternative— that he could have marched some two hundred miles across desert and rock to parallel the Canyon until he could launch in the benign waters of Grand Wash Cliffs or below. Other factors complicate the story further. White had stolen horses from Indians near Fort Dodge, an army post in southwestern Kansas, before heading into Arizona Territory, so he had a good motive for lying about his exact whereabouts. But the absence of corroboration must forever leave the truth unknown. Powell scoffed at the idea that a man clinging to some hastily bound logs could have washed through the Canyon, more like a piece of driftwood than a sentient man. As with much of the other reports he had received, he discarded what he believed fallacious, White's story among them.

On the top of Powell's mind was whether the river hid any expedition-devouring falls. Absent credible information, he simply did not know. Yet he was too meticulous a planner not to have given considerable thought to the possibility. A single brief clue may shed some light on his thinking. Years later, a friend recorded a conversation in which Powell was asked this very same question. The aged Major pulled on a cigar and looked into the faces of his friend and other rapt listeners. "Have you ever seen the river?" he asked. "It is the muddiest river you ever saw." He paused. "I was convinced that the canyon was old enough, and the muddy water swift enough and gritty enough to have worn down all the falls to mere rapids." Yes, he certainly expected that rockfalls and debris from tributaries would create rapids, but not significant falls. "I entered the canyon with confidence that I would have no high falls to stop us, although there might be bad rapids . . ." Powell had seen the soft, sedimentary rock composing most of the Canyon walls in the Green River, figuring that the high volume of the river must have smoothed any large irregularities in the soft rock of the riverbed. But he did not know about the hard pre-Cambrian rocks or the volcanic faults of the Canyon's deep inner gorges that could set up ideal conditions for a waterfall. The truth was that neither he nor anyone knew what lay down the Green and Colorado rivers.

The press took scant interest in the expedition. In May 1869, just three days before they started, the *Chicago Tribune* opined that the entire business "savors of foolhardiness" in the light of White's experience. It "will result fatally," the paper grimly advised. One lone voice raised a more serious accusation. In June, the geologist John Strong Newberry took to the *Tribune* to question Powell's claim that "it is doubtful whether these canons [*sic*] have ever been seen by man." The plainly irritated Newberry, who had pressed into the Canyon with the Ives and Macomb expeditions, pointed out that the Franciscan priest Silvestre Veléz de Escalante had crossed the Colorado north of the Grand Canyon in 1776, not to mention Newberry's own experiences and those of James White.

Newberry's anger was not misplaced. By bad luck, his geological reports on his visits to the Canyon, delayed by the Civil War, did not see print until after Powell's expedition returned. They would contain astute geological observations about Grand Canyon country, particularly how the defining sculptor of these arid lands was, paradoxically, water. Indeed, Powell had clearly overstepped with his claims of uniqueness, the unhappy product of his passion to sell this bold journey to the Senate, the Smithsonian, and ultimately, to the public. He intended to make history—and this would not be the last time he would bend details to fit a storyline. Yet even given Newberry's work, or if White was in fact the first through the Canyon, the encounters of human beings with this unique landform had still been only brief or accidental. No one had penetrated its inner sanctums and seen it completely from the water's edge. In the big picture, Powell was correct.

Some of Newberry's animus may well have arisen from professional jealousy, for every serious geologist knew that the Canyon offered a spectacular opportunity of their career. No other place on earth so dramatically reveals the layers of the planet's history in such a compressed space. Newberry was right about that. The dean of geological science, the great Charles Lyell, was among the most eager of those awaiting news of Powell's expedition.

Perched on the Green River near the influx of Bitter Creek in Wyoming Territory, Green River City was less than a year old and had already seen better days. Abandoned, mostly roofless, adobe structures crumbled in the baking sun under Castle Rock Butte. Green was a misplaced adjective for this lonely outpost, flashes thereof appearing only in the spring on the sagebrush and prairie grass. The river itself turned a sickly shade of that color for a few days as the snowmelt washed in before the river returned to its slow muddiness.

In 1862, the postmaster general created a stage station on the south bank of the Green River as part of the Overland Trail, a southern alternative to the often more dangerous Oregon, California, and Mormon trails leading west. Samuel Clemens—not yet fully Mark Twain—enjoyed a breakfast of hot biscuits, antelope meat, and coffee there in 1862, "the only decent meal we tasted between the United States and the Great Salt City." In 1868, the transcontinental railroad reached this outpost, crossing the river on a trestle bridge built from logs floated down the Green and sawed into boards at the Bitter Creek lumberyard.

An enterprising businessman saw dollar signs with the coming of the Union Pacific. Jake Field had found some earlier success with the Jackass Express—a slight mockery of the already-defunct Pony Express—which bore its colorfully painted metal boxes packed with mail and strapped on muleback to far-flung towns and outposts. Field platted out his would-be city, which by then had attracted some two thousand expectant souls. Also smelling easy money, Theodore Hook, the mayor of the equally new railroad town of Cheyenne, abruptly quit his job to set up in Green River. But the Union Pacific and its lawyers had other ideas than filling the pockets of those they dismissed as squatters, declining to build a switching station there and launch Green River as a serious enterprise. Instead they threw up a new town twelve miles to the west on Black's Fork. By the time Powell's recruits started to arrive in the spring of 1869, Field's dream had shriveled, the town now containing a hundred people or so, his Union Pacific Railroad Eating House and Outfitting House its only going concerns.

While Powell raced to nail down the expedition's final details, the three recruits he had secured in Middle Park the summer before—Jack Sumner, Oramel Howland, and Bill Dunn—had made their way leisurely from the White River winter camp through Brown's Park and Fort Bridger, feasting on an endless supply of "duck soup and roasted ribs," and generally having fun, as Sumner remembered it—a continual binge that boiled up when they hit Green River: "We camped and awaited orders, and in the meantime tried to drink all the whiskey there was in town. The result was a failure, as Jake Field persisted in making it faster than we could drink it."

From Fort Bridger, a military outpost not far from Green River, also came Sergeant George Bradley, whom Powell had met and recruited in 1868. A bullet in the thigh at Fredericksburg had not deterred him from signing up for more service after the war, but a soldier's life that centered on keeping Indians from harassing railworkers had offered little but crushing boredom. The sergeant, who sported a handsome handlebar mustache, told Powell that he "would explore the river Styx" if that could get him out of the army. Powell queried Grant about releasing the soldier from active duty and was obliged quickly, despite the president's busy schedule. Powell found in Bradley an able, if a bit excitable, comrade interested in his geologic work. He would become the most entertaining and prolific of the journal keepers on the trip stretching before them. Sumner warmed immediately to the man who "had been raised in the Maine codfishery school, and was a good boatman, and a brave man, not very strong but tough as a badger."

While awaiting the Major's arrival, one Sam Adams dismounted at the campsite with word that Secretary of War Edwin Stanton had officially sanctioned him to take Powell's place. The startled explorers examined official-looking papers, then shrugged and gave him a place at their mess. On May 11, Powell steamed up on the Union Pacific, leading his brother Walter and a young unnamed greenhorn recruit, along with four specially crafted wooden rowboats. Taking one look at Adams and his letters, Powell politely told Adams to leave, which he did immediately. A liar of gargantuan proportions, Adams would later turn up in Washington with a request for funds, backed by the bald-faced assertion that he, not Powell, had descended the Colorado—and came close to getting what he asked.

Much to his irritation, Powell found the waiting expeditioners hungover and crotchety, but he quickly sorted them out, setting them to unload the three freight and one scout boats from the flatcars and onto the banks of the Green. The rowboats, although sleek and narrow, contained double ribbing, added planking, and bulkheads that increased their durability, but made them quite heavy, as the men would soon find out. Field gave them permission to camp on a willow-choked islet about a mile below the railroad bridge, just out of the view of curious townspeople. Powell next turned the men to caulking and painting the boats, and preparing the seven thousand pounds of food and supplies for transit. The young recruit whom Powell had brought along soon left, scared off by the practical joking of the rough fellows whom he had planned on joining. This left Powell with seven men besides himself—not enough to crew four heavily laden boats, each of which ideally required two oarsmen.

From the banks of the Green, Powell struck up a conversation with a nineteen-year-old man hauling firewood in a homemade boat. His youthful ebullience, underscored by a pair of twinkling deep-set blue eyes, suggested a life already richly lived. Andy Hall had come to America from Scotland at seven; at fourteen, he left his widowed mother to become a bullwhacker, the lowest job on great wagon trains running west, trudging alongside to spur the reluctant oxen onward. No bitterness appeared to sour this light-hearted wanderer, who regarded life as one great lark. Powell signed him up on the spot.

Powell would hire another man he encountered in Green River City, a red-cheeked Englishman named Frank Goodman with a broad face and receding chin, who had fought in the New Jersey Volunteers, then become a Hudson's Bay Company trapper in British Columbia. He had eventually worked his way down the Columbia River to Walla Walla, in the Washington Territory, and thence up the Snake and over the mountains, arriving in Green River only a few days before. The tall, twenty-five-year-old widower, who proudly wore a beaver hat of his own trapping and sewing, sold off his furs for enough to set him free from the hard work of the trapper. Powell believed that his geniality and fine health would be assets for the hard voyage. Goodman signed on right there, the promise of adventure too good to turn down. Powell now had the nine-man crew he desired.

On first inspection, his recruitment choices—both in number of men as well as their character and background—make little sense. Ten men appear inadequate to operate four heavily laden rowboats. The three larger boats worked best with two oarsmen and one to captain and possibly steer the boat through rough water. The scout boat could get by with a crew of either two or three, bringing the ideal complement to eleven or twelve. Finding volunteers had not been a problem on his two earlier trips out west, so he appears to have intended to have ten men all along. Fewer men certainly meant less supplies, both reducing cost and weight. But another possible explanation for the small number of men is equally plausible, even if a bit grimmer: Powell, the master of logistics, worked into his plans the serious likelihood of losing a boat and all its supplies. He indicated that by writing into the contract with Sumner, Howland, and Dunn that hunting would not be possible "should it be necessary to proceed on the journey without delay on account of disaster to boats or loss of rations." Such a scenario would mean that three remaining boats would need to accommodate the crew of the lost boat, if they survived. That would lead to dangerous overcrowding if the complement was too large to begin with. Any additional men would also draw heavily on limited supplies.

The ragtag group of men swatting mosquitoes next to the small mountain of supplies on that islet would have inspired little confidence in a casual observer. The band of hungover frontiersmen did not appear disciplined enough to mount so daunting an expedition. Powell had not pursued the scientifically trained or men with past surveying, engineering, expedition, or even boating experience. His brother apart, not a single man had served under him during the war. Nor did he invite a single member of the 1867 and 1868 field trips, although someone like Keplinger would have made a fine addition. Instead he crafted a volatile, but extremely tough, body of field-tested outdoorsmen and former soldiers. None but Powell were married; most were in their twenties. They had not trained together, nor had anyone but Powell and Bradley sat at the oars of a rowboat for any length of time. He did not have the money to mount a large expedition—but he had drawn the acute conclusion that any group on such a large undertaking into an inhospitable environment can readily become their own worst enemies, a lesson repeatedly imposed by war. Unlike a column, this small band could move fast, and if necessary, regroup quickly.

If they shared a common quality, their leader not excepted, it was sheer cussedness, an attitude and bearing that fueled fierce self-reliance. Every man, with the exception of the Englishman

Goodman, exhibited an unrelenting resilience that would armor them to face almost unthinkable physical challenges. More important, all shared the deep belief that—as Americans—they were destined to write their names large on this still unshaped continent. In another light, such overwhelming confidence in their skills and mission would have bespoken arrogance. They liked to tell wild tales around roaring driftwood fires, wrote Powell, having "seen such in the mountains or on the plains, and on the battlefields of the South." They could take hardship without complaining, improvising when new challenges arose. While Powell's choice of men proved to be brilliant in the aggregate, it also would nearly prove the expedition's undoing. Working with independent-minded and authority-bucking characters came with a downside.

These men had volunteered for different reasons—personal enrichment, adventure, merest boredom, some genuinely detecting the possibility of touching something great. And their leader, entrusted to organize every detail of this perilous journey, had his own particular motivations. He was not moved by the prospect of naked conquest or wealth, but came to the task as an inquirer, particularly in the new science of geology. He did not look for thrills or search for glory but dreamed of matching himself against a great physical and intellectual challenge and overcoming it, especially if it had been previously declared insurmountable.

"We are quite proud of our little fleet," wrote Powell in his journal as their preparations drew to a close. He had named the lead scouting boat after his wife. A stiff breeze whipped and snapped the American flag above *Emma Dean,* "the waves rocking the little vessel, and the current of the Green, swollen, mad and seeming eager to bear us down through its mysterious canyons. And we are just as eager to start." For all his advance work, the river trip still amounted to a dangerous gamble. He would need to deploy all his logistical savvy, all his courage, all his planning acumen and leadership to pull this one off. He would need a good deal of luck also, but he had long known that fortune favors the prepared.

On May 24 at 1 p.m., the Colorado River Exploring Expedition, "thoroughly tired of our sojourn at Green River City," as Walter observed, began their journey in high spirits. "After much blowing off of gas and the fumes of bad whiskey, we were all ready," noted Sumner. They waved nonchalantly to the townspeople who had assembled by the bank, then pushed their four stout vessels into the wide, muddy current. Seated on rowing benches, two men in each boat pulled at oars secured by iron oarlocks. Walter raised his deep baritone in a melancholy song—indeed, the men would come to call him "Old Shady"—and all roared along in hearty chorus, commencing to pull downstream. Powell described with excitement the Uinta Mountains to the south as "high peaks thrust into the sky, and snow fields glittering like lakes of molten silver, and pine forests in somber green . . ."

Powell captained the smaller, sixteen-foot-long pine scout boat, which took the lead of this small flotilla. His crew consisted of Jack Sumner and trapper Bill Dunn. George Bradley commanded *Maid of the Cañon*, which he and his boatmate Walter Powell had decided to christen as befitting two bachelors. The two youngest— Billy Hawkins and Andy Hall—took to the oars of *Kitty Clyde's Sister,* a popular song of the time whose refrain ran: "For if ever I loved a girl in my life, / 'Tis Minnie, Kitty Clyde's sister." Finally came *No Name,* commanded by Oramel Howland and crewed by his brother Seneca and the Englishman Goodman. Sumner's description of the boat—"No Name (piratical craft)"—hints that it may have been christened not out of a lack of imagination, but in reference to a currently popular sea story. Major newspapers and magazines had covered the sensational escape of Confederate secretary of war John C. Breckinridge and the naval officer John Tyler Wood after war's end from Florida to Cuba in a small unnamed sloop, weathering storms and pirates. When Cuban custom officers sought the name of the boat, Wood replied: "No Name." The epic of so small a craft overcoming such deadly odds—"the manner of [Wood's] escape from the coast of Florida savors of the romantic," observed the *New York Herald*—might well have inspired the Howland brothers to give their plucky little rowboat the same nondescript moniker.

Their lack of experience afloat became immediately apparent when Hawkins and Hall ran aground a mile or two below their launch point. The others guffawed as the two clambered out of *Kitty Clyde's Sister* to wrestle her back into the river. Andy Hall muttered how his boat handled about as well as an unbroken mule. Not long after, someone broke an oar fending off a rock, which sent the vessel reeling into an eddy. "In the confusion two other oars are lost overboard," wrote Powell, "and the men seem quite discomfited, much to the amusement of the other members of the party."

But in the relatively slight rapids, the boats performed admirably, shooting through "with the speed of the wind," wrote Oramel Howland—others commenting that they flew like a blue-ribbon railroad train going flat out at sixty miles an hour. They came nowhere near the power of steam, of course—the strongest current in the largest rapids averages twenty miles an hour, only on occasion does the Grand Canyon's most violent waters reach thirty miles an hour. Yet that perception of uncommon speed comes frequently to those who race close to the surface on which they speed, their freeboard only inches from the surging waves, like a sledder whose face rides mere inches above the ice of a steep run.

"The boats seem to be a success," wrote Powell with some qualification, "although filled with water by the waves many times, they never sink." They were all Whitehall rowboats, named after the street in New York City from which they were first launched to ferry goods and sailors to ships at anchor in the harbor. These keeled boats handled the choppy water of New York Harbor and later the Great Lakes well, tracking faithfully and moving smartly. One contemporary observer, who braved Lake Michigan when the waves ran high in a Whitehall, proclaimed that "in the great billows it was so constant" that its company was "satisfied that the boats could ride any sea . . ." Tight for money, Powell had been forced to skimp on many things, but in the choice of boats he wisely did not pinch pennies. The Whitehall's hull design remains very sophisticated and difficult to build even today, employing complex, compound curves that are particularly hard to fashion from hard oak. The Whitehall boasted a carvel-style construction, in which the hull boards lie side by side without overlap.

But a whitewater river—and certainly the Green and Colorado—did not behave like open water, the hydraulics of its tumultuous motions governed by entirely different forces. "Running" whitewater had not yet been seriously contemplated, even among the French voyageurs in their large rabaska canoes of the century before on the St. Laurence, or the Algonquins in their birch-bark vessels along eastern rivers. Even these brave and skillful boatmen portaged the worst waters, not eager for thrills or to wreck boats that had consumed so many resources to build. They often used materials on the bank for repairs; Powell could not assume that his party would find sufficient wood to craft a replacement boat within the inhospitable canyons. The tough fur entrepreneur William Ashley had attempted the Colorado in round Indian bull boats, but the first touch of serious whitewater had quickly taken them out of commission. Frémont had experimented with a four-chambered raft made from rubberized linen on the rapids of the North Platte in present-day Wyoming as far back as 1843, but the craft flipped, and one or more of the air chambers had ruptured. Ives had shown that even iron hulls could not withstand repeated pummeling by granite boulders.

Powell's selection of the Whitehall design made sense, given what he knew at the time. But even they would ultimately prove not ideal craft for whitewater. The very qualities that enabled them to travel fast in a straight line, prevented them from doing exactly what the boaters would need most in the turmoil of whitewater rock gardens: the ability to swing and pivot quickly, letting the oarsman rapidly pick a zigzag through and around multiple obstacles. Andy Hall summed it up best when he commented that his boat would not "gee nor haw nor whoa worth a damn." When the whitewater grew its worst, as the canyon walls narrowed, offering no place to pull over, the boats' handling characteristics would drag the expedition into mortal danger.

Yet Powell had taken some sensible precautions to make his Whitehalls "stanch and strong" by doubling the number of ribs and their stemposts and sternposts. He added bulkheads fore and aft to provide waterproof compartments and flotation, leaving an eleven-foot-long cockpit amidships. The bulkheads' placement distributed weight farther fore and aft, unfortunately thus making the boats even less agile. When waves filled the cockpit, as often they did, the Whitehalls became virtually unsteerable, although the waterproof bulkheads prevented them from actually sinking. The liquid ballast lent a certain stability, but proved fickle and dangerous when a rapid violently shifted the water trapped within the boat.

The notion of an oarsman facing downstream—something now taken for granted today by whitewater river runners—had yet to be formed. The standard rowing stroke derives its most efficient and powerful mode by harnessing the broadest muscles in the back, trunk, and thighs, achieved traditionally by rowers facing upstream. But placement and negotiation in the grip of a tumultuous rapid is far more crucial than power. Rowing with their backs downstream would effectively blind an oarsman—even if they could glimpse the conditions downstream over their shoulders—and leave them unable to respond quickly to rapids that so often reveal themselves in a startling moment. The party's journals give no indication that they used a steering rudder, or sweep, which would have significantly enhanced their ability to maneuver.

Powell had taken other important steps in anticipation of bad water: He had *Emma Dean* built five feet shorter than the other three, and out of lighter white pine to be more nimble, so it could serve as a scouting boat. Aware that the river's deafening rapids might drown out effective voice commands, he brought along red signal flags, a means of communication that worked effectively during loud artillery duels during the war. Powell planned to stand when *Emma Dean* approached a rapid and read the current for "a clear chute between the rocks" while the oarsmen backwatered. Should he see a clear passage, the scout boat would run the rapid, then immediately pull ashore. He would then use the flag to indicate the optimal course between the rocks, standing waves, and holes. If the rapids appeared unrunnable, the scout boat would pull ashore. A flag waved right and left, then down signaled "land at once." A rightward motion meant "keep to the right" and vice versa to the left. Boats were to keep one hundred yards between them. It all made logical good sense on dry land, but the wild river, like conditions during a battle, would find a way to disrupt the best laid plans.

The Green flows through southern Wyoming's desertscape of rocky, nondescript hills patched with grass and scrubby greasewood thickets, these punctuated every few miles with small clumps of spindly cottonwoods and cedars. "Country worthless," groused Sumner. Far to the west, the expedition could faintly discern the Wasatch Mountains, to the south rose the Uintas, toward which the Green drove, its surface now and again broken by riffles. The pair rowing each boat began to fall into a rhythm; they could now straighten their bows quite effortlessly with light adjustments when the current pushed them off center. Despite heavy rains, spirits remained high.

On their third day, having rowed and floated some sixty miles, they crossed into modern-day Utah, and the current accelerated. They passed into the upper canyons of the Green, through the outlying hogback ridges of the Uintas. The fiery-red Chinle and Moenkopi sandstones of the justly dubbed Flaming Gorge loomed above them, beds of orange, ocher, and ruddy remnants of the 200- to 250-million-year-old Triassic, when dinosaurs and the earliest mammals first appeared on Earth. They camped just inside the uppermost canyon, Bradley scribbling in his journal that the river "winds like [a] serpent through between nearly perpendicular cliffs 1200 ft. high but instead of rapids it is deep and calm as a lake." The veteran would record his impressions with almost boyish immediacy and excitement. When they camped over for a few days, Bradley went out exploring in the morning, walked too far, and got caught in a blinding rainstorm, only struggling back to camp after dark "tired and hungry and mad as a bear." The canyon's walls block out direct sunshine for most of the day, dropping temperatures significantly, conditions that favored Ponderosa pines and Douglas firs, which appeared like apparitions at the water's edge.

Flaming Gorge opens onto the tight hairpin of Horseshoe Canyon and then gives way to the soaring ivory Weber sandstone of Kingfisher Canyon, thronged with the thick-necked, large-billed fish-eating bird. The canyon's narrowing now speeded up the river, creating riffles but little whitewater, the sandstone riverbed smoothed for so long by the racing river. Marveling at this steep and narrow Uinta country, they floated past the immense rock dome of Bee Hive Point, honeycombed with small, eroded holes, in which swallows nested. The lithe birds flitted about the rock with the industry of bees.

They came upon the name "Ashley" painted onto a rock wall just before some rapids, along with the date 1825. Powell had been able to gather few details of this fur entrepreneur's journey, but someone had told him about a group floating down the Green that had capsized in the rapids. Some had drowned. "This word 'Ashley' is a warning to us and we resolve on great caution," he wrote.

Conditions grew less benign all of a sudden as the river crossed the Uinta Fault where Red Canyon begins, the soft sandstones giving way to the hard Uinta Mountain Quartzite. Inescapable to all of them—and to all others who would later paddle the western canyonlands—is that hard rock most often equates with rapids. Chunks of fire-hardened quartzite, which had splintered from rock walls in side canyons, had eventually been washed into the main river, forming dangerous rock gardens, which the expedition now named Skull Creek, Ashley Falls, and Red Creek.

But this was no more than they had anticipated. For the next week, they encountered exhilarating whitewater: "We plunge along, singing, yelling, like drunken sailors, all feeling that such rides do not come every day," wrote Sumner. He reached deep to find an apt metaphor, comparing the passage to "sparking a black eyed girl—just dangerous enough to be exciting." They learned the elemental truth of whitewater: Rapids begin when the channel narrows and the walls vise inward. No matter how great the pressure, water cannot compress; consequently when unyielding rock walls close upon a river, the water can only do one thing: increase in velocity—often furiously, not unlike what happens when a thumb is pressed over the nozzle of a hose. When that focused stream of water smashes into a natural dam of rock and boulders, a river will exhibit its exhilarating, but violent, side. "Here and there the water would rush into a narrow gorge, the rocks at the side rolling it to the centre in great waves, and the boats would go leaping and bounding over these like things of life," Powell recalled.

Here the Major deemed their first rapid too dangerous to run, so the men "lined" their boats. After climbing out, several of the party would grab hold of the boat's bowline, then scramble down the bank paying out rope, trying as best they could to slow the path of the bucking vessel downstream. The men suffered their first ankle bruises from staggering along the rocks. Loaded boats proved hard to control while lining, so they often had to unship an entire cargo and carry that as well. Of necessity, they were all becoming students of the river, interrogating its constantly shifting personality for clues as to what kind of obstacles lay ahead. They learned quickly that a boat caught broadside in fast water often becomes jammed on a rock, the river pinning it down with thousands of pounds of force, making it extremely difficult to dislodge. Experience taught them that lighter boats danced best through the rapids, so they became diligent in bailing the cockpits.

Once in camp, they settled into routines. First order of business: Sumner helped Powell fix two of three surviving barometers, damaged on the trip west. This entailed pouring mercury into a glass tube, then boiling it over an alcohol lamp to create a vacuum. The glass too often burst, spraying its poisonous contents. Although the Smithsonian had provided these James Green field barometers—the finest then available—the thirty inches of glass tubing protectively encased in brass remained fragile, needing to travel upside down in a leather case. To get a reading, the men suspended the barometer beneath a tripod.

Of all the scientific instruments, Powell counted most on the barometer, which provided elevation data crucial to mapmaking and enabled him to measure the heights of features along the river. This instrument gave accurate altitude, thus enabling him to calculate the remaining drop in their overall 6,000-foot descent, which he could match with estimates of the distance left—then he could, in a rough manner, guess the drop per mile. Like counting cards in blackjack, barometric readings do not predict the next play—what kind of rapids may come up over the next mile—but rather give some sense of the overall trend of the river's rate of drop.

The expedition grew used to Powell heading up into the cliffs to "geologize" the moment they pulled ashore for the day. His restless imagination was starting to come alive in examination of the rocky features. If they followed him, they might find the Major lying on his side, staring intently at a far prominence. "I had found a way," he later explained, "to judge of altitude and slope as I could judge distance and trend along the horizontal." He compared the experience with a stereoscope in which a pair of lenses focuses on two identical objects fused into a three-dimensional image. "The distance between the eyes forms a base-line for optical triangulation."

On June 2, after ten days on the river, the canyon walls melted away, and they entered the anticipated outlines of Brown's Park, a valley bounded by steep mountains on either side, running twenty-five miles in length and four miles in breadth, named by a Hudson's Bay Company trapper four decades earlier. By the time Powell's team entered that remote tract, cattle rustlers, outlaws, and horse thieves had already known about it, their visits evident by shacks and signs of cattle grazing. By the turn of the twentieth century, Butch Cassidy and his Wild Bunch used this distant spot as a hideout from which to terrorize southern Wyoming, eastern Utah, and western Colorado. Indeed, some in the expedition had camped here on their way to Green River City. It provided a welcome taste of familiarity.

At the park's lower end, the meandering Green abruptly changes character, inscrutably cutting south by punching through the mountain's flank into a yawning mouth of immense, dark canyon walls. All of a sudden, its gates rise precipitously, a full thousand feet higher than the Empire State Building from the flat confines of the park, sandstones fused by the heat of the Earth's core into hard, shiny quartzite. At its threshold into the canyon, the Green again forsakes the softer sedimentary and volcanic rocks of the Tertiary to embrace the far older and harder Pre-Cambrian bedrock, a recipe for truly dangerous water.

Daylight found Powell extolling the beauty of the vermilion cliffs, but the setting sun brought shadows that encouraged correspondingly dismal thoughts: "Now it is a dark portal to a region of gloom—the gateway through which we are to enter on our voyage of exploration to-morrow. What shall we find?" These Poe-like words, written years later at his comfortable desk, smack of melodrama. Yet something about the Canyon deeply troubled him: Why had the river sliced so directly into the mountain, instead of continuing to meander gently to the end of Brown's Park? Pour water into a sandbox and it will take the easiest course, certainly not undercutting the wooden sides. This set the confounded Powell onto a line of questioning that would lead him to generate revolutionary ideas about the formation of rivers and mountains, evoking the huge and ancient forces that must have riven the landscape. At that time, orthodox geology explained the creation of canyons with the theory of catastrophism: The Earth simply cleaved apart under some cataclysmic force, rivers implacably spilling through the resulting cuts. Powell would turn that theory on its head, arguing powerfully instead that the rivers themselves had carved the landscape as titanic forces pushed the plateau up against them.

If Powell revealed his roiling speculations to the others and brought to their attention the daily geological revelations unveiled by this journey, their journals do not reflect it. But even with so much to ponder, Powell would have to turn his attention almost exclusively to getting down the next eighteen miles of river, a ten-day effort that would try each expedition member's strength and determination—and bring near disaster.

On June 8, they stripped to their long underwear and shirts, and kicked off their boots in full anticipation of a soaking ride. The bright red flannels that Goodman had bought in Green River City jarred particularly loudly upon the ancient cliffs. One by one, the boats pushed into the river, Powell and *Emma Dean* of course in the lead, passing through the billion-year-old gates. As they traveled, they named features they encountered, imprinting some form of humanity on this inhuman landscape. This Canyon would earn the sobriquet Lodore, after Robert Southey's 1820 poem, "The Cataract of Lodore," in which the poet uses onomatopoeic rhymes to describe a falls in northwestern England. In the poem, the water crashes, moans, groans, tumbles, claps, slaps, foams, rushes, and flushes. Sumner complained that "the idea of diving into musty trash to find names for new discoveries on a new continent is un-American," but Powell liked the idea anyway, so Lodore it became, and remains to this day. From then on, they would use no more Old World inscriptions for the many hundreds of memorable features that they would christen on their voyage.

All that morning they rode rapids, Powell pointing out paths around boat-eating rocks with his flag. They lined what is now known as Winnie's Rapid, formed by a spray of boulders fallen from a grotto in the right river cliff. After lunch in the shadow of that rose-colored, 1,500-foot wall, they set off again; only a half mile later, *Emma Dean* encountered a set of double rapids squeezed by quickly narrowing canyon walls. The first rapids, which drop only two or three feet, seemed runnable, although beset by large standing waves. The second rapids, immediately thereafter, startled the men with its violence: It tumbled down twenty or thirty feet in a channel choked with dangerous rocks that broke the waves into whirlpools and beat them into foam. Should any crew lose control of its boat in that upper rapid, no amount of effort could save it from smashing into the head of a cigar-shaped islet of sand and gravel dividing the lower falls. The Green drops thirty-five feet in little over half a mile.

Powell pulled *Emma Dean* ashore, then signaled *Kitty Clyde's Sister* to do the same. He gave the flag to Dunn to signal the next two boats, himself walking downriver to scout. A cry rose behind him and, looking upriver, he saw *No Name* madly pulling for shore—but from too far out to make it. Somehow Oramel Howland had not caught Dunn's signal in time. In swift, powerful current, oarsmen must anticipate rather than respond: Reaction most often means action too late. Perhaps still woozy from a big lunch, they had been sloppy at their bailing. Riding too low in the water, *No Name* could respond only sluggishly to the oar. Powell watched as *Maid of the Cañon* pulled over safely. But by this time *No Name*, or what was left of it, was in serious trouble. Oramel, Seneca, and Frank were fighting for their lives.

No Name had shot into the first rapid, the center of which held a threatening, large boulder. The bow smacked the rock, throwing men and oars into the water, although they managed to cling to its sides and climb back into the now-swamped boat. Powell recalled that the first rapid was not so bad, "and we had often run such"; but now *No Name* spun out of control toward the far deadlier second rapid. It hit the islet with such force as to crack the boat in two, its occupants left clutching the severed bow section. Once in the water, all vantage is lost—the waves slap the face and jerk the body unnaturally. Time takes on a different quality altogether, the sheer violence of the water overwhelming one almost faster than the brain can process events. Adrenaline charges mind and limbs for action, but they respond hopelessly out of step.

Goodman lunged for a barrel-sized rock while Oramel jumped for the islet; Seneca waited a beat before flailing for its most downriver tip. Below this sliver of sand and rubble, the water turned even more savage as it rushed toward the overhanging cliff walls on the right bank; no man, even with a life jacket, would likely survive that "perfect hell of waters," wrote Sumner. The wreckage of *No Name* disappeared into the foam as if swallowed by some insatiable beast.

On the islet, Oramel reached for a dead tree root, which he swung out toward the boulder upon which Goodman precariously clung. The Englishman jumped for it, and Oramel pulled him gasping onto the sandy gravel. Their ankles were bloody from bat-tering on the rocks, their stomachs bloated from inhaling the muddy water, their long underwear and shirts clinging like a sec-ond skin. Shouting to be heard, Oramel and Seneca lit a pine trunk on fire with some matches that miraculously had not gotten wet. Goodman sat still, all but the shadow of life sucked right out of him.

The others scrambled downstream, staring across the narrow channel—only a couple of dozen feet but a violent froth separating them from the marooned trio. The others emptied *Emma Dean*, then lined it down to a point on the bank just above the islet. Sum-ner climbed in, then pulling with all his strength "right skillfully," remembered Powell, just made the islet. The four men dragged the boat to the most upstream end of the island. Sumner instructed the rescued men to lie in the bottom of *Emma Dean* while he alone manned the oars to cut hard and sharp across the narrows. The others pulled the boat safely to the main bank.

"We were as glad to shake hands with them as if they had been on a voyage 'round the world and wrecked on a distant coast," wrote Powell. But the tone of comradely bonhomie in which he cast the story was intended for the benefit of a readership far removed from that remote, wave-crashed riverbank. Anger had quickly overwhelmed the relief Powell felt at having the men back alive: Within two minutes, and only two weeks into the trip, two thou-sand pounds of provisions—nearly one-third of their entire complement—had vanished, along with half the mess kit, Ora-mel's maps, three rifles, and a revolver. Powell lost his writing paper. The river had also swept away the bedding and clothing of the three survivors, who were left with only a shirt and pair of drawers apiece. Goodman, who had lost his new buckskin trousers and shirt, a buffalo robe, a blanket, a blue army overcoat, and his beaver hat, seemed particularly spooked. He would later describe to a friend that his long underwear bottoms dropped down to his ankles and made swimming virtually impossible. It had been a very near thing. There would be none of his usual singing or story-telling that night.

Powell confronted the still-dripping Oramel. Why had he not acted on the signal? Surprised at the Major's thinly veiled accusation, Howland responded rather prickly that he had not seen it in time. Who was Powell to question his judgment after he had just returned from the edge of death? Howland was not used to a challenge like this. Such a confrontation with a fellow mountain man risked a fist or pulled knife.

But Powell could just not understand how this could have happened. The bend before the rapid was gentle, the sound of the whitewater loudly audible long before it came into view. Two other boats were clearly visible ashore. Howland should not have even required a signal to warn him. Of the three freight boats, only *No Name* had a free passenger in it, one who could devote himself entirely to peering downstream. Of all the boats, Howland's should have been the most vigilant. Like Powell, Oramel could stand up to survey the situation. How could he not have been paying steady attention? Powell had trained entire batteries to execute complicated maneuvers under the extremity of battle—why could this man not follow simple instructions? Howland had no answer, aside from claiming that the boat had been full of water and unresponsive. Why had he not bailed the boat, as they had done before? It seemed that Powell's obsessive planning—the scout boat and the flag system—had gone for naught.

At least Powell had clearly divided food and supplies equally among the boats. All, that is, except for the three barometers, which were packed aboard *No Name,* and now were lost. For Powell, these were the most galling casualties. The very reason for the expedition—accurately mapping the river's course and riparian topography—was now impossible to complete. The loss of the barometers represented so severe a setback in Powell's eyes that he seriously considered undergoing a grueling trek to Salt Lake City to replace them. Their adrenaline still surging from the rescue, the others must have wondered about the Major's hardhearted-ness in seeming to place a shiny bronze tool above the lives of his crew.

A few days afterward, Oramel Howland wrote that the calam-ity had resulted "owing to not understanding the signal." What-ever the ultimate reason—whether he had missed the signal or just failed to understand it—Howland's mistake proved devastat-ing. Most likely, he had simply underestimated the force of the water. These mountain men, of necessity individualistic, naturally resisted being told what to do, especially by a rather officious Ma-jor who, while battle tested, had little experience in the uncharted West, and whose planning seemed excessive and often unneces-sary. Howland had relied on wits and guts for years. He had grossly underestimated these ferocious waters, taking Powell's warnings more as recommendations than as imperatives for stay-ing alive and preserving the expedition's resources. His had not so much been willful neglect as a habitual placement of his own judg-ment into any process.

The men lined *Emma Dean* another half mile down shore, and discovered part of the stern cuddy stuck on a rocky shoal in mid-river. Sumner immediately volunteered to get it, but Powell over-rode him, uninterested in risking further mishaps on an already disastrous day. They returned to the other two boats at the top of the rapids to set up their pallets. Underneath scrubby mountain cedars, they ate a quiet supper of bread and bacon, the roar of the water now taking a more sinister note than before.

But troubling questions haunted Powell that evening, and despite his exhaustion, he could not fall asleep. He recognized more starkly than the others how far the risk equation had shifted. Many adjust-ments were now necessary to complete the journey safely. While he certainly had anticipated—even planned for—a scenario like this, the accident had nevertheless thinned their safety margin far too early in their trip. The odds of the expedition surviving the loss of a second boat—which would catastrophically diminish food supplies as well as seriously overload the remaining boats—were slim indeed. Powell would now direct his expedition to line and portage even more frequently to minimize the chance of another devastating wreck, exertions that would push them all to the edge of their physical capacities.

The next morning, they lined the boats down what they would soon name Disaster Falls. When they spotted more wreckage on a rock, Powell permitted Sumner to investigate. Sumner powered *Emma Dean* single-handedly out to the crushed remains. Upon reaching them, he whooped with joy. While he had indeed found the barometers, his exultation came from the recovery of a keg of whiskey, which Oramel had smuggled aboard without Powell's knowledge. "The Professor was so much pleased about the recovery of the barometers that he looked as happy as a young girl with her first beau," wrote Sumner. They also came across the traces of another unknown party—perhaps Ashley's. The wreck of a boat, along with the lid of a bake pan, tin plate, and further abandoned supplies, suggested that this party had camped here after a similar debilitating accident—and then left the river altogether.

To every foray into the unknown—whether into the jungle, across the sea, over the pack ice, or deep into a desert—comes a moment of reckoning, which often declares itself with savage immediacy in the form of a storm or sudden death or bad accident, polar frostbite or tropical fever, equipment breakdown or just plain failure of leadership in the face of unanticipated hazards. Optimistic anticipation must rudely encounter rough, cold realities. Human vulnerabilities suddenly reveal themselves, often in stark detail—the veneer of even the toughest can crack. Good cheer alone, even buoyed by formidable skills and fortitude, may not be able to overcome such misfortune. To survive, all adventurers must then acknowledge that they exercise far less control than they thought. To survive, the party must join together far more cohesively than before.

Such thresholds of adversity break many such enterprises, but they also offer an opportunity for a party to discover its deeper purpose. Relationships shift, stretch, and strengthen. On the river, roles were clarifying—Sumner's most notably, as he repeatedly stepped up to take leadership in difficult situations. Powell certainly remained the overall leader, but the genial trapper had already begun to keep the men focused and working together, his decisive action crucial to the group's survival.

Their bodies now reeked of the earthy river. Each man nursed a variety of physical insults: strained backs and ankles, myriad cuts and bruises, stomachs churned by too much coffee. The stress of uncertainty—what new dangers awaited them around each bend?—chewed on them day and night. The river was unquestionably their master now. The only way to survive contact with such power is not to fight it but to find a way of working with its overwhelming force.

Bradley, so recently a soldier, hinted at the transformation that took place among the men at Disaster Falls. "The red sand-stone rises on either side more than 2,000 ft., shutting out the sun for much of the day while at our feet the river, lashed to a foam, rushes on with indescribable fury. O how great is He, who holds it in the hollow of his hand and what pygmies we who strive against it."

Indeed, they now faced powers greater than they had the temerity even to imagine.

John Wesley Powell at age thirty-five in 1869, the year that he made his famous descent down the Green and Colorado rivers. *(National Park Service)*

A *Harper's Monthly Magazine* engraving depicts Powell's battery during the Vicksburg Campaign, Mississippi, in 1863. *(Illinois Wesleyan University)*

John Wesley Powell's wife, Emma Dean Powell. *(Bill and Wendy Krag)*

Lieutenant Joseph Ives's 1858 exploration up the Colorado River ended when his 54-foot steamboat *Explorer* violently struck submerged rocks. *(Illinois Wesleyan University)*

Powell filled his 1868 collecting expedition to the Colorado Rockies with eager college students, including Lewis Keplinger (back row, left), who would help the Major make the first ascent of Longs Peak. *(National Anthropological Archives, Smithsonian Institution)*

Jack Sumner at about age twenty, circa 1860. *(Raymond V. Sumner family collection)*

Jack Sumner and Powell first discussed running the Green and Colorado at Sumner's trading post near Hot Sulphur Springs in Colorado's Middle Park in 1867. *(Denver Public Library)*

Powell's brother Walter (left) and cook Billy Hawkins pose in Green River, Wyoming Territory, before the Colorado River Exploring Expedition set off in May 1869. *(Nolan Reed)*

Shortly after the Union Pacific Railroad completed its trestle bridge over the Green River in Wyoming Territory in 1869, Powell shipped four rowboats there to begin the one-thousand-mile river journey that would lead through the Grand Canyon. *(author collection)*

An ember from the cook fire ignited dry vegetation on the banks of the Green River during the 1869 river trip, causing near disaster for the expedition, as illustrated in a January 1875 issue of *Scribner's Monthly*. *(Illinois Wesleyan University)*

Scribner's Monthly immortalized George Bradley's daring rescue of the one-armed Powell as they "geologized" after a long day on the river. *(Illinois Wesleyan University)*

Oramel Howland, whose decision to abandon Powell's 1869 river expedition and cross the desert led to his death and that of two others. *(Kenneth Barrows)*

Seneca Howland, Oramel's younger half-brother and veteran of Gettysburg. *(Kenneth Barrows)*

Only two weeks into the 1869 expedition, Oramel Howland's carelessness led to the loss of the freight boat *No Name* and a third of their supplies, depicted here in a *Scribner's Monthly* article. *(Illinois Wesleyan University)*

Powell with a Paiute Indian on the Kaibab Plateau near the Grand Canyon. *(Smithsonian Institution Archives, #2002-10682)*

Powell and Jacob Hamblin meet with Paiute Indians on the Kaibab Plateau in the Arizona Strip, circa 1873. *(National Anthropological Archives, Smithsonian Institution)*

Photographer E. O. Beaman captures Powell's second Colorado expedition just before they departed from Green River City, Wyoming, in May 1871. Powell stands above the others on the deck of the center boat. *(National Archives)*

For the second expedition, Powell had an armchair attached to the deck of *Emma Dean*. *(National Archives)*

William Henry Holmes's *Panorama from Point Sublime* appeared in Clarence Dutton's *Tertiary History of the Grand Cañon District* in 1882. *(Library of Congress, Geography and Map Division)*

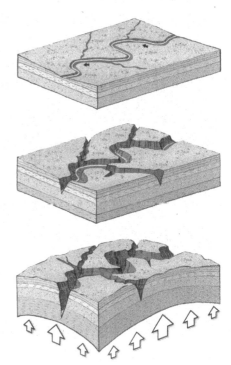

An illustration of canyon creation on the Colorado Plateau: 1. A river flows over the landscape. 2. As geologic forces uplift the plateau, the river cuts into the landscape. 3. Differential uplift causes the center of the landscape to rise faster, but the river's incision keeps pace. *(Grand Canyon Association, Carving Grand Canyon: Evidence, Theories, and Mystery, 2nd edition by Wayne Ranney)*

Federal surveyor and geologist Clarence King.
(Smithsonian Institution Archives, #SA-859)

Lieutenant George Wheeler (seated at center) at Diamond Creek on the southern end of the Grand Canyon in 1871.
(Library of Congress)

Geologist Ferdinand Hayden (left) on his survey of the Colorado, 1873. *(Smithsonian Institution Archives, #MAH-37799)*

Although he retired at sixty-two in 1896, Powell still ran the Smithsonian's Bureau of Ethnology and wrote a 400-page tome on the philosophy of science.
(Smithsonian Institution Archives, #94-12600)

Jack Hillers organizes his wet-plate photographic equipment in south-central Utah in 1872. *(National Archives)*

E. O. Beaman took this photograph of Fred Dellenbaugh on the Green River in Lodore Canyon while on the second Powell expedition in 1871. *(National Archives)*

John Wesley Powell (far left) and Thomas Moran (with hand on face) in the field in the summer 1873. *(National Anthropological Archives, Smithsonian Institution)*

Thomas Moran's *The Chasm of the Colorado*, 1873–1874. *(Smithsonian Museum of American Art, Washington, DC/Art Resource, NY)*

Charles Schott's map "Rain Chart of the United States" shows how rainfall dramatically trails off near the 100th meridian, which influenced Powell's thinking about the limits of non-irrigation farming in the West. *(author collection)*

Senator William Stewart of Nevada clashed bitterly with Powell over land development issues in the West, finally persuading Congress to cut off funding for Powell's irrigation survey in 1890. *(Library of Congress)*

Members of the Great Basin Mess celebrate the Major's retirement from the U.S. Geological Survey in 1894, including Charles Walcott and William Henry Holmes (seated behind Powell on the right), W. J. McGee and G. K. Gilbert (across from him). *(Smithsonian Institution Archives, #75-5228)*

Geologist Clarence E. Dutton served as one of Powell's closest associates until they parted ways after Dutton's damaging Senate testimony in the irrigation survey hearings of 1890. *(National Oceanic and Atmospheric Administration/Department of Commerce)*

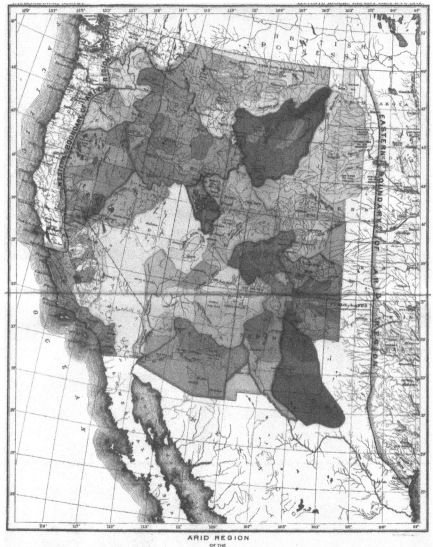

ARID REGION
OF THE
UNITED STATES
Showing Drainage Districts.

Powell's map of the "Arid Region of the United States," which he presented to the U.S. Senate in 1890, offered a radical new vision of the American West centered on watersheds rather than on traditional political boundaries. *(author collection)*

CHAPTER 6

The Canyon

L odore Canyon continued to pound them. Even Disaster Falls paled beside the ferocity of Hell's Half Mile, which drops at a pace of more than sixty feet a mile. They found themselves out of the boats more often than not. The men hefted the heavy frames upon their shoulders and worked them awkwardly down and around the rapids. Then they would wearily clamber back up the same path and repeat many round-trips to ferry their supplies downstream. Every yard became a hard-fought contest.

Where they could, they lined the boats, but that presented its own challenges. All too frequently one of the Whitehalls would wedge tightly between rocks, requiring all hands to push, pull, and coax it free. If a stuck boat filled with water, liberating it could take half an hour or longer. Even those sturdy boats began to show wear: The rapids stove a hole in *Kitty's Sister* and the seams on all the boats began to leak. The men themselves took a beating. Pulled repeatedly off balance, they frequently lost their footing. Bradley gashed his forehead above the left eye, blood pouring ghoulishly down his face. Their leather boots split open under repeated immersions and hard wear, very often leaving toes battered and bloodied.

In one section of Hell's Half Mile, five men lined the empty

Maid of the Cañon through the tumultuous water right along the bank, liberally paying out the bowline. Whenever a boulder blocked *Maid*'s path, they released even more line so it could skirt the obstacle. At one such obstruction, they let out too much: *Maid*'s bow touched the main current, which jerked it savagely out into the river, ripping the line out of their hands. The boat, wrote Sumner, tore "off like a frightened horse," shooting to the far side of the river and out of sight. Sumner and Hawkins leaped into *Emma Dean* and took off through the rapids in pursuit. By a special providence, the intrepid pair discovered the runaway craft circling lazily in an eddy below that awful cascade. *Maid* had shipped much water and also now bore a sizable hole in its stern, yet it remarkably remained afloat.

They patched *Maid* up. Nerves continued to fray. Bradley confided to his journal that he felt like a galley slave. "The major as usual has chosen the worst camping ground possible," he complained in the time-honored tradition of expeditioneers grumbling about their leader. "If I had a dog that would lie where my bed is made tonight I would kill him and burn his collar and swear I never owned him." Nothing stayed dry for long, so the querulous sergeant now kept his journal and some family daguerreotypes under his hat.

On June 17, the ninth day in this dark canyon, they pulled onto a small beach running just under a cliffside, choked with willows, cedar, sage, and grass. They had just enough room to strip off their wet clothes and hang them to dry on the vegetation. Hawkins lit a fire to boil coffee while the rest joked around and discreetly examined their cracked and bruised hands and feet. Powell walked off along the cliffside, searching for a way up so he could study the rocks.

A sudden gust of wind keened down the river course, blowing embers from the cookfire into the scrub. In seconds, the desert-dry beach vegetation and driftwood flared into a conflagration, catching the men flat-footed. They grabbed their drying shirts and pants, many of them already on fire, shaking them furiously as they ran along the narrow beach. The panicked Hawkins embraced the mess kit, stumbled to the water's edge, and stepped into shallows, or so he thought. The bottom fell away, pitching him into the river. The kit flew from his grasp into the water. Before Bradley could dive into the river, flames singed his ears and mustache, burned off his eyebrows, and set his shirt on fire.

From above the camp, Powell heard cries, and peering over the cliff edge, he was astounded to see his party in complete disarray: his men tumbling helter-skelter into the boats, which they frantically pushed off the bank and into the current. Attempts to land farther down the beach failed as the fire outraced them. Instead the boats, with bows pointed every which way, shot into an unscouted rapid, the men just managing to grab their oars, but still unable to direct their course.

They flew through the rapids backward and sideways, somehow emerging unscathed in an eddy below the torrent. "One of the crew came in hatless," wrote Oramel Howland, "another shirtless, a third without his pants, and a hole burned in the posterior portion of his drawers; another with nothing but drawers and shirt, and still another had to pull off his handkerchief from his neck, which was all ablaze." But these men were not easily spooked: Bradley's ghostlike countenance sent them all into howls of laughter.

Hawkins at last got supper going while the elder Howland inventoried their remaining cooking equipment and eating utensils: "One gold pan, used for making bread; One bake-oven, with broken lid; One camp-kettle, for making tea or coffee; One frying-pan; One large spoon and two tea spoons; Three tin plates and five bailing cups." And, he added with a flourish, "One pick-ax and one shovel"—the cook using "the latter article for a spoon, the former to clean his teeth after our repast is over." They now had to sip their coffee from a bailing cup each shared with another man, but that did not dim their spirit as their laughter roared for an hour.

"Went to bed and were lulled to sleep," wrote Sumner casually, "by the rain pattering on the tent."

Lodore released them the next day, its cliffs falling back steadily from the river, the long hours of shadow also melting away to bright sun. As they left the hard, ancient rock of the Uintas, the rapids burbled and sparkled, requiring no lining or portaging. The boats swept effortlessly downstream, the men giddy with their reprieve. As they laughed and sang, Powell studied the low cliffs in amazement. The chaotic violence of the water seemed to have jumped right into the cliffs, which now exhibited sinister-looking formations. One cliff face, its horizontal cake layers of rock thrust skyward by some titanic force, appeared like a rain-swollen paperback, its alternating red-and-white stone layers improbably bent. Powell puzzled over the elemental forces that had lifted and carved, eroded and twisted that alien landscape. Where his men saw only rock and color, he saw patterns that posed more questions about Earth and its long history. Powell looked at each new feature, not only as a geologist but also with a further rarer quality that he himself would later describe as "the instinct for cosmic interrogation," the power he believed that most animated the evolved human mind. "It is easy to be lost in a maze of hills and a confusion of mountain peaks," he later wrote, "unless the grand topographic forms on which the hills and mountains are sculptured are seen with a mental vision that reaches further than the eye. He who can see a mountain range, or a river drainage, or a flock of hills, is more rare than a poet."

After they had passed this anomaly, they rowed into what they would name Echo Park, where the Yampa falls into the Green from river left. Across from the Yampa's dramatic entrance, Sumner glimpsed the prettiest rock wall he had ever seen, an immense 700-foot chunk of ivory-colored Weber Sandstone rising abruptly from the water's edge. They pulled onto the gentle bank opposite this shark fin–shaped monolith, which they would dub Echo Rock, and set up camp.

The journal entries written just after the terrors of Lodore now began to reveal each man's survival strategy. Oramel Howland adopted a tone of confidence verging on bluster. "Danger is our life," he wrote. "As soon as the surface of the river looks smooth all is listlessness or grumbling at the sluggish current, unless some unlucky goose comes within range of our rifles. But just let a white foam show itself ahead and everything is as Jolly and full of life as an Irish 'wake' or merry-making, or anything of that sort. Jokes generate faster and thicker than mosquitoes from a bog, and everything is as merry as a marriage bell."

Bradley could not muster Howland's level of apparent self-confidence—but relied instead on a native optimism fused with keen observation. The Yampa swelled the Green's volume, he noted, creating a wider channel less likely to get blocked by boulders. Lodore Canyon, he wrote, "has been the worst by far and I predict *the worst we shall ever meet*." It would not be so. As the rapids grew more and more perilous by the day, Bradley would mark almost each new one with the mantra that it was the worst they would face. Somehow this willful thinking got him through each day—sincerely believing that things had to be looking up.

Sumner found it best to remain in the present, not wasting time looking backward or forward, choosing instead to fill his journal with the human accounts of the party blowing off steam caterwauling at Echo Rock (today's Steamboat Rock). But not every man was coping. The Englishman Goodman, who had signed up on a lark, had come closest to drowning—and probably to breaking down— the river ripping away his dignity and everything he owned save his red flannel underwear. But he counted himself lucky to have even that—and his life. After he clambered aboard the next boat, he promised himself that he would leave the river and the expedition at the first opportunity.

Powell later filled in his journal with more flourish and swagger than he almost certainly felt at the moment: "This has been a chapter of disasters and toils, notwithstanding which the Canyon of Lodore was not devoid of scenic interest, even beyond the power of pen to tell." He took mental refuge from the continually demanding river by puzzling over its display of geological enigmas—and periodically drew back from the incessant strains by writing about the significance of their undertaking, not just for science, but for a nation just getting to know itself fully.

After running south continuously from its source, the Green hooks northward around Steamboat Rock, thus crossing Mitten Fault, where much older rock has been thrust up to river level. The geology suddenly became even more fascinating as the expedition crossed what later would be named the Pennsylvanian Morgan Formation, eye-catching alternations of gray limestone and orange-red sandstone. For a man who endlessly examined the landscape for clues, the formation was indeed transfixing. As clearly as words on a page, it told of titanic battles between ocean and land. Some three hundred million years before, as scientists today reckon it, the vast shallow sea covering the still-forming North American continent began to recede. When the inland sea thrived, the calcium-rich skeletal fragments of uncountable marine organisms—shells, corals, algae—sank to the bottom, forming a layer eventually compacted into limestone. As that sea receded, terrestrial sand and debris spread over the calcium layer, themselves duly forming sandstones. The alternation of strata bespoke to Powell the comings and goings of that sea over long stretches of time—and evidence of multiple beachheads in the struggle of water and sand. In all nature, few examples exist so clearly of Earth's dynamism and how its surface has so radically altered over time.

Now they entered Whirlpool Canyon, its steep walls closing in on the Green to create "a gloomy chasm, where mad waves roar," noted Powell. The river exhibited new and disturbing patterns in the form of tight, circling whirlpools that clutched at the boats and sent them spinning like the minute hand on a clock face when they caught them. If denied a place to land and scout a rapid, they bounced the boats along the cliff walls, grabbing at even slight rocky protuberances to slow their passage. They hunted for crevices or breaks in the rock wall in which they might scramble up to a shelf from where they could line their boats once more. At the end of Whirlpool Canyon, the milky-white layers of Weber Sandstone dove below the river's surface. Passing over and across a fault in the rock, they emerged into what they would name Island Park. As with Brown's, the river cuts right through a mountain at the end of the park's open area. If the entrance to Lodore is dramatic, then the entrance to Split Mountain Canyon bends the mind, the river acting like a cinched wire ten miles long to cleave the peak perfectly in half from crest to base.

This phenomenon of the river again deeply puzzled Powell. Why would a river choose this less than economical route? To consider the problem, he peeled back the landscape. Today, geologists identify Split Mountain as an anticline, a structure formed by two opposing pressure points pushing against one another, thus upthrusting the midpoint into an arc of strata, not unlike the effect of pinching the loose skin on one's arm. Had that pressure been exercised before or after the river formed? What had the land looked like then? The answer to this three-dimensional puzzle lay in understanding the battery of forces that had shaped, and is shaping, the Earth's surface: mountain building, erosion, river formation, deposition. "We think of the mountains as forming clouds about their brows, but the clouds have formed the mountains," wrote Powell, pulling the pieces together. "Great continental blocks are upheaved from beneath the sea by internal geologic forces that fashion the earth. Then the wandering clouds, the tempest-bearing clouds, the rainbow-decked clouds, with mighty power and with wonderful skill, carve out valleys and canyons and fashion hills and cliffs and mountains. The clouds are the artists sublime."

On June 28, the Green once more spat the expedition out of a rocky canyon passage: "All at once the Great Uinta Valley spread out before us as far as the eye could reach," wrote Sumner. "It was a welcome sight to us after two weeks of the hardest kind of work, in a canyon where we could not see half a mile, very often, in any direction except straight up." They had been on the river now for a little more than a month and had traversed 258 river miles. They beached near the confluence of the Uinta and Green. Forty miles upstream lay the newly established Uinta Indian Reservation, their last chance to contact civilization, however rough it was.

Powell sent Walter and the young cook Hawkins to the Indian Agency, promising to follow in two days, once the rest of the crew had finished notes for newspapers and private letters. At Powell's request, Sumner wrote a list of the forty-one bird species and families that they had seen, including sandhill cranes, eagles, loons, and woodcocks. Oramel Howland assembled his recollections for the *Rocky Mountain News,* while Andy Hall scribbled a note to his brother: "We had the greatest ride that ever was got upon the countenent, the wals of the canone where the river runs through was 15 hundred feet in som places. i think we ar through the worst off the water now . . . The major is from Bloomington, Ill. I suppose you never herd of him and he is a Bully fellow you bett."

That same day, while they dried out, relaxed, and took stock, a curious story surfaced in the *Omaha Herald,* which would have left them whooping in disbelief. The paper reported that all but one member of the Powell expedition had perished. The news blazed across every major U.S. newspaper over the following week, picking up speed and somehow even more lurid detail. A couple of days later, the survivor was named as Jack Sumner. But then, John A. Risdon burst into the story, a liar of such temerity that he walked his fantasy into the Illinois governor's mansion at Springfield. Governor John Palmer bought Risdon's story, which the *Chicago Tribune* printed verbatim on July 2 under the headline, "Twenty-one Men Engulfed in the Colorado in a Moment." Risdon inflated his bona fides, first by claiming three years of war service under Powell, then asserting to have signed on as a "chainman" on the recent expedition. He blithely invented a roster of expedition members that included a "half-breed" Indian guide named "Chick-a-wa-nee," who had convinced the Major to abandon his three boats for a twenty-foot birchbark canoe.

Governor Palmer sorrowfully explained to the *Tribune* how Risdon had tried to dissuade the Major from a suicidal river crossing, but Powell had laughed this off, replying, "We have crossed worse rapids than these, boys. You must be getting cowardly." While Risdon reputedly guarded the horses and wagons on the bank, the boat pushed out into the current, "the Major standing in the stern steering." A moment later, the canoe started to whirl about out of control. Risdon saw it "like a living thing dive down into the depths of the river with its living freight, Major Powell standing at his post. . . ." For two hours, he claimed, "I lay on the bank of the river crying like a baby." He discovered Powell's carpetbag before taking two horse teams on an eight-day journey back to civilization. It was all so vividly detailed.

At the *Rocky Mountain News*, William Byers took exception to Palmer's characterization of Risdon as an honest, reliable man, insisting instead that he should be hung for his lies. A letter from Emma to the *Detroit Post* declared the "whole story glaringly false." Risdon claimed the disaster had occurred on May 8, while she had a letter from her husband dated May 28. But so compelling a story of a martyred hero and his party would not die so easily. "Ambition had a strong hold upon reason," waxed a Chicago newspaperman. "Judgment was laid aside, and the Napoleonic major, with his brave band of faithful companions, saving one who was ordered on shore to report, in case the failure none believed in did occur: These high-minded men, bracing their courage well up, made every preparation, and then entered death's portals—the awful, treacherous portals of Hell's Gate. We can only say they must have died as they had lived—heroes all; yielding up their spirits with the same quiet indifference and pure faith manifested during the horrible descent of the rapids in Brown's Hole."

Finally, however, a few actual facts caught up with Risdon, of whom the *Springfield (IL) Journal* reported on July 10: "The 'Sole Survivor' of the Powell Expedition Arrested and Lodged in Jail." Risdon, it turned out, had stolen a horse, blanket, overcoat, quilt, and shawl.

But the fabricated story had accomplished one thing certainly by bringing the Powell expedition national attention, the *New York Times* alone featuring eleven stories about it. "Up to the circulation of RISDON'S hoax," a late July edition wryly noted, "the country had taken hardly any interest in the exploring party, which has started out on its daring and dangerous adventures. But since then, the entire country has taken the deepest interest in the Powell expedition. The newspapers have eagerly printed every item they could get hold of about the party, and every letter or note from any of the members has been universally read."

America craved a hero—and news from this exotic locale. "Nothing that can be written is so interesting to the casual or constant reader as historical sketches, incidents, actual realities and occurrences of the new and undeveloped country west of us," read the *Tribune*'s preface to Risdon's story. "The new discoveries, hairbreadth escapes, astonishing revelations are often of such a nature as to be almost incredible and beyond belief." The *Times* chimed in: "The ascent of the Jungfrau or the Matterhorn will be nothing to the descent of that watery *Montagne Russe*."

But of this hubbub, Powell and his men knew nothing.

When the Major walked to the Uinta Agency with Hawkins and Goodman, he discovered that the agent had gone off to Salt Lake City. More disturbing, the ramshackle outpost contained scant supplies. In a letter posted there, Powell confided that nearly half their rations were gone, while the rest lay on the verge of spoiling from constant wetting. Nor had his plans panned out to supplement supplies by hunting. At the agency, Powell could secure only three hundred pounds of flour. The loss of *No Name* two weeks earlier now loomed more ominously than ever.

The once-exuberant Frank Goodman pulled Powell aside to announce his intention to leave the expedition, a defection that the Major probably welcomed, not only because of Goodman's half-hearted contributions, but because it meant one less mouth to feed. They parted amicably, Powell moving on to buy some items from the Ute Indians before heading back to the river with the cook, Walter, and Andy Hall. He brought no letters from the agency, for none had come. The Indians lent them a pony to transport the flour.

The men who had stayed riverside noted the slim resupply with disappointment—and, years later, some of the expedition members would criticize Powell harshly for not bringing away more—a rather unfair charge, as Powell knew all too well that their food supplies were growing thin, but the agency had nothing more to sell. And there was no going back now. In 245 miles, the Grand, coming in from the northeast, would unite with the Green to form the Colorado. From this camping spot in the Uinta Valley, they would now press into truly unknown territory.

On July 6, after a seven-day break, they pushed off again, relieved once more to be in motion. After less than two miles, the

White fell in from the left, the same river along which many of them had overwintered the year before. In a couple of days of easy water, they floated fifty miles downstream of the Uinta, when the walls started rising again, the water quickening and rapids beginning as the river crossed from the Uinta Plateau into the Tavaputs Plateau. "The canyon is very tortuous, the river very rapid, and many lateral canyons enter on either side," noted Powell, establishing the perfect conditions for whitewater by creating what geologists call debris fields (or debris flows), which so often force the current into the opposite wall. The Green abandoned its languorous drop rate of 1 foot per mile, increasing to 6.2 feet per mile for the next 75 miles, pounding through 68 brief but difficult rapids.

Scant vegetation and gray shale walls lent an ominous countenance to the first large canyon, which they appropriately named Desolation, as well as the second, named Coal. Even the few juniper trees, Powell wrote, looked like "ugly clumps . . . war clubs beset with spines." Adding to this bleak scene, the wind did not let up. "A terrible gale of dry hot wind swept over our camp and roared through the cañon mingling its sound with the mellow roar of the cataract making music fit for the infernal regions," wrote Bradley. "We needed only a few flashes of lightning to meet Milton's most vivid conceptions of Hell." The wind drove the sand with such ferocity that it stung exposed skin and soon covered their bedding. But at least it kept the flying insects away. When the wind abated, one of the men joked about encountering a very large mosquito, which had asked him for his pipe, knife, tobacco, and a light.

Near the entrance to Desolation Canyon, after an exhausting day, Bradley joined Powell on an afternoon geologizing trip, scrambling up and over broken rocks and geologic benches to reach a point eight hundred feet above the river, only to meet a sheer rockface. Searching about, they finally located a steep but climbable pitch. Nearing the crest, Powell jumped to gain a foothold and grabbed a rock overhead. He found himself stuck, unable to move forward or backward "for I dare not let go with my hand, and cannot reach foot-hold below without." Absent a right hand, he could not feel for another purchase. A sixty- to eighty-foot, potentially fatal, drop awaited him. He yelled for Bradley, who had climbed to a ledge above. Just out of reach, Bradley searched for a stick but could find nothing.

Powell's muscles began to tremble from the strain. Above him, Bradley could think of nothing to do; but then, with an electric burst of inspiration, he ripped off his long underwear bottoms and dangled them over the edge.

Leaning backward, Powell let go and—while falling—grabbed the formless rag with his one hand. The underwear sagged and stretched, but miraculously held. Bradley struggled to keep his grip on the other end, but still managed to swing Powell to solid footing. In moments, characteristically without discussion, they resumed their climb. From one thousand feet above the river, they took barometric readings as they surveyed a "wild and desolate" scene: a lonely, dark, and deeply cut chasm threading its way through a broken-rock moonscape.

The rapids now seemed to press upon them one right after another, at each one Powell choosing whether to run, line, or portage. More often than the men liked, he erred on the side of caution, a strategy that often set Bradley and the others to grumbling. Perhaps Powell heard the grousing, for he decided to run one set of rapids in *Emma Dean* with Sumner and Dunn, at either Steer Ridge Canyon or just below it at Surprise Rapids. Waves washed over the boat, filling it before it crashed into a large wave, which immediately sent it rolling and flung the crew into the chop. Unable to grip the boat, Powell struck out for the bank, later writing that his crude life preserver made swimming "very easy"—but surely this was a stretch, even for an able-bodied man. Sumner and Dunn managed to swim the boat ashore, considerably downriver. They lost the crew's bedding, a barometer, and two rifles. Gone, too, were *Emma Dean*'s oars and "$800 worth of watches," wrote Sumner. Building a bonfire to dry out, they selected a large piece of driftwood from which they sawed out new oars. The following day, a wave knocked Bradley off *Maid of the Cañon,* his foot catching on a rope just as the boat plunged into a rapid. With *Maid* now trailing the half-drowned soldier, Walter valiantly wrestled the oars to prevent a collision with a nasty overhanging cliff. Bradley emerged from the ordeal wet, battered, and his leg badly bruised, but otherwise unhurt.

That afternoon, they exited Desolation Canyon, only to enter the drab gray-shale and brown-sandstone confines of Coal Canyon, which Powell named after the seams of lignite in the rock. (He would later rename it Gray Canyon.) Almost immediately, they pulled to the bank above a section of the river that broke through low but sheer vertical walls and offered no possibility of lining or portaging. They huddled to discuss options, eventually devising a dangerous, but ingenious solution: a technique of leap-frogging the boats down midstream. Lashing all three boats together, they maneuvered this raft over to a large boulder, just before the rapid. Dunn climbed into *Emma Dean,* which they untied and guided downstream by paying out its bowline until it reached another midstream boulder upon which Dunn leaped. Then they let down the second boat, which carried the third boat's still-attached bowline, to *Emma Dean.* The last boat then let go from the top rock, the second boat's crew pulling her to the others. Dunn guided *Emma Dean,* its crew members holding the second boat's bowline, down to the end of its tether. The second boat floated down, somewhat controlled by the men in *Emma Dean,* who let it pass a full line below them. The third was similarly let down until it had passed the second, three 130-foot rope-lengths from the second rock. By this time, the third boat had reached a cove in which the crew secured it.

At Powell's signal, Dunn, on the second rock, dived into the whitewater, holding *Emma Dean*'s line. The others pulled the two boats and the struggling Dunn to safety below the rapid. At any point, this experiment could have gone wrong, but the expedition members worked together seamlessly. After a short portage, they collapsed exhausted on a beach. That night the wind blew fiercely, piling sand over their prone bodies until, wrote Powell, "we are covered as in a snow-drift." Then in casual understatement that belied that long evening's misery, he simply wrote, "We are glad when morning comes." Everyone now bore several kinds of injury: sunburns, sore backs, cuts and gashes that would not heal, along with cracked fingers and toes, sprains, and lost toenails.

Next morning, they came out of the 120-mile gauntlet of Desolation and Gray canyons into one more desertscape, which let them run forty miles through easy rapids that day. Moods visibly relaxed, Bradley even reflecting that a stranger coming into their camp that night would quickly recognize "the cool deliberate determination to persevere that possesses every man of the party . . ." Gone was their boasting and easy confidence, replaced instead by tempered, even humor. They understood clearly now that only a small mistake lay between them and catastrophe.

On July 15, they entered Labyrinth, the first of two flat-water canyons with little current, which left them to row. The heat mounted, measuring more than a hundred degrees ashore. "The sun was so hot," complained Bradley, "we could scarcely endure it." They worked hard, covering twenty-five miles that day, but their effort gained them only eleven miles, as the crow flies, such were the undulations of that crooked canyon. Yet another circuit in Labyrinth twisted so severely for nine miles that the flotilla returned to within six hundred yards of where they began.

On July 16, at 5:30 p.m., they reached the meeting of the Green and the Grand, the latter the very river that went past Hot Sulphur Springs in Middle Park. "Hurra! Hurra! Hurra!" scribbled Bradley in his journal. They had reached the halfway point in river miles. Sumner wrote that the river formed "an apparently endless cañon in three directions—up the Grand, up the Green, and down the Colorado; the walls 1250 ft. high."

At the confluence, Powell and Sumner sifted the remaining flour through mosquito netting to remove the moldy lumps. Repeated soakings and dryings had ruined more than two hundred pounds, leaving only five to six hundred pounds for the rest of the journey. The heat had turned most of the bacon rancid. All looked at the dwindling supplies with alarm. In seven weeks, they had eaten, discarded, or plain lost eight of the ten months of rations that they came with. Geese shot here had proven so scrawny and weak as to lack the muscle to fly. Beaver meat helped, as did the occasional mountain sheep they shot, but the meat quickly spoiled. If they could not rely on hunting, how long could they last? They had descended a little more than 2,000 feet of the 6,000-foot descent. Would the remaining 4,000 feet take another seven weeks or more?

Few activities burn more calories than portaging heavy, water-soaked wooden boats over terribly uneven, often slippery terrain. Even with an abundance of food, consuming enough replacement calories would be difficult. Yet the men met this new challenge with continued good humor, Powell writing that the cook "takes instruments to determine the lat. and long. of the nearest pie."

But despite such rather forced levity, starvation now loomed large. Each one knew the grisly story of the Donner Party's ordeal when trapped by a heavy, early snow in the high Sierras in 1846. When supplies vanished, many of the emigrants resorted to cannibalism. In one of the first reports, a California newspaper described how a woman watched as some party members cooked her husband's heart, while another ate other parts of him and her brother. Such graphic images could not have been far from anyone's minds as Powell and Sumner tossed clump after clump of green flour into the current.

Ever the practical military man, Powell adjusted his calculus yet again on how they must attack the next stretch of whitewater. Rapids offered them the opportunity to increase speed and deliver them faster to journey's end—reducing the odds of starvation. But running bad rapids magnified the odds of a catastrophic accident that could drown them all. Even a fairly benign capsizing that endangered neither crews nor boats, could spoil the remaining food supplies. The pressure mounted on Powell to make just the right decision at each new rapid. The vise tightened. And only now were they approaching some of the journey's worst—by far—whitewater.

Five miles below the confluence, the channel narrows into Cataract Canyon, which delivers a quick succession of rapids over fourteen miles. On July 23, they camped just above this mess. The scouters delivered bad news: They must portage most of the rapids. But they also found a curious fossil, which the Major believed to be an alligator. Bradley joked that the creature must have been on an independent exploring expedition: "All I have to say is he was sensible to die before he attempted to assend the next rappid for it has an almost direct fall of from 15 to 20 feet. We have met nothing to compare with it before."

Powell turned to techniques that had enabled him to negotiate other tight situations—cramming and furious studying. He spent an hour that same day trying to divine the waters' secrets. "The waves are rolling, with crests of foam so white they seem almost to give a light of their own," he recalled years later. "Nearby, a chute of water strikes the foot of a great block of limestone 50 feet high, and the waters pile up against it and roll back. Where there are sunken rocks the water heaps up in mounds, or even in cones. At a point where rocks come very near the surface, the water forms a chute above, strikes, and is shot up 10 or 15 feet, and piles back in gentle curves, as in a fountain." He could make little sense of it. River runners of the following century would coin terms for these curious hydraulic features: haystacks, pillows, rooster tails.

Engorged by the junction of the Green and Grand, the Colorado begins to do things not seen on such a scale in virtually any other river. A steep mountain stream may share some superficial similarities in the behavior of whitewater created when gravity hurls water at rock, but such whitewater is a different animal altogether from what the men now faced. When the irregular riverbed spins and twists the immense volume of the Colorado, the water piles into fifteen-foot standing waves, falling away into improbably immense holes, upwelling in violent boils, and torquing in forceful whirlpools. One whirlpool whipped *Emma Dean* around "like a roulette wheel," reported Sumner. He and Dunn pulled hard on their oars, but could not break the boat from the current's fierce grip. Finally, Sumner executed a well-timed jump with bowline in his teeth toward a rock thirty feet away. "I was able to pull the bow of the boat out of the swirl, whereupon it shot ahead like a scared rabbit."

They faced other strange river features, including the "keeper hole," which river runners dread today. Rushing over a rock or boulder at the surface or near it, the water dives to the bottom of the river, creating a perpetual hole behind it, which water must fill. The river improbably races back upstream: It can slam boats abruptly and hold them there. The Colorado's immense power and volume create gigantic holes capable of swallowing large motor launches, twisting frames and stripping everything from them, and spitting boaters out like pieces of popcorn in hot oil. A keeper can spin a swimmer like a reverse Ferris wheel, all underwater except at its highest point. The struggling victim can only gasp for a half breath before being sucked underwater—an ordeal that repeats itself, often until the body and mind give up the struggle.

Soon the small flotilla reached what modern boaters now reverently describe as Cataract Rapids numbers 21, 22, and 23, or simply the "Big Drop." The worst of these—Big Drop 3—narrows to a thin but ferocious path of water shooting between two boat-eating holes, which in modern times at high water so regularly flip boats that park police often station a rescue vessel below it. Pressed by the need to make better time, Powell decided—mistakenly—to run Big Drop 1. *Emma Dean* proved no match for the huge standing waves, which battered and filled its cockpit before discarding it into a whirlpool. "[I]t is with great difficulty we are able to get out of it with only the loss of an oar," wrote Powell with characteristic understatement.

The chastened Major called the other boats off—and they began the exhausting business of lining and portaging the entire Big Drop. The boats displayed worrisome signs of wear, causing Powell and four others to climb the riverside cliffs in search of pine tar with which to caulk leaky seams. The attempt proved long and hot, all but the Major turning back. Powell eventually reached a patch of pine trees high above the river, where he scraped up two pounds of pitch, stuffing them into his empty shirt sleeve. On the way down, a storm broke from the south, releasing a torrential rain so violent as to nearly wash him off the cliff face. He clung to the rocks one-handed for half an hour until the rain lifted and the sun came out. His relief soured almost immediately at the sight of "a thousand streams rolling down the cliffs on every side, carrying with them red sand; and these all unite in the canyon below in one great stream of red mud."

He skidded down the wet slickrock to warn the others, all the time watching the newly created river break into waves, "several feet high and fifteen or twenty feet in width." The sand soaked some of it up, but another wave came, and another after that. Powell streaked into camp, yelling at the others to strip the camp before the flash flood burst over them. From higher ground, the shaken party watched the cliff-borne river "roll on to join the Colorado." The lesson for Powell, as it is for anyone who witnesses such a flash flood, is that canyon desert, no matter how arid it appears, is most fundamentally shaped by water.

Somewhere near the end of Cataract Canyon, the mission hit its nadir. It began when Bill Dunn, who had been standing near the river's edge making a barometric measurement, fell into the water when a line caught his foot as the current shifted the moored boats. Even he—the strongest swimmer of the bunch—barely escaped the river. The dunking ruined Powell's gold Elgin watch, which Dunn had in his pocket to make time notations for the barometric readings. Powell observed that among all his other chronometers, this was "the only instrument on which I could rely."

The crush of errors brought by carelessness and exhaustion had mounted steadily over the past two months—Howland's missed cue costing them *No Name* and a third of the supplies, the maps drenched and ruined, and the steady attrition of rations. And now, Powell's favorite watch, which doubled as the expedition's most accurate chronometer, had also gone, imperiling their ability to collect mapmaking data.

To date, the largely self-controlled Major had mostly kept his irritation at these mishaps to himself. But now he snapped. Even as the overwhelming challenges had forced more and more of their energies toward plain survival, Powell had clung tenaciously to maintaining the expedition's scientific work—their barometric readings, mapping, their calculations of latitude and longitude, the observations about the landscape. Any semblance of this being a scientific expedition had now vanished. The endeavor had degenerated into a madcap dash down a terrifying river, its sole object now getting its members through alive. Powell had come so far, only to watch his grandest dreams wash away as the shaken party raced through some of the most remarkable geological features on Earth.

Powell lashed out at Dunn, demanding irrationally that he pay $30 on the spot for the ruined watch or leave the party forthwith. On the river the men had overheard their leader bicker repeatedly with the elder Howland over his often-sloppy mapmaking and difficulty in keeping the maps dry, but they were aghast at this merciless ultimatum. Powell knew that Dunn did not have that kind of money on him—so he was in essence telling him to leave, a virtual death sentence. Yet the Major spoke in deadly earnest. Powell gave Dunn such a tongue lashing, wrote Sumner, "that I think only the fact that the Major had but one arm saved him from a broken head, if nothing worse." When Dunn sputtered that he had almost drowned, Walter Powell unhelpfully quipped that it would have been better if he had.

Hawkins would claim in his dotage that Walter and Dunn had fallen upon each other, and that he had saved the day by furiously yanking Powell's brother off the trapper by his hair, then throwing him in the water and holding his head down. But the musings of a then old man, as so often happens, fill with memories that inflate his own importance in an unfolding drama. In their daily journals, Sumner, Bradley, and Powell make no mention of such a tussle. Four decades after the expedition, Hawkins held that Walter stormed off to get his gun, only to be blocked by Andy Hall hitting him in the side of the head. A scuffle of some sort had probably taken place, but these animosities broke as quickly as a wave dashing against the bow of a Whitehall, under bigger concerns than brawling. Their survival now clearly lay on the line. Most of them probably felt relief that tensions had finally boiled to the surface and discharged. Sumner wrote that afterward "everything was as smooth as with two lovers after their first quarrel and make-up." Even so, some resentments would not go away so readily.

Dunn and the elder Howland now firmly believed that the Major did not give a whit about the men he led. The truth on that riverbank that day, while a ragged band of frightened, desperate men eyed one another, was certainly far more complex. Their hard-as-granite leader, who had never before lost control, clearly had that day—and this, more than anything else, had scared the spirits out of everyone. The men might not always like their sometimes autocratic leader, but they knew that he was the key to their survival.

A few days later, they finally emerged from Cataract Canyon. "Now that it is past," recalled Powell, "it seems a very simple thing indeed to run through such a place, but the fear of what might be ahead made a deep impression on us." Soon they entered the serene waters of Glen Canyon, "a curious *ensemble* of wonderful features—carved walls, royal arches, glens, alcove gulches, mounds, and monuments," all now lying beneath the waters of Lake Powell. The few riffles they encountered required no portaging or lining. They came across a four-roomed Anasazi house, the ground about it littered with pottery shards. "How they contrived to live is a mystery to me," wrote Sumner, "as the country around is as destitute of vegetation as a street."

On August 5—the expedition's 74th day—3,100 feet above sea level, the expedition finally pushed off into the Grand Canyon, just downriver from today's Lees Ferry, nine miles south of the present Utah-Arizona border. They had half the vertical distance left to descend, but only one-third of the mileage in which to do it. Several days earlier, Bradley noted that only fifteen pounds of bacon remained. About that time, Sumner had shot a mountain sheep, the last of the game they would find. Although unaware that they had entered the Grand Canyon they certainly understood that something was up. "With some feeling of anxiety we enter a new canyon this morning," recalled Powell. "Below us are the limestones and hard sandstones which we found in Cataract Canyon. This bodes toil and danger." Powell could now read the canyon walls with increasing sophistication. Horizontal rock layering, he noted, often meant an absence of rapids. When those same layers tilted downstream, they generally signaled that the river would flow faster, although probably not arousing any serious whitewater. But when the layers inclined upstream, the river often turned violent.

At Lees Ferry, the whitish-gray Kaibab limestone at the water level would provide a benchmark of sorts for the next three hundred miles. The Canyon would altogether cut downward through nineteen distinct rock formations, some of them many hundreds of feet deep. Each new layer pushed the Kaibab higher until it gleamed a mile above their heads. No geologist—or non-geologist for that matter—had been able to experience the unfolding of Earth's history in such a fashion. From the merely 270-million-year-old Kaibab they would push deeper and deeper into the past, until they encountered the so-called basement rocks, hard granites and schists that had lain there for 1.7 billion years— among the oldest exposed rocks in the Southwest and nearly half the age of the Earth. Their descent left them feeling that they were penetrating the very bowels of the Earth.

Powell turned to literary metaphor: the Grand Canyon as the "library of the Gods . . . The shelves are not for books, but form the stony leaves of one great book. He who would read the language of the universe may dig out letters here and there, and with them spell the words, and read, in a slow and imperfect way, but still so as to understand a little, the story of creation." This book was replacing the narrative in Genesis. The stories of Adam and Eve, and the great flood, were yielding to visions of dinosaurs roaming the Earth, of great inland seas, volcanic disruptions, mountains thrust up and worn away. Powell could read it all in the rock. Even to a man of Powell's formidable imagination and ability to confront the unknown, the experience proved overwhelming. Powell would not be the first to feel the cold realization of humanity's relative newcoming, yet few would experience it so viscerally as did Powell that summer of 1869. It would force him to reflect in powerful new ways about the relationship of humans and the natural world.

In the Canyon, the Colorado River Exploring Expedition would encounter 360 rapids and the worst whitewater of their journey. The men entered the Canyon a ragged mess, not one of them owning a complete set of clothes. Nor were their boats in any better shape.

Now, at most every stop, they caulked leaky seams. On August 7, after running ten bad rapids and portaging three times in Marble Canyon alone, they replaced the ribs of one boat. Never had they worked so hard, and now they had to cut rations even more. Portaging admittedly became easier with fewer supplies to haul, but their steadily weakening bodies now made more mistakes. Two days earlier, the exhausted men had dropped *Emma Dean* while portaging, busting a hole in its side that required major repair.

The lightened boats did appear to ride the waves better. On August 10, Powell seemed to brush away some degree of caution; and so they ran thirty-five rapids—some of them bad ones—in fourteen miles, emerging from Marble Canyon where the Little Colorado River comes in from the left. Here they took a two-day break, Powell taking the latitude by fixing on the North Star, which indicated that they were as far south as their destination, Callville—"so that what we run now," noted Bradley, "must be west from this point."

They now prepared to enter the Inner Gorge, the core of the Grand Canyon. Years later, in the sanctuary of his government office, Powell would mark that pivotal moment with the words for which he is best known: "We have an unknown distance yet to run, an unknown river to explore. What falls there are, we know not; what rocks beset the channel, we know not; what walls ride over the river, we know not. Ah, well! We may conjecture many things." Grand sentiments indeed. He noted that the men joked before setting off, "but to me the cheer is somber and the jests are ghastly." In that day's journal, Bradley reported that the men were "uneasy and discontented and anxious."

After running fifteen miles in two hours of near-continuous whitewater, they heard a roar unlike anything they had encountered before and quickly pulled ashore. Powell climbed the cliffs to scout what others would later call Hance Rapid, returning with somber news. A mile downriver, the Colorado passed over hard granite—a situation the men would come to dread, for it often equated with hellish whitewater. The river's course through softer sedimentary rock, which they had run and labored through since Green River City, now yielded to metamorphic rock, forged by continental-scale pressure and heat from within the Earth's interior to come out as hard, sharp, and unforgiving. The jet-black Vishnu Schist seemed to suck the light from anything near it, except when occasionally—and surprisingly—veins of raspberry sherbet–colored Zoroaster granite shot through it. Unable to erode this unyielding rock as easily as the sedimentary formations, the river becomes a caricature of a whitewater passage, cutting through vertical walls now thousands of feet high. "No rocks ever made can make much worse rapids than we now have," noted Bradley gloomily. The jagged rock gnawed on their ever-weakening boats.

The next morning, "emphatically the wildest day of the trip so far," wrote Bradley, they lined and portaged Hance, then ran a bad rapid at its foot. Two miles later they heard the throaty rumble of yet another menacing rapid, so thunderous that they had to shout to be heard—"a long, broken fall, with ledges and pinnacles of rock obstructing the river," wrote Powell, the torrent breaking "into great waves on the rocks" and lashing itself "into a mad, white foam" for a third of a mile before the river turned sharply to the left and out of view. Sumner, never one to show fear, noted that a line of fifteen-foot standing waves made his hair curl. The steep walls offered no point of purchase to line the boats or any places to portage. "We must run the rapid," wrote Powell, "or abandon the river."

"Who follows?" Sumner shouted. The young men, Andy Hall and Billy Hawkins, yelled back, "Pull out! We'll follow you to tidewater or hell." Sumner, Powell, and Dunn shoved out into the turbulence, riding one wave to its top like a roller coaster, then dropping precipitously into the trough. Again and again they bounced and thrashed through these mad waves until they struck the crest of one as it broke. The boat plunged underwater, its center compartment filling completely, Sumner and Dunn desperately trying to avoid the rocks. Powell frantically bailed as best he could. A whirlpool spun them, but the boat did not sink, and somehow came through.

"I have been in a cavalry charge, charged the batteries, and stood by the guns to repel a charge," wrote Sumner. "But never before did my sand run so low. In fact, it all ran out, but as I had to have some more grit, I borrowed it from the other boys . . ." They named the rapid Sockdolager, a nineteenth-century term for a bare-knuckled knockout punch. They had just entered what later boaters call Adrenaline Alley—forty miles of chaotic whitewater. That night, denied any place to lie down, the men wedged themselves painfully into niches in the wall.

Mistakes and mishaps piled up. The day after Sockdolager, Oramel Howland lost his notes and river map; then *Emma Dean* broke her bow rib on a rock. The following day, the cook knocked the baking soda tin into the river, so their musty bread would now also be unleavened.

Near constant rain, which often turned torrential at night, served as its own plague, extinguishing their driftwood fires almost immediately. For several nights, they huddled two to a blanket, shivering against the cliff until dawn. Powell wrote that they were more exhausted by the night's discomfort than by the day's toil. No matter what they did, they could not keep their food dry. The constant alternation of soaking and heating had ruined their bacon, leaving them with a thin ten days' rations of flour, some dried apples, but plenty of coffee at least.

On August 18, after three portages in four miles, the men pulled bankside to weather a furious rainstorm that continued all night. "The little canvas we have is rotten and useless," observed Powell. "[T]he rubber *ponchos* with which we started from Green River City have all been lost; more than half the party is without hats, and not one of us has an entire suit of clothes, and we have not a blanket a piece." The river had become so muddy they could no longer drink from it, so they relied instead on rainwater pooled on rocks. For the first time, Powell contemplated leaving the river and hiking to a Mormon settlement. Misfortune had emphatically put an end to the scientific documentation of their expedition. No barometers worked, leaving them unable to tell how much farther they needed to descend. When Powell scouted downstream, all he saw was a "labyrinth of deep gorges." They had ten days of rations, with no clear idea about how many miles remained. A few days later, Powell noted with gallows humor that it had "come to be a race for a dinner." On that they all could agree.

Heavy rain continued to hammer them the following day. When another furious rapid appeared, its absence of rocks encouraged Powell to run it. But almost immediately, a standing wave flipped *Emma Dean* like a toy, pitching Dunn, Sumner, and Powell overboard, although they managed to hang on. The gasping men righted the boat below the rapid.

On August 21, after a thrilling run of ten miles in the morning, they encountered yet another massive rapid, requiring a long, grinding portage. But once below it, they could see the dark granite giving way to limestone walls. "Good cheer returns," wrote Powell. "We forget the storms and the gloom and the cloud-covered canyons, and the black granite and the raging river, and push our boats from shore in great glee."

To these exhausted, bruised, and hungry men, all anticipating the Canyon's end around every turn, the sky and river then combined to deal a series of cruel blows: Not only did the heavy rain resume but the river cut back through the sandstone, completely reversing direction, and thus sending them into the granite again. One of their last working tools—a compass—now indicated that they headed northeast, directly away from their destination. On that day water soaked their little remaining flour.

But the following afternoon, the river resumed its westward course, and they returned to the limestone, which enabled them to run a dozen rapids in a similar number of miles. At midday they passed an odd rock in the middle of the river, like nothing they had seen before: a fifty-foot plug of dark volcanic basalt standing as a silent marker to a world that would transform itself just a mile downstream. They pulled up shortly thereafter at the head of a massive rapid, today known as Lava Falls.

Everywhere black lava coated the older rocks like tar. Gone was the symmetrical limestone and sandstone layering, now yielding a geological chaos. Beginning about 850,000 years before, waves of molten rock had erupted from numerous vents both on the rim and within the canyon, flowing through the side canyons, then pouring into the main river channel. The expedition bestowed the name Vulcan's Throne to a cinder cone volcano, its 4,000-foot peak sitting high above on the north rim on the boaters' right. Some thirteen lava dams had blocked the lower canyon, one of them filling it to a height of more than two thousand feet, another flowing eighty-six miles down the river course. "What a conflict of water and fire there must have been here!" wrote Powell. "Just imagine a river of molten rock running down into a river of melted snow. What a seething and boiling of the waters; what clouds of steam rolled into the heavens!"

The formidable hydraulics of Lava Falls forced them once again to line and portage. But afterward, the whitewater eased and they swept along for thirty-five miles. They began on their last sack of moldy flour.

The next day, they again traveled thirty-five miles, which elicited a glimmer of optimism. But the river was not yet done with them. The following day, August 27, the Colorado darted south, then west, then south again. Worst of all, the dreaded dark granite reappeared downriver. The hope blooming among these desperate men withered, then blacked out altogether when they heard the roar of a rapid that made all of the others pale in comparison.

They pulled over and gazed silently at it. Two side canyons entered the river nearly opposite one another. The river first bounced through boulders washed out of the side canyons coming in from the left, then hit rapids caused by the rocks from the canyon on the right. A granite reef reached one-third of the way across the river. The resulting Z-shaped rapid had no apparent way through. "The spectacle is appalling to us," wrote Bradley dramatically even for the master of the superlative. "The billows are huge and I fear our boats could not ride them if we could keep them off the rocks."

That morning and afternoon they spent climbing the rock walls, first from the right bank, then the left, searching for a path around this monster. Scrambling for a mile or more over the granite, they found their way entirely impeded. A portage would work only if they could haul the boats up eight hundred vertical feet then come back down, which Powell calculated would take ten days, an impossible feat with only five days' rations left. They had already wasted half a day on the search itself. Three more rapids—all looking equally formidable—loomed below this one. "[T]o run it would be sure destruction," Powell wrote plainly. The vise had tightened, closing off whatever slight room for maneuver they had enjoyed before. "We appeared to be up against it sure," wrote Sumner.

Before sunset, Powell climbed down the cliffs to announce a plan that he and Sumner had worked out. They would lower the boats on the rocky bank to avoid the first falls, then run to the head of the second, which they would try to skirt through a chute on the right side. Then they would try to cross to the left to avoid a boat-destroying boulder. An iffy plan at best, but it was all they had. They ferried across, then sat down to drink coffee and chew on half rations of tasteless, unleavened balls of bread, the rush of the river loud in their ears. "This is decidedly the darkest day of the trip," scribbled Bradley in his journal.

After this slim repast, Oramel Howland asked Powell to join him on a walk. Up a short distance into a side canyon, out of earshot of the camp, he urged Powell to call off the expedition. He informed Powell that he, his brother Seneca, and Dunn had decided to abandon the river.

Somewhere not too far downstream—but still at an unknown distance—the Virgin River fell into the Colorado. Twenty miles up that tributary stood a Mormon settlement. An overland hike to such an outpost from where they now stood would entail crossing some seventy-five miles of desert, but Howland believed the recent rains would have left enough water pockets to keep them going. And they might find some game along the way. For the elder Howland, the odds of surviving such a desert journey looked much better than running the next rapid, and who knew how many more after that. The five days of half rations could easily rot away with another wetting. The granite showed no signs of abating any time soon. Howland had reviewed his best odds for survival—and they pointed away from the river. Powell could not disagree that the expedition had reached a critical juncture.

"Of course I objected," Powell wrote later, "but they were determined to go." The time for glorious speeches invoking the national importance of the mission had long since passed. Nor could Powell force them to stay: His only authority lay in the trust built up over the past three months, which had eroded steadily with the loss of *No Name,* and the drenching of the maps, and ruin of the instruments. Even the Major's legendary powers of persuasion would fail him now if he attempted to use them. Powell knew that it was not a matter of bucking up Howland's courage and resolve. Unlike Goodman, Howland had demonstrated over and over again that fear did not dominate his actions. He was as brave as they came. At his core as a commander, Powell understood that he had to honor the Howland party's decision—the expedition was not a military unit but a mishmash of volunteers serving at their whim. Neither had Howland challenged Powell to abort the trip in front of all the men nor tried to wrestle away power and become the new leader. This was no mutiny, although Powell most certainly regarded this act as desertion.

Both men returned to the camp not having shared an angry word; neither spoke about their conversation, although the others knew that something was brewing—and that it centered on aborting the expedition. "There is discontent in camp tonight," noted Bradley, "and I fear some of the party will take to the mountains but hope not."

Without a working barometer, Powell could not determine altitude, and thus how much drop there remained in the river. But he did sight a sextant on a celestial object, Sumner illuminating the dial with a mesquite-brush torch, to determine their latitude, which corroborated his dead reckoning that the Virgin ran about forty-five miles away downstream as the crow flies. He then sensibly doubled the length to take the river's meanders into consideration. Explorations by the Mormons had already indicated "comparatively open country" for many miles above the Virgin's mouth. In his pre-trip preparations, Powell had secured the diary records of the Mormon guide Jacob Hamblin, who had floated unscathed from Grand Wash just below the Canyon to the Virgin in April 1867. If they could get to Grand Wash, then the rest of the river would prove easy. By his calculation, therefore, they were quite close to getting through the Canyon.

As river runners have now done for many decades, Powell scratched out the expedition's location in the sand, indicating where he thought the Virgin came in, and the placement of the settlements. Although no evidence reveals Sumner's thought processes, Powell would have wanted his buy-in. And there, in the flickering light of the small torch, peering over a crude map of sand and rocks, Sumner indicated his intention to remain on the river, a decision crucial to the expedition's continuation. Jack had proved the field leader on the trip, quelling disaffection and keep-ing up morale, taking charge of the lining and portaging, and stepping into the riskiest positions as rescue or fast action de-manded. He gave a mountain toughness to the group dynamics.

Powell woke Oramel and showed him the crude map. They spoke briefly. Sumner made a pitch for him to stay. Decades later, Sumner recalled that he did what he could to "knock such notions" out of Howland's head. "I fear that I did not make the case very strong," he would confess—doubt that would haunt him badly for the rest of his life. But Howland's mind was made up, even with the strongest in-dications that their perilous journey neared its end.

Howland lay down again. All that night Powell paced a slight stretch of sand along the river, turning over in his mind whether to abort the expedition. He took no one else's counsel. At one point, he decided to quit the river, but soon enough changed his mind. Much later he would write that "for years I have been contemplat-ing this trip. To leave the exploration unfinished, to say that there is a part of the canyon which I cannot explore, having already nearly accomplished it, is more than I am willing to acknowledge, and I determine to go on."

He woke up Walter and told him his decision, but his brother's dedication to him he would have taken for granted. The young men, Hawkins and Hall, when shown the sand map, agreed to continue. Bradley agreed also, his innate optimism shining through. "'Tis the darkest just before the day," he mused, "and I trust our day is about to dawn."

The men spoke little during their meager breakfast, nothing about the impending split that now hung ominously over the party. After breakfast, Powell asked Howland if he still intended to leave. He did. Dunn did, too. Seneca had misgivings, but agreed to go when he saw his older brother's conviction. Three men would walk out, the remaining six having "come to the determination," wrote Bradley, "to run the rappid or perish in the attempt."

They parted amicably, if sadly; "each party," reported Powell, "thinks the other is taking the dangerous course." Hawkins divvied up the remaining rations. Powell gave copies of the journals to Howland. The Howlands and Dunn took two rifles and a shotgun. Sumner solemnly handed Howland his pocket watch, the one article he had safeguarded through nearly three months of demanding travel, with explicit instructions to deliver it to his sister Libby Byers in Denver should he not make it back. Powell gave Oramel a letter to Emma. The Howlands and Dunn entrusted no letters to the six who were continuing on.

Powell left *Emma Dean* tied to the bank, also abandoning most of their scientific equipment and collections—the broken barometers, boxes of fossils and minerals, and most of their remaining ammunition that the men who were leaving had not claimed. The boats thus lightened would prove far more buoyant, increasing their chances of surviving the cataract ahead. If they could not travel more than a few miles a day, their food would run out in the gloomy confines of their granite prison—and they would probably have no way to climb out.

The three men soon to depart helped the others manhandle the two freight boats over a twenty-five-foot boulder and lower them into a tiny cove just below. Powell recalled a rather solemn parting. "They left us with good feelings," recorded Bradley, "though we deeply regret their loss for they are as fine fellows as I ever had the good fortune to meet." The trio climbed a crag to watch the others in a final gesture of goodwill.

Powell joined Andy Hall and the cook aboard *Kitty's Sister,* which then pushed off into the current, shooting along the rock wall, then dangerously grazing one large rock. Just before reaching the second fall, they pulled directly into the smooth tongue of water that poured into the mouth of the whitewater. But an unseen hole caught them, their boat filling with water, and they smacked into a giant wave. But in a second, the boat punched through the wall of water.

Pulling their oars for all they were worth, Hall and Hawkins mus-
cled *Kitty's Sister* across the river with Powell shouting commands,
narrowly avoiding the great, dangerous rock in mid-channel. They
slammed through in little more than a minute. *Maid* followed
the same line through the uproar; both boats escaped damage.
Scouting—and hard-earned experience—had paid off with their
lives.

Below the fall, the exhilarated men signaled the Howlands and
Dunn to join them, hoping they might follow in the small boat. But
the trio turned away to begin their journey. Powell would name
this spot Separation Rapid. "Boys left us," he noted simply in his
journal. They would never be seen again.

All that morning the remaining two boats battled down a series
of terrifying rapids, until at midafternoon they encountered yet
more volcanic rock and an unrunnable section of whitewater that
they would dub Lava Cliff Rapid. They determined to line the rapid
by tying together several lengths of rope. Bradley volunteered to
keep *Maid* off the rocks from within the boat. Walter and Sumner
carried 130 feet of rope and scrambled up the rocky cliff, Bradley
soon obscured by the overhang. With Bradley fending off the rocks
and walls with his oar, the boat lurched foot by foot as the men
high above paid out the rope. *Maid* rolled and tumbled, the now-
soaked Bradley fighting for balance. In short order, as the men
climbed even higher above the river, the rope ran out. Walter
wrapped the end around a rock knob, while Sumner dashed back
for more. Meanwhile Bradley bounced violently in *Maid*.

The boat shuddered badly each time it slammed against the
rock; Bradley realized that he did not have much longer. With remarkable coolness—"just as I always am, afraid while danger is
approaching but cool in the midst," as he himself admitted—
Bradley unsheathed his knife, ready to sever the line, all the time
desperately scanning the foaming cataract downriver for "the best
channel through." He paused for several long moments, waiting for
the men above to deal him more slack, but none came. At the exact

moment he leaned forward to cut the line, the force of water ripped the stem post right out of *Maid*'s bow with such violence that it flew thirty feet into the air, still attached to the rope.

Like a rocket, *Maid* shot forward into the maelstrom, Bradley getting off a first, then a second stroke to swing the bow into the waves before the water took complete control. Just when the men above glimpsed *Maid,* it plunged into a deep hole and disappeared. In the next instant, *Maid* spat out, crested a massive standing wave, only to smash into yet another wall of water. Narrowly skirting some rocks, due more to luck than to Bradley's flailing efforts, *Maid* then simply vanished into the madly foaming whitewater. "We stand frozen with fear, for we see no boat," remembered Powell. "Bradley is gone!"

But then, far below, a dark object emerged from the froth. Somehow the boat, with its man still in it, had come through intact. The hard-breathing Bradley waved his sodden hat in exultation. But he had not yet quite escaped; a massive whirlpool swung *Maid* in its steely grip. Not aware of how badly *Maid* might be damaged—was it in fact sinking?—Powell yelled for his brother and Sumner to get Bradley a line. In the most dangerous, impulsive decision of the trip, Powell, Hall, and Hawkins raced down the cliff face—then all jumped into *Kitty's Sister* and frantically pushed off to the rescue.

On this journey, Sumner had always been the one engineering emergency descents and rescues, but this time Powell took charge. So the one-armed Major and the expedition's two youngest members drove right into the river's maw, not quite able to swing their bow directly downstream. Powell realized the impetuousness of his decision the moment they smashed headlong into the first wave. He thought he had seen a line through the rapid, but the waves washed away any such plan in an instant. At the foot of holes, waves act like animate beasts: Depending on when a boat hits it—often a matter of mere seconds—a wave may let it pass, but at other times will bend a boat so forcefully as to crush and collapse it back into the hole. What exactly happened then to *Kitty's Sister* was lost in the madness of the moment. Bradley watched as they came inches from dashing themselves to pieces against the rocks. Powell later would reconstruct their passage as best as he could: "A wave rolls over us and our boat is unmanageable. Another great wave strikes us, and the boat rolls over, and tumbles and tosses, I know not how."

Bradley, who had escaped the whirlpool, now turned to rescue the rescuers, pulling each floating man into the safety of the eddy. Only the watertight compartments of each boat had prevented it from sinking. It is doubtful whether the vessels, if heavily loaded, could have survived that awful tumult.

They righted and bailed *Kitty's Sister*, then climbed aboard and rowed over to the bank to await Sumner and Walter coming down the cliffside. Only luck had saved them this time from Powell's most impulsive bid. Bradley, who had for months proclaimed almost every new rapid to be the worst encountered, left no doubt about this one: "It stands A-No. 1 of the trip."

There was nothing else to do but shake their heads and turn their drenched, aching bodies downstream once again. In two or three miles the river turned northwest and passed out of the granite. By noon the following day, August 29, the cliffs dropped away, the mountains receded, and they entered a valley they knew to be the Grand Wash. They had finally left the Grand Canyon behind them, a little more than twenty-four hours since the others had started their overland journey.

As he wrote his expedition report in the safety of his study, Powell would reach for an apt metaphor to voice the relief the entire party felt after three months of "pain and gloom and terror." Those claustrophobic days brought to mind the time he spent in the makeshift hospital at Shiloh, battling the tides of pain from his shattered arm. It is a rare disclosure of feelings for a man who rarely acknowledged them:

"When he who has been chained by wounds to a hospital cot until his canvas tent seems like a dungeon cell, until the groans of

those who lie about tortured with probe and knife are piled up, a
weight of horror on his ears that he cannot throw off, cannot forget,
and until the stench of festering wounds and anesthetic drugs has
filled the air with its loathsome burthen,–when he at last goes out
into the open field, what a world he sees! How beautiful the sky,
how bright the sunshine . . ."

That evening they stayed up past midnight, reveling in their
freedom, but deeply concerned for their three comrades. No one
could dismiss the cruel irony of the situation. "Are they wandering
in those depths, unable to find a way out? Are they searching over
the desert lands above for water? Or are they nearing the settlements?" asked Powell.

On August 30, while fishing from the bank where the Virgin
meets the Colorado, Brother Joseph Asey and his two sons beheld
a most remarkable sight. Weeks earlier, Brigham Young had directed that Mormons building a new town at the confluence keep
an eye out "for any fragments or relics of [Powell's] party that
might drift down the stream." But here were no remnants, but an
almost biblical vision of the Israelites emerging from the desert:
six bearded, mostly naked men crowded into two battered boats,
paddling slowly and clumsily with driftwood oars. The apparitions
croaked out the question, Is this the Virgin River? It was.

The Aseys welcomed them into their home. Upon hearing the
news, the Mormon bishop of St. Thomas, James Leithead, piled a
wagon high with mail and melons and drove to meet them. The
famished men "ate melons till the morning star could be seen."

On September 1, the party split one last time, Powell and his
brother riding in a wagon with the bishop to St. George, the other
four deciding to continue downriver to seek their fortune. Powell
gave them some of the money he had left, along with the two remaining boats. George Bradley and Billy Hawkins would jump off
the river at Fort Yuma, Bradley heading west to San Francisco,

Hawkins to the north. Young Hawkins would outlive them all, dying at the age of seventy-one in 1919 in the Arizona Territory. He had lived a full life, bringing up a family of six boys and serving as a justice of the peace.

The record on Bradley goes cold until 1885, the last year of his life. Until then, he may have survived as a laborer, and perhaps owned a nursery in San Diego. He never apparently brought up his part in the expedition or attempted to leverage it to his benefit. He never sought to publish the journal he had kept, the longest and richest of all written on the 1869 expedition. In late 1885, Bradley's nephew helped the recently crippled fifty-year-old return to his hometown of Newberry, Massachusetts. He spent his last few months with his sisters, who do not appear to have known about his participation in the now-famous Colorado expedition of sixteen years earlier. No obituary or mention of his life accompanied his quiet passing. But he had brought his journal East—and thirty years later, a relative would donate it to the Library of Congress, so only then would the world hear Bradley's bright voice describing that hellish descent into the unknown.

The irrepressible young cook, Andy Hall, would accompany Jack Sumner all the way down the now-gentle Colorado to where it spilled into the Gulf of California. Hall returned to the Arizona Territory as a mule driver. Robbers gunned down the thirty-two-year-old in 1882 as he escorted a mule train into Globe, which was carrying the Wells Fargo gold payroll for workers in the Mack Morris Mine in Gila County. Eight bullets were found in his body. Later, a lynch mob strung up the three bandits who had shot him on a sycamore tree outside the Saint Elmo Saloon in Globe.

Jack Sumner would go on to become a prospector and trapper, but would have little to show for it over the next three decades. He would have a contentious marriage with a wife angry at his drinking and frequent long absences. One thing he knew in his bones to be true and clung to desperately: his unbreakable grasp of the frontier ethic, in whose service he himself carried the torch of the independent, remarkably rugged outdoorsman, spinner of tall tales, but fiercely honest and loyal to his friends. In the Southwest, he would become known as the last of a dying breed of frontiersmen.

In 1901, a Denver newspaperman gently poked fun at Sumner, "Any building higher than a Mexican adobe house reminds him of the treacherous box canons that are the terror of the old prospector," he wrote. The newspaperman then turned to quote Sumner himself and his observation that a "train's bad enough, but these elevators make a fellow think he's drowning and falling over a cliff at the same time." The old West, as epitomized by this old-time mountain man, now generated robust parodies of itself.

In late May 1902, a few days shy of the thirty-third anniversary of the 1869 river expedition start, Sumner found himself throwing back forty-rod in Green River, Utah. The whiskey somewhat eased the many pains in his back and legs, but did not quiet his roiling memories. One evening, he stumbled out of the saloon to watch the muddy waters of the Green River roll on as implacably as they had when the Colorado River Exploring Expedition paused here so many summers ago. He pictured it like yesterday. The shapes and voices of Oramel, Seneca, and Bill, were caught in his imagination as they would always be—young and strong, at the peak of their vitality. Three decades later, no one still knew exactly what had happened to Sumner's good friends after they set off from the river. No bodies were ever recovered, nor their possessions.

For a third of a century, Sumner had felt a numbing regret at not doing more to save his three friends, living over and over again the fateful moments at Separation Rapid when he had missed his chance to prevent them from leaving. He had failed them, he felt, and for that crippling guilt consumed him. If only he had tried just a little harder. Or, why had he not stood up to Powell? He could not escape the feeling that he ultimately shouldered blame for their deaths.

Over the years, the weight had grown unbearable. Alone and despondent that evening, Sumner pulled out his knife, which he had honed to razor sharpness, then dropped his pants and calmly castrated himself. At noon the next day, a townsperson found him unconscious in a pool of blood. Twenty-seven-year-old surgeon Knud Hanson, an immigrant from Norway, sewed him up. Sumner miraculously survived, living for another five years. When Hanson filled out a surgeon's certificate that Sumner would use in an application for army disability, he could not hide a professional admiration for the cool precision in which Sumner used his knife: "Testicles:—Both testicles have been removed by himself. Operation was very successful. Done at a time of supposed temporary insanity." Anything less than a perfect incision would have led quickly to massive blood loss and rapid death. Such careful mutilation suggests a clearly premeditated act, not a flailing, drunken attempt at self-destruction.

While no one can know what courses through the mind of someone set on so terrible an act, the juxtaposition of place, looming anniversary, and precision suggest a purposeful—even strangely courageous—act, symbolic of deep expiation for guilt borne for so long. In the all-too-applicable vernacular of the western frontier, Sumner believed that he did not have the balls to stop his friends from marching off to an early death. Perhaps by this act of self-mutilation, he was atoning for his perceived sins. And coursing through it all was a sense of loss also for the storied frontier West, which had been so much of him, and now had gone. He died five years later, broke and alone in Vernal, Utah.

Once off the river, the Powell brothers passed over the Beaver Dam Mountains to St. George by wagon, where they recuperated for a few days. Here Powell inquired about the Howlands and Dunn, but no one had heard anything. A friend wrote William Byers in Denver that Powell was "anxious about the others."

On September 8, while the Powells traveled by coach to Salt Lake City, the *Deseret Evening News* published the contents of a dispatch received through the Deseret telegraph line from St. George. A friendly Indian reported that the Shivwits, a small band of the southern Pauite, found the three starving men five days earlier, fed them, and sent them on their way to one of the two nearby Mormon settlements. The three, the reporter explained, had then come across a squaw gathering seeds and shot her. Angry Shivwit men had pursued and killed them.

Other reports surfaced that the woman had been raped. Powell immediately rejected this storyline: "I have known O. G. Howland personally for many years and I have no hesitation in pronouncing this part of the story a libel. It was not in the man's faithful, genial nature to do such a thing." And indeed, such behavior does not fit with any of those men's character.

On September 29, nine days after Powell had arrived in Chicago, the Salt Lake paper reported that Mormon president Erastus Snow had telegraphed from St. George upon completing a thorough investigation of the matter. They had not molested a squaw, but "were killed by an enraged Shebitt, some of whose friends had, a short time previously, been murdered by a party of miners on the other (east) side of the Colorado River." The Mormon elder oddly did not order the bodies recovered or see to the arrest of any guilty Indians.

The Mormons assured Powell that they would mount a search, which seemed to satisfy him. It was not characteristic for this man of action to let others do his bidding, although he may well have concluded that the Mormons could conduct a more thorough investigation than he could, especially now as he was worn out and light on funds. Had a certain cool practicality trumped a devotion to his men? Did he not, as Howlands and Dunn suspected, really care for his men at all? Were they merely pawns in his larger machinations? The debate goes on today, among river runners sitting beside campfires on the Colorado and in blogs and chat rooms populated by often well-read, independent historians. Some paint him as an Ahab-like figure, a crippled psychopath so consumed with his task that he would do anything to attain it. No one would doubt his focus and determination. But did a heart beat inside his chest?

What exactly transpired at Separation Rapid, when the walls closed in and the water roared, the flour petering out, will never be known. But that sort of uncertainty and the prospect of death most definitely unleashes powerful demons inside even the strongest men. And it is never possible to tell, when sitting around a bar in town, how one or another will react under the throes of such extreme privation and challenge. One might easily conclude that the Howland brothers and Dunn were cowards, who could no longer face the river, but that is not something that Powell believed. He had seen firsthand that they were not.

But neither would he, unlike Sumner, acknowledge any regret for not changing their minds. He had certainly tried. But he also knew with crystal clarity that they had broken a solemn compact that day. They had parted not with bitterness and rebuke, but with clear thought, a decision that Powell accorded them the freedom to make. But once they made that choice, those three men no longer were part of the expedition—and, thus, no longer his responsibility. Perhaps, in the retrospect of more than a century, this can appear as cold calculation. But when they left the river, they did so under their own will. And while certainly their relationship with Powell had deteriorated, it was not the predominant factor for their leaving. On that dark, difficult day, it boiled down to a very basic decision about survival. Oramel Howland had clearly determined that their odds of living were better off the river. As simple as that.

Battle decisions by commanders become the fodder of armchair generals for years after the event. Did a commander exercise enough care about his men, while also keeping his eyes on the big prize of winning the battle? Powell had watched up close as Grant had exercised difficult command decisions during the war, enduring the slings of those calling him a butcher, but somehow managed to do what he must. Of course, the descent of the Colorado was not war, although it certainly turned into a life-and-death struggle. Neither was Powell as deft a field commander as Grant. But leadership under significant duress requires difficult decisions. Real leaders must understand that and cannot look backward. And that may well be the best lens through which to look at Powell's decisions on the river.

As for how Powell ultimately regarded Oramel Howland's spearheading the trio's departure, the Major left no written record, aside from that comment in his report about each party thinking the other was taking the dangerous course. Did he ultimately regard their act as a betrayal or as the unfortunate collateral damage of so risky a venture? Or had he recognized that the expedition was better off without them, like he had with Goodman? He had never represented that the expedition came under anything like military rule. Honoring the independent traditions of the West, Powell would have understood that anyone could leave should they so desire. Even so, Powell would get the last word. Several years afterward, when he sat down in Washington to write up the narrative, he searched for a way to portray Oramel and finally reached for Shakespeare: "When busily employed he usually puts his hat in his pocket, his thin hair and long beard stream in the wind, giving him a wild look, much like that of King Lear in an illustrated copy of Shakespeare which tumbles around camp." Powell could well have believed that the comparison stretched beyond mere appearances. Doomed by his own folly, Lear is one of literature's most powerfully tragic figures. Certainly, too, Oramel had brought tragedy upon himself by his own actions, starting with the wreck of *No Name,* caused either by his inattention or willful disregard of the flag signals, then his fateful decision to abandon the river. Powell not so subtly hinted that Oramel, like Lear, had crafted his own fate through prideful arrogance and misplaced allegiances.

It would take a year before Powell returned to the area to conduct his own investigation into the disappearance of the missing party, but by this time he was well on his way to the next big task.

Salt Lake City turned out a hero's welcome for the somewhat surprised Powell. Just three months earlier, he had been an obscure midwestern academic with improbably bold plans. But a horse thief's outrageous fantasy about the expedition's tragic end had enthralled the nation—and now his return from the dead in defiance of this crazy fiction was simply too compelling a story to ignore. As the details emerged of the expedition's epic struggles, the voyage would thread its way into the fabric of the American story. Powell's emergence undaunted from that colossal cut in the Earth had somehow enlarged the entire nation, plain flesh and will overcoming the unyielding, ancient hardness of rock and the force of violent cataract. The Canyon journey would become a telling moment in the mighty struggle of Americans with their continent.

From the moment Powell stepped off the river, his journey and its story no longer belonged to him and his expedition members alone, but to America itself. Audiences now gathered, hungry for details. But as the clamor rose to hear the stories of the handful of men battling nature in their pitifully small boats, he wanted mostly to talk impersonally in the language of scientific pioneering—about geology, deep time, how rivers carve the landscape, and the little-known lifestyles of the desert Indians. He wanted to be useful, awakening his audiences to a sense of their land, not inspiring the heroic, but his story now lived beyond his desire to shape the narrative.

Powell addressed a packed house at the Thirteenth Ward

Assembly Rooms in Salt Lake City, a reporter observing that he had "endured the fatigues and anxieties of the trip remarkably well." That evening, he traveled to Chicago, where he submitted to a *Tribune* interview, which glowingly noted that "so important a contribution to geographical and geological knowledge has not been made in a long time." He lectured at the Chicago Academy of Sciences, the Great Bethel Fair in Cincinnati, his father's Wheaton College, and in Brooklyn, New York. Back in Chicago, a choir prefaced his talk at the Teachers' Institute. "The adventures of the party were related," noted a journalist, "the sad fate of some who fell at the hands of Indians was mourned, and a handsome tribute was paid to the cool intrepidity and daring of Bradley, an old sailor of the party."

The *New York Herald* noted that his demeanor fell far short of a public lecturer's—he spoke in a low and indistinct tone of voice, but had "a very pleasant conversational style of telling what he has heard and seen." Another newspaper described him as "erect as a pine, and compactly built, brown hair and whiskers, the latter cut in Burnside fashion. In manners affable—his style of delivery is free from affectations and display. . . . He excels in freshness, originality and compactness of idea and expressions, rather than oratorical finish and flourish."

Powell did not feel different, even though others now beheld him so. Yet the experience had indeed changed him. Not because he had stared into death's maw—he had done that before at the Hornet's Nest and under the surgeon's saw. Certainly he now offered convincing proof that so badly a maimed man could overcome formidable challenges and be useful to his nation. But far more important, this steady descent into Earth's hard-rock history had extended his imagination into surprising new dimensions, greatly reorienting his perspective. He may not have realized it then, but the experience capped an education that had begun so many years ago in an Ohio streamed with Big George. Powell would now be pivoted into a true American visionary, the Canyon's lessons exercising as tangible an influence as the ancient lava-flows of the Inner Canyon had wrought on the river's course.

No other scientist had ventured a mile deep into a scar slashed into the Earth and observed layer upon layer of rock—evidence of the planet's history—revealed so nakedly and clearly. It was not so much that he encountered new formations and previously undescribed convulsions of Earth history—he had—but rather the overwhelming general impression that he had formed was the truly astounding dynamism of Earth's long history. Far from static, or created in a single, divinely inspired instant, the Earth's form had never ceased changing, morphing, upheaving, eroding. The Grand Canyon had forced upon him a new consciousness.

Powell had long been a student of landscape, accumulating knowledge of midwestern rivers necessary for collecting his mollusks, or when deciphering the topographic curvatures and vantages at Cape Girardeau. But his understanding of the land now encompassed a far deeper appreciation of how those contours had arisen—and continued to morph—in the assault of ever-changing forces. The form of the Earth's surface may seem frozen at any moment in the perspective of a human being standing atop a mountain, but seen through the lens of deep time, it revealed huge flux and change, a continuum of major disruptions and a world constantly remaking itself.

This journey would stimulate Powell to develop brand-new theories about river formation and to coin the term "geomorphology," the new science that examined how Earth's topographic features formed through geologic processes. Geologic history would no longer be read only in the rocks alone, but in the landforms and in the paths of rivers.

Along with the geomorphological issues of river formation and mountain building, this new kind of understanding would force him to think deeply about how humanity and nature intersected, how each reciprocally acted upon the other, and would nourish an original vision of sustainability, ecology, and environmental stewardship. When the exhausted Major disembarked in Callville, the journey that counted had only just begun.

CHAPTER 7

Encore

The story of the great conquest of the Colorado was now everywhere, the moniker "Powell of the Colorado" evoking steely courage and unimaginable endurance. But Powell took little satisfaction in the congratulatory handshakes and beaming faces that now always welcomed him. In ways he could probably admit only to Emma, he concluded the venture a failure. They had indeed made it through, but his expedition had been a wild adventure in which three men had been lost and the others left starving and battered, their scientific equipment ruined. The voyage had located the general course of the Colorado and the Grand and Green confluence. And indeed, while held in the Canyon's thrall, Powell had experienced an epiphany about the ancient depth of the Earth's history; but what he had encountered would take years to sort out and make sense of. Simply to come out the other end had never been his only goal.

Virtually all his barometric readings and the maps—the data that would prove the Colorado River Exploring Expedition to have been a serious scientific undertaking—had been destroyed by water. He could not therefore create an accurate map, his prime object all along. From the moment that he stepped onto land at Callville, the river water not yet dried from his emaciated form, he knew with piercing clarity that he must return to the river—and do it right this next time, not as a hero but as a scientific explorer.

As he mused over the experiences of the first descent, the precariousness of their food supply stood out. Even his conservative calculations had not insulated them from near starvation. Ten months of food had dwindled to a few pounds of moldy flour in only three months. The food shortfall had weakened them, forcing them to move downriver faster—and more dangerously—than Powell felt comfortable and afforded them less time to rest, perform critical measurements, and explore their surroundings.

Clearly a successful second expedition would hinge on resupply. Completing their scientific observations would require spending even more time on the river than before. The relatively well-known stretch of the Green River presented few problems; the Uintah Indian Agency forty miles from Brown's Hole and Gunnison's Crossing at present-day's Green River, Utah, would provide opportunities to bring in supplies. Downriver, the Crossing of the Fathers in lower Glen Canyon and the mouth of the Paria also provided points to deliver food, but that left a long inhospitable run between Green River, Utah, south through today's Canyonlands National Park and the deadly difficult Cataract Canyon. Powell knew that the Dirty Devil River, which his first expedition had named, falls into the Colorado from the north just below Cataract. That canyon could provide an ideal avenue for a loaded mule train.

But therein lay the problem. No one knew the location of the Dirty Devil's headwaters, and the entire region lay within an unmapped tangle of desert land that remains to this day the most remote, difficult topography of the entire continental United States. If roughly mapping the path of the Colorado had brought acclaim to Powell on his first expedition, then solving the daunting labyrinth of southern Utah and the Arizona Strip—the nearly three million acres of high desert north of the river to the present-day Utah border—would become the key to the second.

A big factor in Powell's fateful decision to continue downriver at Separation Rapid had been Jacob Hamblin's journal. In 1867, that enterprising Mormon guide had floated down the Colorado from Grand Wash just below the Grand Canyon to Callville. No non-Indian knew the canyonland of southern Utah and the Arizona Strip better than this fifty-one-year-old "buckskin apostle"—and Powell could not hope to find a better guide to solve his resupply problem. Hamblin had become Mormon leader Brigham Young's eyes and ears in the lands south of the Great Salt Lake, learning Ute and southern Paiute languages, and even taking a Paiute wife. Powell determined to seek him out. Overall, the Mormons would need to figure large in his plans. The Church of Jesus Christ of Latter-day Saints would plant some five hundred settlements in the Southwest during the late nineteenth century, eventually sowing the Colorado Plateau with farms and towns, telegraph stations, banks, sawmills, and warehouses, the skeleton of a critical infrastructure upon which Powell would come to rely.

Before he could head west to solicit Mormon help, one last critical piece of business remained. The 1869 expedition, as well as the two earlier field trips, had limped along on a shoestring budget. He had begged funds from Byers and others, skimped where he could, reached into his own pocket, made large promises to furnish specimens to midwestern institutions in return for grants, and depended on the largesse of the army to provide supplies free or at reduced cost. If he intended now to prosecute the important science crucial to the nation's westward advance, he needed more stable funding—and after the much-publicized 1869 descent, he could make a powerful case. By then, every congressman knew his name. In the summer of 1870, he traveled by train to Washington, D.C., to pitch Congress. In July, the national legislature granted him $10,000; a victory certainly, but nowhere near enough to cover even basic expenses—he would still need to supplement it with his salary and return to Washington the following year with hat in hand. But with this direct appropriation, Powell had crossed a major threshold: No longer a private citizen individually prosecuting his explorations, he had now joined the thin, elite ranks of federally supported surveyors, which included such well-established heavyweights as Clarence King, Ferdinand Hayden, and George Wheeler.

In early September 1870, Powell took the train west to Salt Lake City. From there, he rode down to the southern Utah town of Parowan to join Mormon president Brigham Young on a trip to the Paria River and the tiny Mormon community of Kanab. The forty-three-person complement included many Mormon Elders, such as Erastus Snow, who had investigated the disappearance of the Howlands and Dunn. Powell would accompany them for four days, during which he would secure Young's blessing to hire Hamblin for $50 a month.

On September 5, Powell and Hamblin shared a midday meal of baked chicken with John D. Lee, who oversaw a ten-man squad escorting the party. The two Mormon men could not have been more different. Lee, a stout, heavyset man with a low forehead and short, thick neck, was blunt-spoken, straightforward, uncomplicated, and not unlikable, but trailing dark rumors that he had taken part in a barbaric, holy massacre a little more than a decade earlier. This ruthless, devoted foot soldier of a patriarchal religion struggling to survive in a wild land vividly contrasted with Hamblin, a western leatherstocking, who had come to devote his life to understanding the native cultures and forging peace with them.

In Hamblin, Powell found a kindred spirit. Hamblin, too, had spent his teenage years in southern Wisconsin before converting to Mormonism at twenty-two—to his parents' horror—and following his faith west. In his early thirties, while leading an expedition against hostile Indians in Utah's Tooele Valley, his guns as well as those of his entire party had misfired during a skirmish, and arrows had passed harmlessly through his hat and coat. "The Holy Spirit forcibly impressed me that it was not my calling to shed the blood of the scattered remnant of Israel," he wrote, "but to be a messenger of peace to them." Shortly thereafter Young called upon him to work with the Paiutes of southern Utah—no easy task, as Indian and Mormon relations had been fraught from the beginning.

Sometime after 1000 AD, Numic-speaking Indians had moved into the Great Basin, displacing the ancient Anasazi and Fremont peoples across Utah, eastern Nevada, and northern Arizona. By the time the Europeans appeared, small bands of southern Paiutes ranged across a huge crescent reaching northwest from the southern California deserts to Utah's Sevier Lake and south to the confluence of the San Juan and Colorado rivers. These hunter-gatherers derived a thin living, foraging for roots, seeds, berries, insects, and hunting small and large game. Living close to the land, eking out what little the harsh climate might yield, the southern Paiute were isolated, dirt poor, and late to adopt the horse.

The southern Paiute, as most contemporaneous commentators noted, were a rather timid and reclusive people, among the last continental tribes to enter into sustained contact with the white newcomers. Navajo parties from the south, and Ute from the north and east, frequently raided their settlements, bearing off captives to sell as slaves among the Spanish settlements of New Mexico and California. The Kaibab Paiute themselves traded their own children for horses, which they more often ate than rode. While the Mormons ended the slave raiding, the incursions of their Indian neighbors had affected the southern Paiute little in comparison with the arrival of the LDS. Hamblin had seen firsthand how Mormon livestock had devastated the seed-bearing vegetation upon which the Indians depended. Savaged by starvation and disease, their water sources and farmlands appropriated by whites, the southern Paiute had died in droves. Those left were reduced to utter poverty. In short order, the LDS had subjugated virtually all southern Paiute communities. One of the more numerous southern Paiute bands, the Tonequints, had simply vanished in less than a generation.

As the large party pushed toward Kanab, Powell shared a campfire one evening with Young. The latter-day Moses of the Mormon faith, who had led the largest single emigration in American history, improbably establishing a vast empire over the arid lands of what would become Utah and Arizona, sized up the tough, one-armed thirty-five-year-old. Although a vast chasm separated the scientist and prophet, they shared a pugnacious resolve and formidable streak of practicality. Young quizzed Powell about the petrified tree trunks that the party had seen, once so clearly wood, but now beautifully crystallized. At another point on their journey, a rock fall had revealed a perfect bed of petrified oyster shells. Young queried Powell about the mineralization process. The Major "philosophized a little upon it," remembered Young, eventually asserting that the shells had turned to stone over the course of 150 million years. Tantalizing the Mormon leader even further, Powell pointed to the night sky, rhapsodizing on the many thousands of years that starlight took to reach their eyes.

In a sermon three weeks later, Young brought up his conversation with Powell. But, he asked, why could not the petrification process have taken eighteen years? "All that can be said of such things is that they are phenomena, or freaks of nature, for which the knowledge and science of man cannot account." But Powell had opened up rich questions for Young to mull over. No one as shrewd as the Mormon leader could doubt that science was reshaping the world. Young soon began to urge that Mormon children be taught mineralogy, geology, and chemistry. "There are branches of knowledge which we ought thoroughly to understand and are particularly adapted to these mountain regions," he wrote.

Also on that brief journey, Young would learn information of a different sort that would further shake the Mormon world. While Powell and Lee rode with Young south to Kanab, Snow informed Young about Lee's culpability in the Mountain Meadows Massacre, one of the most bloody, bizarre crimes in American western history. Thirteen years earlier, in September 1857, during the Utah War that had Mormon settlers facing off against the U.S. cavalry, a group of LDS dressed up as Indians, along with a handful of Paiutes, had attacked the Baker-Fancher wagon train as it rested in southwestern Utah. The pioneers circled their wagons and put up stiff resistance. After five days of fighting, the embattled emigrants surrendered to Lee, who presented himself as a peace broker between them and the Indians. He claimed to have negotiated safe passage for them. An LDS militiaman escorted each of the weaponless men out from the corralled wagons. The order was then given, "Halt!"; then "Do your duty!" Each Mormon tender delivered a single shot to the head of his prisoner. Every emigrant older than five years old was slaughtered, the youngest spared only because they could not bear witness. All told, about fifty men died, along with twenty women and another fifty older children and adolescents. Mormon families took in the tiny, dazed survivors. No proof exists whether Young directly ordered the attack or whether zealous militia leaders had misinterpreted possibly unclear orders from higher-ups, but it had been a Mormon-initiated action from start to grisly finish. The Mormons blamed the Indians for the slaughter, even though most of the Paiute had departed long before the massacre took place.

Justice was slow to catch up. The frontier realities of plodding communication and hard travel compounded by a national civil war had stymied a sustained federal inquiry for many years. Snow later explained that Young's tardiness in bringing Lee to justice occurred because the Mormon leader believed Lee's lies that Indians alone were culpable. Snow had learned of Lee's involvement from recent interviews he had conducted. He recalled that Young reacted with "great astonishment," even though it strains credulity to believe that he knew nothing. As the party rode toward Kanab, the president pulled Lee aside, giving him "some kind of Fatherly council," encouraging him to gather his wives, sons, and daughters and move yet farther south and out of sight into the Arizona Strip. Young had already determined that Lee must shoulder the blame for the outrage, despite telling evidence that two of Lee's superiors had given him direct orders to kill the gentiles. Two weeks later, after Young returned to Salt Lake City, the church excommunicated Lee for "extreem wickedness."

The party pressed on to Kanab, crossing the twisty Paria Creek some twenty-one times, finally arriving at the tiny settlement and its crude fort. The following morning Young and the elders selected a site to the northeast of the fort on an elevation protected from the wind. A surveyor marked out blocks, while another man located well sites. Powell joined the surveyor, noting that the out-lots were fenced as one great farm. The townspeople would collectively own the water ditch and farm fence. Powell later observed in an article for *Scribner's* that the Mormon towns in Utah were thus "woven together by a net-work of communal interest."

Powell became deeply impressed by the Mormon success in settling the desert, particularly in their collective management of water resources. While most Americans might dismiss the entire Mormon "experiment" out of hand, he cast no judgment on them, nor the Indians, studying them both intently for clues as to how humans survived in arid, inhospitable lands. Practicality certainly played a part—he could not afford to alienate the Saints and jeopardize his upcoming plans—but his overall attitude toward them appeared to be one of genuine curiosity. The observations of outlier cultures would fundamentally shape his evolving vision for the large-scale sustainable development of the West.

From Kanab, Young and his party headed back north, while Powell, Hamblin, and the southern Paiute chief Chuarumpeak, whom Powell would come to call "Chuar" as their friendship deepened, continued on. The rabbit skin–robed chief fondly called Powell "Kapurats," or "one arm off." When Powell inquired about a way down to the Colorado, the Paiute assured him that no one could get to the water's edge from this side of the Canyon, but that he would happily show them the springs and water pockets on the way to the rim. Two recruits to the upcoming river expedition joined them at the tiny Mormon cattle settlement of Pipe Springs: Francis Marion Bishop, a former student of Powell's and devout Christian, and Powell's cousin, Walter Clement Powell. The small party continued southwest toward the river into the Uinkaret Plateau, now part of the Mount Trumbull Wilderness. Powell would name the dominant lava-capped peak in honor of the Illinois senator who had helped him secure federal support. Mount Trumbull rises some twenty miles north of the Grand Canyon, and about sixty miles from Kanab, close to the area where the Howlands and Dunn had vanished. Shuts, a "one-eyed, bare-legged, merry-faced pigmy," recorded Powell, joined them, too. While Chuar rode a pony, Shuts preferred scampering about, often taking shortcuts so that the party would turn a corner and come across him sitting on a rock, "his face a rich mine of funny smiles."

Thus guided by Shuts and Chuar, the party jumped from one water pocket to the next, enabling them to cross the scorching desert and negotiate the deep ravines that headed the canyons leading into the Grand Canyon. Powell was amazed by the Indians' geographic understanding: "My knowledge is general, only embracing the more important features of a region, that remain as a map, engraved on my mind. But theirs is particular; they know every rock and ledge, every gulch and cañon, and just where to wind among these to find a pass, and their knowledge is unerring." In due course, they reached the base of a great volcanic eminence that Powell later dubbed Mount Dellenbaugh.

Nearby lay a Uinkaret Paiute village. That evening, under tall pines around a roaring campfire, Powell asked the Uinkaret elders to tell their traditional stories, even though such expositions usually took place during the winter. They obliged, the storytellers speaking in a special sweet, soft, and musical language. A "scene strange and weird," Powell recorded: "by the fire, men, old, wrinkled and ugly; deformed, blear-eyed, wry-faced women; lithe, stately young men; pretty but simpering maidens, naked children, all intently listening, or laughing and talking by turns, their strange faces and dusky forms lit up with the glare of the pine-knot fire." The legend of Stone Shirt ended well beyond midnight. Afterward, Powell pulled Chuar aside and explained that he sought information on his three expedition members who had disappeared into the mountains some thirty miles to the west, in the territory of the Shivwits Paiute. Could he summon the Shivwits to a meeting? Chuar agreed to arrange a powwow.

The following morning, Powell and the party, along with a Uinkaret guide, left their pack train and most of their gear to ride out to the Colorado, and they managed to reach the Grand Canyon's northern rim, probably some sixty miles north of Separation Rapid. The precipitous descent to the river proved impossible for their horses, so they clambered down on foot with much difficulty. Powell considered this a possible avenue of resupply, but the logistical challenges appeared insurmountable. Many laborers would need to bear heavy loads on their backs down that treacherous face. Retracing their steps, they passed again by a "stinking water pocket" so foul that their ponies had refused to drink from it on the way over. But after thirty hours without water, the animals drank rapaciously, while the men strained out "loathsome, wriggling larvae" to make coffee.

When they limped into the Uinkaret village at sunset, the Shivwits had gathered. Powell was immediately struck by how primitive they appeared.

When the Howland party abandoned the river, they had headed up into the large, steep-sided Separation Canyon, which drains the entire Shivwits Plateau, an elevation of land so enormous that it bends the very Colorado, deflecting it south until it meets the plateau's eastern flank, then west around the southern tip, to run northwest. Several tributaries feed into it, but its tall, steep walls would seem to doom most attempts to climb out. But Powell's men were tough, experienced mountain men, who were also desperate.

In the twentieth century, a hiker discovered possible evidence suggesting that the party did scale the walls. On the 7,000-foot summit of Mount Dellenbaugh, the very mountain at the base of which Powell would powwow with the Shivwits, lies a worn, faint inscription carved into the volcanic rock. The words "Dunn" and "1869" seem certain. A less-distinct word appears to be "water" with an arrow pointing north. Should this relic prove authentic, the men had indeed managed to climb out of the Canyon, some five miles southeast of the mountain, on the edge of the Canyon's rim. Mount Dellenbaugh's summit may have offered them the chance to orient themselves. This carving, some eighteen miles as the crow flies from the river, could be the last physical trace of the three doomed men. Powell was close—perhaps very close—to where they had disappeared.

After dinner, Powell, Hamblin, the Shivwits, and Uinkarets gathered around a campfire. Powell lit his own pipe and passed it. When Powell accepted the Shivwits chief's pipe, he found its mouthpiece wrapped in a saliva-soaked mass of chewed buckskin and sinew. He refilled the bowl, then passed it along without taking a puff.

As Hamblin translated, Powell explained that he wished

neither to trade nor negotiate for land, but only to travel in safety and be considered a friend. A quiet, reserved man, Hamblin spoke slowly and so softly that all gathered had to lean in to hear his words. Powell expressed curiosity about their traditions and habits, and also wanted to learn about high-desert animals and plants. As with Young, he wound a fanciful tale, regaling the Shivwits with stories about African and Chinese peoples, and strange creatures that lived in the sea.

"Your talk is good," replied the Shivwits chief, "and we believe what you say. We believe in Jacob, and look upon you as a father." He described how his people owned no horses and had little to give: "You must not think us mean." The white man was wise, and they were ignorant. Without missing a beat, the chief then voluntarily confessed to murder:

"Last year we killed three white men. Bad men said they were our enemies: They told great lies. We thought them true. We were mad; it made us big fools. We are very sorry. Do not think of them; it is done; let us be friends. We are ignorant—like little children in understanding compared with you. When we do wrong, do not you get mad and be like children too."

The chief confided his dread about the prospect of white men coming in great numbers. "When they stop killing us, there will be no Indian left to bury the dead." Indians required little, he said. "Our children play in the warm sand; we hear them sing and are glad. The seeds ripen and we have to eat and we are glad." He ended by declaring, "We will be friends." Presents were dispensed, all shook hands, and the council broke up. Powell watched Hamblin pull one of the Shivwits aside. The Indian told Hamblin that after his people fed the trio, they had pointed them toward the Mormon settlements and sent them on their way. An Indian from the other side of the Colorado implicated them as the same miners who had killed a squaw in a drunken brawl. Angry Shivwits warriors had pursued the white men and killed them with their arrows.

These explanations and apologies satisfied Powell, who recorded that he slept well that night "although these murderers of my men, and their friends, the Uinkarets, were sleeping not 500 yards away." He had taken the Shivwits' confession at face value, although he must have confirmed the course of events with Erastus Snow on their recent journey to Kanab. Powell's disinterest in pressing the Shivwits for exact details—for instance, where the bodies lay or whether the trio's possessions might be returned—may have stemmed from his desire not to challenge the chief's request to put the unfortunate business behind them. To produce evidence of the deed in the form of bones or artifacts would open up a path of possible retribution that neither Powell nor the Shivwits desired.

Still the simple logistics bear a closer look. Would a generally timid band of southern Paiute, armed only with bows and arrows, attack three rifle-bearing backwoodsmen on the basis of a rumor passed along by someone from another tribe? By then, the Shivwits clearly understood that violence directed at white men would only bring misery crashing down upon them. That they might risk the wrath of these powerful white men to avenge the honor of a squaw from another band lacks plausibility.

Others not present at this council would argue, when no bodies came to light or material objects surfaced, that non-Indians might be involved in the murders. Jack Sumner, although not a friend of Native Americans, concluded that the Mormons had perpetrated the crime. With the Mountain Meadows Massacre still unprosecuted, a case can be made that the Mormon militiamen mistook the three armed men for federal marshals and killed them—and then pinned it on the Indians. Only days before the powwow, Young had exiled John D. Lee to an especially forlorn corner of the desert. Had the chief confessed to the murders in exchange for valuable consideration from the leadership in Salt Lake City? Some conjecture that Hamblin purposefully mistranslated the chief's statement to deceive Powell. While not as fluent as Hamblin, Powell credibly claimed to know some five hundred Ute words, so it is difficult to imagine that Hamblin could have accomplished such misdirection. A later missive from Hamblin to Young contains no whiff of conspiracy. Aside from the admission by the Shivwits chief, no definitive evidence exists one way or the other as to whether Indians or the Mormons did the slaughtering of Oramel, Seneca, and Bill.

In the end, the most simple explanation probably suffices. The appearance of the three strangers in the remote Arizona Strip, far from any town, without supplies, water vessels, horses, or mules—as though they had been dropped from the heavens—most certainly would have alarmed the Shivwits. No one—white or Indian—wandered this land without support of some kind. Lacking means to communicate effectively, misunderstandings might well have caused the violence. Had for instance the desperate white men pointed their guns to demand water, the Shivwits could not be blamed for responding with arrows. Powell also knew that violence often erupted on the frontier for irrational reasons. Some tragic intersection had probably occurred—and Powell did not intend to continue the cycle of violence.

After meeting the Shivwits, Powell continued with his exploration of the Kaibab Plateau and search for an effective route to the river. But increasingly his fascination with the plateau Indians drew him away from his logistical planning. While only a handful of towns and roads interrupt the Arizona Strip even today, the signs of ancient human habitation abundantly reveal themselves: faint outlines of prehistoric adobe houses overlooking dry lake beds, tiny granaries tucked high in cliff walls, lines of broken rock walls, and enigmatic petroglyphs. They beckoned Powell and further inflamed his curiosity in the early Indian presence in the arid lands.

The tradition of American explorers studying the Indians dated back to Thomas Jefferson, who had sent Lewis and Clark west across the Louisiana Purchase with elaborate instructions to gather ethnological and linguistic data on the natives they encountered. Every federally sponsored mission since—from Long's 1819 Expedition to the Rockies to the railroad-route surveys of the 1840s and 1850s—were tasked to collect all sorts of relics of the aboriginal peoples. Powell had embraced the spirit of Jefferson's directive with zeal. But unlike the earlier explorers, his interest did not stop at collecting Indian "curiosities" or making superficial observations about Indian dress and appearance. Powell instead sought to understand the nature of those with whom he had shared campfires— and put on record descriptions of lifestyles and summaries of creation myths that were crucial to understanding the American Indian vision of the world. Powell would push beyond mere description to examine how the tribes treated their insane and elderly and raised their children. His accounts about Indians reveal not just compassion but also a genuinely deep interest, with a scientific distance highly unusual for his day.

In mid-October Powell set out to visit the chain of Hopi pueblos perched atop high mesas south of the Colorado, sending ahead his two recent arrivals, some Indians, and Mormons down the Paria to the Colorado, their packs full of lumber, with instructions to build a crude ferryboat. After Powell himself reached the river, the whole party crossed, their horses swimming behind them. They worked their way along Echo Cliffs, traveling mostly at night to avoid Indian horse rustlers. After five days, they reached the largest of the Hopi towns, Oraibi, one of seven collectively known as Tusayan, a cluster housing some 2,700 inhabitants. Of all the Indians he would meet, the Hopi fascinated him the most. Perched securely on high cliffs, defensible against marauding Apache or Navajo, their multifloor stone-and-plaster houses sometimes reached six stories. The Hopi lived principally atop their houses, noted Powell, making "a merry sight to see a score or two of little naked children climbing up and down the stairways and ladders, and running about the tops of the houses engaged in some active sport." He marveled at the young women, dark black hair parted in the middle, each lock carefully braided or twisted, then rolled into a coil and held by wooden pins over their ears.

Powell recorded Indian life neither exhaustively nor comprehensively but with openness, empathy, and a memorable absence of judgment. In *Scribner's Monthly,* he described the Hopi as a people harboring a vast store of mythology and an elaborate, ceremonious religion. He climbed down into a kiva and sat naked for a twenty-four-hour marathon honoring the Hopi rain god, much of which he described in careful detail. His willingness to shed his clothes, join in the sacred event, and carefully recall the entire experience in detail, count among the earliest examples of American participatory anthropology.

After two weeks of reveling in the Hopi culture, Powell agreed to join Hamblin on a visit to Fort Defiance, a U.S. Army outpost in northeastern Arizona, on his way to Santa Fe and back East. Hamblin wanted to talk peace with the Navajo, who would be gathering there to receive their federal annuities and rations. No Mormon had yet negotiated successfully with them and tensions between the two remained high.

Powell agreed to ride ahead of Hamblin to the fort, with a twenty-five-year-old Mormon guide and translator, Ammon Tenney, and a Hopi guide, to arrange for a meeting with the Navajo chiefs. Not two hours after they had ridden out, two Navajos on fine stallions fell in behind them, horse and men alike bedecked in gaudy silver ornamentation. "[T]he glitter radiating in the noonday could be seen for miles," wrote Tenney. The silent presence of these two powerful figures threw Tenney and the Hopi into a panic, but "the Major seemed calm." They rode on.

The trail soon descended sharply into a shallow valley, then moved parallel to an elevated benchland. Then all of a sudden, recalled Tenney, "our ears were saluted by a (terrible) war whoop which reverberated from one corner of this elevation to the next corner which made it appear to us that we were surrounded by an army of our wood be [sic] assassins." They soon saw two other warriors leaping down toward them from rock to rock. Their two mute companions moved in close—a threatening action, thought Tenney. The Hopi guide's face turned a "deathlike hue." The young Mormon half cocked his repeater's trigger.

When the two approaching warriors came within twenty-five yards, the mounted Navajos rode forward and spoke calmly to them. The other two laid down their arms. The Major dismounted, pulling two sacks of tobacco from his pack, and held them out to Tenney, saying, "This is the kind of arms I carry. Put your guns down Mr. Tenney." He walked over to the newcomers, thumped them on the shoulders, and with a loud and hearty laugh handed them the gifts. The tense moment defused, the party rode on for several days, reaching the fort at the end of October, a miserable collection of abandoned adobe buildings and a log stronghold standing on an elevation near the point where Bonito Canyon cuts through a swell of naked sandstone hills.

The eight thousand Indians encamped before Fort Defiance created a wild spectacle, thought Powell, clumps of Indians gambling, others intent on horse racing. At night, the plain glowed with bonfires. In his later writings about this visit, Powell would end his description at that point, neglecting to record what happened next.

The Indian agent Frank Bennett, known affectionately to the Navajo as "Big Belly," informed the Indian chiefs that Powell and Hamblin desired to talk peace. No doubt Powell served as an important neutral buffer. By the time Hamblin rode into Fort Defiance, the plans were all set. "The throng was immense," Tenney told his journal, adding that Powell represented the U.S. government—a stretch by any interpretation.

At 2 p.m. on November 5, Powell, Hamblin, and Bennett joined the Navajo chief Barboncito and twenty-eight Navajo headmen in a spacious room inside the fort. Bennett called the parley to order;

Powell opened the conversation by declaring his gladness at meeting the Navajo, then explained how white people now spread from ocean to ocean, their taxes supporting not only the government, but the rations and gifts that the Navajo received annually. He reported that the Great Father in Washington would send troops to protect the Mormons—and that he would make war for any depredations committed upon Mormons or any other settlers. He then introduced Hamblin, who spoke slowly and solemnly for about an hour. The Navajo, he said, had stolen many horses—Mormon young men had wanted the elders to declare war, but President Young was committed to peace.

Barboncito spoke next, recalling how he had seen the massacre, betrayal, and starvation of his people over many years. He would do his best to stop Navajo raiding. By guarding the two Colorado crossings, the Mormons could turn back non-Navajos from raiding north into Utah.

"Today," summed up Powell, "peace and friendship is planted, but it will not grow unless the Navajos cultivate it." Barboncito replied, "That is true." They wrapped up some details of an agreement, which included a pledge that the Navajo would no longer cross into Utah. This unofficial pact would largely end Navajo raids on Mormon stock, ushering in a long period of trade and relative goodwill between Mormon, Navajo, and Paiute. While Powell never publically spoke of his part in the successful negotiations—perhaps because he had represented the United States without authorization—the affair bespoke a growing confidence in the former school teacher, as he boldly climbed into whatever role he was called to play. He could wear a personality to match the occasion: the practical scientist-philosopher with Brigham Young; the honest, steady go-between for the Navajo; the bluff backslapper calming two hostile warriors.

But even more clearly, Powell felt responsible for telling new Americans about these native peoples—and shape how they might regard them. Too often, he observed, the white men viewed the

Indians in one of only two ways. Some merely took into account Indian barbarities, seeing the Indians as demon hordes standing in the way of solid Victorian progress, and therefore to be destroyed. But others, however, idealized some concept of the noble savage, focusing only on virtues, and wondered "that a morally degenerate, but powerful civilization, should destroy that primitive life." Neither perception did service to the Native American peoples, he argued. Here the college lecturer and school principal, honed by later efforts explaining geologic intricacies, turned that same eye to gain an unvarnished understanding of Indian cultures.

Powell left the fort for Santa Fe, instructing Hamblin to collect Hopi material and to continue searching for a lateral canyon that could serve as a resupply route for the upcoming river journey. In a couple of months, Hamblin would send Powell "one Cochena suite, 6 fancy legging strings, 2 Cwawa's or womans belts, one fancy belt, one stone mortar, one stone axe, 1 pr moccasins, one fancy Blanket, one large blanket, 2 images." He had enticed the Hopi leader Tuba to come to Kanab with his wife and create a set of their people's bridal clothes. But he had still not found a resupply route.

Powell stopped in Denver to see Byers, who pronounced himself surprised and gratified to receive the now nationally famous explorer. No doubt Powell told him about his council with the Shivwits. For the Major, this report closed the case on the disappearance of the Howland party.

This visit went far toward easing Byers's irritation with Powell, which had mounted ever since his brother-in-law Jack Sumner had written bitterly about how Powell had left him without the means to overwinter and get back to Denver. Powell had a snippy note from Byers in December 1869 demanding that he repay a $7 loan, then informing him that "we hear nothing & fear the worst" for Sumner, who was "destitute" in country "entirely occupied with

Indian difficulties." Seven months later, Byers again wrote Powell, this time asking that he send Sumner a railroad pass from Owens Valley in California to Cheyenne. When Sumner finally arrived in Denver on August 8, nearly a year after the Colorado expedition had officially ended, Byers took out his frustration in the *Rocky Mountain News*. He praised Jack's fearlessness, asserting that he had been the voyage's "leading and ruling spirit, the commander of the signal boat which led the way through the canon and rapid, and torrent. . . ." He then took a direct shot at Powell. "The expedition was a success, thanks to the dauntless man who *led* it, as much as to him who has clothed a portion of its history in the elegant diction of the lecture room." What's more, Byers wrote mockingly, "We promise a new unwritten chapter in the history of the Powell expedition which will demonstrate that truth may really be stranger than fiction." Byers would never write that story, keeping mum for the rest of his life. Something shut him up, very likely plain self-interest: Byers conceding that Powell's work that past summer and fall had yielded promise in yet another sphere of inquiry. "He has found a practicable railway route from northern Nevada eastward, crossing the Great Colorado about midway between the mouths of the Little Colorado and the San Juan." Powell had even outlined how the Colorado crossing would need to be "a suspension bridge of about twelve hundred feet span, three thousand feet above the water." As land agent for the Denver Pacific, Byers had taken great interest in Powell's explorations. His friend John Evans, lately the Colorado Territory governor who had joined Powell at Sulphur Springs in 1868, was currently serving as president of the Denver and Pacific Railroad, which was seeking to connect with the Union Pacific Eastern Division (Kansas Pacific) and, to the north, with the Union Pacific. Such likely connections suggest that Powell may well have supplied important survey information, possibly in some sort of exchange for the free railroad passes and other considerations he was receiving for his expeditions.

Back in Washington, Powell sent Byers a fancy watch for Sumner that would handsomely replace the one he had given to Oramel Howland to pass on to his sister: "A very fine present," replied Byers, "and I know he will appreciate it highly."

For the second expedition, Powell would not select leather-tough mountain men. Such backwoods resilience no longer seemed quite so critical. Nor did he pick professional scientists. He now mostly chose men he knew or was related to, men from back home in Illinois on whom he could depend. Loyalty appeared paramount. His second-in-command, the Illinois school superintendent Almon Harris Thompson, was married to his sister Nellie and, at thirty-two, was second oldest to Powell. "Prof," as Thompson was called, had accompanied Powell on the first trip out west in 1867 as head of entomology. On this expedition, he would learn on the job, serving as "chief geographer, astronomer and topographer." Most important, his loyalty would rarely waver through thick and a whole lot of thin.

In early May 1871, Powell and Thompson brought their wives to Salt Lake City for the summer, Emma clearly showing in the fifth month of pregnancy. Some bad news arrived that Sumner—the only original crew member to receive an invitation for the second expedition—could not join them. He had spent the winter trapping in the mountains. Deep snow, and probably some ambivalence about joining another river trip with Powell, prevented him from getting to Green River City, Wyoming, in time for the departure. But the new expedition would carry Sumner's 1869 journal.

Powell met a strapping German-born teamster in Salt Lake City, whom he signed up on the spot, much as he had Andy Hall two years before. The tall, red-haired Jack Hillers had fought for the Union, staying in uniform until 1870, when he found himself working in the Mormon capital. Life in the City of the Saints had not panned out well for the whiskey-drinking twenty-seven-year-old with an affable manner and a penchant for the ribald. Powell liked "Jolly Jack" from their first handshake, which began a long friendship. With Powell's patronage, Hillers would rise to become one of America's most prominent photographers.

The three men arrived in Green River City on May 16, 1871, where the rest of the crew were readying. Powell had commissioned three new Whitehalls, the design identical to the original craft except for the addition of a third waterproof compartment, plus a steering oar placed astern for more responsive turning. Powell bought a captain's chair from Jake Field's store, which Hillers bolted on top of the center cabin of the latest version of *Emma Dean.*

Six days later, eleven men left Green River City on three boats. Powell had broken the trip into two sections. In summer and fall of 1871, they would row down the Green and the Colorado until they met the Paria at the head of the Grand Canyon; the following summer, they would finish, running from the Paria through the Canyon to Callville. Compared with 1869, in which the expedition raced the thousand miles from Green River City to Callville in three months, the 1871 party would take two months longer just to reach the Paria. Hamblin, still searching for the Dirty Devil's canyon, would coordinate their resupply along the way.

During the trip, the seventeen-year-old Fred Dellenbaugh, the son of a rich Ohio doctor, manned the oars below Powell's feet, listening to the Major's stories. The starstruck young man reveled at Powell's "magnificent will, his cheerful self-reliance, and his unconquerable determination to dominate any situation." On the river, Powell sang constantly, noted Dellenbaugh, fragments ranging from arias in *The Marriage of Figaro* to *Way Down upon the Suwannee River,* his voice rising exuberantly whenever they approached a rapid.

In calm water, the expedition sometimes rafted together, the Major regaling them with his readings of *The Lady of the Lake.* At camp, they read more Walter Scott, and Longfellow's *Song of Hiawatha,* prompting photographer E. O. Beaman to write: "Imagine a group of rough, unkempt men, surrounded by the wildest and grandest solitude, with all the rude appurtenances of camp-life about them listening to the musical rhythm of Hiawatha's wooing, intelligently read."

Thompson described how they confiscated young Dellenbaugh's gun at night for fear of his frequent nightmares about Indians and large white snakes, which once caused him to half throttle a comrade while sleepwalking. Most all expedition members scratched down daily journals. At Brown's Park, Powell dismissed Frank Richardson, who despite his flute-playing prowess, did not possess a strong enough constitution to continue. They discovered the wreck of *No Name* below Disaster Falls, plus an eerily preserved copy of *Putnam's Magazine* and a bag of flour.

The second expedition brought little of the suspense of the first, but plenty of grueling work—the extremely cautious Powell insisting that they line or portage even mildly perilous rapids. They methodically took the measurements necessary to map the river. Thompson, aided by his assistant, Vandiveer Jones, a principal of the Washburn, Illinois, schools, sighted ahead at each bend with prismatic compasses to estimate the length of the river's reach, the height of walls, and the width of the side streams. Every forty-five miles, Thompson took astronomical readings with a sextant. From these measurements, Bishop drew the double-lined course of the river on paper, accompanied by notes in a tiny, cramped hand indicating noon stops and evening campsites. It made slow work, not enough to keep the men sufficiently busy.

With Clem Powell's assistance, Beaman photographed the river and its canyons. The state-of-the-art wet-plate Collodion photographic process, which had replaced the daguerreotype—the first practical photographic technique—in the late 1850s, required equipment weighing a ton or more. The best panoramic vantage often demanded that photographer and assistant climb several thousand feet above the river, lugging a large, heavy box containing the darkroom—a five-foot-tall tent of yellow cloth lined with green calico—and tripod—two wagon bows cut in two, reversed, then fastened together with hinges—in addition to the large-format camera with two side-by-side lenses, bags of processing chemicals, and fragile glass plates. Beaman found himself abandoning the tripod and foraging for sticks to construct the tent. Even significantly lightened, Clem cursed that "infernal howitzer on my back," which several times caused him to fall.

While the cumbersome Collodion process may have required extraordinary patience in setting up, the processing was all about speed. Once he coated the glass plate with wet chemicals, the photographer had ten minutes or less to expose and process it. Wind or rain could destroy a morning's work in a moment, as could an improper mix of the chemicals or contamination by dirt. The sand and dust, compounded with alkali, made it "hard to elude that great pest to the photographer, *pin-holes*," wrote Beaman in frustration. "[W]e often have to station a man at the tripod to keep the camera from going down the cañons on an exploring trip of its own, carried by the frequent whirlwinds which visit us during the calmest days." Clem bickered with Beaman constantly.

Long exposure times prevented such "action" shots of a rowboat caught in fearsome waves. But this collection—Powell would bring 250 images with him to Washington that winter—were powerful, not only for capturing the vast expanse of the western canyonland, but for the sheer alien quality of a landscape whose only human touch was a boat or the rigid outline of a man sitting in a natural amphitheater—images that would join an increasingly sophisticated arsenal that Powell would use to explain the West to the rest of America.

On July 6, Thompson reported that the Major "had decided to go on ahead to Uintah as he says, but to Salt Lake as I believe." By now, Emma was in her seventh month of a difficult pregnancy, and he wanted to be with her.

When the rest of the expedition reached the Uinta River on July 15, they found a rusted oyster can containing a note from Powell telling them to stay put; so wait they did, for eight days. On his way back from Salt Lake, Powell met Jacob Hamblin, who still had not located the Dirty Devil. The Major hired Pardon Dodds, the former Indian agent at Uinta, to help him. By July 23, Powell had rejoined the men at the river, but told them to continue without him; he would meet them at Gunnison's Crossing in the Utah Territory. By then, the monotony and hard work had worn on morale, and Beaman and Clem were not the only ones not getting along. Most complained about the cook and his food, while others flinched every time John Steward opened his mouth, such was the color and vigor of his profanity. In late August when Powell rejoined the party at Gunnison's Crossing, even Thompson was not happy to see Powell, who had managed only to secure a rather slim resupply of flour, sugar, and meat. That would have to last for some time, because Powell still had not been able to locate the Dirty Devil, not that "the Major made any serious effort," grumbled Thompson. In fact, Powell had traveled across the West Tavuts Plateau south of the Uinta Valley on his way to the Sevier River drainage, examining rocks and studying the Indians. Those he interviewed had confirmed Hamblin's premise that the Dirty Devil did not offer a viable path for a mule train. "I do not care a cuss whether he comes with us or not on the river," wrote Prof, "but it makes one mad to wait and then have him come in and report a failure." He added as an aside that he should not complain, having known what the situation would be like before leaving on the trip. Like all secondary commanders in the field, comfortable when the leader is gone, Powell's reappearance—once again sitting kinglike in his chair and calling all the shots—irritated him.

The expedition set off through Labyrinth Canyon, then to the intersection of the Green and Grand, and on to the bad whitewater of Cataract Canyon, which Powell dreaded seeing again. By the end of September, they reached the foul Dirty Devil, but did not find Hamblin and supplies waiting there. Powell decided to cache *Canonita* in a shallow cave some two hundred feet back from the river. They had less than a week's worth of flour left. They would travel faster and more easily with two boats, although over-crowded, and could retrieve *Canonita* later.

Much to the Major's disappointment, their dwindling food supplies forced them to skip the chance to climb the mountain Powell had named after Oramel Howland (today's Navajo Mountain). They did stop at the Music Temple in Glen Canyon, a beautiful grotto with high walls, in which Powell showed them where the Howlands, Dunn, and others from the 1869 trip had carved their names. In silence they inscribed their own.

A week later, they reached the Crossing of the Fathers, where Dodds waited with food and supplies, including a pair of heavy shoes and overalls for each man. They had cut it close. Two days later, Powell again, this time with Hillers, set out for Salt Lake City to meet his month-old daughter, named Mary Dean after his mother.

The rest of the party continued downriver to arrive on October 23 at the influx of the Paria—and found no supplies awaiting them. They camped and waited. Five days later, down to half rations, they heard an "Indian yell" from across the river. When they rowed over, they met Hamblin, who was leading a party of nine Navajo, along with Isaac C. Haight and George W. Adair, both participants in the Mountain Meadows Massacre, on a trading visit to the Mormon settlements. After Hamblin had shared a dinner of beans with the hungry rivermen, all enjoyed an evening filled with Navajo song and dancing. One expeditioneer wrote of the friendly Haight: "Can it be that he would sanction and assist in the murder of women and children?"

Several days later, their supplies finally arrived. The pack train had gotten badly lost. Thompson left for Kanab with two sick men: Jones, plagued by rheumatism, who had also injured his ankle; and Steward, inexplicably unable to stand or eat. The others cached the boats, some equipment, the instruments, and the oars for the following season. The first section was complete.

Powell overwintered the expedition at Kanab. The small Mormon town had filled out since his visit with Young a year earlier, now hosting almost fifty families. Fruit and shade trees grew, watered by irrigation ditches that ran down either side of the wide streets. For men who had labored alone on the river for five months, Kanab glowed as a bastion of civilization, especially when Emma arrived with the new baby, accompanied by Nellie Powell, and Fuzz, their tiny terrier.

Before the congressional appropriation committee in Washington, Powell had promised not only to map the river, but also to complete a survey of the Colorado Plateau itself, west of the Colorado River to the Sierra Nevada, an area encompassing southern Utah and northern Arizona. From Kanab over that winter and spring, Powell and his expedition would begin the demanding survey work. In mid-December, Powell and Clem rode six miles south of town into the Arizona Territory, then selected a flat stretch of desert in which they would establish their nine-mile "baseline," the surveying marker that would anchor all their subsequent readings. Once this baseline was laid out, they could take bearings on any feature in the distance from both ends of the baseline, creating a large triangle. Basic geometry then enabled them to determine the length of the two other sides of the triangle by knowing the triangle's angles. From that first triangulation they would extend others, and others off those, until they had covered a large swath of the Arizona Strip. These measurements, along with barometric readings to determine the elevation of topographic features, would provide the key data points for accurate mapping.

Other members of the party soon followed, setting up a tent

camp, complete with conical sheet-iron stoves. Dellenbaugh especially remembered the sorghum molasses-soaked bread desserts, but Bishop started complaining: "Sent over in Utah to hunt a place for a lunatic-asylum—for if I ever see a lot of men working on a bigger piece of tomfoolery than this, measuring baseline with 3 fourteen foot rods, I am going to petition the powers for an asylum for the insane."

Prof Thompson took a theodolite sighting on Polaris to determine the true north-south, but before he could use it, snow and rain started coming down heavily. Difficult weather would continue to hamper their efforts. Bishop crafted three fourteen-foot wooden rods, connected by pins at each end. These would be laid down, two always on the ground to prevent accidental shifting by the often-whipping wind, so they could measure the exact distance of the baseline they were creating. Bishop created molds into which he poured molten lead to form the plumb bobs necessary to level the rods.

They started to measure out the baseline just after Christmas, using a zenith telescope to determine latitude at the north end and longitude by telegraphic signals with Salt Lake City, finishing by February 21. From there, small groups rode out to mark points with cairns, every twenty-five to thirty miles, the angles of triangles thus formed were then measured with a seven-inch theodolite. Secondary triangles were added, then others extended from those. They fought snowstorms and the landscape itself, Thompson at one point climbing a 125-foot-tall tree to take a bearing. By May, their invisible triangles covered Arizona to the Grand Canyon, and southwest of Kanab to Mount Trumbull, west from there to the Nevada border. The unmapped portion of the unwelcoming Arizona Strip slowly yielded to their determined work.

In February, the Major prepared to return to Washington to seek another year's funding. Although contracted to the expedition, the photographer Beaman had bristled at Powell's constant demands, eventually deciding that he could do better on his own.

He sold 350 stereoscopic glass plates to the Major and all rights to his eight months of work for $800, then headed off to photograph the Hopi towns. On his way east, Powell stopped for a week in Salt Lake City to have prints made from 250 stereoscopic plates. The expedition's specially designed camera took two simultaneous shots at slightly different angles, about the same distance that lies between two human eyes. These two images were printed side by side on a single card, which was then slipped into a device with a lens and viewed, the images popping into startling three-dimension. At a time when publishing photographs in newspapers or magazines had not been fully worked out, such stereoscopic photography cards proved extremely popular in American parlors. These stereographs served as important gifts to the influential politicians who determined Powell's further funding.

Powell liked the genial if sickly technician at Charles R. Savage's gallery who took so much care in making the prints. On the way back through Salt Lake City, he hired James Fennemore as expedition photographer. On his return to Kanab, Powell found he had lost yet another employee. After complaining at length that Powell and Thompson had been living in luxury compared with the others, Bishop quit the expedition. Powell paid him $400 in back wages and gave him a railroad pass to Illinois—which Bishop never used, for he stayed on instead in Kanab. The man who once described the Mormons as "vile, miserable sinners with but few exceptions," fell in love with a Mormon woman and converted, settling in Salt Lake City, eventually became a bishop in fact as well as name, and science professor at the University of Deseret.

Without Bishop, Beaman, and Steward on the payroll, Powell still struggled to support the survey, even to pay for the weekly hundred pounds of flour they consumed. But in Prof, Powell had picked an extraordinary worker, who somehow managed to keep the venture fed and occupied, though he, too, considered quitting at times. For long months in early spring 1872, Powell did not respond to his repeated queries by telegraph. At one low moment, Thompson wrote to him, claiming that he had not acted squarely or honorably. But by June 10, Powell's hard work had paid off: Congress appropriated $20,000 to complete the survey.

Powell bought a modest row house in Washington at 910 M Street, which he and Emma would call home for the remainder of their lives. He tendered his resignation to the Illinois State Board of Education as curator of the museum on the Normal campus. He was moving fast along a path that opened up to him with each larger task he embarked upon. It meant sometimes leaving his supporters in the lurch, such as the vast confusion over unclear ownership of some of the collections he had sent home. And though he made some attempts at sorting things out, it was not enough, and so soured some of his early relationships. But something far bigger than collecting specimens had possessed his imagination.

The finishing river season for the second expedition proved somewhat anticlimactic. Where Hamblin had failed, Thompson had succeeded. He and a few other expedition members not only located the Dirty Devil canyon but also named the last mountain range to be discovered in the continental United States—the Henrys. The route down the river gorge proved too difficult to navigate, so Thompson and his men skirted it, making it down to the *Canonita* cache on May 25. Several men stayed behind to caulk the boat, then emblazoned its stern with bright red lettering and rowed down to the Paria confluence by July 17, where they awaited the others.

The place now held permanent residents, the exiled John D. Lee and his family, who operated a ferry across the main river. One of his wives dubbed the spot Lonely Dell, but it would soon become known simply as Lees Ferry. A journalist had kicked up trouble trying to track Lee down, so he did not welcome non-Mormon outsiders. But when Thompson's group arrived, identifying themselves as part of Powell's undertaking, he invited them to dinner, where they found him quite pleasant. While awaiting the Major, the visitors helped Lee out in his garden and fixed some of his irrigation canals, cracking uncomfortable jokes about Mountain Meadows just within earshot of Lee.

On August 13, Powell arrived, eager to continue into the Canyon. Given the number of dropouts, they no longer needed a third boat, so they gave *Nellie Powell* to Lee for his ferry. Fennemore the photographer, who had gone down the Colorado with *Canonita,* had already fallen sick and proved too weak to continue. His assistant Jack Hillers proved a quick learner, so Powell tapped him to succeed Fennemore. The former teamster would shoot more than three thousand photographic glass plates of the Colorado River area between 1872 and 1878, completing twenty thousand more for the U.S. Geological Survey and the Bureau of Ethnology over the rest of a productive career.

Only seven took to the river again: the teenage Dellenbaugh and Hillers, along with Powell in *Emma Dean;* Thompson, Jones, Clem, and Andy Hattan in *Canonita.* Fennemore and the others headed back to Salt Lake City. Five years after Fennemore had enjoyed a meal at John D. Lee's table, he would famously photograph Lee sitting on his coffin moments before a firing squad executed him for his role in the Mountain Meadows Massacre, the only person held accountable for those unspeakable crimes.

On the river, Powell could see that the water was running eight to ten feet higher than before, rainfall steadily adding to it. With seams dried out from months of disuse, the boats leaked badly. Rain soaked everything, forcing them to raise a tarp over the fire. "The party seems dead," wrote Clem, "—nothing but work and danger, hard beds and worse food—a little bread, a few peaches, jerk and coffee." To make matters worse, a many-legged insect had infested their beef jerky.

On September 3, Powell and Hillers flipped *Emma Dean* twenty-four miles downriver from Bright Angel Creek. Hillers flew six feet headfirst into a whirlpool, followed by Powell, who both were immediately sucked out of sight. The swirling water stripped Hillers of his hat, shoes, and stockings. He claimed that Powell owed his life to his lifejacket, but it was he who had pulled Powell to safety after the boil finally brought them spluttering to the surface. "We joked him a good deal about his zeal in going to examine the geology at the bottom of the river," wrote Dellenbaugh, "but as a matter of fact he came near departing by that road to another world." The river was fast, muddy, turbulent, and ever more dangerous.

Four days later, the crew arrived at Kanab Creek, south of mile 143 of the Canyon, slightly more than halfway through, where they met three Mormon packers with much-needed supplies, but also with the disturbing news that whites had killed some Paiute near Mount Trumbull. After breakfast that day, the Major called the expedition off. Everyone "felt like praising god," wrote Hillers.

While the others scattered, Thompson and Dellenbaugh stayed on in Kanab to integrate all their accumulated measurements into a map. Dellenbaugh would roll up the completed document on February 28, insert it into a tin tub, and send it off to Powell in Washington via Wells, Fargo & Co. The map was a solid topographical achievement, accurately delineating at two miles to the inch the heretofore unmapped section of the remotest reaches of the Colorado Plateau. Powell was no longer just the tough, heroic conqueror of the Colorado, but a world-class scientist/surveyor of America's far western lands.

Even though he had finished his objective of mapping the Colorado River and some of its surrounding area, he was not finished. Now he set his sights on securing more robust federal funding to survey the rest of the Colorado Plateau. He would come up against stiff competition.

CHAPTER 8

Fighting the National Surveys

Ever since Congress had created the U.S. Army Corps of Topographical Engineers in 1813, the military had conducted the young nation's official business of exploration and surveying. After Polk appropriated Mexican territory, the army naturally stepped in to help redraw new national borders. It made sense: During peacetime, the army directed much of its effort toward surveying army roads west, siting forts, and determining reliable supply routes. When the transcontinental railroad gelled into an important national priority in the 1850s, the army only naturally undertook five large-scale expeditions to evaluate the best path west. Their Pacific Railroad Surveys produced thirteen quarto volumes weighing some eighty-three pounds, more than seven thousand pages long, not including maps and hundreds of full-page lithographs. Much natural history found its way inside these tomes, but only as an afterthought to the main purpose. Before the war, civilian-led explorations had been limited to the state level.

But in late 1866, when Powell the Illinois schoolteacher had only begun to contemplate a field trip west with his students, the military dominance in national surveying would be challenged by a twenty-five-year-old Yale graduate, who walked into the halls of Congress with a bold, unprecedented plan for a large-scale geological survey of the American West. Clarence King laid before the congressmen a proposal to survey eight hundred miles between the Rockies and the Sierras, a hundred-mile-wide swath along the Union Pacific transcontinental railroad now being built. He seductively dangled in front of legislators the promise that these lands contained coal, oil, and precious metals. Should not the nation know what it possessed? King argued convincingly that only an experienced civilian geologist could properly accomplish this kind of work. King would later boast that the year 1867 marked a turning point in the history of national geological work "when the science ceased to be dragged in the dust of rapid exploration and took a commanding position in the professional work of the country."

The short, dapper Clarence King represented everything that Powell was not. While Powell had wandered from college to college across the Midwest, searching for mentors who might slake his intense thirst to understand the natural world, King had matriculated at "The Sheff," Yale's new school of science, which would award the nation's first PhDs in geology and engineering. King studied under James Dwight Dana, listening raptly to America's foremost geologist tell stories of his travels with Charles Wilkes's world-circling United States Exploring Expedition in the 1830s. King learned firsthand about the latest European topographical mapping techniques.

Whereas Powell often appeared more detached, King commanded a room when he entered, not only by his fine dress, which often included silk gloves and colorful polka-dot ties, but with his captivating stories. In drawing rooms, or around cards and a bottle of whiskey, men and women gravitated to him naturally, delighting in his tales of evading Mexican bandits, surviving a lightning strike that left half his body brown for a week, or crawling into a grizzly's den. Somehow his stories of sexual conquests of dark-skinned women did not come off as boasting, perhaps because his jokes were usually at his own expense. Bouts of recited

Romantic poetry also seemed to offset any vulgarity. Writer Henry Adams recognized in his great friend so many of the manly attributes in which he felt himself lacking. "He had in him," wrote Adams, "something of the Greek—a touch of Alcibiades or Alexander." Indeed, King personified the grandest ambitions of a nation pressing into new lands rife with promise and unlimited possibility, and embracing these with gusto, unbounded confidence, and largesse of spirit. "I regarded the brilliant and beaming creature before me," wrote William Dean Howells, "simply as a promise of more and more literature of the vivid and graphic kind."

King's survey request fell at a propitious time. Congress eagerly wanted to get back to business after the war. He solicited support from the pioneering economic geologist Joseph Whitney, on whose California survey King had cut his teeth, Spencer Baird at the Smithsonian, and scientific notables from Yale to send letters to key senators and Edwin Stanton, the secretary of war. On the last day of its second session, March 2, 1867, the outgoing 39th Congress authorized King as the U.S. Geologist of the Geological Exploration of the Fortieth Parallel, under the supervision of General Andrew A. Humphreys of the Corps of Engineers. King could expect to receive $100,000 to finance the work over three years, and engage two assistant geologists, three topographic aides, two specimen collectors, a photographer, and needed camp assistants. King's directions, which he drew up himself, included a dizzying list of activities that included the examination of all rock formations, mountain ranges, detrital plains, coal deposits, soils, minerals, ores, and saline and alkaline deposits. His team would make barometric and thermometric observations, collect plant and animal specimens, and establish the necessary data points for a topographic map.

"Now, Mr. King," the secretary of war told him, "the sooner you get out of Washington, the better—you are too young a man to be seen about town with this appointment in your pocket—there are four major-generals who want your place." Powell would be a beneficiary of King's precedent-setting work when he received an appropriation of $10,000 in July 1870 for his second Colorado trip. Civilian geologist Ferdinand Hayden would also vie for congressional dollars to survey the West. The army's topographical corps was not about to abandon its long exploring traditions either. Lieutenant George Montague Wheeler of the Corps of Engineers would also enter the fray. These four charismatic men would clash and compete, setting off a fierce, sometimes vituperative arms race for the chance to direct scientific surveying after the war. Their personalities and passions would deeply shape American science as it emerged after the war, and their competition would turn cutthroat: They would badmouth one another, steal one another's talent, and compete for limited appropriations. Much lay on the line. The high stakes would soon put the four on a dangerous collision course.

Officially, the federal government had given the four authority for the rather straightforward task of exploring and surveying the West. Congressmen viewed them as little more than instruments of plain aggrandizement who served as the cutting-edge truth seekers of Manifest Destiny. The mountain men, railroad captains, westward-traveling journalists and editors, and politicians each had a self-interested take on the still little known West. But the surveyors would serve as far more than mere wayfinders across a largely still alien landscape. They would become explainers and interpreters of lands that defied easy understanding, and had yet to find purchase in the American imagination. In every report, map drawn, or photograph framed and captioned, they shared their vision of the West, how best it could fit into the larger emerging consciousness of a truly continental nation. Their findings might launch new gold rushes, stimulate entire new economies, and open new frontiers of wealth and prosperity.

The search for scientific fame and fortune certainly motivated these four players, but, more important, their main competition revolved around an argument that would form one of the most significant struggles in America for the three decades after the Civil War, a contest over the nation's very soul. Would America develop her rich, promising western lands with the public interest in mind or hand development over to selected, well-connected, and wealthy individuals to exploit, and worry about the consequences later? How would the federal surveys choose to assess the economic value of public lands larger than European empires? And how would that influence the General Land Office, the bureau in which America distributed its land to its citizens?

Powell came late to the game, after the other three had already secured large annual appropriations, an underfunded dark horse who at first glimpse did not stand a chance of surviving against the others. Although famous for his river trip, he had published nothing from his expedition aside from some letters to newspapers. But the Major had been underestimated before. The new competition would stoke the furnace in which Powell would hone and develop new keen ideas. He had something the others did not: a developing large-scale vision of what exactly was at stake.

In 1869, when Powell and his nine men started down the Colorado for the first time—and as King prosecuted his survey west into Utah—the geologist Ferdinand Hayden received a large appropriation and leadership of the United States Geological Survey of the Territories, the next great federal survey after King's. Hayden's star had risen two years earlier as Nebraska had gained statehood. Funds designated for the now-defunct territorial legislature lay unspent, prompting Congress to decide that these $5,000 might best be used for a survey of the state. When the Smithsonian's Spencer Baird learned this, he contacted Hayden, then a professor of mineralogy and geology at the Medical Department of the University of Pennsylvania, who had served as a Civil War surgeon. Baird had known him before the war when the ambitious medical student had devoted summers to collecting fossils out west. Hayden took his degree, but never seriously considered going into practice, spending the next seven years privately exploring the geology and geography of the upper plains, cleverly winning patronage from the American Fur Company, the Smithsonian, and the U.S. Army Corps of Topographical Engineers. "I feel as though I could endure cheerfully any amount of toil, hardship and self-denial provided I could gratify my strong desire to labor in the field as a naturalist," explained the excited twenty-three-year-old.

He often traveled alone through dangerous Sioux lands collecting fossils. The Indians left this strange figure alone, naming him "He Who Picks Up Stones Running." Hayden wandered beyond the Dakota Badlands and the Black Hills to explore the Yellowstone River and the Missouri's major tributaries in Montana. Hayden sent natural history specimens back east to Baird, as well as fossils to academies in St. Louis and Philadelphia, particularly to his mentor, the University of Pennsylvania's Joseph Leidy. The soft-spoken Leidy had shocked scientific circles in 1847 by uncovering evidence that the horse had once thrived in prehistoric North America before going extinct.

The Late Cretaceous dinosaur teeth and bones that Hayden sent from Montana enabled Leidy to identify many new species, notably the duck-billed dinosaur and armored ankylosaur, firmly establishing dinosaur paleontology in America. Recognizing raw talent, Baird set Hayden up in a Smithsonian Castle office during the off season, and secured him positions on two military explorations of the upper Missouri just before the war broke out. Hayden's impatient, confrontational style, however, had already begun to grate on other scientists. He made no friends when he waged a bitter war of words and influence over rather obscure boasting rights about who first discovered Permian rocks in America.

Born out of wedlock to an alcoholic father, Hayden grew up poor and suffered frequent humiliations, developing within him a ruthless ambition and unsleeping restlessness. The notorious womanizer exhibited impatience bordering on rudeness, his self-promotion at times embarrassing to those around him. Nonetheless many admired him for his energetic and consuming curiosity, which left few others better able to communicate the sheer excitement of the western lands.

With Baird's support, Hayden became head geologist of the Geological Survey of Nebraska, during which he exhibited a striking ability to win over powerful men. He would grow into the job, and expand his survey into the largest, most famous of the postwar years, eclipsing even King's. Like Powell, Hayden excelled at cobbling funds and patronage into ever larger projects.

In the spring of 1871, Hayden attended a lecture in Washington by a Montanan who had explored the upper Yellowstone the year before, returning with breathtaking accounts of bizarre geothermal features. The speaker urged that this strange area become a park of some kind. Hayden was intrigued. In 1860, Hayden had traveled with Jim Bridger, the legendary mountain man, who told him wild stories of Yellowstone's exploding mudholes, boiling springs, and a mountain of yellow rock and glass. Few had believed him, so wild were his descriptions. But with the recent story appearing in *Scribner's Monthly* and Congress now starting to pay attention, Hayden saw a ripe opportunity. It was time for a formal federal survey to visit Yellowstone—and, of course, he should lead it. Relying on his already strong congressional connections, he pressed the idea and Congress bit, increasing his appropriation from $25,000 to $40,000. Congress would not be disappointed with this outlay.

In the summer of 1871, Hayden enlisted a highly talented retinue—the photographer William H. Jackson and the topographical artist William H. Holmes, and painter Henry W. Elliott, who was the private secretary of the Smithsonian's Joseph Henry. Then a piece of luck fell into Hayden's lap. The thirty-four-year-old landscape artist Thomas Moran was also desperate to get out to see Yellowstone for himself. The painter borrowed funds from railroad financier Jay Cooke as well as the editor of *Scribner's*, the latter in return for a pledge to deliver watercolors. An agent of Cooke's asked Hayden whether Moran might accompany him.

With the painter's expenses already covered, Hayden agreed. The cadaverous artist, weighing only 110 pounds, had never ridden a horse before, but his oils of Yellowstone's odd features would create a sensation back East and vault Hayden into star status.

During that summer of 1871, Hayden conducted a first mapping of the Upper Yellowstone. But it would be Jackson's stunning photographs, along with a satchel full of Moran's work, published in *Scribner's* and passed around to congressmen, which, with Hayden's strong lobbying efforts and support from well-placed friends, would move Congress to enact a bill making Yellowstone America's first national park. President Grant signed the bill into law on March 2, 1872. In later years, Hayden would claim near sole credit for the park's creation—a huge overstatement, yet it is unlikely that without Hayden's work that this unprecedented initiative would have passed through the Congress that spring. Moran worked up a monumental 7-by-12-foot canvas of Yellowstone Canyon, which Congress would buy for $10,000—the entire amount that the body had voted Powell for his surveying activities in 1870.

In 1872 Hayden was back in Yellowstone for a second season, the same year that King had completed his field survey work along the 40th parallel. But Hayden had no intention of wrapping up his survey, cleverly defining his objectives only in the widest possible terms as parts of a "Survey of the Territories." By 1872, ten western territories still remained unsurveyed. "General Garfield told Governor Potts and other citizens of the West that my exploration would be continued as long as there was any of the public domain to be explored, so we might as well strike out as free as we can," wrote Hayden.

The third entrant into the federal survey contest, the twenty-four-year-old Lieutenant Wheeler of the Corps of Engineers, had graduated from West Point in 1866. The world's best-trained army had demobilized quickly, its million soldiers melting away to barely twenty-five thousand regulars by 1867. Few academy graduates chose an army career, their chances for advancement and glory limited in the Reconstruction era to Indian fighting and enforcement duty in the South. But Wheeler, who graduated sixth in his class, decided to stay on anyway, becoming an assistant engineer on the Point Lobos survey around San Francisco Bay.

In 1869, Wheeler, while not yet in command of his own survey, rode twenty-four thousand miles throughout southeastern Nevada and western Utah to find an efficient route for moving troops from the northwest to the Arizona Territory. He did so, and his report included the suggestion for a general military survey of the western territories. The civilian scientists' maps, he argued, were "controlled by the theoretical considerations of the geologists." Army maps would provide only practical information. Geologic and natural history would be treated as "incidental to the main purpose." Wheeler would become the U.S. Army's champion against the civilian savants now inflexibly asserting their rights to survey and map the west.

The Corps of Engineers approved a $50,000 budget for Wheeler in 1871, with the authority to hire ten assistants, and further employees not to exceed thirty. The authorization unleashed a whirling dervish: That year, Wheeler and his teams would cover an astounding 72,250 square miles across southern and central Nevada, eastern California, southwestern Utah, and much of Arizona. Wheeler raced across Death Valley, even though the Briers Party had explored it as far back as 1849, driving his men to exhaustion, he himself admitting that marches had often "extended from fifty to sixty or even eighty hours, with scarcely a single halt." He did not hesitate to invoke the strict articles of war to enforce discipline. Stories emerged in the press of Wheeler's leaning hard on the Indians, including a report that he tied four Native American guides to the ground so they would lower their demands. When one got loose under the sweltering sun, Wheeler's men just shot him. Other stories whispered of men gone mysteriously missing, perhaps murdered by an unknown hand, and of a young Indian boy strung up by the thumbs. Perhaps some of these tales were told by someone with an ax to grind—and certainly fewer enterprises ranked tougher that running a survey in the American West, but such charges of bad management and racism boiled up everywhere Wheeler led his men. In October 1871, he left the surveys for two days with two prospectors, visiting thirty mining locations and staking his own claims.

After his race through the Mojave desert, Wheeler turned to challenge Powell directly by pushing up the Colorado. Powell had yet to publish the results of his 1869 trip, and so perhaps Wheeler felt the region fair game. Three flat-bottomed boats arrived at Camp Mojave from San Francisco close to the point where the Colorado passes into California. Thirty-five men, including geologist G. K. Gilbert, the photographer Timothy O'Sullivan, whom Wheeler had borrowed from Hayden, and a number of Mojave Indians started out on September 16, 1871, intending to work their way up into the Grand Canyon as far as Diamond Creek. Powell had already covered this stretch going downstream, and Lieutenant Ives had already bulled his way upriver. Perhaps Wheeler feigned ignorance that Powell's second expedition would row downriver again that season. He may have placed too much stock in James White's story of washing downriver—and that determined upstream boaters could make their way. He may have dismissed Ives's and Powell's stories of rough water, feeling that a strictly disciplined enterprise could complete the task. More darkly, he probably intended to usurp Powell's work. Wheeler simply wanted to crush the competition.

The river quickly beat any exultation right out of Wheeler and his men. Weary and demoralized, they reached Diamond Creek thirty-three days after starting out, having rowed, but more often dragged and shoved, their boats two hundred miles upstream. A little over a week before they finished, one of the boats swamped in a rapid. Wheeler lost the stout case in which he kept all his personal papers, including the expedition's astronomical and meteorological observations. Only Wheeler's threats and Gilbert's persistence kept the expedition pressing on overland, and now on reduced rations.

Once back at Camp Mojave, Wheeler sent O'Sullivan to Washington with his glass plates to show the politicians about their trip. But nearly all three hundred of them broke in transit. Despite his negligible success, Wheeler brashly reported to Congress that "the exploration of the Colorado River may now be considered complete," an odd statement considering Ives's and Powell's efforts—but he directed a growing army, intent on recovering what the army claimed by right.

In America, the Gilded Age was blossoming. In an 1871 newspaper essay, Mark Twain satirically proposed that the chief end of man was in getting rich. What's the best way? he quipped. "Dishonestly if we can; honestly if we must." Few examples better illustrate the Gilded Age's hunger for quick, fabulous wealth that the West appeared to offer than the Great Diamond Hoax. In 1871, two Kentucky hucksters walked into the office of a prominent San Francisco businessman carrying a bag of diamonds, which they claimed to have found in Colorado. They swore him to silence, but the secret, just as the two men planned, lasted only seconds after they left. Selling interests in the diamond fields, the pair themselves bought more rough-cut diamonds and rubies, then salted a remote, unnamed Colorado field. Smelling chicanery, Clarence King carefully read a report about the so-called discovery by mineralogist Henry Janin, deducing that "there was only one place . . . which answered to the description," and it lay within the confines of his 40th parallel survey. King located the spot with several of his men, discovering that some of the jewels were in anthills and that they carried cut marks on them. King brought his findings to San Francisco. "We have escaped, thanks to GOD and CLARENCE KING, a great financial calamity," crowed the San Francisco *Morning*

Bulletin on November 27, 1872. Had the hoax gone undiscovered, the paper continued, no less than 12 million dollars' worth of stock would have gone on the market.

In the early summer of 1872, Congress appropriated $75,000 to fund the U.S. Geographical Survey West of the 100th Meridian, under Lieutenant Wheeler. Four national surveys now operated in the western lands. And many people were paying attention to what they were finding.

That spring, in the wake of the landmark Yellowstone legislation, but before heading west for the second leg of the river trip, Powell had set his sights on luring Moran away from Hayden. It had not taken long for the national surveyors to realize the importance of taking artists and photographers along with them. As Powell had discovered with his stereographs, visuals could turn congressmen into supporters far faster than written reports. Visual documentation also served a greater function in educating the public about these exotic lands. Based only on scattered accounts of explorers and a handful of illustrations, long before the photography of Ansel Adams, the filmmaking of John Ford, the stories of Zane Grey, or the frontier thesis of Frederick Jackson Turner, Americans to the east and south had virtually nothing by which to comprehend the scope, detail, and raw intensity of the American West. For most it remained vaguely alien and dangerous, perhaps unable to be assimilated into the national story. Americans needed someone to explain the West to them, not only to discern more clearly what it contained but to interpret its very significance.

The American public hungered to learn more. By the 1870s, more than four thousand inexpensive weekly magazines had appeared, the beneficiary of railroad delivery, cheap postal routes, availability of the cylinder printing press, and rising literacy rates. The first illustrated story from the great surveys came out several weeks after Powell completed his first voyage. *Harper's*

New Monthly Magazine published "Photographs from the High Rockies"—thirteen wooden engravings describing the travels of John Samson—the pen name of Timothy O'Sullivan—with King's 40th Parallel Survey since 1867.

Powell had watched Hayden's annual appropriation increase and Wheeler poach on his territory. He needed to move boldly. On May 22, 1872, he offered Moran the chance to join him out west so that he might create a fitting painting of the Grand Canyon. Powell could pay $500 for a trip to last four months and cover his railroad ticket from Chicago to Salt Lake City. Wheeler also approached Moran with an offer.

The following month Moran sent a note declining Powell's invitation. He had already committed to illustrating a chapter of the book *Picturesque America*. He also turned down Wheeler, as well as Hayden's invitation to the Grand Tetons. But he did keep Hayden apprised of his interest in joining him the following summer. Like a good negotiator, he dropped the hint that Powell tried to lure him away with "great inducements." But Hayden did not yet consider Powell a threat. His play for Moran seemed the work of an ill-funded wannabe.

Tensions ratcheted up in early 1873. After spending several hours with Hayden in January, Garfield wrote in his diary: "I am troubled to know what to do with the large number of exploring expeditions Congress has on hand." He mused that "there should be a consolidation of all the geological and geographical expedition[s] in their work under one head." Hayden understood that events pointed toward a showdown—and only one surveyor would come out on top. "The Engineer Bureau is the only real foe we have," he wrote to a recent survey recruit in February 1873. With King's present work closing, he and Wheeler were in head-to-head competition to determine whether the War Department or the Department of the Interior would control the federal surveys. Eight days after Garfield's worried diary entry, Hayden wrote his boss, Secretary of the Interior Columbus Delano, formally requesting $100,000 for the 1874 field season, unilaterally switching his efforts from the sources of the Missouri and Yellowstone rivers to Colorado. He knew Wheeler had shifted his survey into southern Colorado—and wanted to get there first. In the letter, he attributed the change of plans to the large expense of working in an area without railroad transportation. He also complained about the hostility of the Indians, who had attacked one of his survey divisions the past season in Wyoming, although no lives or property had been lost. The bold letter glossed over far more significant strategic reasons for the realignment. He must confront Wheeler, he felt, or his congressional funding might dry up. The maw he must feed annually demanded that he deliver new, colorful discoveries, and he had already plucked the ripest fruit from his seasons surveying Yellowstone. Colorado would give him new fields of discovery. If he played it right, Colorado would extend his survey and guarantee him continued support for years to come.

As Hayden planned for the summer of 1873, he decided to send one of his surveying divisions, accompanied by Jackson the photographer, down the Green and Colorado to the Grand Canyon, yet another challenge to Powell. He mentioned the idea of visiting the Grand Canyon to Moran, which thrilled the painter. Moran could use Jackson's images to create drawings, or they could serve as research toward perhaps a new large oil to rival the Yellowstone painting. "I saw Wheeler's photos from the Grand Cañon of the Colorado today," Moran wrote Hayden in May. "They are poor and Jackson will knock spots out of them."

That spring, Hayden abruptly pulled Jackson and a team from visiting the Grand Canyon, sending them instead to Colorado's high peaks, part of his strategy to beat out Wheeler. He told the acting assistant surgeon general of the United States to pass along a curt message: "You can tell Wheeler that if he stirs a finger, or attempts to interfere with me or my survey in any way, I will utterly crush him—as I have enough congressional influence to do so, and will bring it all to bear." That summer, Hayden's and Wheeler's men literally came to blows. In Colorado's South Park on July 9, a Wheeler survey team headed by Lieutenant William Marshall encountered one led by Hayden's men. According to Marshall, the parties agreed to operate on opposite sides of the upper Arkansas River. But he claimed Hayden's men had ignored the agreement. The two parties closed upon one another and fists flew.

When he had raced out of town in June to resume his survey, Hayden neglected to bid farewell to a now thoroughly miffed Moran. "Under the impression that you would go [to the Grand Canyon]," wrote the painter, "I made a number of contracts to furnish pictures of the region. . . ." Hayden had left him in an embarrassing predicament. With regret, he wrote, though his tone does not suggest it, he would instead accompany Major Powell. Even though Powell had left long ago for the West, his offer to Moran remained open; he may even have upped the inducements.

This good turn of events for Powell came just in time. While peddling a book about the 1869 expedition, Powell had received an editor's note that such a manuscript would need full-page engravings and vignettes to make the book more publishable. The Riverside Press editors looked nervously on Powell's thick prose and heavy emphasis on geology. Moran's sketches would change that. When the painter went west, he did so with a passel of commissions: "70 drawings for Powell, 40 for Appleton, 4 for Aldine, 20 for Scribner's . . ."

Two months after Dellenbaugh sent the map back east in February 1873, Powell traveled west to Salt Lake City to set up the next phase of his survey. On the way he received a telegram from Secretary Delano that would significantly alter the summer's survey plans. Delano had appointed him a special Indian commissioner, and charged him, along with southern Nevada Indian agent George Ingalls, with evaluating the "conditions and wants" of the Utah and Nevada Indians and making recommendations on reservation policy. President Grant's Peace Policy had fallen apart after Modoc Indians had murdered a U.S. general in southeastern Oregon. Delano feared that the violence would spread into the southwest. In Washington Powell had reassured him that the Pauite and Ute were unlikely to mobilize in force against the whites, but the secretary remained unconvinced.

From the outset, Delano's task proved a tall order. Assembling a formal census of the southwestern Indians was daunting enough, but putting together a coherent legal and humane policy for settling the Utes (Utah), Paiutes (Utah, northern Arizona, southern Nevada), Shoshones (Idaho and Utah), and western Shoshones (Nevada) into reservations verged on the impossible. But Ingalls and Powell turned to their task with energy, traveling throughout Utah in May and June to many places without railroad or stage lines. The commissioners divided up in September, Powell to Las Vegas, Ingalls to southern Nevada. All told, they identified more than one hundred tribes, each independently governed and named, counting 10,437 individuals, half already living on reservations. Powell took along photographer Jack Hillers. Although later criticized for questionable practices—Hillers and Powell were not averse to providing some of the poorer Paiute with colorful headdresses and clothing for their portraits—the images form an important documentation of the southwestern Indians on the cusp of tumultuous change. Powell also amassed considerable ethnographic and linguistic material. If he worried that his work for the commission would subtract from his survey efforts while Hayden and Wheeler furiously prosecuted their own, he never showed it. Increasingly Powell had been drawn to ethnology—and this opportunity gave him an ideal chance to put that interest to practice.

Although tired from the hard travel and countless councils required of his commission work that spring and summer, Powell met Moran and *New York Times* reporter Justin Colburn at Salt Lake City in July. After securing interviews with Brigham Young and a number of elders, the small party set out south along the Wasatch range. The skinny but wiry Moran, in a full blond beard and wearing his trademark black felt bowler, took cheerfully to the hard life on horseback or in a Mormon farm wagon behind two mules. After a grueling climb up Mount Nebo—then considered the Utah Territory's highest peak—from which they could almost see the Grand Canyon's rim, Moran reported, "It was the most magnificent sight of my life," strong words indeed for someone who had seen Yellowstone and Yosemite. After returning to base camp, all but the painter got sick and vomited from the exertion and altitude. Moran pointed out with satisfaction that even Powell himself had retched.

Powell sent Moran and Colburn on ahead with teamsters bringing supplies to Kanab, telegraphing to Thompson and Hillers to take the painter and correspondent to the next Mormon town of Grafton, to see the great West Temple of the Virgin, an immense natural edifice of naked rock, which shimmered in the summer sun. They rode up the Virgin River and thence to Mu-koon-tu-weap, more commonly known by the Mormons as Little Zion. Moran's sketches, soon after to appear in *The Aldine* magazine, became the first published images of what would become Zion National Park nearly a half century later.

Powell broke away from his work—this time with the Pahvant Ute—to rejoin Moran in Kanab, intent on guiding the painter to the Major's favorite distant prospect of the Canyon. On August 14, they headed south across the desert into the Arizona Strip, then climbed into the high forest of the Kaibab Plateau, which Powell knew well, then toward a small plateau connected to the north rim by a narrow isthmus known as Muab Saddle. After negotiating this, the team climbed up Powell Plateau, an eight-square-mile thumb of mesa jutting out into the Canyon, a veritable sky island of Ponderosa pine. A mile below curves the river, a seeming afterthought in this grandly sculpted landscape. On the Canyon's far side rises the San Francisco range, while a twenty- to thirty-mile view stretches both up and down the Canyon. "The whole gorge for miles lay beneath us," wrote Moran to his wife, "and it was by far the most awfully grand and impressive scene that I have ever yet seen."

Colburn declared himself equally awestruck, then wrote, clearly prompted by Powell's eloquent characterizations of what they were seeing: "And yet the force that has wrought so wonderfully through periods unknown, unmeasured, and unmeasurable, is a river 3000 feet below." Ever the teacher, Powell explained and analyzed, offering his observations and singling out features far in the distance with his good arm, and describing how erosion over millions of years had shaped this impossible landscape. Moran hurried home eager to get to work on his commissions, declining Powell's offer to take him into the Canyon for a water's-edge vantage.

That fall, Powell returned to Washington to complete the commission report, which he submitted on December 1, 1873, to the secretary of the interior. A thoughtful, reasoned document, the report argued against the military policing of Indians, recommending instead that committed civilians protect and oversee the reservations—which should not be "looked upon in the light of a pen where a horde of savages are to be fed with flour and beef, to be supplied with blankets from the Government bounty, and to be furnished with paint and gewgaws by the greed of traders, but that a reservation should be a school of industry and a home for these unfortunate people." Here the practical reformer shines through, Powell arguing that the government should provide conditions under which Indians could learn to live productive lives. A man of his Victorian times, Powell regarded their customs as barbaric. Indians could move toward civilization and enlightenment only by forsaking their hunter-gatherer traditions and becoming self-sustaining farmers. Paternalistic to be sure, yet his views encompassed a genuine concern for these uprooted people and revealed a sympathy often seriously lacking in that day. To attain such Indian independence, he argued, the federal government must go beyond giving out blankets. It must buy out white settlers who squatted on prime cropland and controlled critical water supplies. The commission's report advocated enlarging some of the reservations so that some tribes long hostile to one another would not have to live in proximity.

But the reservations never saw the commission's recommended compensation. The white men would not leave the lawfully designated Indian reservation land, nor did the Indians come. Powell would reveal some of his anger and frustration in a letter in the summer of 1878 to the commissioner of Indian affairs: "The promises made by Mr. Ingalls and myself have not been fulfilled . . . I am constrained to protest against their neglect and against a course which must sooner or later result in serious trouble." Solving the so-called Indian Question remained out of reach by any single person, even for someone such as Powell, whom the Smithsonian's Spencer Baird described as knowing "more about the live Indian than any live man."

While the commission work may not have spurred much federal action, it had a bracing effect on Powell's interest in ethnology. Whereas before he had concentrated on collecting, whether of stone axes or words, he now worked on knitting together the relationships of Indian words, and furthermore generally assembling their "systems of consanguinity," a term very recently coined by another pioneering ethnologist. Powell also began to discern the lines of evolution of Indian myth, poetry, art, language, and religion. The following year, Powell would request—for the first time—a specific congressional appropriation to prepare an ethnological report. Although only $3,000, it would mark a personal commitment to so recently an invisible science, which would only continue to grow, until he founded the Smithsonian's Bureau of Ethnology in 1879. He would turn this tiny initiative into one of the world's premier anthropological organizations.

On April 30, 1874, Thomas Moran's huge painting of the Grand Canyon went on public display in Newark, New Jersey. The contrast between this and his equally large oil of Yellowstone could not be more distinct. In the Yellowstone work, blue skies shine brightly above sunlit rocks; in the foreground, two human figures view Yellowstone's Lower Falls and blue-watered river. Conversely, few would call Moran's Grand Canyon scene beautiful: A dark abyss drops away just feet from where the painter has situated the viewer. Stunted dead trees, cacti, and shrublike plants cling to a rocky ledge. A small snake writhes on the rock, while the tiny shadow of a bird appears faintly in the far distance. Life is peripheral here, brushed off to the side and permanently insignificant. Immense rock pillars, buttes, boulders, and sheer rock faces dominate every prospect. In the mid-ground, storm clouds unleash torrents of rain that lash the rock and throw up vaporous clouds. Boulders in the foreground appear ready at any moment to topple into the chasm. Although this rockscape has an eternal quality, the landscape appears dynamic, a patch of blue sky in the upper right corner suggests the passing of the storm. While not beautiful, the scene, like the Canyon itself, inspires awe. The Irish intellectual Edmund Burke once drew a distinction between beauty and sublimity—and few other vistas illustrate his point better than the Grand Canyon. Beauty delivers thoughts of wonder and joy, while sublimity brings unsettling, often frightening, emotions. And yet, as Burke pointed out, contemplating the sublime can awaken deep joys beyond reason.

Of all of America's natural spectacles, from the sweep of the mile-wide Mississippi and Denali's peak cutting the heavens to the thunderous roar of Niagara Falls and California's groves of towering redwoods, nothing but the ocean itself matches the Grand Canyon in its sheer, incomprehensible power and scale. A mountain range becomes visible long before a visitor reaches its base, but the Canyon confronts its visitor abruptly. One can stroll to within ten yards of its lip and still not know it is there. A newcomer experiences the Canyon's gaping absence and dizzying drop-off like a slap in the face—no poetry comes to mind, but rather one feels an over-whelming sense of the raw, primeval, and vertiginous—as if one is a voyeur peeking at some unfinished handiwork of God. Only after some minutes does the Canyon's true scope force itself upon the visitor with a sort of mild horror. By 1874, still only a handful of Americans had experienced the Canyon in person, but now, for the first time, a talented artist had brought the Canyon to life in brilliant color on canvas.

Early critical comments of Moran's painting were mixed. Clarence Cook in the *Atlantic Monthly* repeatedly compared the painting with Dante's portrayal of hell, observing that "here, there is no loveliness for hundreds of miles, nor anything on which the healthy human eye can bear to look (the scientific eye excepted), and this scene is only the concentrated ghastliness of a ghastly region." Yet something did touch Cook deeply enough to acknowledge the Canyon's grandeur in a scene appearing as if the "raging ocean had suddenly turned to stone." With Moran's painting, so deeply influenced by Powell's thinking, ideas about the Grand Canyon's worth would begin to change.

White men, from the conquistador Don García López de Cárdenas, who stared down into the Grand Canyon in 1540 and rapidly looked away, to the West Point surveyors who did so just before the Civil War, all deemed the Canyon worthless—hostile even—and to be avoided at all costs. Powell would claim and unveil the Grand Canyon as a national treasure through his tireless advocacy in his writings, his congressional lobbying, and as a result of his hiring renowned painters, photographers, and illustrators. He would give the nation what it needed to "see" this New World's new world. "It seems as if a thousand battles had been fought on the plains below," he wrote, "and on every field the giant heroes had built a monument compared with which the pillar on Bunker Hill is but a mile stone. But no human hand has placed a block in all those wonderful treasures. The rain drops of unreckoned ages have cut them all from the solid rock."

Indeed Powell gave Americans a way of coming to terms with this frightening chasm, a way to understand it—and begin not only to appreciate it, but come to regard it as one of nature's most stupendous displays. Only then could it become "our" Grand Canyon, and perhaps America's most iconic natural feature. Only a man of outsized imagination, immense powers of communication, and burning curiosity could spread the word about this nearly incomprehensible, gigantic feature into American visual consciousness—something that all could wrap their heads around, and embrace as their own. This former vision of desolation now emerged as a distinctive, American landscape, which reflected a further sense of the nation's growing understanding of itself as exceptional.

When the organizers of the Centennial Exposition in Philadelphia requested that the Capitol loan them Moran's two great canvases, they wrote, "[W]e do not know of any paintings about this Capitol which are more characteristic, which are more strictly national, which would be more interesting or more instructive to submit to foreigners visiting this country than those pictures of Moran." The *Chasm* would hang in the Senate for years, then eventually make its way to the Smithsonian American Art Museum, where it is today.

Yet even so, the passage that the Grand Canyon would undergo to become one of the most-visited and iconic of America's national parks would take time. Whereas Yellowstone became a park only a few years after Hayden's visit and survey, the Grand Canyon would not become a national park until 1919, fifty years after Powell's first visit. Part of this had to do with the Canyon's sublimity.

Powell returned that fall of 1873 to find a subdued capital. The postwar boom had finally crashed in September, setting off the Panic of 1873. Between 1866 and 1873, the nation had seen 35,000 miles of new track built, railroads becoming the nation's second-largest employer, only after agriculture. This new business required high levels of risk taking, not just in laying rails over insufficiently known terrain, but in building a massive national infrastructure, so large as to require federal government intervention in the form of liberal land grants and subsidies. In modern parlance, the railroad sector had become a "bubble," which burst when the banking firm of Jay Cooke and Company, a federal agent in the government financing of railroad construction, declared bankruptcy in September. Other overextended banks and companies collapsed: 89 of the 364 railroads failed, as did 18,000 other businesses, within two years. By 1876, unemployment had soared to 14 percent. The depression, exacerbated by European monetary policies, would extend through 1880.

The often overlapping work of the three remaining federal surveys still in the field—King had wrapped up his fieldwork by 1872—could not help but come under congressional scrutiny in these increasingly lean times. In May 1874, the House Committee on Public Lands launched an inquiry, known as the Townsend Hearings, into the duplication of federal surveying. The details of the Wheeler-Hayden feud now became public. Hayden came out swinging: ". . . as far as my own party was concerned, it was generally rumored and believed that the avowed purpose of Lieutenant Wheeler in coming into Colorado was to precipitate a conflict which had been hanging over us for three years." The two prideful principals would stain the hearings with name calling, Wheeler attacking Hayden as "unable to perform, or intelligently direct" the data gathering necessary, while Hayden charged back that it had not been "the love of science, but of power, that has induced [Wheeler] to precipitate this conflict." The proceedings quickly turned into a referendum on whether military engineers or civilian scientists could more effectively manage a consolidated survey. Powell quietly stepped into the proceedings, and began methodically to undermine the army's case,

Wheeler, Hayden, and the army's chief of engineers, General Andrew A. Humphreys, underwent a full week of contentious testimony, the record revealing a growing confusion among the congressmen about the details of surveying, which they had earlier regarded as a simple process. Wheeler's testimony came off as angry and belligerent, dismissive of any congressmen's interest in matters of which they knew little. He flat-out refused to even outline War Department policy. When Powell took the stand one Monday morning, he extended a guiding hand to the committee: "I have therefore brought a blackboard for the purpose of drawing diagrams for illustration." The congressmen watched as Powell fell comfortably into his role of intense but dispassionate professor, his chalk clacking and flying across the board, dust settling over his wool suit.

He lucidly explained Wheeler's archaic technique of "meandering," which relied on rolling an odometer or simply counting the steps of a horse, and compared it with the highly exact modern method of triangulation, perfected by Clarence King, and now adopted by him and Hayden. The War Department, including Wheeler's survey, had simply not embraced modern surveying techniques and technology. Wheeler's astronomic work, Powell conceded, "ranks with the best that has ever been done in this country . . ." but then he inquired whether he might show the bemused committee "why his map is so inaccurate as not to be available for geological purposes." On the blackboard there appeared a cross-section of the Pangwitch Canyon, a river gorge cutting through volcanic rock, which showed economically why Wheeler's technique could not describe it accurately. He also illustrated a plain to the southwest, reputed to contain rich coal beds. Wheeler's map, Powell calmly demonstrated, displaced the location of the beds, thus giving the impression that the coal lay under 2,500 feet of sandstone, limestone, and shale. In reality, the beds lay on the hillsides, many of them already claimed and opened by settlers. Powell backed off slightly, adding that Wheeler had probably not intended to create an accurate topographic representation of the country, but rather a general sense that the country was broken and mountainous.

During the previous field season, Wheeler had covered a prodigious 72,500 square miles in four states and territories. A geologist who would quit Wheeler's survey to join Powell's a month later would complain about the speed of his old chief's surveying. "To study the structure of a region under such circumstances was to read a book while its pages were quickly turned by another, and the result was a larger collection of impressions than of facts," G. K. Gilbert wrote. In Wheeler's surveys, the business of surveying roads and finding clear routes for supply trains trumped all else.

Powell argued that no great unexplored region remained in the United States, so such exploring surveying expeditions were no longer necessary. Powell implied that the army-surveying era had ended. "A more thorough method, or a survey proper, is now demanded," he added in case the congressmen had missed it. The growing nation needed tools that the army could no longer provide.

The Townsend Hearings censured Wheeler and Hayden for bad manners, but declined to recommend any wholesale changes or consolidation. Competition among various surveys—as long as it remained civil—encouraged good work, the committee stated; and more survey teams could cover greater swaths of ground more quickly. President Grant's support of Wheeler and the army's role in surveying probably shielded this officer for the short term. However, the days of army participation in surveying and mapmaking neared an end. Congress shifted Powell's survey from the Smithsonian to the Interior Department, ostensibly under Hayden's auspices, although Powell did not report to him directly.

But Hayden would soon recognize with a growing sense of alarm that Powell, not Wheeler, stood as the biggest obstacle to his securing the job of running a consolidated survey.

In this competitive environment, the pressure to publish grew extreme. Hayden's office would push out hundreds of volumes in the 1870s. Before the Townsend Hearings in 1873, James Garfield, now the House Appropriations Committee chair, asked Powell why he had not published a history of the original exploration of the Grand Canyon. The Major answered that he had no interest in publishing it as a work of adventure, but rather as a work of science. Garfield gently chastised him, saying that he must either submit a report or lose funding altogether.

Powell believed somewhat naively that all interest in his 1869 expedition had faded after the explosion of daily press articles. Unlike Clarence King, who missed no opportunity to weave his personal experiences into a clear, powerful western epic, Powell rarely sought to write—or speak—about himself. Even given a healthy ego and strong if rather impersonal ambitions, Powell unemotionally let science override any desire to put him at the center of a story. Indeed, he had never felt comfortable in the media-bestowed guise of a hero, even though his fame enabled him to conduct further scientific investigations. This, along with his intensely private temperament—he rarely, if ever, gave others any chance to gain purchase on his inner life—misled many, who came then to regard him as a wooden titan or haughty patrician. Such two-dimensional sketches obstruct any full understanding of Powell to this day.

The pressure for Powell to publish his account grew even more intense in mid-April 1874 when *Appleton's* printed the photographer E. O. Beaman's account of the second river expedition. No one else from Powell's first or second river ventures had yet published accounts besides letters. Even though the prickly photographer had only accompanied the first leg of the second expedition, entirely missing the Grand Canyon, publication in such a popular venue finally moved Powell to pursue a publisher more aggressively. Riverside Press, Harper Brothers, and Ticknor & Fields had all turned the project down, objecting to the author's devotion to impersonal science and far too few details of the journey itself. The publication of Beaman's nine-part series—"The Cañon of the Colorado, and the Moquis Pueblos: A Wild Boat-Ride Through the Cañons and Rapids—a Visit to the Seven Cities of the

Desert—Glimpses of Mormon Life"—coincided with the Townsend Hearings. Beaman's account included not only the river but also the same Hopi villages visited by Powell. In a real way, Beaman challenged Powell more than Wheeler by threatening to steal the thunder he needed to keep up appropriations in the face of steep competition from Hayden.

By July, Powell had finally worked out a deal with *Scribner's Monthly* for a three-part series of his own, one installment on the 1869 river journey, a second on his travels in the Arizona Strip and the Mormon settlements of southern Utah, and a third section on the Hopi, whose lifestyles appeared particularly interesting to eastern audiences.

"Please send one or two more incidents of the expedition of a bloodcurdling nature," Powell's editor pleaded. The Major no doubt bit his lip but complied. The moment when Bradley rescued him from the cliff face with his dangling long underwear—an insignificant event in Powell's eyes and one that he would prefer to forget—proved one of those sensational moments the editors craved. In Powell's and Bradley's journals, the event received only the briefest mention, but most definitely grew far more lurid on the editorial desk. *Scribner's* commissioned a woodcut of the very moment when Powell hung from Bradley's drawers. The image came entirely from the artist's imagination of things western, but with an eastern propriety: Bradley somehow remained fully clothed even after pulling off his underwear. This deeply powerful combination of courage and indignity could easily have graced the cover of a best-selling dime novel.

Even so, Powell did not buckle entirely to his editors, his mode of telling stories retaining much of his characteristic focus on task, not on personality and emotion. He certainly waxed clumsily about the beauty of the land through which he passed, but little of it could be described as personal. "You do not once (if I recollect aright)," recalled his friend Thomas Moran, "give your sensations even in the most dangerous passages, nor even hint at the terrible &

sublime feelings that are stirred within one, as he feels himself in the strong jaws of the monstrous chasms." Yet the understatement in Powell's narrative gives the story a riveting power absent in Beaman's overwrought prose.

After the hearings, Wheeler and Hayden redoubled their efforts, covering more miles and collecting yet more samples, while building ever more complex organizations. In 1874, Wheeler oversaw nine surveying parties ranging across Colorado, Utah, Arizona, and New Mexico; his complement, only down slightly from 1873, totaled eighty-nine officers and assistants. Hayden mounted much the same. As their surveys expanded, Powell made no attempt to match them, choosing instead to keep his survey small, inexpensive, but of high quality, never operating with more than six to eight professional men and a few field assistants. He restricted his survey to geology and ethnology, eschewing the expensive collecting and transportation costs associated with botany, zoology, ornithology, and paleontology. Neither did he investigate mining opportunities, or like King experiment in metallurgy or chemistry. He did not request that the government pay for the costs of transporting his men, instead still relying on the railroad's free or discounted passes. Neither did he require military escorts. For many years, Powell operated the survey out of the cramped but inexpensive confines of his M Street home.

Powell's no-nonsense focus both on physical and social science started attracting first-class talent. Tired of Wheeler's disregard for geology, G. K. Gilbert quit his survey in 1874 to sign up promptly with Powell, beginning a productive, almost brotherlike friendship that would last to the end of their lives. In 1875, Powell persuaded his old friend Ulysses S. Grant to assign him the geologist Captain Clarence Dutton, a polymath cigar-smoking lover of Macaulay and Twain. Dutton, Gilbert, and Powell would become fast friends, putting out some of the finest geological work of the late nineteenth century. One of Powell's greatest strengths lay in identifying talent that would complement his own, then giving them the widest latitude possible. Whereas Powell drew bold, intuitive geological ideas, Gilbert came up with a brilliant, if less colorful, systematization. And so, too, with Dutton, whose evocations of the geology of the Grand Canyon will never be surpassed in the minds of many.

Dutton would later recall the bond of affection and mutual confidence that connected the three men, describing their work as a labor of love. "[T]his geological wonderland was the never-ending theme of discussion; all observations and experiences were commonstock, and ideas were interchanged, amplified, and developed by mutual criticism and suggestion." These three, aided by the visual genius of Moran, and later by the illustrator William Holmes, would begin to make the Grand Canyon's deep rifts and alien landforms more and more comprehensible.

The year 1875 would prove a watershed for the Powell survey, the Major able to rely on a cadre of professional scientists for the first time. While Prof Thompson certainly understated his proper pride for his men after completing the map in 1873, writing to Powell that "we done middling for greenhorns," Powell from the early days in Colorado had drawn upon amateur talent. Now he assigned Thompson, Gilbert, and Dutton each to lead a team to the Colorado Plateau. While Wheeler's teams ranged far, wide, and thinly, and Hayden moved out of Colorado to skim other fertile fields, Powell continued to center his survey work on the plateau.

Such talent offered the added benefit of enabling Powell to focus on Washington's always uncertain politics and devote himself to getting his survey work ready for publication. In mid-June of 1875, Congress published Powell's "Exploration of the Colorado River of the West and Its Tributaries, Explored in 1869, 1870, 1871, and 1872." The original 1869 trip took up half of the book, while the rest offered chapters by Thompson on searching for the mouth of Dirty Devil, two by Powell on Colorado River Valley topography, and a third section on fauna, by scientists not part of either team. The report proved a near-instant success, the Government Printing Office going back to press almost immediately after the first three thousand copies ran out quickly. In 1895, Powell would publish the report in book form—with some changes and packed with Hillers's photographs and woodcuts of Moran's illustrations. The book would never go out of print and has become one of American history's most enduring stories of exploration.

The report, and book in some eyes, however, contains a damning flaw. Although the title mentions that the explorations took place in 1869 through 1872, the text, aside from Thompson's chapter, makes no mention of the hard work performed by those in the second expedition—indeed no direct mention of that effort at all. The omission provoked a deep bitterness, Thompson describing Powell as not "a fair and generous man—to put it mildly." In a letter to Dellenbaugh years later, he asserted that Powell "was generous, sympathetic, and possessed all the estimable qualities you and I assign him but you will notice neither you nor I speak of his justice or loyalty." This omission feeds the notion among some that Powell had little appreciation for those who worked for him.

But again, the story is more complicated. Pulling both trips into a single narrative, especially when one soared with the drama of a virgin descent while the other crawled sleepily under the methodical demands of scientific measurement, would have required more writing skills than Powell possessed. Garfield wanted details of the first expedition—as had the *Scribner's* editors—so he delivered that story.

Yet the omission does reveal elements of Powell's character, particularly his lack of interest in assigning or taking credit. Gilbert described the Major as "phenomenally fertile in ideas . . . absolutely free in their communication, with the result that many of his suggestions—a number which never can be known—were unconsciously appropriated by his associates and incorporated in their published results." In Powell's mind, everyone worked in subservience to far more powerful masters than mere ego: the greatest of them all, science and the nation. Therefore, Powell did not undertake the account to mete out credit. It simply did not occur to him to do so. His undoubted generosity in some ways was matched by a blunt indifference in others. It would have cost him nothing to acknowledge the men of the second expedition. If someone had queried him about their work, he would have responded with praise for their dedication. Nonetheless, this omission remains a black mark, a failure ultimately in leadership.

But Powell was not one to dwell in the past. While Wheeler and Hayden traded insults in front of the Townsend committee, Powell set about hijacking the agenda and taking the reins of the conversation. Just as he could see landforms where others only saw one more range of hills, Powell had begun to think far beyond what pure surveying might mean, far beyond a mere surveyor's interest in laying out roads or railroad paths, finding extractable coal or gold. His dawning realization appeared here nationally for the first time: The key to developing the West centered not so much on what evanescent treasures it contained, but rather on what it did not—water.

CHAPTER 9

A Radical Idea

When the International Centennial Exhibition in Philadelphia opened its gates on the overcast day of May 10, 1876, to commemorate the signing of the Declaration of Independence, nearly 200,000 visitors poured into the fairgrounds by the Schuylkill to commence the showiest national birthday celebration in American history. Although earlier heavy rains had turned much of the grounds into a muddy mess, it had not slowed the huge crowds flocking to the southern edge of Fairmount Park to see the Main Building—the world's largest wood, iron, and glass structure—which stretched for more than six football fields. The entire 190-building complex sported 5 main exhibition buildings and many pavilions, each of the latter devoted to such topics as women, Turkish coffee, the Bible, and cigars—in all some 30,000 exhibits. Nine foreign governments had erected structures, along with seventeen American states. Visitors could see a Nevada quartz mill and New England log house. Alexander Graham Bell demonstrated his newly patented telephone, in its first public appearance, while a young Thomas Edison exhibited an "automatic telegraph system" and "electric pen."

That first day, an engineer switched on the 1,400-horsepower Corliss steam engine, the largest ever built, its surprisingly quiet mechanism powering every exhibit in Machinery Hall, all turning on in a chorus of metallic sighs, groans, and swishes. The poet Walt Whitman stopped speechless for half an hour in front of the Corliss, bewitched by the engine's two enormous walking beams moving in quiet, perfect rhythm. Over five months, nearly ten million national and international visitors—this in a nation numbering forty-eight million souls—came to gawk at the Corliss and numerous other examples of America's muscular engineering and inventive prowess. The press of visitors so overwhelmed the whole city that one company even bought Oak Cemetery, transforming it into a campground after hastily carting away the headstones.

A modest, cross-shaped United States Government Building, while far smaller than the Main and Machinery Hall buildings, offered some of the fair's most popular exhibits. Visitors encountered a vast window composed of William Henry Jackson's photographs taken on the Hayden survey, printed on panes-of-glass positives. An *Atlantic Monthly* correspondent wrote that the "geological outlines are formidable, redoubtable, in their fantastic forms; there are horrible crags which look like fossil fungi or groups of petrified penguins of gigantic size." The West's alien outlines still confounded this viewer: "[B]eauty is overpowered by more stupendous forces, which make it a relief to return to the machines and maps to see what man can do." The integration of the West into the American consciousness had begun but was far from complete.

Hayden's survey exhibit drew the most attention of the three existing federal surveys, which all had displays at the fair. The publicity-minded Hayden had detailed Jackson to work full time on the grandly entitled United States Geological Survey exhibition. The photographer turned to the task with gusto, lining up a rich display of maps, publications, water colors, chromolithographs, and artifacts. In addition to the windows, photographs adorned the walls, and visitors could pore through albums. Jackson took great pride in his plaster models of the southern Colorado cliff dwellings he had created from photographs taken over the previous two years.

Powell devoted little effort to representing his pure survey work, although a journalist noted that silver-print photographs taken on his expeditions hung on the walls. Powell gave his energies mostly to the Smithsonian Institution section, laying out southwestern Indian artifacts, clothing, baskets, and beadwork. A contemporary guide breathlessly urged its readers to see the display in the Interior Department section, which included famous—and infamous—representations of such Indians as Captain Jack, Split Oak, Dull Hatchet, Clumsy Moccasin, "in all the glory of life-size papier-mâché and stuffing, streaked on the face with red paint. . . ." The Indian displays proved among the exposition's most popular, but evoked bitter feelings among many. The United States still had a fighting frontier.

While the exposition welcomed record crowds, events out west took a chilling turn when Lakota Sioux and Cheyenne killed Lieutenant Colonel George Custer and his main command at the Little Bighorn. That lopsided Indian victory perhaps explains some, but certainly not all, of the fury of the *Atlantic Monthly* editor W. D. Howells's comment that the Indian as represented at the exposition "is a hideous demon, whose malign traits can hardly inspire any emotion softer than abhorrence." Howells advocated the immediate extermination of the native American so that the "peaceful and industrious" Americans could get on with their nation building. Indeed, the counterpoint between the stone axes and moccasins of the American Indian and the powerful machinery of industry in Philadelphia that year left little doubt where the future of American progress lay.

While the Centennial Exhibition proved an unparalleled success, tonic for a nation still reeling from the Panic of 1873 and the consequent economic depression, the federal surveys locked ever more intensely into a struggle for survival. Talk of consolidating these three remarkably different entities into one had only grown louder since the 1874 Townsend Hearings. In these financially pressed times, Congress lacked the appetite to devote taxpayer money to support not just the four large enterprises—King still received funds to finish his publications—but also smaller autonomous surveys of the General Land Office under the Interior Department, as well as the Treasury Department's Coast and Geodetic Survey. In 1876, the House had cut funding for Wheeler's survey entirely, probably because of Hayden's lobbying, only to find the Senate restoring it. One scientist assembled a list of Colorado mountains, each bearing two separate names given by Wheeler and Hayden, respectively. That year, Congress had clipped the Powell appropriation.

But the Hayden juggernaut rolled on. The Centennial Exhibition revealed the extent to which Ferdinand Hayden outclassed Powell as publicist and raconteur. Congress simply adored Hayden, unanimously voting the funds to print his annual and final reports in ever larger numbers. His handsome *Atlas of Colorado* had appeared to a storm of positive reviews. Powell had profited out of selling Beaman's stereoscopic photographs, but this amounted to peanuts compared with the products that Hayden's machine regularly pushed out by the truckful. Hayden worked with the publisher Louis Prang to package fifteen chromolithographic prints of Moran's Yellowstone watercolors into a portfolio for sale at the Centennial. The expensive set, which included an introduction by the survey leader, won a medal. In the chute for that summer, Hayden had arranged for two of the world's most eminent botanists to accompany him on a western tour, informing all major media outlets, of course, well ahead of time. The well-respected paleontologist Charles White, who had made known his disdain for Hayden while working for Powell, joined Hayden by the promise of more funding. Hayden also started a new entomological commission.

Hayden's brilliance in public relations, however, would prove his Achilles heel in the long run, as he returned year after year to the Hill to ask for larger appropriations to match his increasingly unrealistic promises. Despite recruiting some good talent, he started turning out reports so furiously that the science and accuracy suffered considerably. Even his large field parties had grown unwieldy, forcing him to split them into as many as five divisions. Duplication and inefficiency flourished. Even so, his appropriations grew. By 1879, Congress had cumulatively appropriated $690,000 for Hayden, $368,000 for King, and $449,000 for Wheeler. Powell had received only $259,000 to date. Powell oversaw the fewest staff and could offer only a relatively modest list of publications—three short reports and two books, *The Exploration of the Colorado River of the West* and one on the Uinta Mountains' geology. Despite surveying almost six million acres and making a reconnaissance of twenty million more, he still had published few maps.

In early 1877, as Powell prepared one more request to Congress, he heard disturbing news of an initiative that might end his survey. Columbia geologist John Strong Newberry told him that a member of the appropriations committee, W. S. Holman of Indiana, would move to defund all but Hayden's survey. Holman's son had joined one of Hayden's field parties. Little stood in the way of Hayden's rolling effortlessly over Powell's small outfit. "I fear that it will be a tight squeeze for us this year," he wrote Newberry two days later. Whatever animosity that Newberry harbored about Powell had been long forgotten as they joined together to fight for the place of geology in the surveys.

Powell dived into the political fray, turning to Clarence King, whose timely exit from the national survey horse race had shielded him against much of the mudslinging. King had met Powell in 1870, when the Major lectured in Washington on his river trip the year before. (On that same occasion, King met Henry Adams, who would soon become another lifelong friend.) "I beg of you to come and help me pull through this year," wrote Powell. "You can do me great good in exactly the direction in which I am needing assistance." The two would form a rewarding bond—one that would yield fruit for both in their coming skirmishes against Hayden. Whether bidden by Powell or otherwise, Newberry wrote letters sharply disparaging Hayden to key members of the appropriations committee, Abram Hewitt and Garfield. Hayden had disrespected his former mentor, and so Newberry's words rang with particular animosity: "Hayden has come to be so much of a fraud that he has lost the sympathy and respect of the scientific men of the country and it may well be questioned whether he and his enterprises should be generously assisted as they have been." Newberry further charged Hayden not only with being a "political manager" but "giving employment to the relatives of those by whose influence he was assisted." He then leveled the most damning accusation: Hayden's work had "deteriorated." Powell's work, on the other hand, was high quality, inspired by true scientific enthusiasm and honesty.

On March 3, 1877, the last full day of Congress, the Powell survey found its appropriation doubled, to $50,000, but even so his future was far from certain. That spring President Rutherford B. Hayes appointed the strongly reform-minded former senator Carl Schurz to head the Interior Department. The German-born Schurz had escaped his country during the 1848 revolution, settled in Wisconsin, and gone on to serve as a general in the war, then becoming a senator and leader of the Liberal Republicans and a fierce critic of the Grant administration. No government agency had suffered the black curse of scandal during Grant's tenure more than the Interior Department, under which both the Powell and Hayden surveys worked. Grant's much-touted Peace Policy, which concentrated on moving American Indians to reservations— the moral underpinning of much of his administration—came crashing down in part with revelations of widespread graft throughout the Interior's Bureau of Indian Affairs. Indian agents, who drew their appointments often with slight experience and even fewer ethics, viewed their jobs fundamentally as a license for self-enrichment at the expense of their charges.

In the summer of 1875, the Yale paleontologist O. C. Marsh stumbled on such self-dealing in the Black Hills. Ogalala Sioux chief Red Cloud showed Marsh the spoiled supplies and shoddy goods coming from the Indian agent. Upon returning east that spring, Marsh found a letter from Red Cloud saying that the Ogalala Sioux had received no supplies at all. Articles in the *New York Herald* exposed this and a rat's nest of other widespread Indian Bureau fraud. An outraged nation forced Grant to accept the resignations of Interior Secretary Columbus Delano and Indian Commissioner John Q. Smith.

Things began to heat up between Hayden and Powell. On April 26, 1877, Hayden asked the incoming secretary to give his survey funds from the Indian Bureau to support what he called "the most valuable and important collection of this character in this country." While Hayden had certainly done important ethnological work—consider Jackson's photographs of the pueblos alone— Powell had made such work a centerpiece of his survey. Hayden had a right to ask for the funds, but the timing suggested that he was moving in on Powell, just as he had earlier on Wheeler.

A month later, Powell responded with a letter to Schurz suggesting a compromise between the two surveys. It caught Hayden by surprise. Both he and Hayden, Powell wrote, should keep at work on geology, but one should focus on ethnology, the other on all other fields of natural history. Powell had little interest in pursuing zoology, paleontology, and the other natural history disciplines, but wanted to keep a bulldog grip on ethnology. He had already worked out a deal with the Smithsonian's Joseph Henry to turn over the institution's ethnographic material to him.

Seeing no need to compromise and sensing an opportunity to destroy Powell, Hayden reiterated his need for ethnologic funding because his collection was "unique in importance as well as in extent," claiming to have 1,500 negatives depicting 75 to 80 tribes, as well as other material. Schurz did not buy Hayden's appeal, reminding him sharply in August that he had yet to respond to the secretary's presentation of Powell's compromise. By late September, Hayden grudgingly conceded the ethnological sphere to Powell, while reserving "the right to elaborate what matter I have already in hand."

Clearly stung even by this small concession, Hayden spent two months brooding and repeatedly drafting a letter to Schurz. By November he had the epistle he desired. In it, he submitted to the need for economy and reform among the surveys, proposing that only one Interior survey should perform all the geology and non-ethnographic work. "I would therefore respectfully suggest that Major Powell be desired to devote himself exclusively to Ethnographic work and its cognate branches after the present year . . . and that all geological and geographical work may be assigned exclusively to the survey under my charge." But before Hayden's countermove could come into play, other matters intervened.

In April 1877, the normally staid proceedings of the National Academy of Sciences' annual meeting in Washington took a dramatic turn. For two weeks, members had listened to the nation's most distinguished scientists speak on topics ranging from lunar theory to the structures of organic acids. Members enjoyed "Results of Deep Sea Dredging," by the son of the recently deceased scientist Louis Agassiz. The Academy had invited G. K. Gilbert to deliver a paper, "On the Structure of the Henry Mountains," so named in honor of the Academy's president by Powell's survey. On the final day, the geologists took the floor, whereupon erupted a furious discussion of the American West. The rub lay between those who studied the fossils and those who examined the rock strata, each drawing wildly different conclusions about the age of their subjects.

Such was the fervor of the discussion that the geologists soon jumped to their feet in animation and anger. "[W]hat they might do if they once went fairly on the rampage, it is impossible to say," wrote one correspondent. Hayden rose to argue that no great degree of difference existed between the two sides, but others immediately shouted him down.

Yet while the rather scholarly debates over dating and provenance might animate the geologists, that day would be remembered not for these petty theatrics, but for an address Powell delivered. In it, the Major stepped away from the fields of geology and out of academic realms to address a topic that pressed right to the heart of American democracy. During the Townsend Hearings three years earlier, he had raised the issue of the West's extreme aridity and the difficulty of irrigating much of it—but he had thought a lot more about it since then, and the map he now unrolled in front of America's top scientists carried startling implications. He had bisected the map of the nation from Mexico to Canada with a vertical line rising from central Texas up through Kansas, east of Nebraska, and through Minnesota, roughly approximating the 100th meridian. At this line the arid West begins with startling consistency, the tall prairie grass cedes to short grass and less fertile soils. Trees appear rarely west of the line, except at high altitudes and in the Pacific Northwest, while forests dominate the east: The 100th meridian elegantly divides two separate lands, one composed of wide horizontal vistas, so much of the other defined by its vertical prospects.

The land west of the 100th meridian, Powell announced, could not support conventional agriculture. Surprise met this bold statement, for the line clearly indicated that much of the great plains—including all of Colorado, Montana, Wyoming, and Idaho, plus Arizona and New Mexico—was essentially unfarmable. Here was the professor at his best: clear, authoritative, dramatic. He had everyone's attention.

Powell had drawn an isohyet, a line connecting areas that experience equal volumes of annual rainfall. The relatively humid lands to the east of this line experience twenty or more inches of annual rainfall, the unquestionably arid lands to the west receiving less than that, except some narrow strips on the Pacific coast. The twenty-inch isohyet offered a valuable generalization—conventional agriculture simply could not work without twenty or more inches a year, unless supplemented by irrigation. Except for some lands offering timber or pasturage, the far greater part of the land west of the line was by itself essentially not farmable. Access to the transformative powers of water, not the availability of plots of land, proved a far more valuable commodity. By now, any land through which streams passed had all been acquired, some of these owners charging those less fortunate for irrigation water. "All the good public lands fit for settlement are sold," Powell warned. "There is not left unsold in the whole United States land which a poor man could turn into a farm enough to make one average county in Wisconsin."

Much of what Powell reported was not exactly new, but no one had presented the data so comprehensively and convincingly—and not anyone so famous as the Major. Few, of course, doubted the region's aridity. But in one powerful moment, Powell had claimed that the nation's traditional system of land use and development—and thus America's present push west—simply would not work. The debate that Powell provoked that late April day drew immediate and blistering response. The land agent for the Northern Pacific Railway, itself the beneficiary of a government grant of nearly four million acres, hammered back at Powell's "grave errors." "[P]ractical farmers, by actual occupancy and cultivation, have demonstrated that a very considerable part of this 'arid' region, declared by Major Powell as 'entirely unfit for use as farming lands,' is in fact unexcelled for agricultural purposes." Others responded similarly. Powell clearly had touched a raw nerve. Over the next several years, he would have much more to say on the matter, igniting a veritable firestorm. While the other surveyors limited themselves to covering as much ground as possible, Powell now wrestled with the startling implications for the ongoing development of the West—and what that meant for the American democracy he had fought so hard to save.

For most of the first half of the nineteenth century, eastern America's conception of the western portion of North America could be spelled out in three words: Great American Desert. That originated during the Long Expedition of 1819, when President James Monroe directed his secretary of war to send Stephen H. Long of the U.S. Army Corps of Topographical Engineers with a small complement of soldiers and civilian scientists on a western reconnaissance. Secretary of State John Quincy Adams had just negotiated a treaty with Spain that ceded Florida to the United States and drew a border between the two countries running across the Sabine River in Texas, west along the Red and Arkansas rivers, and all the way to the Pacific. Eager to know more about the border and the new western territory, Monroe had the secretary of war direct Long to follow the Platte River up to the Rocky Mountains, then trace south and back east along the new border.

The energetic New Hampshire–born West Pointer envisioned himself the successor to Meriwether Lewis and William Clark—indeed, over the course of five expeditions, he would cover twenty-six thousand miles, and mount the first steamboat exploration up the Missouri into Louisiana Purchase territory. His name would grace the peak that Powell was first to climb. On this expedition, Long split his group into two, sending one party along the Arkansas while he with the rest headed south to chart the Red River. Long's men, often parched and starving, battled a violent hailstorm, sometimes resorted to eating their horses, and negotiated their way past a band of Kiowa-Apaches. But the maps they carried were so atrociously inaccurate that the river they followed for weeks was not the Red at all.

Three years after Long's party returned home, expedition member Edwin James published the three-volume *Account of an Expedition from Pittsburgh to the Rocky Mountains*. Long's ordeal imbued him with little affection for the "dreary plains" they had traversed. The Great Plains from Nebraska to Oklahoma he found were "wholly unfit for cultivation and of course uninhabitable by a people depending on agriculture." He added: "The traveller who shall at any time have traversed its desolate sands, will, we think, join us in the wish that this region may forever remain the unmolested haunt of the native hunter, the bison, the jackall." The accompanying map labeled the area a "Great Desert," terminology that soon fully flowered into the "Great American Desert," a colorful appellation that would stick to the indefinable sections of the West for the next generation. Long believed that this desert wilderness served as a natural limitation on American western settlement, acting as an important buffer against the Mexican, British, and Russians, who claimed the western lands beyond. That compelling assertion seemed to resonate in the public imagination, locking into place the notion of a vast desert dominating the nation's western midsection. "When I was a schoolboy," wrote Colonel Richard Irving Dodge in 1877, "my map of the United States showed between the Missouri River and the Rocky Mountains a long and broad white blotch, upon which was printed in small capitals "THE GREAT AMERICAN DESERT—UNEXPLORED."

Even though some early trappers and mountain men had brought back word of a land often far from desertlike, the idea persisted. In 1844, when U.S. naval officer Charles Wilkes published his five-volume *Narrative of the United States Exploring Expedition*, it included a map of upper California. Inland from the well-detailed Pacific coast lay the Sierra Nevada, while the front range of the Rockies marked the map's eastward extension. In between the ranges lay a vast, wedge-shaped blank space, without a single physical feature delineated. Unable to leave such a realm blank without remark, Wilkes had inserted a simple paragraph reading "This

Plain is a waste of Sand. . . ." Like the sea monsters inhabiting the unknown sections of medieval maps, he—like Long—had condemned the entire region, the dead space not even worthy of a second look. Eleven years later, a Corps of Topographical Engineers map had sought to add additional detail, but could only insert a tenuous dotted line that indicated some cartographer's wild guess about the Colorado River's course.

Cracks started appearing in the notion of a Great American Desert during the early 1840s expeditions of Charles Frémont, son-in-law of that powerful advocate of Manifest Destiny, Senator Thomas Benton. With his backing, Frémont led both a four-month survey of the newly blazed Oregon Trail in 1841 and an audacious fourteen-month, 6,475-mile circuit of the West, beginning in 1843. Frémont's subsequent reports combined a deft mix of hair-raising adventure with scientific discovery, thrilling its readers with images of guide Kit Carson and the so-called Pathfinder himself running up a flag atop a vertiginous Rocky Mountain peak. The maps accompanying the reports furnished emigrants with an accurate road map for the journeys that thousands would take west in the 1840s and 1850s. Frémont's reports indicated that the intercontinental west certainly contained stretches of truly arid land, but that it was no unbroken Sahara. Yet even so, the pioneers and gold seekers understood that great opportunities lay not in this parched region, but beyond, at the end of the trails, in Oregon and California. Most of the West still remained no more than a place to get across.

In the late 1850s, a rather startling shift had turned the idea of the Great American Desert on its head. "These great *Plains* are not *deserts*," wrote William Gilpin in a late 1857 edition of the *National Intelligencer,* "but the opposite, and are the cardinal basis of the future empire of commerce and industry now erecting itself upon the North American Continent." Gilpin, the electric-tongued son of a wealthy Philadelphia Quaker paper merchant, would do more than any other single individual to persuade his fellow citizens that America's great midsection was a garden only waiting to be plowed. Whereas the term Manifest Destiny had been coined as a justification for conquering great swaths of the continent at gunpoint, Gilpin transformed it into a more wholesome interpretation that pulled peoples across the nation. It also had the weight of the Enlightenment's commandment, articulated by philosopher John Locke that God and reason commanded humans to subdue the earth and improve it. As Civil War soldiers returned home, all America could climb on board with Gilpin's fantastical promises, any threatening idea of a great desert now disregarded. He had given America what it most wanted to hear: the promise that its growth was unlimited, its western lands a never-ending buffet of opportunity and growth, limited only by a lack of imagination and courage.

Gilpin had impressive credentials: Not only had he joined Frémont and Kit Carson on their expedition to Oregon in 1843, but as an army officer he had fought the Seminoles in Florida, served as a major in the First Missouri Volunteers during the Mexican War, and marched against the Comanche to keep the Santa Fe Trail open. A columnist for the *Kansas City Star* observed that "his enthusiasm over the future of the West was almost without limitation." He became a disciple of Alexander von Humboldt, the great German geographer, who published the early volumes of his *Cosmos* in the late 1840s, elaborating the thesis that geography, climate, and biota incontrovertibly shaped the growth of human society. Gilpin pressed the Humboldtian idea that much of North America lay within an Isothermal Zodiac, a belt some thirty degrees wide running across the Northern Hemisphere, which contained climatic conditions ideal for human civilization to blossom. Herein lay the justification for Gilpin's remarkable, if fanciful, theory that rationalized American exceptionalism. In three letters to the *National Intelligencer* in the late 1850s, later developed into an influential book, Gilpin outlined how North America's convex shape had determined its grand destiny. The Mississippi Valley drained the bowl that was defined by the Appalachians to the east and the Sierra Nevada and Rockies to the west. By contrast, the Alps of Europe and the Himalayas of Asia rose in the center of their continents, forming insurmountable barriers to any continental unity. The geographical realities of Europe and Asia broke them up into small states and away from common centers, forcing upon them a history of unending warfare. North America, Gilpin grandly declaimed, had a national, unified personality. Thus endowed with a centripetal, unifying geography that encouraged a single language, the easy exchange of ideas, and favored the emergence of a continental power, North America stood ready to achieve world primacy.

Gilpin claimed that America would fulfill its destiny in the so-called Plateau of North America, the region between the main Rockies and the Sierra Nevada, "the most attractive, the most wonderful, and the most powerful department of their continent, of their country, and of the whole area of the globe." Here Gilpin shone at his most incandescent, piling sheer fantasy built on pseudo-science and hope ever higher. As the war ended, most Americans had embraced the West as an untapped Eden, not as the barren edge bounding the American nation, but as the very place in which it would fulfill its national destiny.

Certainly other forces supported such a change of heart about the West. The railroads—America's most visible instrument of Manifest Destiny—adopted such sentiments with enthusiasm. To encourage the largely authentic, nation-building efforts of the railroad companies, the federal government bestowed vast swaths of public land abutting their tracks onto these rising great powers, many now laying track furiously across the continent. Their long-term interests hinged on the high value of the land they penetrated. The West as garden, rather than desert, suited their ambitions far better, and railroad publicists rolled out a relentless tide of promotional material. Utah was a promised land, proclaimed the Rio Grande and Western Railroad. "You can lay track through the Garden of Eden," said Great Northern Railroad's founder J. J. Hill, "[b]ut why bother if the only inhabitants are Adam and Eve?"

A new, supposedly scientific, idea arose to support the vision of productive dryland farming. The "rain follows the plow" theory became chaplain of the western movement. Simply cultivating the arid soil, this theory postulated, will bring about permanent changes in the local climate, turning it more humid and thus favorable to crops. The climatologist Cyrus Thomas, who had founded the Illinois Natural History Society that had given Powell his chance, became one of the theory's strongest advocates. "Since the territory [of Colorado] has begun to be settled, towns and cities built up, farms cultivated, mines opened, and road made and travelled, there has been a gradual increase in moisture . . . ," he wrote. "I therefore give it as my firm conviction that this increase is of a permanent nature." Hayden, along with many other national personalities, endorsed this intoxicating, but deeply flawed theory.

In 1846, Gilpin addressed the U.S. Senate, asserting that "progress is God" and that the "destiny of the American people is to subdue the continent—to rush over this vast field to the Pacific Ocean . . . to change darkness into light and confirm the destiny of the human race. . . . Divine task! Immortal mission!" Even at a time lit up by fiery eloquence, Gilpin stood out, his giddy pronouncements seismic in their appeal, emotionally resonate, wrapped in morality, and nationalistic in self-praise. Few could resist so powerful an appeal. And few did.

Gilpin and Powell had met at least once, in Denver City, on the Major's first trip west in 1867. The ex-governor had probably waxed about the great promise of the West, perhaps even suggested that the Colorado River lay open to exploration. No record exists of their conversation, but Powell did not seek out his help or opinions after that. The Major found himself more comfortable with William Byers's gritty practicality.

Indeed, Powell had no truck with the "rain follows the plow" theory. He believed that the Southwest was indeed a desert, one that could be cultivated, but only with the careful marshaling of the limited resource of water. Powell's urging for caution solicited widespread groans and charges that he was backward-looking. That summer, he quietly ordered his senior investigators west to establish data on irrigation practices. Ostensibly traveling to northern Utah to classify land, Gilbert would examine Mormon water-delivery technology in the Great Salt Lake drainage area. Dutton would continue his geologic studies on the Colorado Plateau, but take some time off to survey irrigable lands in the Sevier River Valley and measure the river's flow.

On March 8, 1878, Representative John Atkins of Tennessee, chair of the House Appropriations Committee, introduced a resolution that called for the secretary of the interior to submit a report summarizing the operations, expenses, and overlaps of the work conducted by geological and geographical surveys over the past ten years. During the consequent hearings, Wheeler, Hayden, and Powell testified about their surveys.

Powell's young secretary would recall how Wheeler appeared dignified but aloof in his testimony. Hayden came on like a freight train, bitter and at length. He immodestly championed his work above the others and claimed that no duplication among the surveys had occurred. Once Hayden had finally finished his statement, the exhausted committee turned to Powell. In silence, the room of congressmen and a large assembled audience waited as Powell paced back and forth in the chamber, his stump clasped behind his back. All expected an impassioned speech denouncing Hayden's claims one by one. But Powell ignored the earlier testimony. He gave a calm, even-keeled appraisal of his own work, applauded the achievements of the others, and then contended that much overlap between the surveys had occurred. Soon the entire committee was following his every word. "It was plain to see," noted his assistant, "that the day was won."

But even the ascendency he gained at the congressional hearings did not satisfy Powell. Never one to sit back, he prepared to make the riskiest, most brazen gamble of his career—even eclipsing the decision to run the Colorado. One of his greatest intrinsic strengths lay in realizing that opportunity so often arises out of good timing. The timing now—with the survey consolidation in full press and congressional discussion bubbling away—offered an optimal chance to take hold of the narrative and change its course. The report he would release was nothing less than explosive. He would reach far beyond his own survey work, indeed push so far beyond the bounds of a federal bureaucrat as to astound observers, seeming to shoulder the whole American experiment and bear it westward.

While Hayden and Wheeler conducted their fieldwork during the summer of 1877, Powell had stayed home, working assiduously on a document that built on the ideas he had presented to the National Academy of Sciences the year before. His *Report on the Lands of the Arid Region of the United States,* delivered to Interior Secretary Schurz on April 1, 1878, would be monumental and astonishing, and, in the words of a respected mid-twentieth-century historian, "[o]ne of the most remarkable books ever written by an American." Starting with Charles A. Schott's meteorological observations, buttressed by Gilbert's and Dutton's ground measurements of water requirements necessary for irrigation, Powell presented a formal, prescriptive plan for developing the West. In this report he integrated a lifetime of thought and observation, ranging from his childhood experiences in the Wisconsin grain fields to his close study of Mormon irrigation techniques, and informed by the network of ancient Pueblo canals and customs of Mexican water sharing. The thousands of miles he had walked, ridden, and climbed in the West keenly but invisibly shaped the document. At its core lay the realization battered into him on his first journey down the Colorado about humanity's impermanence in the face of geologic time and how the Earth remained in a

continual state of flux. It was more manifesto than scientific report, many of its conclusions based on incomplete evidence, much
of the data hardly better than educated guesses.

Yet the conclusions have since proved ecologically sound and
indeed remarkably spot-on. The report opened with a lengthy appraisal of the topography of the American West, including estimates of the amount of potentially irrigable land, timberland, and
pasturage, before launching into a full-frontal assault on the current land-grant system, still rooted in the 1862 Homestead Act's
stipulation that any American adult could receive 160 acres, con-
tingent upon demonstrating an ability to live on the land and improve it. While that system might work well in Wisconsin or
Illinois, Powell argued, the arid West could not successfully support 160-acre homesteading. Those westgoers flocking into the
arid lands beyond the 100th meridian would see their dreams
dashed by spindly crops. Powell had directly contradicted Gilpin's
soaring promises. America could not have everything it wanted.

Powell's recommendations focused first on classifying lands,
then directing their use accordingly: Low-lying lands near water
that were west of the 100th meridian should be available in
80-acre lots, while water-limited areas should be parceled into
2,560-acre units for pasturage. High mountain tracts under an
abundance of timber should be made available to lumbermen.

He did not deny that drylands could be redeemed, but the limiting factor, as he noted before, was water. Irrigation could "perennially yield bountiful crops," but the West contained few small
streams that could be diverted by canal to fields, and those available were already being exploited to the limit in Utah and Arizona. Such large rivers as the Colorado ran through deep chasms
and hostile ground, mostly far from any potential cropland. Only
"extensive and comprehensive" actions—dams and distribution
systems—could deliver the water, and only those with the means
to undertake the task—not individual farmers, being poor men—
could pursue it. If not carefully planned, wrote Powell, the control

of agriculture would fall into the hands of water companies owned by rich men, who would eventually use their considerable power to oppress the people. He painted a truth that still rankles many today who believe in the myth of the rugged, independent westerner. He asserted that the development of the western lands depended not so much on the individual landowner as on the interdiction of the federal government, the only entity that could survey and map the land, build dams and other reclamation projects, administer vast swaths of public lands, oversee federal land grants, and tackle the displacement of the indigenous peoples. The lone cowboy taming the land with lasso and fortitude may fit the myth of the West, but the reality was quite different. Put simply, the West's aridity required that overall public interest trump that of the individual.

The man who had previously limited himself to describing the topographic and geologic formations of the western lands had now waded directly into populist politics, driven by isohyets and tables of rainfall-per-acre statistics. Powell believed that the very republican dream of the small farmer was at risk under the crushing power of monopolistic interest. Such resistance aligned with his core childhood beliefs. He had seen the local grain operator in Wisconsin abuse powerless farmers with impunity. The stakes, as he saw them, were of the highest order, threatening the country's very fulfillment. With the *Arid Lands* report, Powell had taken on not only Hayden and his congressional supporters, Wheeler and the army but also the General Land Office, the railroads, and the likes of William Gilpin—an overwhelming front of entrenched beliefs, myths, and nation-building passion, the very patrimony of Manifest Destiny. He had taken a hard shot directly at virtually unchallengeable assumptions about the unlimited wealth of American resources and the bright future of the great West—and also at who would have access to whatever wealth the West had to offer.

Powell saw that arid cultures stood or fell—and mostly fell—not on their absolute amounts of water, but on how equitably political and economic systems divided limited resources—and could evolve in the face of climatic and societal changes. To Powell, the Homestead Act, which imposed an arbitrarily eastern 160-acre parcel regardless of topography, rainfall, nearness to water, altitude, and other critical factors, appeared the height of folly, the blind, reflexive policy of a nation with outsized optimism drunk on the seemingly infinite resources available to it. Above all, he argued that the nation's trustees needed to listen to the land itself—and respond accordingly.

Two days after Powell submitted his *Arid Lands* report to Schurz, the interior secretary forwarded it along to the House, which ordered 1,800 copies printed. After exhausting that print run quickly, another 5,000 copies printed afterward disappeared equally fast.

A month after Powell delivered his report, Abram Hewitt of Appropriations inserted a resolution into the Sundry Civil Expenses Bill that referred the question of consolidating the surveys to the National Academy of Sciences. The Academy's president, Joseph Henry of the Smithsonian, had died five weeks earlier, leaving leadership to its vice president, the Yale paleontologist O. C. Marsh, who had a rocky relationship with Hayden and many others.

Hayden and Powell alike had already run afoul of the bitterest, most personal, and long-standing scientific rivalries in American history, between the pioneering paleontologists Marsh and E. D. Cope. They were once friends collecting together in western New Jersey in 1868, and were beckoned by the rich dinosaur beds in Colorado and Wyoming with such a bounty of fossils that it remains hard to fathom how two men could fight so viciously amid so much opportunity. They argued over who had found bones first, named the same species differently, accused one another variously of stealing, appropriating assistants, and plagiarizing the other's descriptions. The national surveys fueled their careers, Cope collecting mostly for Hayden from Texas to Montana through the 1870s, while Marsh rode with King, with whom he had attended Yale's Sheffield School of Science. Under King's patronage, Marsh published his discovery of a sequence of fossilized horses, which Darwin declared to be one of the finest examples of natural selection.

As Marsh went about selecting a committee to examine survey consolidation, he felt little inclination to help Hayden's cause, which continued to support his nemesis, selecting geologist John Strong Newberry, who had also come to loathe Hayden, among six other scientists.

In mid-October of 1878, as he finished up fieldwork in Utah, Powell learned that Marsh had requested a report on his survey's activities. He hurried back to Washington. The document Powell then submitted to the Academy marked another tour de force. Compared with Hayden's anemic, not-quite-two-page summary, and the equally pallid reports from the Office of the Chief of Engineers, and the commissioner of the land office, Powell's exhaustive document ran thirteen pages. In reply, Hayden lamely argued for business as usual, but based upon "the organization now under my charge," along with an increase in his own funding. In contrast, Powell again plunged right into the heart of the matter, calling the competition among the organizations unscientific, excessively expensive, and vicious. Such an environment, he argued, actually worked against amassing comprehensive, thorough, and honest research, leading to an unhealthy rivalry that produced sensational and briefly popular works rather than solid and enduring results.

The Major then turned his attention to the General Land Office, the century-old institution that the government used to parcel federal lands to the public. At that time, sixteen regional surveyor-generals operated independently and nearly autonomously, directing the work of an army of deputy surveyors in the field, none salaried but instead paid by the number of townships they surveyed, creating a situation in which the personal pursuit of wealth stood in the path of accurate scientific work. The government had already spent $23 million on shoddy work, the surveyors often marking township boundaries on trees soon cut down, by little heaps of raked earth easily dispersed by wind, or by wooden stakes that rotted away, a formula for leaving the land as unsurveyed as when the Europeans had first come. "A heritage of litigation relating to boundary-lines has been bequeathed to posterity," Powell wrote. All this survey work had yielded little scientific benefit. And because the land system required surveys to be continuous—each new section line one mile parallel from the last—surveyors happily overlayed the deserts with townships that would never arise. "Many millions of acres have thus been parceled without the slightest necessity, the land being worthless, and the land marks have been allowed to perish, and all useful results have perished with them."

Scientific triangulation methods, he argued, would solve all these problems, which, when coordinated by the federal government and operating with salaried workers, would eliminate wasteful old land surveying altogether. Proper surveying would not only benefit development of the country's arid lands but also help engineering interests nationwide, such as guiding the federal government in sculpting the land by draining millions of acres of Florida swampland, along the Gulf Coast, and around the Great Lakes to create valuable agricultural land. In the midst of this exposition, he asked the academicians to contemplate massive changes to the landscape. "The time must soon come when all the waters of the Missouri will be spread over the great plains, and the bed of the river will be dry."

He devoted the last two pages of his letter to ethnology, arguing that federal government support for ongoing research could help solve the "Indian problem." He understood that many of the present difficulties could not be avoided. However, many could. A lack of knowledge about the Indian was a major obstacle in the nation's ability to address these issues. Here Powell did not argue that a systematic recording of Indian languages should be an end in itself, or be performed just for the sake of scientific knowledge, but pitched his argument instead in real-world terms: "The attempt to transform a savage into a civilized man by a law, a policy, an administration, through a great conversion, 'as in the twinkling of an eye,' or in months, or in a few years, is an impossibility . . ." Ethnographic work, quite simply, would prove critical to the humane administration of Indian affairs.

Ultimately this letter made an effective argument for the central leadership role that the sciences should play in the federal government, at a time when the permanence and continued deep funding of government science agencies was by no means certain. With these words, Powell would add a late-nineteenth-century twist to the long-standing American friction between Hamiltonian federalism and Jefferson's modulated states' rights vision. A strong vein of populism ran through this midwesterner, which in due course would burst out. While he recognized that only the full power of government could bear on great engineering and other problems, he would also claim that only local control could best manage available resources responsibly. He outlined a necessarily complicated prospect for a fast-changing world, part naively utopian, part clear-eyed toward issues both human and environmental. Generations of dueling developers and environmentalists have claimed him as a their guiding star.

The Academy committee incorporated much of Powell's report into their own, nevertheless watering it down considerably by passing over ethnology and his ideas about engineering the landscape. They recommended that the General Land Office's surveyor generals, along with the three current federal surveys of Hayden, Wheeler, and Powell, be subsumed under two civilian-run agencies in the Interior Department. All land-measurement operations

would fall under the Coast and Interior Survey, while all investigations of geology and natural resources, together with land classification, should fall under a new consolidated geological survey.
It also recommended that the president appoint a blue-ribbon commission to investigate public-land laws in order to create a new
land-parceling system in the arid West, where traditional homesteading was both impractical and undesirable.

On November 6, 1878, the entire Academy approved the report
with only one dissenting vote, that of Marsh's bitter rival Cope.
Powell focused next on the congressional backlash that the Academy's report would surely elicit. After all, it cut out the War
Department—and diminished the power of the General Land Office's sixteen surveyors general and their contractors. And then, of
course, Hayden remained capable of hijacking all Powell's work.

Powell launched a major lobbying effort, calling upon Newberry
and Clarence King in late November to sway congressional opinion away from army management of the surveys. Ten days before
the Academy presented its report to Congress on December 2,
Powell decided not to seek the directorship of the new consolidated
survey that Congress would most likely authorize. His deputy
Clarence Dutton had written a friend ten days earlier with news
that his boss "renounces all claim or desire or effort to be the head
of a united survey." A close observer much later wrote that "no one
episode illustrates more strongly the character of the man—to
pass voluntarily to another the cup of his own filling when it was
at his very lips."

Noble sentiments may have in fact prompted Powell to step
aside, but sheer fatigue with the political infighting could also have
played a factor. But Powell had also grown shrewd in politics, anticipating full well that as architect of the survey and land-office
reform approach, he would feel the wrath of the vested interests. A
general awareness that he was seeking to take the directorship
might put the whole endeavor at risk. He now carried great ambitions for two mighty unfolding powers—the nation and

science—but not comparable ambitions for his own wealth, power, or glory. When fame came, as it had with the descent of the Colorado, he would harness it to help overcome his next challenge, not to leverage into higher speaking fees, a larger house, or political office. His distaste for self-aggrandizement embodied the Wesleyan requirement of modesty. Work done was for God's glory, not the individual's. While Powell worshipped at a different altar, his work, not himself, remained the center of his life. But that did not mean he had stopped fighting to get someone installed to carry on the mission of science in good form.

In his eyes, Hayden had come to stand for the culture of Grant-era corruption after the war. Hayden's often shoddy science, Powell believed, sent the interests of the United States squarely in a damaging direction. Hayden's ascent to the position of senior federal scientist would doom land-grant reform. With his willingness to play up to senators and his suspect optimism about the unlimited possibilities of the West, Hayden stood flatly in the way of Powell's struggle to open minds as to what the West actually offered. In this contest, Powell felt that nothing less than democracy lay on the line.

When Congressman James Garfield asked Powell's opinion of Hayden's integrity as a scientist, the Major responded blisteringly that Hayden was "a charlatan who has bought his way to fame." He was a "wretched geologist" who "rambled aimlessly over a region big enough for an empire," shamelessly attempting to catch the attention of "the wonder-loving populace."

Nor had Hayden stood idly by when Congress called upon the National Academy for an opinion: "I presume some great plan will be proposed that will obliterate the present order of things," Hayden wrote a friend, "unless all our friends take hold and help." In another letter Hayden told Joseph Hooker that "Hon. Abram Hewitt is an enemy of mine. . . . We had a hard time this last session and came near being decapitated. . . . We had to cultivate the good will of over 300 members to counteract the vicious influence of the [Appropriations] Committee." Hayden had lobbied members of the Academy to keep John Strong Newberry off the committee.

Clarence King topped Powell's list to run a consolidated survey. King lived in New York, comfortable with seeking his own fortune and happily above the fray as Hayden, Wheeler, and Powell battled it out. He would do little to seek the directorship, but would be only too happy to accept it if offered. On the other side, Hayden launched a forceful letter-lobbying campaign. Unbeknownst to others, he had begun to suffer the effects of syphilis, very likely contracted from his frequenting of prostitutes. The disease, which would kill him nine years later, had already begun to cloud his judgment. His letter writing, however, appeared to be working. Again Powell countered with more lobbying of his own. In early January, Marsh received a letter from Clarence King, letting him know that King felt it was time to submit his credentials for the job.

Hayden still saw Powell as his major competitor, until when— in the middle of January—a friend notified him of Powell's withdrawal; ten days later, Hayden wrote a friend that "all looks well now." Of all the national surveyors, Hayden had published the most, had received more appropriations, and had more friends in Congress—and indeed had the bright feather of Yellowstone in his hat. The directorship was his to lose.

In late December, Powell had finished drafting the legislation that Schurz had requested to turn the Academy's proposals into law. Powell cleverly tied three of the four proposals to appropriations bills, clearly intending to skirt the Public Lands Committee, crowded with western congressmen who would never allow such issues a hearing. Schurz forwarded them to John Atkins, the chair of the House Appropriations Committee, as well as to Abram Hewitt, the committee's most influential member. Both strongly supported the measures. Atkins waited until February 10 to open congressional discussion, whereupon several weeks of vigorous debate ensued. Powell kept at work behind the scenes as a very public debate churned over the role of the federal government in the still largely undefined areas of science. He detailed his staff to bring Garfield books from the Library of Congress so he could cogently draft his position against proposed changes by General Humphreys and the Topographical Engineers.

The former Kansas shoe merchant, Representative Dudley C. Haskell, scoffed at federal dollars going to scientists collecting "bugs and fossils" and creating "bright and beautiful topographical maps that are to be used in the libraries of the rich." Why would Congress reach into public coffers to pay these dubious scientists exorbitant sums to study the public lands? Other opponents of the Academy's plan argued that the western public domain embraced much fine agricultural land. The West, the Montana newspaperman Martin Maginnis joyfully expounded, "contains in its rich valleys, in its endless rolling pastures, in its rugged mineral-seamed mountains, traversed by thousands of streams clear as crystal and cold as melting snow, all the elements of comfort, happiness, and prosperity to millions of men." One congressman after another fumed at anyone so fainthearted as to criticize the extraordinary promise of the West. The "genius of our people," wrote Representative John H. Baker of Indiana, was that they were "bold, independent, self-reliant, full of energy and intelligence," who "do not need to rely on the arm of a paternal government to carve out their won fortunes or to develop the undiscovered wealth of the mountains." Then he came to his real point: "I do not want them in their anxiety to perpetuate those or any other scientific surveys to interfere with our settlers upon the frontier."

With Powell's finger marks all over the Academy recommendations—much clearly pulled from his *Arid Lands* report—he now came under direct fire. Thomas Patterson, a former trial lawyer from Colorado, rose to decry Powell as a dangerous revolutionary, "this charlatan in science and intermeddler in affairs of which he has no proper conception." Atkins's proposal, he continued, was the work of one man, and threatened the West and its landed interests with disaster. Should Congress enlarge the land grants for grazing, then baronial estates would soon crowd the plains, an aristocratic few owning lands sufficient for a European principality and crowding out the small farmer upon which the nation depended. Powell must have been galled when the floor debate took this particular twist, especially when he had so consciously dedicated his efforts toward supporting the interests of the small farmer and preventing the aggregation of land and power that Patterson railed against. Patterson himself would go on to buy the *Rocky Mountain News,* making it a bullhorn for labor rights and the taming of corporate overreach. Indeed both men did not diverge much in their views. But at the heart of the matter lay a considerable foundational debate about who should be shaping the development of agricultural America and how much the government and scientific elite should be involved.

On February 18, 1879, Representative Horace Page of California offered a compromise that agreed to the consolidation of the scientific surveys but made no mention of reforming the land-survey system. Representative Haskell read a letter from a National Academy scientist, which submitted that the Academy debate was actually far more divisive than the one dissenting vote might indicate. The congressman would not reveal the letter's author, most probably E. D. Cope, the missive a ploy by Hayden's people to sow doubt about the Academy's recommendations.

Atkins amended Page's compromise to include the creation of a commission to investigate the land-grant system. The measure passed 98 to 79. The approved Sundry Bill went to the Senate, where no discussion took place. In the Appropriations Committee, Hayden's supporters weighed in strongly, the committee amending the bill so that the scientific surveys were consolidated under Hayden, even taking $20,000 from Powell to finish up his work and giving it to Hayden. The bill then passed to conference committee. When it emerged on March 3, the last day of the session, the Senate's emendations placing Hayden in charge had been cut out, but so had the House reformers' bid to place all the competing agencies under the

Interior Department. The last-minute collection of appropriation bills to keep the government functioning passed and the 45th Congress closed.

Hayden may well have considered this outcome a victory, the Senate indicating its interest in his running the consolidated survey. All he needed now was to take the directorship. But he had not counted on Powell. The Major did not delay, writing at length to Atkins on March 4, pinning blame on Hayden for negatively influencing the tenor of the congressional discussion by raising false issues solely to advance himself personally. Powell then revealed his deepest concern: The appointment of Hayden would effectively end efforts to reform the system of land surveys. He asked Atkins to approach Schurz and President Hayes to obstruct Hayden's bid and to sing the praises of King.

Two days later, Powell spoke with the president, Hayes questioning him in particular on Hayden's methods of securing appropriations. Powell also wrote a lengthy letter to Garfield, furnishing him with a withering analysis of Hayden's published work. He did not hold back, claiming that Hayden's mind was utterly untrained and incoherent, leading him to fritter away federal money on work "intended purely for noise and show." Powell also worked closely with O. C. Marsh, helping to coordinate the flow of letters in support of King. Marsh traveled to Washington and also met with the president.

Cope wrote Schurz in support of Hayden, claiming that "simply shameful" personal grudges had aroused the voices against his friend. As for King, Cope insinuated that his tenure in government service had been sullied by his taking fees from mining enterprises. But Cope's letter could not stem the tide of questions raised against Hayden. King's nomination was officially announced on March 20. "My blood was stirred," wrote Hayden supporter and Brown University president Ezekiel G. Robinson, upon hearing the news. "There must have been some dexterous maneuvering to have brought about a change in the President's mind."

The Senate approved King's nomination with the slightest opposition on April 3. Three days later Marsh wrote Powell, "Now that the battle is won we can go back to pure Science again," then invited him and Gilbert to present papers to the upcoming National Academy annual meeting. When Powell told King he would be pleased to work for the new United States Geological Survey, King responded exuberantly. "I am more delighted than I can express. Hamlet with Hamlet left [out] is not to my taste. I am sure you will never regret your decision and for my part it will be one of the greatest pleasures to forward your scientific work and to advance your personal interest."

King did not last two years on the job.

CHAPTER 10

Taking Over Washington

For all appearances, the events of 1879 had not ended well for Powell. His fierce lobbying results had forced the melding of his beloved survey into a larger bureaucracy. He had failed to bring about a revision of the public land laws. He had engineered himself out of the job for which he had made himself prime claimant by his risky trip down the Colorado River a decade before. The prospect of working under the direction of someone else—even his friend King—held little appeal. Field geology no longer captivated him either, the discipline passing increasingly to the province of such specialists—and younger men—as Gilbert and Dutton, who performed the follow-up detail work that the Major cared little for.

But if some of his congressional antagonists felt relief that this heated reformer would take himself gracefully offstage, they would be mistaken. Powell had yet another big plan in mind: nothing short of rewriting the science of American anthropology. His intentions surfaced as a mere ripple in an innocuous letter to John Atkins, the chairman of the House Appropriations Committee, on February 20, 1879, in which he briefly reviewed the rich ethnological materials his survey had accumulated over the years. "[T]he greater part of this material . . . yet remains in an inchoate condition," he wrote, and needed arranging and editing. The charter for the United States Geological Survey (USGS) contained no provision for such work, so Powell here requested that the Sundry Bill include a $20,000 appropriation to conclude this important work. The federal government's already substantial investment in Indian "vocabularies, grammars, notes and materials on their habits, customs, governmental organization, mythology and religion, arts and industries etc. etc.," Powell implied, would all go for naught without such funding. He urged that the Smithsonian oversee the project. Atkins saw to it that the Sundry Bill contained the funding provision.

But Powell had not the faintest intention of merely tying up loose ends. Quite the contrary. His Geographical and Geological Survey of the Rocky Mountain Region simply became the Smithsonian's Bureau of Ethnology. Even the most liberal reading of the funding provision could not justify congressional authorization of a permanent government organization devoted to the "science of man." Yet Powell set out to make just that happen. By late 1879, he had more than doubled the ethnologists on the new bureau's payroll—six new scientists, the talented artist William H. Holmes, the executive officer James Stevenson, the photographer Jack Hillers, and adequate support personnel, including messengers, clerks, and librarians. Far from wrapping up raw field research, he sent men out west to collect new material.

Nor did he waste time implementing his systematic plan in which he would not only hire scholars and trained men to do research, but persuade academics around the country, as well as promising amateurs, to conduct research under his overall guidance. These "collaborators" would greatly extend the Bureau's reach—for often these men, and some women, did not need full salaries, only an element of financial support and a place to publish. As with the Colorado expeditions, he ran operations on a shoestring. He convinced the U.S. Census, which had once asked him to help classify American Indians by language, to pay the salaries of several anthropologists. The War Department detailed army personnel to the Bureau, notably Washington Matthews, who would conduct studies on the Navajo. The Interior Department gave him much administrative support.

Had any congressman deigned to read Powell's introduction to his six-hundred-page *First Annual Report of the Bureau of Ethnology,* he would have found the Major's ambitions as clear as a winter sky over the Grand Canyon: "It is the purpose of the Bureau of Ethnology to organize anthropologic research in America." Powell's fait accompli came off. The following year, the Bureau received a whopping annual increase to $50,000. With rare exceptions, Congress would raise the Bureau's appropriation by 10 to 20 percent per year all through Powell's nearly quarter-century directorship, which ended only with his death in 1902. Remarkably, Powell built upon this slim justification to create America's foremost anthropological organization, train the next generation of the country's anthropologists, and spin off many satellite organizations. At its center, directing the complicated endeavor, would always be the Major, set upon remaking the study of American anthropology.

Powell might have been happy just to direct the Bureau, but the gales of political change soon blew him right back into public life.

Clarence King quickly discovered his temperament ill-suited for the political machinations necessary to keep a Washington bureaucracy functioning. He did get off to a solid start by hiring real talent and focusing the survey on his true love, economic geology. But his attention soon wandered. He spent long trips at government expense roaming Sierra Madre gold and silver mines, searching for that one score that would set him up for life. The heady promise of the West dispensing overnight riches still held him in its thrall—as it did so many others—but such interests did not bode well for someone seeking to establish the authority of a newly formed federal bureaucracy.

Just a year into his tenure, King started to look for a way out—
and the upcoming change of administrations would give him just
the chance. Under President Hayes, King had enjoyed the support
of his friend and boss, Carl Schurz, secretary of the interior. But
Hayes, who had agreed to serve only one term in the wake of
Grant's unsettling administration, prepared to leave office in
1881, and Schurz most likely would go with him. King drafted his
resignation letter.

Grant's triumphal return from a two-year world tour had
thrown the Republicans into disarray. His hero's welcome deluded
him into running for a third term, Senator Roscoe Conkling of
New York building a nostalgic coalition, known as the Stalwarts,
to reinstall him. Maine senator James Blaine and former Ohio
senator John Sherman, brother of William Tecumseh, challenged
Grant, splitting the party into factions. During the Republican
Convention in Chicago, congressman James Garfield of Ohio served
as Sherman's floor representative. When Grant, Blaine, and Sherman did not each garner enough votes for the nomination, the delegates coalesced around Garfield as a compromise candidate,
despite his own efforts to remove his name from contention. Garfield won the nomination on the thirty-sixth vote in a deal sealed
by the addition to the ticket of the Stalwart Chester Arthur as vice
president. Garfield then narrowly beat the Democratic candidate,
fellow Civil War general Winfield Scott Hancock, by less than two
thousand recorded popular votes.

"I congratulate you and myself on our great Republican victory,"
the anthropologist Lewis Henry Morgan wrote Powell. "It will give
four years of steady encouragement to your work, and enable you
to get it upon a solid foundation." Powell and the president-elect
had become fast friends and allies over the past decade, the latter
as the powerful chairman of the Appropriations Committee who
played a major role in consolidating the surveys. Over six feet tall,
the warmhearted trustee of the Smithsonian had championed geology as far back as 1860, when as a state senator he introduced a

bill to bring back the state's discontinued survey. Garfield shared with Lincoln and Powell the credentials of self-made, frontier intellectuals of strong Whig and Protestant sensibilities bent upon reform. Like Powell, Garfield had worked America's interior waterways—a Horatio Alger book celebrating his life was called *From Canal Boy to President*—and also served at Shiloh.

Amid the whirlwind brought by the federal survey consolidation, Powell had lent Garfield his aid, Joseph Stanley-Brown, on Sundays and holidays to help with the congressman's overwhelming correspondence. When Garfield became the Republican nominee, Powell graciously acceded to Garfield's wish to make Stanley-Brown his personal secretary. "Without my knowledge," wrote Stanley-Brown, "the General had again arranged matters with the Major." Stanley-Brown would become one of the Garfield family, eventually marrying the president's only daughter, Mollie.

A week after Garfield took the oath to become the twentieth president in March 1881, King and Powell met with him at the White House, the president at once accepting King's resignation from the USGS and appointing Powell as his replacement. With "great pleasure," Stanley-Brown sent off the president's letter of nomination to the Senate within half an hour of Powell's leaving the White House. The Senate quickly approved the appointment. Hayden only learned about the transition afterward.

For all his harsh words about Hayden, Powell would maintain King's appointments, including a $4,000 salary for Hayden to finish up his work. The already ailing geologist wrote to Newberry that year that Powell had "been far more than just and magnanimous toward me, and I wish it were in my power to make some adequate returns."

Once King left the USGS, his life shuffled toward a long, disappointing end. None of his mining deals panned out, and his credit and reputation with investors exhausted all but his firmest friendships. Only when he died, broke, from tuberculosis in an Arizona hotel in 1901 did his friends learn of his long-secret marriage to an African American nursemaid from Brooklyn. Ada Copeland had borne him five children, and would be as shocked as King's friends when she learned the details of his life. In a story worthy of his best high-Sierra tall tales, the rather swarthy King had represented himself to Copeland as James Todd, a light-skinned Pullman porter, frequently absent on long railway excursions. The charismatic maverick had done fine work, but ultimately fell cruelly before too-tall expectations of Gilded America's boom and bust mentality. The American West—so infinite in its possibilities, so grand in the wild dreams it nurtured—had chewed him up.

Powell now added a more-than-full-time job atop that of his more-than-full-time job at the Bureau of Ethnology. Certainly Garfield knew that far better credentialed geologists could have taken the reins. But the president, a gifted amateur mathematician and a strong proponent of federal science, understood that his friend would be ideal to build this fledgling organization into a powerhouse. Powell would not let him down, although the president would not live to see it. Four months after Garfield assumed the highest office, the deranged Charles J. Guiteau fired his .44 caliber English Bulldog pistol into Garfield's back as the president entered a Washington train station on his way to his twenty-fifth college reunion. "I did it," Guiteau reputedly said as policemen dragged him away. "I will go to jail for it. I am a Stalwart and Arthur will be President."

"The surprise this morning is overpowering," Powell wrote Stanley-Brown. One of the bullets broke a rib and lodged in the president's abdomen, physicians unable to locate and remove it. The president clung to life, suffering terribly in his White House sickroom from the humid ninety-degree heat of the Washington summer, which no fans could moderate. In desperation, Garfield's physicians approached Powell about cooling the room. On the Saturday night a week after the shooting, Powell enlisted the aid of his friend, the astronomer and mathematician Simon Newcomb. The two graybeards hurried into discussion, agreeing that an electric fan forcing air through cheesecloth dampened with ice water might work. Figuring that they needed to supply 12,000 cubic feet of cool air per hour, they calculated that it would require "the condensation of some 10 pounds per hour," which would require melting 70 pounds of ice. They finished their experiments and calculations by 1 p.m. that Sunday, turning next to devising an icebox capable of holding six tons of ice. This they decided to connect to a coffin-shaped iron box devised by a Baltimore inventor, which held many thin cotton screens, and placed this in the president's office adjacent to the sickroom.

By Monday, the apparatus pumped "cool, dry, and ample" air into the president's sickroom, but the clatter of air forced through tin pipes caused the president great distress. By replacing the metal conduit with pipes made from canvas-covered wire, they quieted the racket. The air in the room settled to a cool fifty-five degrees. Newcomb and Powell's system remains one of the first active, effective air conditioners in history.

Garfield may well have survived the assassin's bullets, but physicians' continued probing of the wound in search of the bullet with unwashed fingers—this in the days before germ theory—introduced infections that led to a fatal aneurysm on September 19, 1881. Powell took it hard; the news, on top of his new responsibilities, conspired to compromise his own health. In early October, inflammation of his iris sent the Major into a dark room, where he lay until late November, his doctor warning that to do otherwise might cost him an eye.

The loss of this most powerful friend and supporter was profound. Chester Arthur immediately fired all of Garfield's cabinet appointments except Secretary of War Robert Todd Lincoln. But Powell did not lie idle in his darkened room, instead working out the details of his ambitious plans for entirely reshaping the consolidated survey. He began with a structural overhaul, replacing

King's decentralized organization of largely independent regional offices with a highly centralized bureau formed around topical divisions. He planned even more sweeping changes on top of that.

After assuming the directorship, King had addressed Congress about the future of the USGS, telling the legislators how the nation's great destiny was tied inextricably to its ability to extract its mineral resources and convert that into wealth. "In the industrial conquest of a continent the tide of victory has never ebbed," he exulted, revving the engines of Manifest Destiny in a gilded age. The survey's purpose, he argued, centered on identifying the nation's mineral wealth "with the highest technical skill and with the utmost scientific economy." King's emphasis on geology for mining reflected not just his own interests but the growing needs of the iron and steel industries, now pinched by an acute shortage of raw materials. King had planned to dedicate the whole survey to mining geology—limiting general geology, topographic mapping, and hydrology to satellite supporting roles; thus the USGS's pursuit of paleontology would be limited to identifying strata containing coal or minerals. While Powell did not doubt that practical geology would unlock wealth, he determined that the USGS's mission must entertain far wider ambitions than simply locating coal beds or other precious commodities. No longer would the survey devote itself to identifying mining centers and developing theories of ore formation.

Right away, Powell committed the survey to focus on paleontology by hiring Othniel Marsh, Lester Ward, and Charles Walcott. Invertebrate paleontology gave indispensable assistance to that generation's geologists in sequencing rock layers and comparing them with similar deposits across the land. King, the man of mountains, was replaced by Powell, the lover of rivers. The Major set up chemical and physical laboratories, built a library and publication program, undertook a thesaurus of American geologic formations, and started a bibliography of North American geology.

When Congress created the USGS in 1879, the bill contained

vague language as to the full scope of its assigned mission. The statute defined the survey's province as the "national domain," an unclear term that could either encompass the entire United States or only the states and territories containing publicly owned lands. Then, the federal government owned more than 1.2 billion acres of land, the greater part west of the Mississippi. Of that, only one-sixth had been surveyed.

As director, Clarence King had asked Congress to clarify its intent, believing that a broader interpretation would give him a better chance to develop national mineral resources. But Congress dithered and made no decision. Fear of legal entanglements and hampered by a relatively small budget—only $106,000 despite a request for $500,000—persuaded King to drop the matter and focus entirely on public lands. He clearly did not have the stomach for an extended congressional fight.

Powell had no such reservations. In his first survey budget, submitted in April 1882, he asked for an increase of $100,000 for western work and an additional $100,000 to extend the survey into the Mississippi Valley and the Appalachians. Powell's ally, the recently displaced House Appropriations chair John Atkins, who proved so critical to creating the USGS, had attached an amendment to the bill as it emerged from his committee the year before, which directed the survey "to continue the preparation of a geological map of the United States." Other congressmen objected to its continental sweep, changing the amendment to read "of the national domain of the United States." But by August 7, 1882, when the Sundry Civil Expenses Bill passed, the amendment to the amendment had lost that added phrasing. That the commission's mapping amendment stayed in at all spoke to the promise that such mapmaking could uncover vast wealth. Powell appeared so certain of this outcome that five weeks before the bill passed, he appointed Henry Gannett as chief geographer to direct the topographic mapping project. Nowhere yet had Powell secured authorization to print the maps.

In the USGS's fourth annual report, he announced with no trace of irony that "prior to the beginning of the present fiscal year it was doubted whether the Geological Survey was authorized by law to extend its operations into the eastern portion for the United States." Congress resolved that issue, he continued, because it required the survey to create a geologic map of the United States. "Authority, therefore, was given to extend the operations of the Survey over the entire country to the extent necessary for that purpose." Powell had again built out one of his greatest ambitions on the merest sliver of questionable authority. By then, the survey had already spread into Massachusetts, Texas, and New Jersey.

The creation of a geologic map requires the prior creation of a topographic survey map, which acts as a template. The most prominent features of a topographic map, of course, are its contour lines, which bunch tightly to indicate a cliff face or stream embankment, but spread apart over the likes of the Nebraska prairie, while some human landmarks—towns, cities, roads—may appear. It is a picture of the Earth's surface. In contrast, a geologic map defies a pictorial conception, noted Earth scientist Preston Cloud, serving as "more of a three- or even four-dimensional conceptual model of the underlying geologic structure and history." Vast amounts of analysis and interpretation go into identifying different rock compositions, their relative ages, and relationships to other strata that may be faulted, twisted, fractured, or eroded around or into them. Brightly colored geologic maps often include many vertical cross-sections of the surface strata.

In relatively short order, the Major had masterminded the first continental federal science project—both the geological and topographical mappings of the entire contiguous United States. Nowhere had Congress explicitly authorized so monumental a project. The 2,600-sheet topographic atlas, drawn to three different scales depending on level of state support and population density, would be engraved on copper with three impressions per plate: relief lines in brown, hydrologic features in blue, man-made features and lettering in black. By the time Powell left the survey after a dozen years, federal surveyors had entered every state and territory, topographically mapping 600,000 square miles, or about 20 percent of continental America. He rightly anticipated that future generations would require a much more detailed scale than the 1:250,000—or about four miles to the inch—that he proposed. When the USGS tackled the mapping of the contiguous United States on a 1:24,000 scale, it took from the 1930s to 1991 to complete the 55,000 quadrangle maps, employing 33 million person-hours at a cost of about $1.6 billion. Powell had described many of the techniques used to print the modern quad maps in 1885.

The economic value of geologic and topographic mapping is immeasurable as it affects countless areas of human activity—from urban and other land-use planning, highway construction, and oil and natural gas exploration to assessing environmental impacts and assisting national security agencies to planning against terrorist attacks on the nation's infrastructure. Powell succinctly claimed that "a Government cannot do any scientific work of more value to the people at large than by causing the construction of proper topographic maps of the country." He had correctly understood that without maps, a nation could not truly know itself. Without maps, America could not reach its potential.

Needing more space as his payroll ballooned in 1884, Powell convinced Congress of the survey's need to rent space in the six-story Hooe Iron Building at 13 and F Streets, a twenty-minute walk from his M Street home and just a couple of blocks from the White House. Washington's largest cast-iron-fronted structure, the Hooe was also the city's largest privately owned office building. American Express operated out of a storefront on the street level. Powell had chosen a fashionable block indeed, especially given its proximity—just sixty feet away—from the city's most elegant hotel, the mansard-roofed Ebbitt House, with its immense gas-fired chandeliers, imposing marble-and-walnut lobby, and constant stream of politicians and military figures. Large flamboyant white script spelled out *United States Geographical Survey* on the transom over the Hooe's elegant main entrance. The USGS, like Powell, had finally, and completely, arrived.

Practicality, as might be expected, equally marked Powell's choice of location. The city's infamous Newspaper Row lay only a block away, an anarchy of a dozen small houses packed with journalists, all anchored by the Western Union office on the corner of 14th and Pennsylvania. The telegraph office would enable Powell to communicate with his far-flung staff. The taverns jamming nearby Rum Row, where journalists, politicians, and lobbyists gathered, offered the latest information and gossip. He could not have chosen a better place at the center of the Capital's influence peddling.

Moving the survey into a roomy building also helped Powell support his perpetually stretched Bureau of Ethnology. With the survey now boasting a budget ten times that of the Bureau, Powell set out to work an economy of scale on behalf of the smaller organization, moving himself, his personal secretary, and several Bureau personnel to the survey payroll. The survey paid James Stevenson's salary, even though he served as the chief executive officer of both organizations. Artist William Henry Holmes and photographer Jack Hillers reported to both, although they were paid only by the survey. In practice, this meant that Powell and the others had doubled their workload for no additional salary. The interior secretary acceded to Powell's request to become the sole arbiter of the survey's budget, becoming the "Special Disbursing Agent of the United States Geological Survey" on August 24, 1882.

From his second-floor corner office in the Hooe, Powell held court like an unkempt monarch, his door open to any who might wander in. Senators and congressmen dropped by to chat or pick up handsome illustrated copies of survey publications. Scientists visited fresh from the field, while other impromptu gatherings might find the discussion centering on Hopi dance or a recent discovery of toothed bird fossils. Time had played its ravages on the Major, now approaching fifty, who resembled an odd hybrid of mad scientist and rumpled professor, yet his left hand reached out in welcome to deliver a nearly uncomfortable grip. The immobility enforced by his iritis had fattened his frame. His stump continued to deliver near-constant pain, which caused his friend Samuel P. Langley, the secretary of the Smithsonian after Baird, to describe him as "a stoic who suffered long years of pain in silence." Deep lines etched his face. An unruly, graying red-brown beard always seemed dusted by ashes from an ever-present cigar. His hair grew long, combed back without a part. He was fond of formless wool suits, looking as though he had slept in them, and conforming to no recognizable fashion. Yet his deep-set bright gray eyes still twinkled, and never seemed to miss the least detail. He had the gift of making others feel that he registered and carefully weighed every word they uttered. Many felt elevated after a conversation with him, inspired to dig deeper into their work, perhaps with the benefit of some new perspectives. Powell had a gift for opening up new contexts; his intellectual abilities, noted one of his friends, lay in "seeing analogies and making comparisons, of coupling observations and thoughts which to most people seemed not at all related to each other until by him placed in a certain light."

Not all survey employees jumped eagerly aboard Powell's train, particularly such close friends of King's as the geologists Samuel Emmons and George Becker, who detested the free-form sharing of ideas. They liked to remind Powell that Congress had established the survey primarily as a vehicle to develop mineral resources. Powell listened courteously, but with only half an ear, yet still kept both on staff. Emmons reported a conversation he had with Gilbert, who commented on Powell's general decision process: "He will think it over for a few days, come to half a dozen minds about it, and then decide suddenly without any reference to what we had said about it." Powell's general open-mindedness would eventually bring Emmons around to supporting him.

Powell's eclectic hiring practices defied any sort of consistency—a pastiche of political motivation, the desire to engage influential scientists, and warmhearted regard for the self-taught. He gave his scientists wide latitude to focus on their particular interests. As the survey grew, he drew in remarkable numbers of America's top scientists. Between 1882 and 1892, the USGS collaborated with more than forty institutions in twenty-six of the forty-four states. Powell's growing influence ensured that every major American university and prominent academic organization would feel his missionary passions. When federal laboratories could not accommodate one aspect or another of cutting-edge science, Powell established new divisions at Harvard, Yale, and the University of Wisconsin. Under Powell's support and guidance, Lester Frank Ward wrote his influential 1,200-page *Dynamic Sociology,* a work that created the political philosophy of social liberalism, and served as a foundation of progressivism in the next century. Among others under Powell's wing would be Charles Walcott, who would serve two decades as a brilliant Smithsonian secretary.

Powell's inner circle met regularly at the Hooe, gaily calling themselves the Great Basin Mess—Dutton, McGee, Holmes, James Piling, Walcott, and Gannett telling stories from their days in the field. Initially an indoor picnic, they ate simple meals on wooden plates with cheap silverware and paper napkins. Most of these men lived not far from Powell's home and supported one another like a band of brothers through many difficult times. One such came early in 1883, when coal-gas poisoning sickened Gilbert's entire family. The survey staff and their wives pitched in to help nurse them back to health. When tragedy struck again that spring, the Great Basin Mess rallied to help. Emma never left the bedside of Gilbert's seven-year-old daughter, Bessie, as she lay dying from diphtheria, her parents too sick themselves to be present.

The men surrounding Powell clearly saw his foibles and idiosyncrasies—yet those very qualities appeared to energize them with zeal for the mission. Like other great salesmen, he did not focus on product details, but rather spun notions of what could be, whether amid a rugged band of adventurers huddled on the banks of the Green, the clumps of young scientists eager to change the world, or in the ranks of senators shaping policy in Washington parlors. He combined skills of a Houdini and confidence man with the contrasting ideas of an idealist committed to salvation. When these qualities meshed with his future-shaping visionary insights into land stewardship and federal science, they created a formidable package.

Observers often described antebellum Washington as a sleepy southern town, but the northern war effort had changed that forever, centralizing great power and emboldening it with enormous economic expansion. The reclaimed swamplands along the Potomac saw its population rise from 75,000 in 1860 to more than 130,000 in 1870 and 175,000 by 1880, newcomers often drawn by fast-rising needs for scientific, professional, and technical work. By 1877, three thousand gaslights illuminated city streets, even more new swampland had been reclaimed, and mule teams drew streetcars along the major avenues. The federal government played an ever larger role in public life.

In the small parlor of his M Street town house, Powell and several others, including Henry Adams, formed the Cosmos Club, with Powell serving as its founding president. The club offered newly forming scientific societies and their members with the social club, assembly hall, and library they needed. Ethnologist Otis Mason described "the scientific minds of Washington" as parts "of an organized, living existence." This community crystallized into new societies, "all of them flourishing and useful." At the Club, "they meet two or three times a week to discuss everything in the heavens above, the earth beneath, the water under the earth, and sociology."

At the Cosmos, the Hooe, and new and old universities across the nation, Powell prosecuted his grand ambition "to make the Survey of such magnitude," as he wrote another scientist in 1884, "that the whole area of the United States can be properly occupied with a corps of topographers and geographers doing efficient work which will be available during the present generation." By the following year, his goal was close. King's staff of 40 had blossomed to 283, working among 10 divisions: topographic survey, geologic survey, economic geology, paleontological laboratories, chemical laboratory, lithological laboratory, physical laboratory, illustration, geologic library, and mineral statistics.

Powell must have known that he would soon run afoul of Congress. Postwar national politicians still espoused laissez-faire attitudes toward federal governance, a general disposition that worked well for the big corporations of the Gilded Era. Politicians gave little thought to science, unless it involved a major inventive breakthrough such as the telephone or railroad, neither of which had resulted from public money. When Congress did wade into these waters, it was moved by singular responses to specific problems. Any endeavor to find an overall role for science in federal government got nary a look or consideration. These attitudes had opened a door through which Powell boldly strode. But that door was fast closing.

A reckoning would come in the 1884–1885 appropriation request for the USGS. By all accounts it appeared a big winner, the Appropriations Committee furnishing the survey with $386,000—a more than 60 percent increase over the previous year, and more than two and a half times the entire budget of all federal surveys in 1878. Yet when the budget passed in July 1884, two items appeared that would lean hard on the survey, one a directive to the Joint Committee on Public Printing to curtail the mounting costs of publications. The year before, the survey's publications expenses for its annual report and myriad monographs and bulletins topped $150,000. The second, more ominous, directive, appeared in the form of a Joint Congressional Commission tasked to secure greater efficiency and economy of administration of the Signal Service, Geological Survey, Coast and Geodetic Survey, and the Hydrographic Office of the Navy Department. With a combined annual budget of approximately $3 million, these four separate agencies consumed most federal science appropriations. The USGS had not been singled out, but Powell understood that some congressional apprehension now focused on the very public survey and its director. The Commission offered the microscope through which Congress could finely examine Powell's fiscal and personnel management.

On December 4, 1884, the first day of testimony before the Joint Commission—known as the Allison Commission after its chairman, Republican senator William B. Allison from Iowa—Powell took a chair at 10 a.m. in the Senate Appropriations room before the six commissioners, three from the Senate, three from the House. If he thought this inquiry would end quickly, he was sorely mistaken. They summoned him again the next day, and then five more times over the next fourteen months. His oral testimony and prepared statements would fill 285 pages of the commission's more than 1,000-page report. Of the six commissioners, Hilary Herbert, an influential congressman from Alabama, would become Powell's most severe interlocutor, his biting asides and caustic questioning of Powell both acerbic and clever. Two more formidable duelists would be hard to imagine. The son of a slave-owning plantation culture, Herbert moved stiffly, his right arm hanging limp and useless at his side from a grievous war wound sustained at the Battle of the Wilderness in May 1864. He had also endured a prisoner-of-war camp.

The war had forged unquenchable fires of nationalism in both men, but their views on reunion were radically different. A "Bourbon Democrat," the Greenville lawyer had won election to the House

in 1866 on a tide of like-minded Southerners who had bitterly resisted federal Reconstruction policies, while Powell had remained
closely affiliated with the Republican Party of Lincoln, Grant, and
Garfield, union and antislavery running in his veins. A month before Powell faced Herbert, the Northern Bourbon Democrat Grover
Cleveland had narrowly won the presidential election, pledging to
reduce federal inefficiencies and waste, and to institute a
government-wide pursuit of corruption. The Allison Commission's
inquiry dovetailed well with Cleveland's agenda, Herbert eagerly
taking a cudgel to what he believed was the inflated presence of
science in federal government. His target came to focus almost entirely on Powell. On trial would be Powell's great visions for science
in the federal service and his ambitious plan to map the continent.
The debate would spill out into the press and soon get nasty.

The Allison Commission began by asking the National Academy of Sciences to weigh in, much as it had earlier in the matter
of survey consolidation. Another bout of iritis cut short Powell's
testimony in front of a newly assembled Academy committee. The
Commission would choose to ignore the Academy's broad-gauge
recommendation—to organize all federal science under a cabinet-
level Department of Science—but the ideas they presented as to
what kind of science the government should conduct marked the
beginning of a federal science doctrine that in its main aspects
endures today.

On the first day's hearings, commissioners questioned Powell
on the difference between geological, topographical, and geographic mapping. At one point, the chairman admitted his confusion; Powell kept explaining. They pressed him as to why a geologic
map needed an exact topographic map to fit beneath it. "Every
error appearing in geographic part or topographic part of a map
projects itself into the geology and vitiates the geologic representation to that extent," explained Powell wearily.

Why then, inquired Herbert, did one need a topographic map if
the land survey plots laying out townships could be used to mark

deposits of coal, iron, and other minerals? What necessity would a map serve that located roads and hills accurately? The Major responded that "we do not usually tell a man, 'You can go and find a mine on such a fraction of a section,' but make outlines of the geologic formations in which ores are found, and every man exploits his own land."

Senator Eugene Hale of Maine detected the elephant sitting in the room. This slight man with a tightly trimmed beard, known for his dapper big city suits and Down East sarcasm, asked whether anyone believed that a line of an appropriation bill delivered the authority for creating a nationwide geological map. "Do you suppose that that carried in Congress, or elsewhere, any expectation of your going on and making triangulation, topographic work, and a complete topographic map of the United States? Do you suppose anybody construed it that way, or expected that?" Powell responded that "the passage of it hinged upon that point; and it was elaborately and fully discussed." But Hale soon circled back.

Hale represented that other senators besides himself had no idea that they were approving a national map of such grand proportions. He most definitely remembered the debates—how could he not, serving on the Senate Appropriations Committee. "Certainly it did not occur to the members of the Senate, it did not to carry the idea, that this was to take upon itself the province of a survey in the old States." He directed his gaze more intently on Powell. "Now, in framing that language, why did not you put it in fairly and in terms?"

Powell dodged the question, cheekily telling Hale that perhaps the distinguished senator did not recollect the whole history of the matter—then delved into the confusing politics of the appropriations bill. "It was in the amendment made by the Senate committee that went back to the House and was there approved under very peculiar conditions," argued Powell. "It went out upon a point of order in the House and was restored in the Senate, and when it came back to the House the House did not even refer it to the conference committee, as I remember it now, but called up that separate amendment and voted upon that question without it being referred to the conference committee." Not willing to drill deeper on this first day of hearings, Hale pressed no further. The House as well as the Senate had ultimately approved the wording. The fog of this non-answer had covered Powell's escape.

Later that day, Herbert asked how long the map would take to complete. Again dodging the question, the Major detailed how he proposed to proceed. Eventually Herbert would extract his answer: Powell thought twenty-four years.

On December 5, Powell was recalled; Herbert waited for several of the others to question him before he dived in to ask for a single practical purpose or new fact that the survey's work had uncovered after already spending all this money. Powell answered that the work had not been completed, but that did not deter Herbert from pressing. For the first time in the proceedings, Powell appeared confused, bringing up the importance of mapping to constructing charts for mariners—the province of the Coastal Survey, not any of his departments. The two men stared at each other from opposite sides of a vast abyss, Powell's unwavering faith in science challenged by an able man. Powell pulled back from specifics to identify why science itself was critical: "Perhaps the most practical value that a great scientific fact or principle may have subsists in its educating power—its power of improving the minds of the people."

Within the hour, Powell had fully regained his form, elaborating on how maps could practically aid the common good—touching on the discovery of minerals, how to determine the most efficient road and rail connections, plan sanitary water delivery, and determine which swamplands might be drained to create fertile cropland. Powell may have bristled internally at Herbert's line of questioning, but it still offered him the stage to speak directly, not only to the importance of his national mapping plan but also to the critical role that federal science could play in America. Had either Hayden or King come under such a grilling, they probably would have fallen back to evoking maps only as tools to exploit mineral resources for the great industrial engines of the Gilded Age. But here Powell shifted the discussion, invoking the need to create an even more informed citizenry. Few scientists of his era, if any, could extol these realities with such specificity, yet while wrapping each one in the noble mantle of science. Clearly frustrated by the end of that day's hearing, Herbert was reduced to muttering snidely, "That must be very useful to Von Moltke"—referring to Prussia's top field marshal—when Powell acknowledged that England's geodetic maps would be as useful to an invading army as to the country's defenders. On that note, the second day of the Allison Commission ended. But Herbert was not finished with Powell.

On August 6, the special committee unveiled its hard-hitting assessment of Coastal Survey operations. Not only had it lost track of valuable chronometers, but it retained "ladies" on the payroll who never worked. The superintendent frequently drank to excess during the day. The embarrassing revelations caused him to resign the next day. A week later, the federal First Auditor J. Q. Chenoweth of the Treasury Department announced an investigation into the Geological Survey, energized by his belief that it operated without congressional authority in seventeen states. Rumors swirled that Hayden had been sent far afield lest the auditor interrogate him. By the middle of September, the inflammatory abstract of a lengthy report, supposedly from a committee established by Chenoweth, found its way to the *New York Times* and *Boston Daily Advertiser,* the former announcing in large headlines "Geological Survey Abuses. A Report Making Charges of Illegal Expenditures and Fraud." The elaborate document challenged the legality of the survey's extending into the "old states," claimed that surveys had been made outside the United States, that fossils collected under the survey's aegis now fattened private collections, and that salaries grossly exceeded appropriations. Chenoweth drew aside a reporter for the *New York Herald* to impart a new twist, with the overall judgment that "if these scientific people cannot show that they have performed real work and of a character that ordinary people can understand, they will not be allowed to continue to draw their salaries." Clarence Dutton wrote a friend that the first auditor had been poking around the survey for the past three months. "The attack arises from a gang of cheap newspaper men backed by a few politicians who want to break down the barrier which keeps the petty patronage of the scientific bureaus from their reach."

Powell hit back hard against the charges, providing the interior secretary with a point-by-point refutation of the "baseless and absurd" newspaper allegations of the last four months. He sent copies to the newspapers concerned.

By late November 1885, a few days before the Allison Commission had returned from a nine-month hiatus, Herbert sought to bring a heavy gun in the scientific community against Powell and the survey. "The time has come when Congress ought to consider seriously whether it ought not to abolish the whole survey," he wrote to Alexander Agassiz, son of the famous biologist. "To me it is very clear that Major Powell is transcending the rule you lay down, that Government ought not to do scientific work which can be properly accomplished by private effort." This document, which he would submit to the Allison Commission, ended with the inquiry: "Please tell me also whether you deem it imperative that the Government geologist should do topography."

A known conservative who had made his fortune in Michigan copper, Agassiz for the most part believed that science belonged to privately funded academic institutions or simply to rich men. As director of Harvard's Museum of Comparative Zoology, Agassiz had had collegial interactions with Powell, but he now replied that he saw no reason why scientists, like others in the pursuit of knowledge, literature, and fine arts, should count on government support. Paleontology should be conducted in universities, in which it could be pursued more efficiently and effectively. States should prosecute topographic work. If the states were not willing to go to the expense of creating topographic maps for themselves, he wrote, then "it seems plain that they don't wish the Government to go to that expense for them." The letter delivered to Herbert his next line of attack, the "wasteful and extravagant" expense of publishing so many volumes at government cost. "There is no end to the kind of interesting documents which the heads of Bureaus could get printed at Government expense, and which very few individuals or societies would print, even had they the means at their command." Agassiz could not abide federal involvement in science, period.

In late January 1886, Powell countered Agassiz in a detailed letter to the Commission, inquiring as to whether only the wealthy should be employed in matters of science. Here is Powell, the passionate defender of the pursuit of knowledge and its implicit rightness, taking to a national pulpit to expand the place of science in a democracy. Whereas possession of property is exclusive, he wrote, the possession of knowledge is not. The knowledge that science uncovers cannot be owned: "Scholarship breeds scholarship, wisdom breeds wisdom, discovery breeds discovery." He certainly agreed that all science was not the province of the federal government, but such projects as providing a topographical record of the nation undoubtedly were. Imagine topographical maps sifting into every college, coming to the attention of every student and professor, for every community to make use of.

For all Powell's eloquence, Herbert's well-targeted attacks, and the mounting criticism in the press, appeared to sway the Allison Commission. In early May, the chairman sent Powell a courtesy copy of the Commission's draft bill, shortly to be submitted to the House, along with Herbert's summary of the Commission's year and a half of work. Powell was aghast. The bill proposed to preclude the survey's spending money on paleontology and work that involved the general discussion of geological theories. The survey could publish nothing more than an annual report. Herbert no longer attacked the survey's legitimacy, but instead more subtly intended to starve it by severely restricting its ability to publish. On these dry bones, Powell could hardly have felt sanguine about his organization's ability to survive: Deprived of its ability to publish, his ability to get information out to the public would be critically compromised. "We think it is clear," Herbert continued in his summary, "that no such ambitious scheme of geology as that we are now pursuing was ever mapped by man." Once more handicapped by his iritis, Powell still mustered his extraordinary resources and returned to the offensive, writing a detailed response to the proposed bill and distributing it to papers across the nation. He extended his lobbying to scientists and politicians alike, enlisting every ally he had ever had in a last-ditch effort to save the survey.

Powell's worst fears came about when the *New York Times* headlined the Commission's report the following day: "Astonishing Growth of the Geological Survey Officially Condemned." Its reporter had gotten matters wrong. The Commission's full six members had agreed only to the wording of the bill, and certainly not Herbert's summary, a clearly minority position. Furthermore, the article mistakenly reported that the full Commission believed that the survey's work on the "elaborate geological map" should be curtailed as well as the "pernicious tendency" of certain bureaus to control the government in the name of science. But the damage was done. Had Powell's boat finally overturned in the rapids of public opinion?

Against Herbert's strong objections—but in acknowledgment of the *Times'* erroneous claims—Allison gave Powell one last chance to testify, on May 13, although the testimony would come too late to make the official Commission report. Powell argued hard that the survey needed to continue its work in paleontology and general geology, but did agree to some restrictions on printing and engraving. The chairman requested that he limit comments to the content of the bill itself, but the Major could not resist the chance to smite Herbert's minority report. Herbert left the hearing early, inescapably realizing then or shortly thereafter that he had overplayed his hand.

On June 8, 1886, nineteen months after the Commission conducted its first hearing, Allison submitted its official report.
Signed by four of the six commissioners, the fifty-three-page document revealed a nearly complete reversal of the earlier bill, and a
repudiation of Herbert's accusations. Powell's last-minute, passionate appeal had yielded rich fruit. The Commission found no
misconduct in the survey, instead declaring Powell's administrative leadership exemplary. The majority reaffirmed the place of
topographic mapmaking as a province of the federal government.
Not only that, but the report asserted that it was "more than prob-
able that this survey will be continued indefinitely," as the nation's
population filled up its vast lands and its needs changed. Herbert's
most persistent charge—that the survey's mapping work would
never end—had undergone a transformation in the eyes of the
majority from a liability to a valuable feature.

The commissioners acknowledged the need to constrict the survey's printing budget, but had wholly revised its opinion upon hearing from Director Powell, and would submit a substitute bill to
Congress. This bill would require an itemized budget for all four
scientific agencies, which would "exert a restraining influence" on
excessive spending, but no specific limits would be entertained.
The report and resulting bill marked not just a conclusive victory
for Powell, but also solidified indefinitely the federal government's
connection to science. Powell had his national mapping project,
built upon years of overreaching appropriations wording, but now
the institution he had shepherded through near famine was a powerful, appreciated arm of federal strength. He had made it through
whirlpools and giant standing waves even more menacing than
those on the Colorado. When Congress enacted the Commission's
bill, it moved the nation far closer to placing federal science in the
budget on an ongoing basis, not just in a series of scrambles from
project to project. It was the Major's finest hour.

"Powell justly feels in very good spirits today," wrote one of his
staff members to Marsh in New Haven, "as he has had a long fight

over the matter." Both must have known how much of an understatement this was. For his part, the director exultantly read parts of the Commission's report out loud in the Hooe to the Great Basin Mess.

Later that year, Powell would be one of forty-two dignitaries receiving an honorary degree at Harvard's 250th anniversary celebration. Few would argue that he ranked among the top of America's most respected and influential scientists; his USGS reached into virtually every major college and university in the nation, dominating and directing the sciences. He had become a major force in forging Washington's reputation as a first-class center for science policy, ensuring that science would become a permanent part of the federal bureaucracy. The year that the Allison Commission vindicated the survey's broad scope of inquiry, Heidelberg University awarded him a PhD in absentia, and he would lend a hand in founding the National Geographic Society. The dynamo so impressive to his Illinois Wesleyan peers long ago had lost little steam, despite the crippling iritis and near-constant pain in his stump. The following year he would become president of the American Association for the Advancement of Science.

Throughout his life, Powell had embraced—or created—roles necessary to respond to the fast-rising challenges of a breakneck-growing republic: soldier, explorer, geologist, bureaucrat, and institution builder. Now events conspired to move him toward his last, greatest, and perhaps most difficult act.

CHAPTER 11

A Tough Opponent

I n the mid-to-late 1880s, the West got hit with a one-two punch—a sockdolager, as Powell himself might have described it. The first, a series of particularly severe blizzards in 1886–1887 slammed across the Great Plains, striking the Dakotas, western Kansas, the Indian Territory (soon to be Oklahoma), and the Texas panhandle. In southwestern Kansas, a man wearing a light linen overcoat froze to death, his pocket stuffed with a flyer advertising Kansas as "the Italy of America." Some one hundred Kansans died, including entire families trapped in their houses by vast snowdrifts. And the storms savaged the newly booming cattle industry with particular intensity, freezing millions of the animals where they stood. Theodore Roosevelt returned to his Dakota ranch to find half his herd dead, so he sold off his enterprise at a loss and sought a different dream. When the snow finally melted, farmers found the bodies of steers suspended in tree branches, their last desperate act having been to climb snowdrifts after the last green leaves.

A cruel, multiyear drought followed directly upon the snow. "The sky began to scare us with its light," remarked Hamlin Garland, invoking the desolation settling over the dry-as-a-bone prairie. By 1890, the drought's third year, between a quarter and a half of the once-hopeful settlers of Kansas and Nebraska had gone, some of them nailing the iconic sign to their wagons, "In God we trusted. In Kansas we busted." Drought struck hardest just east of "Powell's line," reaching from Kansas to the Dakotas where farmers could just get by without irrigation. Families had withstood waves of grasshoppers desolating their crops and myriad other agricultural misfortunes, but no degree of perseverance or courage could overcome persistent drought. The mild weather following the Civil War had encouraged the populations of Nebraska, Kansas, and Colorado to double or triple, all founded on the idea that such favorable conditions would continue indefinitely. They did not. The droughts and national economic setbacks of the 1880s and early 1890s brought social unrest, starvation, and widespread destitution, driving upward of 300,000 people from the arid lands—a drop of 50 to 75 percent—their dreams dashed.

The realities of arid land settled in: Hundreds of irrigation companies founded in the 1870s and 1880s, financed largely by eastern capital, did not survive the decade. The regular mechanisms of American capitalism—private equity, the resilience of the individual—even when injected with healthy doses of Manifest Destiny and the nation's eternal optimism, could not override the challenges of the arid West.

For Senator William M. Stewart of Nevada, the West's least populous state, this added up to calamity. The silver boom of the Comstock Lode, America's first great discovery of silver ore, had tailed off in recent years; many miners and those supporting that industry had left the state. Stewart increasingly felt heat from the Southern Pacific Railroad, Nevada's most extensive private land owner, which feared that drought and the declines in mining would kill the land development upon which it counted. Stewart took his case to the Senate, convinced that the federal government should take part in the irrigation business.

On March 20, 1888, Stewart helped push through a joint resolution directing the secretary of the interior to "make an examination" of the advantages of storing water for the irrigable lands—including the assessment of stream capacity, and the practicability and costs of building reservoirs. The inquiry's objective rested squarely on the arid region's being "capable of supporting a large population thereby adding to the national wealth and prosperity." In so doing, Stewart launched a train of events that would lead him into a bitter confrontation with Powell. Stewart would prove the most formidable opponent that Powell had ever encountered.

A week later, again at Stewart's urging, the Senate asked Powell for his estimate of the costs associated with running an irrigation survey that would examine the practicability of water storage in the arid region, determine what lands could be reasonably irrigated, and identify locations for reservoirs, canals, and dams. In a consequent hearing, the director replied that he would need $250,000 for the first year, but that a careful, responsible evaluation of possibly reclaimable lands would require upward of $5.5 million, most of it for topographical mapping to reveal the drainage system. Such knowledge could then help uncover the most effective means of distributing the limited water available.

During discussion on the floor of the Senate, Stewart reassured his colleagues that the irrigation survey would only identify reservoir and canal sites, not build them. Stewart had long believed that the federal government needed to cede all public lands to the states; the sale of these tracts would finance the irrigation works. Stewart praised Powell as the person to get the survey done, calling him "a very competent and enthusiastic man." While the senator might have initiated the irrigation survey, it had been Powell's *Arid Lands* report that brought the issue of irrigation to the general public consciousness, and paved the way for this new effort.

Six months later, Powell had $100,000 in hand. The bill creating the new irrigation survey included a badly written clause, inserted by a Colorado congressman to prevent speculators from trailing after surveyors and buying up prime land. It authorized the secretary of the interior, at the request of the president, to pull "all lands made susceptible of irrigation" from public entry: or, in other words, take them off the market. A prudent caution certainly, but interpretations of the wording would come to bedevil the whole process. In December, Stewart urged the Senate to create a Select Committee on Irrigation and Reclamation of Arid Lands under the Public Lands Committee. The Senate agreed, naming Stewart its chairman, and appropriating $80,000 for a congressional fact-finding trip out West.

That month, President Cleveland spoke directly to irrigation issues in the last annual congressional address of his first four-year term. Republican Benjamin Harrison had just narrowly beaten him, losing the popular vote but taking the electoral college with wins in New York and Indiana. "I can not but think it perilous to suffer either these lands or the sources of their irrigation to fall into the hands of monopolies . . . ," said Cleveland, "and the public good presents no demand for hasty dispossession of national ownership and control." Harrison harbored no such burning passion and would prove overall a charming but weak executive, whom Cleveland would convincingly defeat in four years, garnering a second term. Two weeks after his inauguration, Harrison issued a proclamation opening the Cherokee Strip to homesteaders as of April 22 at noon. "Sooners" claimed upward of two million acres over a matter of hours in what would be dubbed the Great Land Rush of 1889.

Even before Congress officially appropriated the funds, Powell had already kicked the irrigation survey into high gear, tasking Prof Thompson to handle mapping and Clarence Dutton to head up engineering and hydrographic work. Every unused corner of the Hooe filled with new hires. An annex across the street, plus offices at the Smithsonian and regional locations, just about accommodated the rest. Besides the USGS and the Bureau of Ethnology,

Powell now had another entire agency to run, but no other career official was better positioned to launch so ambitious a program. His organization had experience juggling multiple complex operations, and G. K. Gilbert stepped in to help run things. By the summer of 1889, Powell's men had set up stream-gauge stations on the Arkansas, Rio Grande, Carson, Truckee, Gila, and Snake rivers. By the end of the following June, they had surveyed and identified 147 reservoir sites: 33 in California, 46 in Colorado, 27 in Montana, 39 in New Mexico, and 2 in Nevada. The reservoir sites themselves covered 165,932 acres, which Powell projected might irrigate nearly two million acres of dry land, only a fraction of the 30 million acres that the irrigation survey had designated as irrigable, but still more extensive than all the currently irrigated land in Arizona, New Mexico, Utah, Wyoming, Montana, Idaho, and Nevada combined. The survey coined the terms "runoff" and "flyoff," still in use today. Powell agreed with Stewart that the federal government should provide only planning and estimates. He imagined a series of small dams, rarely more than several feet high, each on a tributary of a major river, which would provide water for local communities. Congress found him $250,000 for the second year, and would have considered more, but Powell said he was not yet ready.

On August 1, 1889, Stewart's entourage left from St. Paul, Minnesota, traveling in style in a Pullman train car. At Stewart's invitation, Powell joined the party, which would travel to the Dakotas, Montana, Wyoming, Colorado, Utah, Idaho, Nevada, California, Arizona, New Mexico, and Texas, covering 14,000 miles and conducting hundreds of interviews. The Major and the white-haired six-foot-tall senator made an odd couple. Stewart had made his mark in Virginia City, earning huge fees litigating the tangled claims of Nevada's (then the Utah Territories') Comstock Lode. An implacable mercenary for mining companies, he had no peer at intimidating, bribing, and cajoling judges, juries, and witnesses.

At one point, the blue-eyed pit bull had forced the resignation of the Nevada Territory's entire judiciary. Several of his most questionable mining deals would dog him for the rest of his life. He came to Washington in 1865, briefly hiring the young Samuel Clemens as a clerk. Clemens, whose pen name was becoming Mark Twain, would later lampoon his former boss in *Roughing It* with a caricature of the senator snarling behind a piratical eye patch. On what would become Dupont Circle, Stewart soon raised a five-story, Second Empire mansion, which boasted a palatial ballroom and room after room crowded with massive Chinese teak furniture and gilded chairs upholstered with Aubusson tapestry. One reporter claimed that "Stewart's Castle" attracted more curiosity seekers than the White House. Stewart, a strong free-silver advocate, reflected his epoch, helping to write the National Mining Law of 1866, which to this day still affords mining interests startlingly favorable terms for developing public lands.

Somewhere along these 14,000 miles, Stewart and Powell's friendly relationship deteriorated. Washington's *Daily Critic* surmised that the senator "grew jealous of the attentions paid the geologic director." These two men made strange bedfellows indeed, drawn together by their agreement that irrigating the west required federal assistance. But as Stewart had begun to realize, they came at this great issue from different universes. The two bull-headed men, each accustomed to getting his own way, proved as compatible as oil and water.

The Dakota Territory delegates at their first constitutional convention wanted to hear from the grizzled USGS director, not from the booming gentleman from Nevada. Powell urged them to keep state control of water rights. Far from extolling western corporate boosterism, Powell preached a solidly populist message: "Fix it in your constitution that no corporation—no body of men—no capital can get possession of the right of your waters. Hold the waters in the hands of the people." That summer, while the committee's

train chugged through the West, events in the field would acceler-
ate the coming Washington showdown between the two men.

Other problems rose up to bedevil the survey. Land speculators
hired their own surveyors to follow Powell's men, then filed on
land and the water rights along the streams and gulches. "Such
monopoly by the speculators promises to defeat the plans of the
government," reported the *Cheyenne Daily Leader*. Shortly after
the irrigation survey designated southern Idaho's Bear Lake as
its first reservoir site, the Bear Lake and River Water Works and
Irrigation Company filed for all the land and water rights throughout the basin—not only the lake, but also Bear River and all its
tributaries—set on diverting the water south to irrigate 200,000
acres of the Salt Lake Basin. The governor of Idaho telegraphed
the secretary of the interior in alarm, demanding that he forestall,
in the newspaper's words, "this great wrong to Idaho."

In August, after checking with the attorney general and the
president, Interior Secretary John Noble invoked the anti-
speculation amendment in the irrigation survey's appropriation
bill, but, instead of merely closing off potential reservoir sites, the
secretary removed all public lands nationwide from entry, shuttered the land offices, and suspended all claims retroactively to
October 2, 1888, when the bill had been signed. With one flourish
of his pen, Noble had closed off hundreds of millions of acres to
settlement and suspended 134,000 filings and entries on nine million acres. Legislators had never meant to concede such sweeping
authority as to seal off the entire public heritage, although the
amendment's muddy wording could indeed be so interpreted. "The
segregation of irrigable lands provided for by the law," explained
the *Rocky Mountain News,* "is not intended in any way as a bar to
their acquirement under the land laws. . . . The only reservation to
be made is in the case of the sites for storage reservoirs. These are
to be withdrawn from public entry to prevent their monopoly by

speculators." Soon the fury of politicians, railroad interests, and
land grabbers exploded into a wildfire, most of it pointed toward
the director of the USGS. "It is doubtful that any modern controversy among men of learning," wrote Wallace Stegner in 1954,
"has generated more venom than this one did."

Though Powell had nothing to do with this draconian measure,
powerful forces understood that he—and he alone—would be the
person to judge for the secretary of the interior when the public
lands would again be open. By the look of it, the president and a
land-hungry nation waited upon Powell's judgment on the matter.
Seldom has so wide ranging a power been dropped into the lap of a
single individual. Asked whether he agreed with Noble's decision,
Powell said that he did. He had always been upfront that the irrigation survey would take several—or more—years to complete.

As the seismic rumblings over Noble's decision began to am-
plify ominously, an old enemy surfaced to blindside Powell. The
paleontologist E. D. Cope had never forgotten the Major's siding
with Marsh long ago. For his part, Powell had met with Cope in
1888, agreeing to put him on the USGS payroll so that he might
finish his book, already more than a decade old. In return, Cope
agreed to turn some of the fossils in his collections over to the
Smithsonian. "I feel much relieved," wrote Cope. A year later, no
fossils—or manuscript—was forthcoming, so Secretary Noble demanded that either he surrender the fossils or forgo salary and
publication.

Cope blew up, livid that he had no say in the disposition of the
fossils in which he had personally sunk $75,000 of his shrinking
fortune. Detecting Powell's hand behind the secretary's threat,
Cope rushed to scandal writer W. H. Ballou, a stringer for the *New
York Herald*. The *Herald's* competition that January was enjoying
a sensational run as their star writer, Nellie Bly, had decided to
challenge the central conceit of Jules Verne's hugely successful
novel *Around the World in Eighty Days*. Traveling by ship, train,
and burro, the charismatic thirty-year-old finished in 72 days,

6 hours, and 11 minutes, steaming into New York Harbor late that month to become a huge star. Tweaked by his competitor's success, the *Herald*'s James Gordon Bennett, Jr., sponsor of such publicity stunts as sending Stanley to find Livingstone in the African jungle, was not about to be bested. When Ballou came to him with Cope's accusations, Bennett went big, publishing a huge headline, "Scientists Wage Bitter Warfare . . . Red Hot Denials Put Forth." The article quoted Cope as alleging that the survey had become a politico-scientific monopoly that operated like a political machine. Ballou claimed that a steaming volcano lay underneath the survey and would soon erupt. Powell responded with a masterful dissection of Cope's character, praising him as a fair systematist who could still do great work, but was unable to see that "the enemy which he sees forever haunting him as a ghost is himself." The headlines died down, but then Marsh reinvigorated them with his own attack on Cope, dredging up a twenty-year-old claim that Cope had placed the skull at the wrong end of a dinosaur skeleton.

The same week that the *Herald* article broke, Powell appeared before Stewart's Senate Select Committee, attending six of its ten hearings between January 17 and March 28, 1890. The Major unpacked his ideas once more, perhaps the most innovative of which was integrating water rights with claims to the land that the water flowed through. Here he displayed a map of the arid lands, separated into colorful circles of various sizes, designating watersheds. He also introduced the idea of irrigation districts, which would manage their own water, neither sending it out of their own watershed nor importing any from another. These communities, established on parcels of the land for settlers at eighty acres, cut in half from the traditional quarter section, would own the water communally, each having an equal voice in its use. Each district would make its own rules and raise capital for building its system of irrigation; the federal government would help only in the fundamental organization and nothing more—whether the construction of reservoirs, dams, or canals. Powell offered an unparalleled understanding of watersheds, rivers and their tributaries, the history of irrigation, artesian water, storm water, and reservoir capacities.

Again and again, Chairman Stewart and his fellow Republicans questioned the extraordinary expense of creating the topographical atlas. Powell never shied from his belief that the correct siting of hydrologic works necessitated such a broad undertaking. Mapping offered the cheapest, quickest, and most efficient means of carrying out this task. Such mapping made it possible to identify the potentially irrigable land at the outset. But why, asked Stewart, could not an engineer simply climb a mountain and eyeball a reservoir or dam site without the benefit of topographic data?

Powell explained the need for exact information, perhaps thinking about the article he had written for *The North American Review* about the recent catastrophic Johnstown Flood. Under heavy rain, the earthen South Fork Dam on the little Conemaugh River had collapsed, releasing a thirty-foot wall of water onto Johnstown, Pennsylvania, and killing 2,200 people. The worst failure of American engineering had shaken the public's faith in dams. Powell had stepped in to reassure. By all accounts, he acknowledged, the engineers had built a sound dam, but had neglected to consider "the duty the dam was required to perform." The engineers had not built the dam to accommodate what nature could deliver under maximum rainfall or snow-melt conditions into that gentle valley. Quite simply, the engineers had failed to reckon the capacity of the entire drainage basin and the slopes and declivities that hemmed the dam in. Establish that body of knowledge, combine it with annual precipitation data, and an engineer could accurately calculate the maximum amount of floodwater—and design a structure capable of containing it. A topographical mapping lay central to such calculations.

This was the linchpin of Powell's argument to the senators: The irrigation survey might certainly designate reservoir sites without the benefit of exact mapping, but many would not be scientifically

sited and thus be prone to disasters. So, too, topographical work
would help determine the location of underground water, obviat-
ing the wasteful need to drill at random. But said Senator Gideon
Moody of South Dakota about experimental well drilling, "what
these people want is . . . the courage of conviction." Give them
money to dig wells and "they will take care of the rest." Powell
would not budge: "I do not wish to give the people courage to lead
them on to failure, to waste their energies in seeking disaster."

Over days of testimony, Stewart turned his legendary powers
of advocacy toward strong-arming Powell into submission or finding a crack in his argument. Again and again he attacked Powell.
Back and forth they went like two exhausted prizefighters in late
rounds. The Major never lost his cool, adopting the demeanor of a
patient teacher with a somewhat dim student, explaining things
over and over again, invoking an example every time. The senator
had come up against Powell's legendarily steely resolve.

On January 31, the fourth day, Stewart understood that he had
drawn to a stalemate. Calling the committee to order, he acknowledged that much valuable general material had been collected.
"What we want now is to hear from any person present who has
practical ideas as to what can and ought to be done to facilitate
irrigation; how it can be directly got at; what aid the Government
can give most advantageously and with the least expense to make
a profitable development of the arid regions." Stewart, like any
western senator, wanted answers right away, not to wait for some
bureaucrat driven by righteous philosophical generalities and taste
for larger payrolls to take as many years as he pleased. Powell saw
the immense costs to the farmer—and American democracy—by a
reckless, ill-considered development of the West. Both Powell and
Stewart agreed that irrigation of the arid lands remained a national priority—and that the federal government needed to aid
that process but should not be involved in the actual building of
the infrastructure. Yet at the root, they held diametrically opposed
perspectives on how to get irrigation done. Any chance of their

working together had now passed. Over the last days of testimony, Stewart's antagonism toward Powell had grown deeply and visibly personal.

Political expediency would have suggested that Powell back down and live to fight another battle, or approach Stewart with a compromise, although by then Stewart would have probably rejected anything that Powell advanced. Anyhow, compromise would not have crossed Powell's mind. Not only did his tenacity kick in, but his deep convictions on these matters would never have let him budge. He felt himself fighting for the very future of the American republic.

In mid-March, the senator would try a new tack to best Powell, finding a weakness not in Powell's arguments, but in one of his subordinates.

By all accounts, Clarence Dutton, the bright Army Ordnance Corps captain for the past fifteen years on permanent seasonal loan to the USGS, had served faithfully as one of Powell's most trusted lieutenants. Dutton, sporting a trimmed Van Dyke and an always-burning cigar, his carriage more soldierly than scientific, brought an unassuming manner but a trenchant intellect to Powell's innermost circle. Powell regarded him as his heir to the survey's preeminent geology department. Along with Gilbert, Dutton had instituted rigorous bookkeeping protocols, which kept the survey out of trouble under repeated congressional inquiries.

Unlike Gilbert, who viewed the Major as something of a father figure, Dutton called his boss "Powell," perhaps a natural result of their common war experience, during which both had served as artillery officers and had suffered severe wounds. Where Powell enjoyed immersing himself in Scott and Longfellow, Dutton tended toward Twain and the humorous aphorisms of Josh Billings—his joke-and-riddle-telling softening Powell's often overtaxed countenance. The Major might be interested, Dutton once wrote from the field, that he had solved a vexing problem, namely "how high and steep and rough a hill a mule can roll down without getting killed." Or he might write to Clarence King how he had found earth faults in flagrante delicto. Later, when the naturalists John Muir and John Burroughs encountered the baffling immensities of the Grand Canyon, they would turn to the surprisingly lyrical exposition of Dutton's *Tertiary History*.

But Powell particularly counted on Dutton's eclectic curiosity, much like the Major's, which always took him off on interesting tangents, whether in studying the volcanoes of Hawaii or the earthquake that battered Charleston in 1886. The same year of the Stewart hearings, Dutton had brought boats to Oregon's Crater Lake—a startlingly difficult feat in those days—to survey it and plumb its depths for the first time. With those data, he theorized about the crater's origin, coming up with an explanation that still stands today.

When the irrigation survey work fell on him rather suddenly, Powell tasked Dutton to run the hydrographic engineering division. Although reluctant to leave the studies he loved, the dutiful captain agreed. This inveterate chess player, capable of playing seven simultaneous games blindfolded, understood that stakes in this particular inquiry had grown steadily higher, so confronted Powell about the propriety of spending irrigation survey appropriations on topographic mapping, when the USGS had already dedicated federal dollars to that purpose. Powell might all-too-convincingly be charged with soaking up irrigation survey funds to water his larger mapping agenda. Powell did not see how these could be separated. The national topographic mapping project remained critical to his current mission—and the success of the irrigation survey.

For all Dutton's abilities, he would prove no match for Stewart's deft cross-examination on March 13. Ever the responsible military man responding candidly to his commanding officer, Dutton acknowledged that his engineering and hydrographic section received less than half the irrigation survey appropriations assigned to the topographical division. Stewart then unwound a long array of pointed questions centering on whether an engineer needed a topographic map to locate a reservoir site. Dutton explained and explained, but Stewart battered away. Finally, the cornered Dutton conceded that mapping was not strictly necessary. Stewart now had what he needed and moved to close the session.

Just before adjournment, Senator James K. Jones from Arkansas stepped in to make sure he had heard right:

Senator Jones: "You say a topographic map is of very little value to the engineer in locating irrigating works?"

Captain Dutton: "I think they are of only general value."

Senator Jones: "And are by no means necessary?"

Captain Dutton: "I do not think they are necessary within the meaning of the law . . ."

At that moment, the extent of his concession dawned on Dutton, the direct contradiction of his boss's outspoken stance. One feels Dutton jarring under the Major's boney left elbow in his ribs even though Powell was not in attendance that day. Dutton unraveled. "The term 'necessary' has a practical interpretation," he stammered, "which is not easy to define." He was no longer making sense. "We are every day certifying that certain things are necessary on our bills and on our vouchers. While in a certain sense and in the ordinary acceptation of the term they are necessary, in an absolute sense they are not."

Senator Reagan ended that day's session by clearly throwing the obviously demoralized Dutton a lifeline: Had the government made a mistake in authorizing "these topographic surveys"?

Dutton vigorously clutched the offering: "No, sir, I think not. I think no money has been better spent." With this last line, he made clear that he believed in the broad mapping project, but that did not matter to Stewart. He now had the apparent defection of a Powell loyalist on the record.

When Powell next appeared before the committee just five days later, he explained "the error which I think Captain Dutton has committed." Each of those subordinates tasked with a given branch of work often overestimated the importance of their responsibilities. It was for him, not Dutton, to coordinate the overall effort. When the Major suggested that committee call upon the actual mapmakers to testify, Chairman Stewart agreed, but requested their testimony come only in writing. Stewart's undisguised venom proved too much for Senator Jones, who dismissed this approach as a "onesided affair," asserting that it was "not right" for the committee to only question witnesses, such as Dutton, who fell on one side of the issue. Stewart was forced to yield the point.

Several days later, the committee heard from Thompson, Gilbert, and a USGS topographer, Willard Johnson. The latter recorded that the engineering surveyors' calls upon him for map data were "continuous, urgent, and annoyingly persistent." Mapping was indeed an "indispensible and unerring guide" to determining long-term reservoir sites and the paths of irrigation canals. As Powell had testified, the engineers could locate valuable reservoir sites, but their efforts were not systematic and "great blunders . . . involving the expenditure of vast sums" could be "avoided by the early expenditure of a very small, relatively insignificant, sum." Do the job right from the start, argued this loyal and well-coached lieutenant, and avoid potentially catastrophic consequences. But Powell and all his subordinates could have submitted to weeks more of inquisition without altering Stewart's mind.

Powell had seriously miscalculated the depth of Stewart's personal animus. He realized too late that Stewart was playing for high stakes. "In the conflict," as Stewart wrote a friend, "there is great danger that the whole matter of irrigation will be defeated altogether. But I would rather be defeated than have the whole country tied up under Powell."

On May 8, the Select Committee issued its report; the majority opinion, written by Stewart with the consent of his Republican colleagues, strongly advocated that irrigation matters transfer from the USGS to the recently created Department of Agriculture. Much of the report centered on Powell's allegedly illegal transfer of funds appropriated for the irrigation survey on topographical work. This report cited expert testimony about the wastefulness of mapping. The minority opinion—from the Democrats Reagan, Gorman, and Jones—fully supported Powell's recommendations, lest lands and waters fall into "the hands of the wealthy few and the farmers themselves will be but hired laborers."

Two weeks later, Stewart pushed a resolution through the Senate requiring the secretary of the interior to document how much of the irrigation survey budget had been diverted to topographical surveying. Despite Powell's firm declaration from the start that topographical mapping remained critical to locating reservoir sites, Stewart clearly prepared to hang him for it.

Powell took his case before the public, telling Washington's *Evening Star* that he was fighting to prevent "a sort of hydraulic feudal system," which would undoubtedly emerge should speculation and "moneyed sharks" gobble up the irrigable lands and waters in the West. Furthermore, he was at a loss to understand how the survey might put together a successful plan for irrigation without preliminary mapping of the region.

The next morning Stewart excoriated Powell on the Senate floor, asserting that his survey had misallocated more than half its appropriation on "vast and expensive surveys of no practical use," not to mention hiring scores of congressmen's sons to exert an enormous, invisible lobby in Washington. Powell's survey amounted to no more than "a mass of humbug and foolishness" and "a great lying-in hospital for lame ducks." And from then on nothing could curb his vitriol. "I have never met so unscrupulous and extraordinary a man," he wrote an influential friend, "ambitious to the last degree, and the most artful, insinuating, and persevering lobbyist known in the annals of this country." To another, he railed that Powell was "ruining the West." And to one more that the Major was "drunk with power and deaf to reason." Nor did he stop there, becoming "a frequent, almost daily visitor to the secretary of the Interior and the president demanding the summary removal of Director Powell," reported *The Daily Critic*. On June 4, Secretary of the Interior Noble categorically denied that any Geological Survey money had been defrayed to the irrigation survey, or vice versa.

Harsh words flew between Stewart and Reagan in a Senate cloakroom one afternoon in mid-June. As he passed the other, an angry Stewart "charged Reagan with falsehood," whereupon the 250-pound, seventy-two-year-old Texan swung a roundhouse at the Nevadan but missed. "[F]or a moment it looked as if the two antiques would indulge in an old-fashioned fist fight of the date of 1800," wrote an eyewitness. Before Stewart could retaliate, bystanders pulled them apart, ushering them to sofas on opposite sides of the room like prizefighters broken in the clutch. Later that afternoon, Stewart visited Reagan to apologize, but the still-smoldering Texan refused to see him.

By July 2, when Senator Allison convened the Appropriations Committee, he mustered a cadre of heavy-hitting western colleagues. Stewart was there, of course, along with Moody (South Dakota), Allen (Washington), Carey (Wyoming), Paddock (Nebraska), Power and Sanders (Montana), and Reagan (Texas). When Powell came in as a witness, even that formidable fighting man and explorer must have recoiled slightly from the hostile atmosphere. Five of the eight senators came from four brand-new western states—North and South Dakota, Washington, Montana—each enclosing great tracts of arid public land. All Republicans, these five senators from rapidly growing states had been alarmed at the closure of public lands. Without sales to homesteaders, these newcomer commonwealths stood to lose considerable tax revenue.

Powell stuck bluntly to his guns, stating that "I think it would be almost a criminal act to go on as we are doing now, and allow thousands and hundreds of thousands of people to establish homes where they can not maintain themselves." Stewart and Moody led a blistering interrogation, repeatedly breaking in on the Major's responses. At one point, Powell told Stewart to either stop interrupting or forgo his questioning.

Director Powell: "Senator, in the first place, you make a statement which you do not mean to make to me—that I have got the whole country reserved. No word was ever said to me about that reservation; that was put in by Congress; nobody consulted me about that in any way. I have not done it. I never advocated it. That reservation was put into the law independently of me. Yet you affirm here and put it in the record that I had it done. What had I to do with it? Nothing."

Even Chairman Allison felt some sympathy for Powell, interrupting his "Brother Stewart" to remind him that he had questioned Powell for nearly an hour to the frustration of his "brethren." Later, in some exasperation Allison told Stewart that Powell had clearly answered that he could not bring off his irrigation surveying job unless he did the appropriate topographic mapping. Stewart shot back that "then we would rather have no appropriation, because we do not want the money spent in that way. The engineers say that this topographic survey is not necessary." Allison asked incredulously, "You do not want the appropriation of $720,000?" Retorted Stewart: "Not if it involves the tying up of the country by topographic surveys. . . . We would rather have nothing than have that plan carried out."

Senator Moody carried on the questioning, shotgunning inquiries about rainfall, locations of tributary outlets, names of rail lines—all designed to stretch Powell to a snapping point. He only grew more frustrated when Powell did not bend, pulling out arcane answers to geographical questions as if from the air. Only Reagan offered support. The rest of the senators of both parties acted as though Powell was a recalcitrant hooligan brought in before a magistrate. They had covered this harsh terrain time and again.

In the spring of 1890, as the hearings ground on, Powell again took his arguments before a larger audience, writing a series of articles for *Century Illustrated Monthly Magazine,* then the most respected, widely read "genteel" magazine of the day. Over the past five years, *Century* had excerpted Mark Twain's *The Adventures of Huckleberry Finn,* Henry James's *The Bostonians,* Grant's memoirs, and Theodore Roosevelt on ranching. *Century*'s editor, Richard Watson Gilder, offered Powell an extraordinary soapbox, three articles to run in three consecutive issues, a testament to Powell's intellectual standing. No outlet would bring him a more influential readership. And Gilder assured, with the three articles, that few of those who counted could miss Powell's implications. Only excerpts from the vast, masterful biography of Abraham Lincoln, written by his personal secretaries John Hay and John G. Nicolay, also earned three installments, but those spread across three years. Over twenty-five crowded Victorian pages, beginning in March, Powell unleashed "The Irrigable Lands of the Arid Regions," "The Non-Irrigable Lands of the Arid Region," and finally "Institutions for the Arid Lands."

Uninterrupted by rapid fire congressional interrogation, Powell could muse and proclaim, warn and inspire, never once referring to the irrigation survey or the passions it aroused. The articles smacked of vintage Powell: clips of badly translated Indian poetry and wandering asides but also stretches of breathtakingly novel ideas, forcefully delivered. In the dozen years since he published the *Arid Lands* report, Powell had further refined his vision. No longer content only to recommend grazing cooperatives and tracts of forestland overseen by lumbermen, the Major now confidently proposed a plan "to establish local self-government by hydrographic basins." The boldly colorful map of the arid West broken up into some 140 watersheds indicated the purview of each proposed commonwealth, each responsible for the water within it. "All the waters are common property until they reach the main canal, where they are to be distributed among the people." The commonwealths would also contain shared grazing and pasture, held in trust by the federal government, but their use dictated by the locals. Inspired by the Mormon achievements across the Utah desert, Powell proclaimed: "The people in such a district have common interests, common rights, and common duties, and must necessarily work together for common purposes." Self-interest would ensure that local owners, for instance, would tread carefully about clear-cutting mountain forests on the slopes of their watersheds, because such activity would not only constrict their water supply but also extinguish steady timber values.

Thus Powell anticipated "the tragedy of the commons," an economic theory coined nearly eighty years later. When a group wins access to a resource held in common—pasture, for instance, fish in the sea, or water in arid lands—a distinct pattern emerges: The overall effect of individuals left free to act independently leads to overexploitation and often the destruction of the entire resource. Without malice or intention, individuals naturally so often work against the common, long-term good of all users. Thus fishermen may overfish their waters, crash fish populations, and end up jobless near a barren sea. Powell structured the commonwealth watershed model to avoid such outcomes, in a belief that "a body of interdependent and unified interests and values, all collected in one hydrographic basin" would achieve a self-controlling mechanism for long-term sustainability. He pressed emphatically that the federal government would not be a major participant: "So dreamers may dream, and so ambition may dictate, but in the name of the men who labor I demand that the laborers shall employ themselves; that the enterprise shall be controlled by the men who have the genius to organize, and whose homes are in the lands developed, and that the money shall be furnished by the people; and I say to the Government: Hands off!" Here he tied land sustainability into a grand American tradition of believing that a local body of people can bring forward the talent to create a just and forward-looking community.

Of all his writings, this presents Powell at his clearest and most passionate, yet ever the clear-eyed, detached scientist reflecting that the complex dance between human beings and their environment did not defer to political boundaries and was always changing. But here, too, is the Manifest Destiny Powell, gung-ho for opening the gates to America's glorious future. The arid country, he urged, contains "the best agricultural lands of the continent," and must be "redeemed because they are our best lands." Remember, the preacher in Powell exhorted, "conquered rivers are better servants than wild clouds." Speaking about putting the Colorado River to human use, he said that "great works must be constructed costing millions of dollars, and then ultimately a region of the country can be irrigated larger than was ever cultivated along the Nile, and all the product of Egypt will flourish therein."

Again and again, Powell drew the reader's attention to the deep differences between East and West. The East had been won by the work of individuals and families on 160-acre parcels of land—the hallowed quarter section—not that far removed from the European ideals of a near feudal yeomanry. Powell understood, as few did, that the quarter section would not repay its owners in the West; but, more important, that individualism, hard work, and private enterprise alone could not overcome the challenge of the arid lands. In perhaps his most important bid to introduce the West to the East, Powell explained how communalism alone made possible democratic success. As the *Reno Gazette* favorably opined about western senators' criticism of the irrigation survey, they believed "that the powers of the National Government are limited and restrained; that they extend only to matters relating to war, to commerce, and to police protection; that the Government is in no sense a paternal one, and that it has nothing whatever to do with the fostering of the great enterprises upon which the prosperity, the wealth and the progress of the country depend." But Powell could see—by the very forces of nature that made it compelling— that right then the West required more federal involvement, albeit that it must be shouldered aside once the commonwealths became self-sufficient. But the mythology of the West, already deeply ingrained, celebrated that fierce individualism more than any other area in the nation: a paradox, because, as Powell foretold, this land would become the most dependent on federal nation-making support—land reclaimed by water stored and dispersed from federally funded hydro projects, the beginning of a colossal system of federal subsidies of agriculture. The scrappy cowboy would not often find himself an independent worker, but more likely a small employee of a huge ranching effort. Other small businesses found themselves dependent on large agribusiness. The fast-rising western cities would become utterly beholden to federal-built dams for their drinking water and energy.

While Stewart deserves sharp criticism, especially for his venal attacks and reflexively self-interested behavior, in other regards he does not. He passionately represented his Nevada constituency, men and women who wanted their shot at a new start and the riches that were promised them for hard work, ingenuity, and initiative. He—and many of those coming into the Silver State—were swept up in a classic boom mentality: This time will be different, the notion that populations and demand for product would rise indefinitely, and that a player can achieve anything beyond his wildest dreams. Simply standing still was the greatest sin of all for them. They just needed one good shot at it—and the senator would help them get their inheritance. Stewart, and so many others, saw the West as the next stage of American ascendency: its fertile, vast, largely empty, and rich lands so endlessly full of promise and possibility. Powell, this righteous bureaucrat from the East, did not deny the West's bright future, but his optimism embraced caution and clear-eyed understanding of consequences. Every answer that Powell gave always seemed to be qualified by "yes, but." And surely this was a direct affront to the American Dream itself. Hearts ached to believe Stewart—that the desert could be redeemed, tender rains would follow the plow, and the fields would bloom like a rose. Powell's long-term practicality and Cassandra-like warnings plucked no such heartstrings. Like the American Indians, he seemed to stand simply in the way of progress. Stewart knew all about the power of shaping nature to newcomers' desires, but paid no heed to the unintended consequences of headlong advance; it was not his concern. For Powell, the fulfillment of the American promise had to include a future-looking stewardship of people and land.

The Major had become a lightning rod, the perfect scapegoat for all that stood in the way of Stewart's vision for a prosperous American future.

The full Senate and House took up the Sundry Civil Expenses Bill in mid-July, but not before Moody got in a few more licks on the Senate floor, dubbing Powell a "tycoon of many tails," then confiding much less wittily to the *Evening Star* that Powell "knew as much about the arid lands of the west as he did about the mountains of the moon, and not one whit more." Powell appeared to get blamed almost entirely for western development's shutting down by the dramatic closure of the public lands. The western senators, who united against Powell, found support from eastern senators reluctant to pour money into expensive western irrigation projects. Powell had finally paddled into a wave he could not negotiate, no matter his prodigious skill and determination.

The Senate cut off funding for the irrigation survey. In late August, Congress as a whole repealed the provision closing all public lands, limiting closure to reservoir sites only. The General Land Office, with all its warts and transgressions and briberies, opened again for its publicly scandalous business. The federal government would not return to classifying lands until the Dust Bowl and farm-surplus crises forced its hand in the 1930s. For Powell, even though the USGS received a record appropriation that year, the closure of the irrigation survey came as the biggest loss of his career. Gone were two years of toil, and his prime opportunity to cast his ideas into the future of western development.

Powell reluctantly discharged dozens of employees. In large part, he was one more victim of the times. The Republicans were undergoing a generational change, virtually trading off its fading patronage of southern blacks and coming to comfortable terms with the powers of the Gilded Age. Even as industry inexorably expanded, workers and farmers saw little increase in prosperity, and those hard times spurred alliances and organizations that mobilized into clamorous political movements pressing for radical economic reform. But Powell had also underestimated the storm of anger breaking over Stewart and pretty much the entire western congressional presence as the whole region underwent one blow after another.

In turn, Stewart won an empty victory: Federal irrigation did transfer over to the Department of Agriculture, but Congress would not fund the effort for another dozen years. In the meantime, a host of private water companies failed. Stewart had let his personal animosity for Powell doom the very goals he and his people sought to attain.

Even with tactical victory in hand, Stewart still spat venom at Powell, spreading malicious rumors in a letter to John Conness, lately a California senator: "Since the receipt of your letter I have made some inquiry and find that his habits with women are scandalous." He would—or could—never substantiate these accusations. Once Stewart felt he had finished with Powell, he went after the Major's brother Bram, who had come to town as superintendent of schools, and eventually hounded him out of office.

Powell's relationship with Dutton became yet another casualty of the hearings. In his treasured associate's entangled testimony, Powell found a deep, unforgivable betrayal. Dutton certainly had not intended to derail the irrigation survey. Nothing suggested that he felt any remotely unusual antagonism toward his boss, although he and others of the Great Basin Mess certainly felt the sometimes-overwhelming presence of the Major, his larger-than-life personality and roster of exploits seeming to reach into every aspect of their work and personal lives. Unlike the Howlands and Dunn, Dutton did not actively decide to walk off the job and crack the continental undertaking. Powell's rebuke must have devastated him.

Another of Powell's protégés, Charles Walcott, who would go on to succeed Powell as head of the survey, and eventually to head the Smithsonian, quietly commented that Powell "likes strong loyalty from those nearest to him." The other side of that cult of loyalty was pride; and once Dutton had crossed the line—on the record in a Senate hearing no less—their collegial relationship ended. In July, Dutton requested full transfer back to the army and was obliged. His superiors dispatched this great talent to anonymity at the San Antonio arsenal. No record exists that he and Powell ever spoke again, although other members of the survey kept in touch.

Powell had lost not only a close friend but a valued professional colleague. These two—more than anyone else—had brought the Grand Canyon in all its splendor before the nation, revising it from a place of horrors and awe into one of spectacular beauty and exceptional presence in the American nation. If Powell had been the protagonist in the Grand Canyon epic, then Dutton was its muse. In his *Tertiary History of the Grand Canyon District,* he described how the individual's perceptions of the great gorge can grow and change—an observation that could well be extended to America's shifting views of the West overall: "Whatsoever might be bold or striking would at first seem only grotesque. The colors would be the very ones he had learned to shun as tawdry and bizarre. The tones and shades, modest and tender, subdued yet rich, in which his fancy had always taken special delight, would be the ones which are conspicuously absent. But time would bring a gradual change. Some day he would suddenly become conscious that outlines which at first seemed harsh and trivial have grace and meaning; that forms which seemed grotesque are full of dignity; that magnitudes which had added enormity to coarseness have come replete with strength and even majesty. . . . Great innovations, whether in art or literature, in science or in nature . . . must be understood before they can be estimated, and must be cultivated before they can be understood."

Yet even Dutton, a colleague and deep friend who had shared so many experiences of the American West, did not ultimately possess the imagination to encompass the future shape of the American West as did Powell.

The most essential element of the man and his successes lay in his forward-going energy, his chessmaster ability to see three or four moves ahead. The West had brought some great changes to America—and far more rapidly than anyone had anticipated; Powell could never cease to feel the land shifting beneath his feet. The charging, sudden continentalization of American power energized Powell into thinking forever bigger, sometimes almost violently forcing upon him a larger sense of the world that was coming to be. This did not dizzy him; it just lifted him from one challenge to the next greater one. At least two generations would pass before others could grasp his ideas. Over the next several years, his voice would resound, lonely but undimmed and defiant.

CHAPTER 12

Last Stand

I n 1891, the Fifth International Geological Congress, the first of its kind held in the United States, convened in Washington. By clever politicking, Powell had shifted the original location from Philadelphia to the nation's capital, a change that made sense as 42 of the 173 American attendees belonged to the United States Geological Survey. Foreign participants came from fifteen nations, for the most part western European, although members from Russia, Peru, and Chile attended. After days spent discussing such weighty topics as the chronological correlation of clastic rocks and the standardization of colors, symbols, and names on geological maps, the well-dined members had a chance to take several tours, the highlight being a twenty-five-day "grand excursion" for ninety guests by rail and stage across the Great Plains to the Rockies, Yellowstone, and Grand Canyon. American geologists could proudly boast not just about the spectacular formations of the West, but also show off the pioneering mapwork undertaken by the USGS, the largest scientific organization in the world. In Salt Lake City, the entourage enjoyed a banquet attended by many luminaries, not least Senator William Stewart.

Dutton's abrupt departure from the survey left no one but Powell to meet up with thirty-six visitors in Flagstaff in late September for a trip into the Grand Canyon. The promised tents never materialized, so the group weathered wind, rain, and hail for ten demanding days. By all accounts, Powell appeared to relish the chance of submitting the distinguished visitors to truly western conditions—and they did not seem to mind either, the Chilean mining geologist Francisco San Román recording that "good humor prevailed." On day two they reached the South Rim, descending into the Canyon to examine Precambrian and Permian rocks. Of all Powell's many descents through or down the Canyon—this would be his last—this distinguished visitation must have struck him with particular resonance. Only two decades earlier, he and his ragged band of adventurers had pushed their way through the unknown Canyon; now he was lecturing eminent foreign geologists on American geology as mapped by American scientists on an unprecedented scale. How much he must have wanted to share this moment with Clarence Dutton as he and his guests gazed out from Point Sublime. American geology, as it became clear to everyone at the Congress—had they not sensed it before—had attained star status.

Another participant, the geographer Emmanuel de Margerie of Paris, delighted in more than the spectacle: "We have nothing comparable to that wonderful display of labor in every direction of geological science; the union of topography and of geology seems specially wise and expedient." He was speaking directly to Powell's transcendent vision for the USGS and the survey's patrons. Three months later, Powell accepted the Cuvier Prize from the Academy of Sciences of the Institute of France on behalf of the survey for its superb mapping and interpretation of the great American West.

The year 1892 did not smile on the survey—or on other federal scientific endeavors. An election year in which Democrat Grover Cleveland returned to office, it came fogged with continuing economic uncertainty, which in a year pushed the nation into the

worst recession of its first one hundred years. The western senators, still brooding over Powell's resistance in the irrigation survey
business, joined with Cleveland Democrats eager to show their
cost-cutting bona fides, and took another hard look at the USGS.
Not surprisingly, change of administration or not, Stewart led the
charge, railing at the survey as "a mockery of science." Marsh's
paleontological work came under fire, particularly his book on the
extinct Odontornithes. The catchphrase "birds with teeth" became
a favorite rallying cry of those bent on eliminating alleged government waste. Surprisingly, many in Congress stood up for Powell,
but the fiscal climate and lack of a standard bearer capable of
checking Stewart did not bode well. The Senate cut the survey's
budget from $800,000 to $400,000.

When that ominous news hit in July, Powell discharged a volley
of telegrams, the one to Marsh reading curtly: "Appropriations cut
off. Please send your resignation at once."

In 1893, a full-blown economic crisis overran the United States,
its root causes international and complex. By July, 560 state and
private banks, as well as 155 national banks, had closed their
doors. Factories shuttered and unemployment soared, while ex-
port markets foundered. A continuing western drought compounded the troubles of states beyond the Mississippi, smashing
farm prices and causing a rash of mortgage foreclosures. Silver
prices declined. In this tense environment, the West's demand for
federal help in promoting irrigation projects came roaring back to
life. While the Stewart-Powell deadlock had stalled irrigation
policy for some time, the economic and ecological disasters awakened new voices. William Smythe, an Omaha newspaperman
turned champion of headlong irrigation in the "conquest of arid
America," launched *Irrigation Age,* one of several such publications that had sprung into creation. He swung high the torch of
William Gilpin, but in a different arc. Aridity was no curse, he

argued, but an actual blessing, because it required the civilizing power of irrigation. His new movement was "not merely a matter of ditches and acres, but a philosophy, a religion, and a programme of practical statesmanship rolled into one." The target of irrigating 572 million acres of public land west of the 97th meridian intoxicated a new generation of boosters. He declaimed that he had science, not bromides, at his back. The answer to the nation's ills lay in the latest modern technologies that would bring abundant grain and blooming fruit trees to the conquered desert, offering prosperity and opportunity to millions in dirty, overcrowded cities. The *San Francisco Chronicle* enthusiastically opined that a comparatively small investment could bring millions to the nation and create thousands of happy homes "where now is but a sterile wilderness."

As economy and environment visibly withered, Smythe organized a national irrigation congress in Los Angeles in October 1893. The *Los Angeles Times* applauded the choice of venue—after all, had not Major Powell, "the well-known specialist on this subject," declared that California boasted the world's finest example of the benefits of irrigation in fostering horticulture and agriculture?

Befitting the importance of the gathering, President Cleveland extended invitations to most major foreign governments. Some seven hundred delegates, including Powell at the head of a delegation from the survey, turned up for the five days' proceedings, the main events held downtown in the cavernous, boomtown Grand Opera House. Across the street, a vacant lot exhibited examples of modern technology. While the first practical internal-combustion-powered car lay two years in the future, the newly reconfigured—smaller and more efficient—gasoline-powered engine promised the capacity to pump groundwater in great volumes that windmills could not. The delegates gawked at gas engines, graders, ditchers, duplex pumps, pipes, special drainage tile, and new water-tank designs. The new-fangled Hellemotor featured large reflecting surfaces that caught the sun's rays to power a pump. Executives of water companies and speculation-hungry capitalists enjoyed free California wines and fruit, cigars, and sandwiches.

Inside the opera house, amidst a riot of bunting and flags, one speaker after another mounted a stage crowded with tropical plants and flowers to speak to the wonders of irrigation. Above their heads hung a streamer bearing the congress's motto: "Irrigation: Science, Not Chance." A festive, celebratory mood prevailed, undergirded by the body's commitment to its keynote promise that homes for "millions of free men could be made on the arid public domain." One evening, in a talk sponsored by the Los Angeles Science Association, Powell lectured about his 1869 voyage. Just after lunch on October 13, Powell climbed the stairs to address the entire congress. Delegates were limited to five minutes, but no one dared constrain the Major, who would speak for three-quarters of an hour.

Pale and gray, the Major no longer radiated the vigorous health of his prime. The long train ride from Chicago had worn him considerably. His stump burned. Yet, looking out over all the adoring faces raised expectantly beneath him, Powell laid aside his prepared remarks, announcing to more applause that they could read his technical paper on water supply later. The Major's gray eyes flamed. Perhaps he knew that the end of his career approached. And then he delivered the most eloquent, impassioned speech of his life.

He outlined his pride in his great nation's enterprise, then confirmed his populist bona fides: "I am more interested in the home and the cradle than I am in the bank counter." But he felt obliged to remind those convened of the West's blunt environmental realities. He was going to make himself absolutely clear: "When all the rivers are used, when all the creeks in the ravines, when all the brooks, when all the springs are used, when all the reservoirs along the streams are used, when all the canyon waters are taken up, when all the artesian waters are taken up, when all the wells are sunk or dug that can be dug in all this arid region," he gravely proclaimed, "there is still not sufficient water to irrigate all the land." All this effort, he continued, could only reclaim a small fraction of the West. The crowd rustled in their chairs, now thoroughly confused.

That no misapprehension should linger, he explained it again. Take all the waters in the arid region, devoting not one drop of it to the public lands, and there would still not be enough water even to moisten all the vast stretches in private hands. With this statement, Powell undercut the Congress's entire platform. The mutterings grew louder. "Not one more acre of land should be granted to individuals for irrigation purposes; there is not water enough." A scattering of boos now met him, sounds the proud Major had never heard before. Yet he plowed on. "There is no more land, owned by the Government in the arid regions, that ought to be used for irrigation, except in about half a dozen little places." Federal land should be used for mining and stock raising. Incredulous, some of the delegates broke in with a storm of questions. Very heated remarks were made, reported an Albuquerque paper. If what you say is true, said one, then "we are here upon a useless mission." Smythe would report that the "first sensation of the delegates was one of amazement, the second one of anger, and the third one of contempt." Powell was sinning against the central American idol of optimism.

Powell explained matter-of-factly that he was not calling the platform a lie; millions more could indeed settle: "I believe that the irrigable land that can be redeemed by waters of the arid region is very great." But still the waters were limited. This is a "simple statement in mathematics, that every man of intelligence will at once see that it must be true." It was simple, but not a single delegate dared accept it.

In the face of a crowd now openly hostile, Powell marched on determinedly, but now venturing into new territory. These issues he had always felt were extremely important to him, but never personal. He got personal now. "What matters it whether I am popular or unpopular? I tell you, gentlemen, you are piling up a heritage of conflict and litigation over water rights, for there is not sufficient water to supply these lands"—a stunning statement by the first and long-standing dean of irrigation, the hero of the Colorado, and the patriarchal director of the USGS.

Prominent delegates countered by citing the power of seasonal floods. Certainly by capturing such tumultuous volumes of water in reservoirs, the desert could be won. But Powell's words, distilled by more experience that anyone in the country, hung like a menacing cloud above the congress. One delegate burst out that not all knowledge belongs to any one man, even if he belonged to many learned societies. Smythe moved to expunge the Major's entire address from the record, lest it discourage settlers. The assembly compromised by allowing speakers to go home and revise their comments before submitting them for publication. Perhaps the Major would come to his senses. But for him, his message made the plainest sense. Like his father ringingly denouncing slavery on the steps of the Jackson County Courthouse, Powell felt constitutionally responsible to speak the truth, no matter the consequences. It was his duty as a patriotic American and a scientist on the cutting edge of his discipline. Nothing could shake him from such obligations.

The Major believed as firmly as anyone that America had a shining future, and that it lay in bending nature to the will of an advancing humanity. "[T]he powers of nature are his servants," he told the Philosophical Society of Washington in 1883, "and the granite earth his throne." He was a man of his times; and yet his vision enabled him to peer far into the future, seeing how the new birth of a nation would be endangered if her citizens did not listen with a scientific ear to what was revealed by ecology, geography, and geology. The Union had nearly fractured during the war. A future that did not contemplate reasonable limits would be lured into swamps of unsustainability: shortages, endless litigation, the demands of infrastructure, feuding water politics—each one a threat to a democratic society the likes of which had never been attempted on so grand a scale. While others saw him as a crank, Powell felt the heat of urgency to speak out: Here the patriarch corrected his children's temptations toward selfish aggrandizement. But this was not a message for which his children were ready. At the end of the *Irrigation Age* article in which he denounced Powell's "sensational" speech to the congress, Smythe simply burst into bold, final capitals: ARID AMERICA IS FIGHTING FOR ITS FUTURE. WHOEVER STANDS IN ITS WAY WILL BE CRUSHED. No reader could doubt at whom the threat was directed. And the *San Francisco Chronicle* concurred, writing that Major Powell and his geological survey have not been in the best of odor for some time. This latest iteration of America's unbridled belief in its unprecedented future would roll over data and reasoning.

In retrospect, Powell would stumble over some hard facts. He deeply underestimated the resources of the western aquifers. Conversely, he would also severely underestimate the amount of water necessary to irrigate arid land. He also believed too optimistically that repeated applications of such water would flush away crop-killing alkalis and other impurities. The opposite has proven true. And his ideas that watershed commonwealths could wrest water control from state and national entities have proven—so far—to be economic and political non-starters.

Yet, in his most basic assumptions, Powell has proven eerily accurate. With Francis H. Newell, he estimated that little more than 40 million arid acres could be recovered—very close to the total under cultivation today, including deep-well irrigation on the Great Plains. And Powell, though wrong about the overall quantity of the fossil water, at least fully grasped how it had taken millions of years—Ice Ages and all—to accumulate. Still, so much of what he preached—of limited water, of the threat of monopolies, of the importance of steady measurement and analysis, of the critical importance of topographical mapping and the indispensable role of federal science, and perhaps most broadly, of the necessity of ecological stewardship, remains presciently to the point, clearing the way for debates to the present day.

In the congress' audience sat the architects of future western water strategy. Among them, the Irish-born engineer William Mulholland, who would design and oversee the construction of the 233-mile Los Angeles Aqueduct, which carried water from the rural Owens Valley to the San Fernando Valley. Finished in 1913, the aqueduct became an essential agent of Los Angeles becoming one of America's largest cities, but it also let loose the California Water Wars. Mulholland's career ended suddenly in March 1928 when the St. Francis Dam, a concrete gravity dam containing a major reservoir for the aqueduct system supplying Los Angeles, failed catastrophically only a dozen hours after he had inspected it.

Senator Francis Newlands of Nevada was a presence also. In 1902, he spearheaded the creation of the United States Reclamation Service, later the Bureau of Reclamation, the federal organization that would launch a fever of dam-building across the West. Powell more than anyone else had laid the foundation for the bureau, yet even he could have never imagined what it would bring. Eventually some 75,000 dams more than six feet high would harness the power of nearly every major western river, culminating in the 726-foot tall Hoover Dam. The dams blocking the western rivers, observed one team of geologists, have become "America's version of the Egyptian pyramids."

Powell's assistant N. K. Newell, a hydraulic engineer good at designing solid dams, became the Reclamation Service's first director. Although the federal government would exert a fundamental influence on western society through the management of water, it never crystallized coherent western water or land development policies. In the final analysis, the Newland Reclamation Act, which created the Reclamation Service, gave legal form to the western boosters' dreams of an essentially limitless western water supply. Powell's careful projection of sustainable management of a limited resource had been dismissed as cowardly and irrelevant.

By 1894, it had become clear to Powell that his continued presence as director might wreck the agency he had worked so hard to create and grow. In the spring he resigned, and immediately underwent an operation on his stump at Johns Hopkins. He remained the head of the Bureau of Ethnology, while his protégé Charles Walcott took over the survey. In one of the USGS reports his quiet successor wrote about Powell's legacy, citing his *Arid Lands* report and ideas as creating a storm center of agitation that served to stimulate public interest in the matter. And, as if he was remembering sitting there in the Great Basin Mess with Powell, Walcott would say that the Major always stressed the great importance of the arid lands in the ultimate development of the country—"and by sheer force of character kept the subject alive."

Four months before Sumner yielded to the ghosts of his past on the bank of the Green, the Major suffered a severe stroke, which prevented him from attending the fortieth Shiloh anniversary that April. But Powell would not be stopped. He struggled mightily to walk again, even if only on the arm of a helper. During his last years, while still nominally head of the Bureau of Ethnology, he had written a philosophical tract that set out to establish a grand theory—a new science of intellection—that would explain how all things are connected to one another. It was a natural conclusion of a lifetime of faith in the bright promise of science to explain everything in the world around him. "Every body, whether it be a stellar system or an atom of hydrogen, has certain fundamental characteristics found in all," he wrote. "These are number, space, motion, and time, and if it be an animate body, judgment." At more than four hundred pages, *Truth and Error, or the Science of Intellection,* published in 1898, is an unwieldy and virtually unreadable tome.

Ever the quick study—whether as to Civil War fortifications or the hydraulics of whitewater—Powell had finally stepped into the province of Kant and Hegel, where he floundered. His driving nature demanded that he take ever greater challenges, each bigger than the last, but this was too large for him—or probably for anyone for that matter.

That spring, the writer Hamlin Garland encountered him on a Washington street, gray and feeble, shuffling along on the arm of a black attendant—most likely Tolly Spriggs, a former Maryland slave and now the Major's companion. Garland watched as this once prodigy of vitality struggled to recall his name, although he remembered the face. "I've lost my memory," said the Major. Their encounter prompted Garland to write "The Stricken Pioneer," a romantic ode to that whole generation of westgoing men, now fading as fast as the setting sun.

By the turn of the century, the old American West that Powell had known had vanished. A decade earlier, the University of Wisconsin historian Frederick Jackson Turner had famously declared the West's frontier dead. The Indian Wars had ended, now William "Buffalo Bill" Cody and his Wild West Show toured the East and even Europe, thrilling audiences with reenacted Indian battles and staged Pony Express rides, the sharpshooting of Annie Oakley, and the solemn pronouncements of the real Sitting Bull. A psychopathic serial killer, William Bonney, was on his way to fond immortalization as Billy the Kid. The new myths of the Old West would soon enough become rich fodder for John Ford's westerns and Zane Grey's novels. America's Manifest Destiny for a while turned from the continent to overseas, first in Cuba, then to the Philippines. Theodore Roosevelt, passed into the White House upon McKinley's assassination, was soon to exercise his muscular brand of conservation on the western lands.

That September of 1902, John Wesley Powell died in Haven, Maine, at age sixty-eight, with Emma and their daughter by his side.

During his life, Powell had refused to regard the West through rose-colored glasses—and that remains one of his greatest legacies. That did not mean he had no wonder for the West's rich gifts, for he stood in amazement at Indian cultures, the extraordinary geography, and the rich promise that the land offered. But as a consummate reader of the landscape, combined with the geologist's long view, he understood that the interplay between the Earth and humanity was indeed a complex, ever-changing, and delicate dance. This battler and risk taker, this scientist and visionary, ultimately asked Americans to temper their desires with a practical understanding of what the land and its climate was capable of—how far it could be pushed and how much it could be used. He did not ask for reverence for the land, but rather—more significantly—he asked for humility when regarding it. It was not then, and not today, an easy message for Americans to hear.

Epilogue

ven the Major would have found it ironic that Lake Powell bears his name. No tree-hugging conservationist—he saw western rivers as a huge plumbing system ready to help build the glorious American future, yet he still would have found Lake Powell a caricature of the ideas he had sown, a monstrosity defying his hard-learned assumptions of a sustainable West and localized control of water. The lake now known as Powell was created by the last of the U.S. Bureau of Reclamation mega-dams, the 710-foot Glen Canyon Dam, which rose on the Colorado fifteen miles above Lees Ferry in 1963. The immense reservoir of Lake Powell that grew behind it became one of the world's largest human-made lakes, stretching 186 miles upriver and flooding the quiet beautiful red rock chasms of Glen Canyon. Drowned now were the heady rush of rapids down Cataract Canyon, and the influx of that Dirty Devil River that Powell had been so determined to locate. Gone, too, were innumerable petroglyphs, grottoes, side canyons, and rock faces. It proved a devil's bargain: The Glen Canyon Dam got passed after David Brower and fellow environmentalists had stopped another dam project on the Green River. The outrageous trade-off sparked the environmental movement and rang the death knell of the mega-dam.

Three hundred miles downriver from Lake Powell lies Hoover Dam. Thus bracketed, the Colorado through the Grand Canyon has

become little more than a canal between these two mammoth hydro-
electric centers. Glen Canyon engineers release cold water from the
depths of Lake Powell into the Canyon for rafters and boaters, this
icy water replacing the warm, muddy river down which Powell ventured. The Colorado has become America's—and likely the world's—
most contested and controlled river, every single drop of it allocated
to serve more than 36 million people in seven states—more than the
nation's population when Powell served at Shiloh—mostly gathered
in massive, often desert cities of Los Angeles, Phoenix, Tucson, Las
Vegas, Denver, San Diego, and Mexicali, and to irrigate nearly six
million acres of farmland. In 1922, Herbert Hoover, then secretary
of commerce, traveled to a Santa Fe lodge to allocate the Colorado's
water among the seven riverine states. The resulting Colorado River
Compact did just that. (Mexico objected, a treaty two decades later
yielded it 10 percent of the river's flow.)

This heavy-handed, central settlement was exactly what Powell
had for so long argued against. The Compact set off a binge of dam-
building by the Bureau of Reclamation. The small-dam system that
Powell had cautiously imagined on the tributaries of western rivers
now looked to dam every major watercourse. Political expediency
now had more weight than environmental or ultimately economic
costs: While engineers put up 85 dams between 1902 and 1930, the
number jumped to 203 during the following 40 years. Bureau staff
soared from a few thousand employees in the 1920s to 20,000 in the
1940s. Every locality wanted a dam project, whether it made sense
or not. Somewhere along the line the dams got even larger, and, as
Powell would have predicted, things got truly out of hand. The states
started canal projects to distribute that water, often lifting it across
absurd distances and over mountains. The Central Arizona Project,
completed in 1993 at a cost of $5 billion, diverts Colorado River wa-
ter through a 336-mile canal system to Phoenix and Tucson. Southwestern cities grew faster than any other region in the United
States, putting even greater strains on the water infrastructure.

Today, there is not enough river water for everyone to take

their legal allotment. The Colorado has not much more to give, yet dependence on its waters keeps growing. Recent droughts have pushed farmers to tap deeper and deeper into the aquifers, some "water mining" now drills 3,000 feet to reach the precious commodity in the vanishing Ogalla Aquifer. The fossil water deep under the ground, which took millions of years to collect, is being withdrawn rapidly—and largely not being replaced.

In 1935, when one of humanity's more remarkable engineering feats—Hoover Dam—was completed, a curious omen befell Washington, D.C. A dust cloud reaching 10,000 feet in the sky blew into town—remarkably consisting of the aerated soil from Nebraska and Oklahoma 1,000 miles to the west—just as the Senate debated the government's responsibility in mitigating the great Dust Bowl. A severe drought across the West had created a new form of weather, the "black duster," facilitated by the indiscriminate plowing of the prairies. The topsoil on more than a million acres simply blew away. Congress and the secretary of the interior were slowly moving to address the degradation with the Taylor Grazing Act of 1934 and a bill establishing the Soil Conservation Service the next year, whose measures, such as planting windbreaks and seeding grasses, did much to head off future black dusters. On that early spring day, the nation's capital became a city on the prairies, infiltrated by great filth that begrimed the windows of federal office buildings. It was the most tragic and most impressive lobbyist to visit those early discussions of climatic disaster.

More recently, a combination of droughts and overdemand has swallowed much of lakes Powell and Mead. A good snowpack one year revives the reservoirs somewhat, but then again Powell would have made clear that such variability is normal, and that one must certainly not hope to escape long droughts. Intensifying the mounting crisis in the West are rapid population growth and global climate change, the latter of which a recent National Climate Assessment report concludes will likely make devastating dryness an ongoing condition.

From the *Arid Lands* controversy of Powell's day can be drawn important parallels—and a still unique perspective—for the current climate debates. The genius of John Wesley Powell—for which his times were not ready—was his sense that sustaining development in the arid lands rested on a broad-front integration of human and physical factors under a so-often-variable climate. It was not enough merely to acknowledge that the land was desperately dry or to seed it with irrigation works; it was also necessary to establish the legal frameworks to tie the water to the land, to design watershed communities, to inform Congress in a way that would keep its usual interventions modest, and to establish mechanisms for monitoring meteorological and ecological factors. At the heart of such large-scale assessments lay Powell's far-reaching programs in topographic and geological mapping, the classification of land, the establishment of regular data monitoring with such instruments as permanent stream and rain gauges, and the ongoing assessments of the land's resources. He could have written the playbook for today's Intergovernmental Panel on Climate Change, the UN-authorized body set out to gather and integrate scientific and economic data on global climate change.

Powell's 1869 river voyage had bestowed on him a geologist's deep understanding of Earth's history—that forces operating on the landscape were destined to shift radically in the face of climatic change. These lessons raised serious doubts about relying too heavily on the stability of climatic conditions. It was not a far step for him to sense the dynamism between earth, climate, and human activities. What Stewart, Herbert, and others missed was that Powell did not look to these efforts as either a bureaucratic power play or simply an obsessive collection for science, but as a serious human commitment to managing the future—an acknowledgment that no future would be entirely friendly to human interests. Indeed, the responses to Powell's ideas in that debate sound much as they do today. C. D. Wilber, first secretary of the Illinois Natural History Society, whom Powell most certainly knew, accused him of producing scientific information that "is consistent only with the all too common practice of public fraud."

Powell's emphasis on watershed commonwealths and local responsibility for water use seems far from crazy after all. "Irrigation emerged as an individual and collective effort at the watershed level," reads *New Era for Irrigation,* a National Academy of Sciences report, "and in many important respects its future will be determined in the watershed. The growth of locally driven watershed activities reflects a promising trend in water management." Indeed, a Bureau of Reclamation report found that western-water stakeholders largely favored decisions made at the local level on issues of water policy.

As in Powell's day, sociocultural beliefs about American enterprise and its golden future can still trample over the dawning realizations of what science is revealing. It took severe drought in his day for the irrigation debate to come onstage—and later for the Dust Bowl to savage great tracts of topsoil to force Congress into taking a more rational view of full-tilt exploitation of the land. It took a good many more years for Powell's ideas to sink in and blossom. The debate over global climate change will also take time— filled as it had been in Powell's day with vituperative national debates clouded by misinformation, the terrors of economic recessions, and unsettling climate fluctuations.

If Powell was here today, he would be at the forefront of climate change, working to inform the public about the relationship of a warming climate and flooding, drought, rising sea levels, and bad storms. The connection would be all too clear for him. But so, too, would his optimism that Americans and the rest of the world can adapt and work to mitigate these challenging conditions. He would—as he had always been—be there to serve his country.

Notes

CHAPTER 1: INTO THE CAULDRON

5 **permanently frost the banks:** Robert Edgar Ervin, *Jackson County: Its History and Its People* (Jackson, OH: Sheridan Books, 2006), 5.

6 **Jackson also boasted:** William Bramwell Powell letter, *Jackson Standard Journal,* January 14, 1903.

6 **whose men worked blast furnaces:** William E. Van Vugt, *Britain to America: Mid-Nineteenth-Century Immigrants to the United States* (Urbana and Chicago: University of Illinois Press, 1999), 98.

6 **this "magic line":** Sarah Hopkins Bradford, *Harriet, the Moses of Her People* (New York: Geo. R. Lockwood & Son, 1897), 30.

8 **frontier of 1800:** Kim Heacox, *John Muir and the Ice That Started a Fire: How a Visionary and the Glaciers of Alaska Changed America* (Lyons, NY: Lyons Press, 2014), 91.

9 **Few other periods of sectarian:** Sam Haselby, *The Origins of American Religious Nationalism* (New York: Oxford University Press, 2015), 120.

9 **newsbearers and moral purveyors:** Donald Worster, *A River Running West: The Life of John Wesley Powell* (New York: Oxford University Press, 2001), 31; Donald G. Mathews, "The Methodist Schism of 1844 and the Popularization of Antislavery Sentiment," *Mid-America: An Historical Review* 5, no. 1 (January 1968): 9.

10 **"crows and Methodist preachers":** Peter Feinman, "Itinerant Circuit-Riding Minister: Warrior of Light in a Wilderness of Chaos," *Methodist History* 45, no. 1 (October 2006): 47.

10 **"reform the continent":** Haselby, 126, 157.

10 **"Beware of clownishness":** Robert Emory, *History of the Discipline of the Methodist Episcopal Church* (New York: Carlton & Porter, 1845), 53.

12 **a veritable Samuel Johnson:** Eugene B. Willard, ed., *A Standard History of the Hanging Rock Region of Ohio* (Chicago: The Lewis Publishing Company, 1916), 370.

12 **General Conference of 1836:** Mathews, 13.

13 **Crookham traveled the countryside:** Cheryl Janifer LaRoche, *Free Black Communities and the Underground Railroad: The Geography of Resistance* (Champaign: University of Illinois Press, 2013), 8.

13 **proximity to Berlin X-Roads:** *Colored American,* July 28, 1838.

14 **Berlin X-Roads came into being:** LaRoche, 79.

14 **owned 150 hogs:** Ronald Shannon, *Profiles in Ohio History: A Legacy of African American Achievement* (iUniverse, 2008), 55–56; *The Philanthropist* (June 29, 1842).

14 **carts full of concealed fugitives:** Entry under "Judge J. A. L. Crookham," *Portrait and Biographical Sketch of Mahaska County, Iowa* (Chicago: Chapman Brother's, 1887).

15 **Joshua Giddings, who was censured:** Mrs. M. D. Lincoln, "John Wesley Powell: Part 1: Boyhood and Youth," *Open Court* 16 (1902): 706.

15 **men emboldened by cheap whiskey:** Willard, 369; William Culp Darrah, *Powell of the Colorado* (Princeton, NJ: Princeton University Press, 1951), 14.

16 **jeers soon boiled:** Ibid., 11; Lincoln, "Powell: Part I," 706.

16 **educate his sixteen children:** Agricultural record, 1850 Federal Census, Crookham, Lick Township, Jackson County, Ohio.

16 **most engaging student:** Lincoln, "Powell: Part I," 707.

17 **poured brine into long lines:** Ervin, 4; J. Michael Stroth, *Salt in Our Blood: The Story of the Scioto Salt Works, 1795–1827* (Privately published by author, 2014); Ohio Department of Natural Resources, Division of Geological Survey, *Geo-Facts,* No. 7, "The Scioto Saline—Ohio's Salt Industry," www.OhioGeology.com.

17 **eleven-foot-long mammoth tusk:** W. W. Mather, *First Annual Report of the Geological Survey of the State of Ohio, 1837* (General Assembly of the State of Ohio, Doc. 26), 97.

18 **five hundred ancient earthworks:** D. W. Williams, *A History of Jackson County, Ohio* (Jackson, OH: n.p., 1900), 22.

18 **a rectangular earthen enclosure:** Ervin, 9.

19 **extensive mineral collection:** "Sketch of William Williams Mather," *Popular Science Monthly* 49 (August 1896): 550–55.

21 **badly beaten body:** LaRoche, 80.

21 **eighth and final child:** 1850 United States Federal Census, Sharon Township, Walworth County, Wisconsin.

23 **a series of willed battles:** "In Memory of John Wesley Powell," *Science* 16, no. 411 (November 14, 1902): 788.

CHAPTER 2: OSAGE ORANGES AND PINK MUCKETS

24 **first plank road companies:** M. G. Davis, *A History of Wisconsin Highway Development, 1835–1945* (Madison: State Highway Commission, 1947), 17; Carl Abbott, "Plank Roads and Wood-Block Pavements," *Journal of Forest History* 25, no. 4 (October 1981): 216; Carrie Cropley, "When Railroads Came to Kenosha," *The Wisconsin Magazine of History* 33, no. 2 (December 1949): 188.

24 **"jirk and jolt":** Sarah Foote, *A journal Kept by Miss Sarah Foote (Mrs. Sarah Foote Smith) while Journeying with her People from Wellington, Ohio, to Footeville, Town of Nepeuskun, Winnebago County, Wisconsin, April 15 to May 10, 1846* (Kilbourn, WI: n.p., 1905), April 28th entry.

25 **"I have often perplexed myself":** Francis Parkman, *The Oregon Trail: Sketches Prairie and Rocky-Mountain Life* (Boston: Little, Brown, and Company, 1914), 9–10.

25 **still lay up for grabs:** Bernard Devoto, *The Year of Decision 1846* (New York: Macmillan, 1943), 9.

26 **"nervous, rocky west":** Ralph Waldo Emerson, "The Young American," in *Ralph Waldo Emerson: Essays and Lectures* (New York: The Library of America, 1983), 216.

27 **soon swelled to 140 acres:** "Productions of Agriculture in District No. 33 Town of Sharon, July 1850," 1850 U.S. Census.

27 **nut-laden trees delivered bagloads:** W. A. Titus, "The Westward Trail," *The Wisconsin Magazine of History* 19, no. 4 (June 1936): 411.

28 **Territory's grain production:** Louise Phelps Kellogg, "The Story of Wisconsin, 1634–1848," *The Wisconsin Magazine of History* 3, no. 2 (December 1919): 200.

28 **nearby Methodist community:** Frank H. Lyman, *The City of Kenosha and Kenosha County Wisconsin: A Record of Settlement, Organization, Progress and Achievement,* Vol. 1 (Chicago: The S. J. Clarke Publishing Co., 1916), 120.

28 **Venomous massasauga rattlesnakes:** A. W. Schorger, "Rattlesnakes in Early Wisconsin," *Transactions of the Wisconsin Academy of Sciences, Arts and Letters* 56 (1967–68), 29–48.

29 **"had been their rabbit preserve":** John Wesley Powell, "Proper Training and the Future of the Indians," *Forum* 18 (1895): 622.

29 **"shelling corn, fanning wheat":** John Muir, *Selected Writings* (New York: Alfred A. Knopf, 2017), 89.

29 **six-day roundtrip journey:** Lincoln, "Powell: Part 1," 709.

30 **crossed Pike Creek:** "Southport—1847," painting by George Robertson in the Kenosha History Center's C. E. Dewey Lantern Slide Collection; Communication with Cynthia Nelson, Kenosha History Center, July 16, 2015.

31 **the longest pier:** David Vaught, *After the Gold Rush: Tarnished Dreams in the Sacramento Valley* (Baltimore: The Johns Hopkins University Press, 2007), 18.

31 **series of droughts:** Western Historical Co., *History of Walworth County Wisconsin* (Chicago: Western Historical Company, 1882), 202; "Injury to the Wheat," *Milwaukee Sentinel and Gazette,* September 5, 1850, 3.

31 **a storm sank:** Lyman, 129.

31 **two hundred angry farmers:** Carrie Cropley, *Kenosha: From Pioneer Village to Modern City, 1835–1935* (Kenosha, WI: Kenosha Country Historical Society, 1958), 23.

32 **"Riot in Southport!":** "By Telegraph. Riot in Southport!," *Milwaukee Sentinel and Gazette,* April 9, 1850, 2.

32 **Walking with hickory canes:** Lyman, 134.

32 **had been "egregiously swindled":** John C. Rives, *Congressional Globe,* Vol. XXI, Part II (Washington: 1850), August 7, 1850, 10.

32 **"Having died with his harness on":** "A Well-Known Pioneer," *Sacramento Daily Union,* September 26, 1884.

32 **"toiled and sweated":** John Muir, *The Story of My Boyhood and Youth* (Boston: Houghton Mifflin Company, 1913), 220.

33 **Wesleyan Methodist camp meetings:** "Camp Meeting," *The Belvidere Standard* (Belvidere, IL), August 16, 1853, 3.

34 **large eastern rattlesnake:** Lincoln, "Powell: Part I," 714.

35 **led them in singing:** Peter Ellertsen, "The untaught melody of grateful hearts in Southern Appalachian Folk Hymnody in Illinois, 1800–1850," *Journal of Illinois History* 5 (Winter 2002): 274.

35 **"better than highway robbery":** Worster, *A River Running West,* 69.

36 **called upon Turner:** Mary Turner Carriel, *The Life of Jonathan Baldwin Turner* (Published by Mary T. Carriel, 1911), 63.

37 **"horse-high, bull-strong":** Ibid., 65.

37 **three great races:** Linda Jeanne Evans, "Abolitionism in the Illinois Churches, 1830–1865" (PhD diss., Northwestern University, 1981), 48–49.

37 **provide land grants:** Donald R. Brown, "Jonathan Baldwin Turner and the Land-Grant Idea," *Journal of the Illinois State Historical Society* 55, no. 4 (Winter 1962): 373–74.

38 **transformation of the Midwest:** James Mak and Gary M. Walton, "Steamboats and the Great Productivity Surge in River Transportation," *The Journal of Economic History* 32, no. 3 (September 1972): 620.

39 **"a young man of enterprize":** Timothy Flint, *A Condensed Geography and History of the Western States, or the Mississippi Valley,* Vol. 1 (Cincinnati: E. H. Flint, 1828), 213.

39 **the summer of 1856:** *Scientific American* 59, no. 7 (August 18, 1888): 103.

39 **"annual processions of mighty rafts":** Mark Twain, *Life on the Mississippi* (New York: P. F. Collier & Son Company, 1917), 18–19.

40 **set the transit record:** Mak and Walton, 632.

41 **French bateaux with pointed bow:** Malcom L. Comeaux, "Origin and Evolution of Mississippi River Fishing Craft," *Pioneer America* 10, no. 1 (June 1, 1978): 76–79.

42 **surface geology and agriculture:** Robert G. Hays, *State Science in Illinois: The Scientific Surveys, 1850–1978* (Carbondale: Southern Illinois University Press, 1980), 24.

45 **Just topping five feet:** National Archives and Records Administration (NARA), Washington D.C., NARA Series: *Passport Applications, 1795–1905; Roll 290–01 Apr 1887–15 Apr 1887.*

CHAPTER 3: THINKING BAYONETS

46 **"the integrity of the Union":** Mrs. M. D. Lincoln, "John Wesley Powell. Part II: The Soldier," *The Open Court* 17 (1903), 14.

47 **a slim meal:** Ira Blanchard, *I Marched with Sherman* (San Jose: toExcell, 2000), 20–21.

48 **"a very extravagant opinion":** Andrew Brown, *Company K. Twentieth Regiment, Illinois Volunteer Infantry. Roster and Record* (Yorkville, IL: Kendall Country Record Print, 1894), 60.

48 **a French village:** John H. Brinton, *Personal Memoirs* (New York: The Neale Publishing Company, 1914), 95–96.

49 **"beautiful girls here":** Charles W. Wills, *Army Life of an Illinois Soldier* (Washington, D.C.: Globe Printing Company, 1906), 62.

50 **critically placed Fort D:** Mary Ann Andersen, ed., *The Civil War Diary of Allen Morgan Geer* (Tappan, NY: R. C. Appleman, 1977), 9.

51 **median age of his recruits:** Worster, *A River Running West,* 89.

51 **did "nothing carelessly":** Brinton, 104.

51 **"One of my superstitions":** David Nevin, *The Road to Shiloh* (Alexandria, VA: Time-Life Books, 1983), 45.

52 **the "efficient officer":** Grant to Captain Chauncey McKeever, from Cairo, October 9, 1861. John Y. Simon, ed., *The Papers of Ulysses S. Grant, Vol. 3: October 1, 1861–January 7, 1862* (Carbondale: Southern Illinois University Press, 1970), 29–30.

52 **"a very beautiful young woman":** (Bloomington) *Daily Pantagraph,* June 7, 1909.

54 **"a disorganized, murderous fistfight":** Shelby Foote quoted in Geoffrey Ward, *The Civil War: An Illustrated History* (New York: Alfred A. Knopf, 1990), 267.

55 **"a great herd of lions":** Winston Groom, *Shiloh 1862* (Washington, D.C.: National Geographic, 2012), 269.

56 **"Men fell around us":** William E. Bevens, *Reminiscences of a Private: William E. Bevens of the First Arkansas Infantry, C.S.A.* (Fayetteville: University of Arkansas Press, 1992), 71.

56 **simply abandoned everything:** Hurlbut to Major John A Rawlins, August 18, 1862, in "Reports of Brigadier General Stephen A. Hurlbut, U. S. Army, commanding Fourth Division, Army of the Tennessee, including correspondence related to the Thirteenth Ohio Battery abandoning its position and equipment during the battle," The Civil War Archive, www.civilwararchive .com/RESEARCH1/1862/shilohusa6.htm.

56 **the Union infantry:** Frederick Welker's Missouri battery, private communication with Stacy Allen.

57 **swung Powell onto the saddle:** Powell letter to Colonel Cornelius Cadle, May 15, 1896, 5, courtesy of Shiloh National Military Park.

57 **a ghastly heap:** John A. Cockerill, "A Boy at Shiloh," *Sketches of War History, 1861–1865: Papers Read Before the Ohio Commandery of the Military Order of the Loyal Legion of the United State*, Vol. 6 (Cincinnati: Robert Clarke & Co., 1888), 25.

58 **"Now, now," gasped Powell:** Darrah, *Powell of the Colorado*, 58.

58 **"Amputations were abundant":** "Extract from a Narrative of his Service in the Medical Staff, XXXVIII," *The Medical and Surgical History of the War of the Rebellion* (Washington, D.C.: Government Printing Office, 1870), 41.

58 **complicated facial reconstruction:** *The Olney (Illinois) Times*, March 12, 1858, 1.

59 **"Retreat? No. I propose":** Bruce Catton, *Grant Moves South* (Boston: Little, Brown and Company, 1960), 241.

59 **"a lump of sugar":** Jean Edward Smith, *Grant* (New York: Simon & Schuster Paperbacks, 2001), 203.

59 **"I wanted to pursue":** Ibid.

60 **"vessel sailing through the air":** Jalynn Olsen Padilla, "Army of 'Cripples,' Northern Civil War Amputees, Disability, and Manhood in Victorian America" (PhD diss., University of Delaware, 2007), 42.

61 **"I can't spare this man":** Smith, *Grant,* 205.

61 **scrawled a letter:** *Decatur Herald*, May 14, 1916.

61 **credited her continued presence:** Lincoln, " Powell: Part II," 19.

62 **"the most hazardous & desperate moves":** Sherman to Ellen Sherman, April 23, 1863, in Brooks D. Simpson and Jean V. Berlin, eds. *Sherman's Civil War: Selected Correspondence of William T. Sherman, 1860–1865* (Chapel Hill: University of North Carolina Press, 1999), 455.

63 **bridges of lumber:** William L. Shea and Terrence J. Winschel, *Vicksburg Is the Key: The Struggle for the Mississippi River* (Lincoln: University of Nebraska Press, 2003), 91.

63 **reassembled their gun carriages:** Manning F. Force, "Personal Recollections of the Vicksburg Campaign," *Sketches of War History, 1861–1865: Papers Read Before the Ohio Commandery of the Military Order of the Loyal Legion of the United State*, Vol. 1 (Cincinnati: Robert Clarke & Co., 1888), 296.

64 **impaled what remained:** Shea and Winschel, *Vicksburg*, 108.

67 **searching the waterfall:** T. A. Conrad, "Observations on the Eocene formation, and descriptions of one hundred and five new fossils of that period, from the vicinity of Vicksburg, Mississippi," *Proceedings of the Academy of Natural Sciences of Philadelphia* 3, no. 11 (September–October 1847).

67 **male family teams:** Janet Hewett, *Supplement to the Official Records of the Union and Confederate Armies* (Wilmington, NC: Broadfoot Pub. Co., 1994–2001), Vol. 79, U.S. Colored Troops (Union)–Infantry, 292–94.

68 **"a straightforward and attentive officer"**: United States War Department, *The War of the Rebellion: A Compilation of the Official Records of the Union and Confederate Armies* (Washington, D.C.: Government Printing Office, 1892, Series 1, Vol. 39, Part 3, 618–19.

68 **pressed Powell into service**: *War of the Rebellion*, Series 1, Vol. 49, Part 2, 780.

69 **"mad as he could be"**: Worster, *A River Running West*, 101.

69 **Of the ten men**: 20th Illinois Infantry Regiment, Company "H" muster rolls, The Illinois Civil War Project, www.illinoisgenweb.org.

CHAPTER 4: FIRST THOUGHTS WEST

71 **"a cripple was a cripple"**: William H. Rideing, "Patched-Up Humanity," *Appletons' Journal* 13, no. 326 (June 19, 1875): 783.

72 **"cripple for life"**: Padilla, 55.

72 **"cruel and bloody Rebellion"**: Brian Matthew Jordan, "Living Monuments: Union Veteran Amputees and the Embodied Memory of the Civil War," *Civil War History* 57, no. 2 (2011): 121, 133.

72 **"cost rivers of blood"**: Ibid., 139.

73 **"nonsense of science"**: Darrah, *Powell of the Colorado*, 72.

74 **"He made us feel"**: J. B. Taylor, "In the Wesleyan, '63–'69," *The Illinois Wesleyan Magazine* 5, no. 1 (April 1900), 68; Helen E. Marshall, *Grandest of Enterprises: Illinois State Normal University, 1857–1957* (Normal: Illinois State Normal University Press, 1956), 119.

74 **"Scientia et Sapientia"**: This means "Knowledge and Wisdom."

75 **"All civilized nations"**: Marshall, 120.

76 **nation's first college field trips**: Worster, *A River Running West*, 118.

76 **display in the museum**: Marshall, 121, quoted from Proceedings of the Board of Education (Normal, IL), March 26, 1867, 10.

77 **"at government rates"**: Simon, ed., *Papers of Ulysses S. Grant, Vol. 17: Jan. 1–Sept. 30, 1867* (Carbondale: Southern Illinois University Press, 1991), 406.

77 **"A party of Naturalists"**: *Scientific Expedition to the Rocky Mountains. Preliminary Report of Prof. J. W. Powell to the Illinois State Board of Education* (Peoria, IL: N. C. Nason, Printer, 1867), 1.

79 **"a city of demons"**: W. H. Dixon, *Collection of British Authors*, Vol. 1 (Leipzig: Bernhard Tauchnitz, 1867), 111.

79 **"dropped out of the clouds"**: Rose Kingsley, *South By West* (London: W. Isbister & Co., 1874), 44.

81 **Byers hit the dirt streets**: Robert F. Karolevitz, *Newspapering in the Old West* (New York: Bonanza Books, 1965), 60–62.

81 **taking Albert Bierstadt to**: William Newton Byers, "Bierstadt's Visit to Colorado," *Magazine of Western History* 11, no. 3 (January 1890): 237–40.

81 **Kit Carson, Jim Beckworth**: Mrs. Wm. N. Byers, "The Experiences of One Pioneer Woman," Typescript in Western History Department, Denver Public Library, Denver, CO.

81 **"except by irrigation"**: *Rocky Mountain News*, December 21, 1864.

82 **"could ride all day"**: Mrs. M. D. Lincoln, "John Wesley Powell, Part III: The Professor" *Open Court* 17 (1903), 90.

83 **"struggle of extermination"**: James Schiel, *The Land Between: Dr. James Schiel's Account of the Gunnison-Beckwith Expedition into the American West, 1853–1854* (Los Angeles: Western Lore Press, 1957), 90.

84 **"We were shooting swiftly"**: Joseph C. Ives, *Report Upon the Colorado River of the West Part 1* (Washington, D.C.: Government Printing Office, 1861), 81–82.

85 **"shall be forever unvisited"**: Ibid., 110.

85 **"Though valueless to the agriculturalist"**: Captain J. N. Macomb, *Report of the Exploring Expedition from Santa Fe, New Mexico, to the Junction of the Grand and Green Rivers of the Great Colorado of the West in 1859* (Washington, D.C.: Government Printing Office, 1876), 54.

85 **"more worthless and impractical region"**: Ibid., 6.

85 **"prospect for a fatal termination"**: John Charles Frémont, *Memoirs of My Life*, Vol. 1 (New York: Belford, Clarke & Company, 1887), 200.

86 **A broad plain opened**: Samuel Bowles, *The Switzerland of America: A Summer Vacation in the Parks and Mountains of Colorado* (Springfield, MA: Samuel Bowles & Company, 1869), 69–70.

86 **"regular hunter's abode"**: Henry Ellsworth Wood, Typescript journal, *Henry Ellsworth Wood Papers, 1854–1932*, The Huntington Library, San Marino, CA, August 4, 1868, entry 27; William Henry Jackson's photographs of Hot Sulphur Springs, shot while on the Hayden Survey in 1874, National Archives, Washington, D.C.

86 **a pocket edition of Kit Carson**: Chauncey Thomas, "Recollection of Jack Sumner," William Culp Darrah Papers, Utah State Historical Society, Salt Lake City, UT, P-2435.

86 **One of eight children**: U.S. Census, 1850.

87 **corporal in the 32nd Iowa**: Guy E. Logan, ed., "Historical Sketch Thirty-Second Regiment Iowa Volunteer Infantry," *Roster and Record of Iowa Troops in the War of the Rebellion*, Vol. 5 (Des Moines, IA: Emory H. English, State Printer, E. D. Chassell, State Binder, 1911), 3–19.

87 **a voracious reader**: "Capt. Sumner is No More," *Grand Junction Sentinel*, July 10, 1907, provided by Ray Sumner.

87 **"after several windy fights"**: Robert Brewster Stanton, *Colorado River Controversies* (Boulder City, NV: Westwater Books, 1982), 170.

88 **"Peaks, Parks, and Plains"**: *Daily Colorado Tribune*, November 1, 1867.

88 **"pleasing and persuasive"**: *Daily Colorado Tribune*, November 6, 1867.

88 **Powell planned to return**: *Rocky Mountain News*, November 6, 1867.

88 **"over two thousand pounds"**: (Bloomington, IL) *Daily Pantagraph*, August 19, 1867.

88 **a human scalp**: *Chicago Republican*, September 3, 1867.

89 **"successful beyond expectations"**: *Scientific Expedition to the Rocky Mountains*, 9-13.

89 **"sixteen hours a day"**: (Bloomington, IL) *Daily Pantagraph*, January 25, 1868.

89 **"the best geological section"**: *Congressional Globe*, Part 3, May 25, 1868, 2564.

90 **"purely one of science"**: Ibid.

91 **would obtain scientific information**: Ibid., 2563.

91 **backdoor way of organizing expeditions**: Ibid., 2564.

91 **"a very novel proceeding"**: Ibid., 2565.

91 **"detrimental to the interests"**: Ibid., 2566.

92 **twenty-three members**: *Chicago Tribune*, July 1, 1868, 4.

92 **to secure sixty-seven pairs**: Wood journal, July 4, 1868, 3.

92 **"knew nothing about mountaineering"**: L. W. Keplinger, "The First Ascent of Long's Peak" in *Collections of the Kansas State Historical Society 1915-1918*, Vol. 14, ed. William E. Connelley (Topeka: W. R. Smith, 1918), 347.

93 **"no more artists"**: *Rocky Mountain News*, July 3, 1868.

93 **"great cañon of the Colorado":** *Rocky Mountain News,* July 14, 1868.
93 **"no living creature":** *Rocky Mountain News,* September 23, 1864.
93 **"a dry-goods counter":** Stanton, 170.
94 **dragging the wagon's party:** Wood journal, August 4, 1868, 27.
94 **buckskin of dark, oleaginous luster:** John Wesley Powell, *The Exploration of the Colorado River and Its Canyons* (New York: Penguin Books, 1987), 120.
94 **"[Powell] doesn't get along much":** Wood journal, August 8, 1868, 31.
94 **enjoyed so much:** Ibid., August 3, 1868, 27.
94 **more than two hundred bird species:** Bowles, *Switzerland,* 82.
95 **Sumner killed three grizzlies:** Powell, *Exploration,* 120.
95 **raspberries and gooseberries:** "Diary of Lyle H. Durley, Aug. 14, 1868," Darrah Papers, Box 3, 9.
95 **"'Tis most stupid work":** Worster, *A River Running West,* 143.
96 **"water of the arid region":** "J. W. Powell-Report [1890]," typescript, Records relating to the Powell Irrigation Survey, National Archives (Washington, D.C.), 57.6.12, Box 1.
96 **"so ignorant of itself?":** Samuel Bowles, *A Summer Vacation in the Parks and Mountains of Colorado* (Springfield, MA: Samuel Bowles & Company, 1869), 84.
97 **"Utes and Prof Powell":** *Springfield (MA) Republican,* October 31, 1868.
97 **"that Arabian presence":** Thomas L. Johnson, *Letters of Emily Dickinson,* Vol. 3 (Cambridge, MA: The Belknap Press, 1958), no. 643.
97 **"The whole field of observation":** Bowles, *Vacation,* 86.
97 **"had fun at our expense":** Keplinger, "The First Ascent," 343.
97 **"a castle with defenses":** Mike Caldwell, quoted in Ruth M. Alexander, "People and Nature on the Mountaintop: A Resource and Impact Study of Longs Peak in Rocky Mountain National Park," A Project funded by the Rocky Mountain Cooperative Ecosystems Study Unit, Rocky Mountain National Park, and Colorado State University, 2010, 1.
98 **Grizzly indeed pitched:** *Chicago Tribune,* September 10, 1868.
98 **"Hello, Jack, what's the matter?":** Keplinger, "First Ascent," 343.
99 **at 10 a.m.:** William N. Byers, personal journal, Byers family papers, Denver Public Library, Denver, CO, provided to author by Raymond Sumner.
100 **"accomplishing what others thought impossible":** Keplinger, "First Ascent," 345.
100 **badly bruising his stump:** *Rocky Mountain News,* September 28, 1868.
102 **"I have explored":** Elmos Scott Watson, *The Professor Goes West* (Bloomington: Illinois Wesleyan University Press, 1954), 24.
102 **"to think was to dare":** (Bloomington) *Daily Pantagraph,* July 1, 1869.
102 **"jovial good fellow":** Powell, *Exploration,* 123.
102 **contributions toward equipment and groceries:** Don Lago argues that Byers gave Powell a series of loans and outright gifts to buy equipment and such. See Don Lago, "New Evidence on the Origins and Disintegration of the Powell Expedition," in *Reflections of Grand Canyon Historians,* ed. Todd R. Berger (Grand Canyon, AZ: Grand Canyon Association, 2008), 121.
103 **receiving $25 per month:** Michael P. Ghiglieri, *First Through the Canyon* (Flagstaff, AZ: Puma Press, 2003), 49.

CHAPTER 5: DESCENT

104 **laid out a city:** W. A. Bell, "Major J. W. Powell's Report on His Explorations of the Rio Colorado in 1869," in *New Tracks in North America,* Vol. 2 (London: Chapman and Hall, 1870): 559.

106 **"the rocks h-e-a-p h-e-a-p high!":** *Chicago Tribune,* July 19, 1869.

107 **century and a half later:** For the James White story, see Tom Myers, "Why James White's 1867 Raft Trip Doesn't Float—At Least through Grand Canyon," and Brad Dimock, "The Case for James White's Raft Trip Through Grand Canyon: The Story of White's Story," in *Reflections of Grand Canyon Historians: Ideas, Arguments, and First-Person Accounts,* ed. Todd R. Berger (Grand Canyon, AZ: Grand Canyon Association, 2008), 125–30, 131–36; Stanton, 3-93; Virginia McConnell Simmons, *Drifting West: The Calamities of James White and Charles Baker* (Boulder: University Press of Colorado, 2007); Eilean Adams, *Hell Or High Water: James White's Disputed Passage through Grand Canyon, 1867* (Logan: Utah State University Press, 2001).

107 **river was high:** Don Lago. *The Powell Expedition: New Discoveries about John Wesley Powell's 1869 River Journey* (Reno: University of Nevada Press, 2018), 25.

108 **"I entered the canyon":** Wm. H. Brewer, "John Wesley Powell," *American Journal of Science,* 4th series, 14 (1902): 381.

109 **"savors of foolhardiness":** "Powell's Expedition," *Chicago Tribune,* May 21, 1869, 2.

109 **"it is doubtful":** "The Canon of the Colorado: A Letter from Prof. Newberry," *Chicago Tribune,* June 4, 1869, 2.

110 **among the most eager:** Henry P. Zuidema, "Discovery of Letters by Lyell and Darwin," *The Journal of Geology* 55, no. 5 (September 1947): 439.

110 **"only decent meal we tasted":** Mark Twain, *Roughing It* (Hartford, CT: American Publishing Company, 1875), 105.

112 **"tough as a badger":** Ghiglieri, 12.

113 **Goodman signed on right there:** E. G. Evans, "Historic Article: Life Story of Francis Valentine Goodman," *The Outlaw Trail Journal* (Winter 2004): 31–39.

114 **writing into the contract:** Ghiglieri, 49.

115 **liked to tell wild tales:** Powell, *Exploration,* 152.

116 **"thoroughly tired of our sojourn":** Walter Powell to editor of *Chicago Evening Journal,* July 3, 1869, "Camp in Red Canon, Green River," reprinted in (Bloomington, IL) *Daily Pantagraph,* July 20, 1869.

116 **call him "Old Shady":** Michael Ghiglieri argues in *First Through the Canyon* that Old Shady was a nickname that Powell gave his brother after his trip, but does acknowledge that Sumner referred to that name years later.

116 **"thrust into the sky":** Powell, *Exploration,* 125.

116 **popular song of the time:** Ghiglieri, 62.

117 **"escape from the coast":** *New York Herald,* June 27, 1865.

117 **give their plucky little rowboat:** Ghiglieri, 61-62; Lago, *The Powell Expedition,* 90-99.

117 **"two other oars are lost":** Powell, *Exploration,* 124.

117 **"the speed of the wind":** *Rocky Mountain News,* July 17, 1869; on the speed of the river, see Edward Dolnick, *Down the Great Unknown* (New York: Harper Perennial, 2002), 109.

117 **"seem to be a success":** Powell to Prof. Edwards (Bloomington, IL) *Daily Pantagraph,* July 19, 1869.

118 **"could ride any sea":** Frederick S. Dellenbaugh, *Romance of the Colorado River* (Mineola, NY: Dover Publications, Inc., 1902), 237.

118 **sophisticated and difficult to build:** Brad Dimock personal communication with author, April 8, 2016.

118 **Frémont had experimented:** Richard Lovett, "White Knuckles in Wyoming," *New Scientist* 184, no. 2475 (November 27, 2004): 48–49.

119 **"gee nor haw nor whoa":** Ghiglieri, 66.

119 **"stanch and strong":** Dolnick, 28.
119 **The bulkheads' placement:** Ghiglieri, 53. He argues that by moving heavy loads away from the boat's center of mass it would cause "the oarsmen to combat a maximum load leverage," which would work against they every time they tried to steer the boat.
119 **proved fickle and dangerous:** Brad Dimock personal communication with author, April 7, 2016. He discovered the unstable "sloshing" while running authentic Whitehalls on a 1999 National Geographic Society trip.
119 **used a steering rudder:** Debate over the years has raged about whether the 1869 crew had stern-mounted oars, which certainly would have helped with their maneuverability. Michael Ghiglieri argues in *First Through the Canyon* that they didn't have them. But Brad Dimock theorizes that they would have quickly figured out the advantage of adding an oar in the stern and retrofitted the boats. Photographs from Powell's 1871–1872 Colorado River expedition reveal the use of stern-mounted oars.
121 **"mad as a bear":** Ghiglieri, 89.
122 **"'Ashley' is a warning":** *Chicago Tribune,* July 19, 1869.
122 **"sparking a black eyed girl":** Ghiglieri, 101–102.
122 **"leaping and bounding":** *Chicago Tribune,* July 19, 1869.
123 **James Green field barometers:** New York City barometer maker James Green provided the Smithsonian for years with his fine pieces. Personal correspondence with Marc Rothenberg, emeritus editor of the *Joseph Henry Papers.*
125 **"What shall we find?":** Powell, *Expedition,* 148.
126 **"diving into musty trash":** Ghiglieri, 135.
126 **now known as Winnie's Rapid:** Roy Webb, *If We had a Boat: Green River Explorers, Adventurers, and Runners* (Salt Lake City: University of Utah Press, 1986), 14.
126 **channel choked with dangerous rocks:** *Chicago Tribune,* August 20, 1869.
126 **cigar-shaped islet:** Webb, *If We Had a Boat,* 14.
127 **"perfect hell of waters":** Ghiglieri, 115.
128 **Goodman sat still:** O. G. Howland, *Rocky Mountain News,* July 17, 1869.
128 **pulled the boat safely:** Sumner described the details of the rescue in Stanton, 177.
128 **"glad to shake hands":** Ghiglieri, 114.
128 **lost his writing paper:** Powell to Edwards, (Bloomington) *Daily Pantagraph,* July 19, 1869.
128 **lost his new:** Evans, *Life Story of Francis Valentine Goodman,* 32.
130 **"not understanding the signal":** *Rocky Mountain News,* July 17, 1869.
131 **"so much pleased":** Ghiglieri, 118.
132 **"The red sand-stone rises":** Ibid., 116.

CHAPTER 6: THE CANYON

134 **bore a sizable hole:** O. G. Howland, *Rocky Mountain News,* August 18, 1869; Ghiglieri, 125.
134 **"If I had a dog":** Ghiglieri, 120.
135 **"One gold pan":** O. G. Howland, *Rocky Mountain News,* August 18, 1869.
136 **"were lulled to sleep":** Ghiglieri, 129.
136 **"instinct for cosmic interrogation":** J. W. Powell, "Sketch of the Mythology of the North American Indians," *First Annual Report of the Bureau of Ethnology to the Secretary of the Smithsonian Institution 1879-'80* (Washington, D.C.: Government Printing Office, 1881), 19.

136 **"more rare than a poet"**: J. W. Powell, "Biographical Notice of Archibald Robertson Marvine," *Bulletin of the Philosophical Society of Washington, 1874–1878* 2 (1880): Appendix X, v.

137 **"Danger is our life"**: O. G. Howland, *Rocky Mountain News*, July 17, 1869.

137 **"the worst we shall ever meet"**: Ghiglieri, 130.

138 **"chapter of disasters and toils"**: Powell, *Exploration*, 163–65.

138 the vast shallow sea: Wayne Ranney's blog, www.WayneRanney.com, entry for August, 19, 2010.

139 **"clouds have formed the mountains"**: Powell, *Exploration*, 393.

140 **"It was a welcome sight"**: Ghiglieri, 124.

140 **"We had the greatest ride"**: Ibid., 152–53.

142 **"Ambition had a strong hold"**: "From the Omaha Republican, July 3," reprinted in *New York Herald*, July 10, 1869.

142 featuring eleven stories about it: William deBuys, ed., *Seeing Things Whole: The Essential John Wesley Powell* (Washington, D.C.: Island Press, 2001); *New York Times*, July 26, 1869.

142 **"almost incredible and beyond belief"**: *New York Times*, July 26, 1869.

143 unite with the Green: Dolnick, 125.

144 **"The canyon is very tortuous"**: Powell, *Exploration*, 191.

144 languorous drop rate: Felix E. Mutschler, *River Runners' Guide to the Canyons of the Green and Colorado Rivers with Emphasis on Geologic Features*, Vol. 4 (Denver: Powell Society LTD, 1969), 46.

144 **"A terrible gale"**: Ghiglieri, 153; Desolation Canyon retains a reputation for being a haven for mosquitoes during the summer.

145 **"$800 worth of watches"**: Ibid., 162.

147 **"as in a snow-drift"**: Powell, *Exploration*, 198.

147 **"cool deliberate determination"**: Ghiglieri, 167.

147 **"Hurra! Hurra! Hurra!"**: Ibid., 171.

148 **"of the nearest pie"**: Ibid., 177.

148 **"cooked her husband's heart"**: *California Star*, February 13, 1847, as printed in "The Virtual Museum of the City of San Francisco," www.sfmuseum.net /hist6/donner.html.

148 Such graphic images: Don Lago, "What's Eating the Howland Brothers," *BQR* 29, no. 1 (Spring 2016): 19–23.

149 believed to be an alligator: Ghiglieri, 178.

149 **"a chute of water"**: Powell, *Exploration*, 218.

150 **"like a scared rabbit"**: Stanton, 188.

150 like pieces of popcorn: Author interview, Colorado River guide Bruce Quayle.

151 **"loss of an oar"**: Powell, *Exploration*, 218.

151 **"a thousand streams"**: Ibid., 223.

152 **"on which I could rely"**: "The Elgin Watches—Testimonial from Major Powell," *Chicago Tribune*, July 17, 1870, 4. Interestingly, there's a rapid in Cataract Canyon called Powell's Pocket Watch.

152 pay $30 on the spot: Richard Quartaroli notes that a gold Elgin watch in 1867 cost $117. Michael F. Anderson, ed. *A Gathering of Grand Canyon Historians* (Grand Canyon, AZ: Grand Canyon Association, 2005), 133.

153 **"everything was as smooth"**: Stanton, 202.

154 **"what might be ahead"**: Powell, *Exploration*, 224.

154 **"a curious ensemble"**: Ibid., 232–33.

154 **"How they contrived to live"**: Ghiglieri, 185.

154 **"This bodes toil and danger."**: Powell, *Exploration*, 234.

155 **"library of the Gods":** J. W. Powell, *Exploration of the Colorado River of the West* (Washington: Government Printing Office, 1875), 193–94. (This is Powell's official report, as opposed to the *Exploration* book he published in 1895, cited as "Powell, *Exploration*" throughout these notes.)

156 **"must be west":** Ghiglieri, 204.

156 **"the cheer is somber":** Powell, *Exploration,* 247.

156 **"uneasy and discontented and anxious":** Ghiglieri, 204.

157 **"No rocks ever made":** Ibid., 205.

157 **"We must run the rapid":** Powell, *Exploration,* 251.

157 **"Pull out! We'll follow you":** Stanton, 196.

158 **"sand run so low":** Stanton, 197.

158 **"[T]he rubber *ponchos*":** Powell, *Exploration,* 263.

159 **"a race for a dinner":** Ibid., 272.

159 **"Good cheer returns":** Ibid., 267.

161 **"up against it":** Stanton, 202.

162 **call off the expedition:** *Hartford Daily Courant,* October 4, 1869.

162 **"Of course I objected":** Ibid.

163 **"discontent in camp tonight":** Ghiglieri, 222.

164 **"knock such notions":** Stanton, 203.

164 **"To leave the exploration unfinished":** Powell, *Exploration,* 279–80.

164 **"run the rappid or perish":** Ghiglieri, 224.

165 **Powell joined Andy Hall:** Although Powell claims he negotiated Separation Rapids in *Maid* in his 1875 report, he is most probably misremembering. Hall wrote his brother just off the river on September 10 that the Major joined him on *Kitty's Sister,* which is more likely.

168 **"A wave rolls over us":** Powell, *Exploration,* 284.

168 **"It stands A-No. 1":** Ghiglieri, 226.

168 **"chained by wounds":** Powell, *Exploration,* 284.

169 **Asey and his two sons:** *New York Times,* September 26, 1869, reprinting article from *Deseret (Utah) News,* September 15, 1869.

170 **Robbers gunned down:** Ghiglieri, 274.

171 **"train's bad enough":** *Denver Republican,* April 18, 1901.

172 **"supposed temporary insanity":** Jack Sumner, Surgeon's Certificate, November 2, 1904, Army pension file, WC-644-311, National Archives, Washington, D.C.

172 **"anxious about the others":** *Chicago Tribune,* December 1, 1869, reprinted letter from J. E. Johnson to Byers.

173 **"killed by an enraged Shebitt":** *Deseret (Utah) News,* September 29, 1869.

174 **not something that Powell believed:** Stanton, 253.

175 **comment in his report:** Powell, *Exploration,* 281.

175 **"When busily employed":** Ibid., 123.

177 **"endured the fatigues":** *Deseret (Utah) News,* September 15, 1869.

177 **"so important a contribution":** *Chicago Tribune,* September 21, 1869.

177 **"the sad fate of some":** Ibid., February 20, 1869.

177 **"erect as a pine":** *Naperville Clarion,* 1869, in Worster, *A River Running West,* 587, n.9.

178 **Geologic history would no longer:** Grove Karl Gilbert, "Powell as a Geologist," *Proceedings of the Washington Academy of Sciences* 5 (1903): 116.

CHAPTER 7: ENCORE

183 **barbaric, holy massacre:** Will Bagley, *Blood of the Prophets* (Norman: University of Oklahoma Press, 2002), 212, 263.

184 **"Holy Spirit forcibly impressed me"**: Jacob Hamblin, *Jacob Hamblin: A Narrative of His Personal Experience, as a Frontiersman, Missionary to the Indians and Explorer* (Salt Lake City: The Deseret News, 1909), 30.

184 **Numic-speaking Indians had moved:** Catherine S. Fowler and Don D. Fowler, "Notes on the History of the Southern Paiutes and Western Shoshonis," *Utah Historical Quarterly* 39 (1971): 98.

184 **traded their own children:** Fowler and Fowler, "Notes," 104.

104 **devastated the seed-bearing vegetation:** Edward Leo Lyman, "Caught In Between: Jacob Hamblin and the Southern Paiutes During the Black Hawk-Navajo Wars of the Late 1860's," *Utah Historical Quarterly* 75, no. 1 (2007): 25.

185 **One of the more numerous:** Lyman, 26, 43.

185 **The Major "philosophized a little":** Brigham Young sermon, September 25, 1870, *Journal of Discourses*, Vol. 13 (Liverpool: F.D. Richards, etc.), Discourse 27, 248–49.

185 **"branches of knowledge":** Worster, *A River Running West*, 216.

186 **bringing Lee to justice:** Sworn statement of Erastus Snow, February 21, 1882, in Elder Charles W. Penrose, "The Mountain Meadows Massacre. An Address by Elder Charles W. Penrose, October 26, 1884" (Salt Lake City: The Deseret News, 1906), 63–64.

187 **excommunicated Lee for "extreem wickedness":** Glen M. Leonard, "The Juanita Brooks Lecture Series presents The 26th Annual Lecture: Revisiting the Massacre at Mountain Meadows," March 18, 2009 (St. George: Dixie State College of Utah, 2009), 26.

187 **"net-work of communal interest":** Major J. W. Powell, "The Ancient Province of Tusayan," *Scribner's Monthly* 11 (December 1875): 194–95.

188 **"bare-legged, merry-faced pigmy":** John Wesley Powell, "Western Exploration," *Chicago Tribune*, October 28, 1870.

188 **"My knowledge is general":** Powell, *Chicago Tribune*, October 28, 1870.

189 **sweet, soft, and musical language:** "The Cities of the Aztecs: Lecture by Major J. W. Powell, U.S.A., Before the Young Men's Christian Association," *Brooklyn Eagle*, February 17, 1871, 2.

189 **"by the fire":** Powell, *Exploration*, 311.

190 **faint inscription carved:** Frank M. Barrios, "An Appointment with Death: The Howland-Dunn Tragedy Revisited," in *A Gathering of Grand Canyon Historians: Ideas, Arguments, and First-Person Accounts, Proceedings of the Inaugural Grand Canyon History Symposium, January 2002*, ed. Michael F. Anderson (Grand Canyon, AZ: Grand Canyon Association, 2005), 146–47.

192 **"although these murderers":** Powell, *Exploration*, 323.

193 **some five hundred Ute words:** "Academy of Sciences. Lecture by Major Powell, the Eminent Explorer," *Chicago Tribune*, October 13, 1869, 4.

194 **Every federally sponsored mission:** Don D. Fowler and Catherine S. Fowler, "John Wesley Powell, Anthropologist," *Utah Historical Quarterly* 37, no. 2 (Spring 1969): 156.

194 **"a merry sight":** Powell, "Tusayan," 204.

195 **"radiating in the noonday":** Frank D. Reeve, "War and Peace: Two Arizona Diaries," *New Mexico Historical Review* 24, no. 2 (April 1949): 124.

196 **a wild spectacle:** Powell, *Exploration*, 353.

196 **an important neutral buffer:** Todd M. Compton, *A Frontier Life: Jacob Hamblin, Explorer and Indian Missionary* (Salt Lake City: The University of Utah Press, 2013), 319.

197 **"peace and friendship is planted":** "Journal History of the Church: 1870–1879, 1870 November–December," Church History Library, The Church of Jesus

Christ of Latter-day Saints, Salt Lake City, Utah, Reel 26, Vol. 83, November 21, 1870.

197 **no longer cross into Utah:** "Journal History of the Church: 1870-1879."

198 **wondered "that a morally degenerate":** Major J. W. Powell, "An Overland Trip to the Grand Cañon," *Scribner's Monthly* 10, no. 6 (October 1875): 677.

198 **"one Cochena suite":** Worster, *A River Running West,* 218.

198 **"we hear nothing":** Byers to Powell, December 1869, William N. Byers Papers, University of Colorado at Boulder, University Libraries, Archives Department, Box 1, Book 3, Letterbooks.

199 **send Sumner a railroad pass:** Ibid., July 1, 1870.

199 **"a new unwritten chapter":** *Rocky Mountain News,* August 9, 1870.

199 **"a practicable railway route":** *Ibid.,* November 19, 1870.

199 **supplied important survey information:** Raymond Sumner communications with author.

200 **"A very fine present":** Byers to Powell, December 16, 1870.

201 **bought a captain's chair:** Hillers diary, May 21, 1871, in Don D. Fowler, ed. *"Photographed All the Best Scenery": Jack Hillers's Diary of the Powell Expeditions, 1871-1875* (Salt Lake City: University of Utah Press, 1972), 24.

201 **Powell's "magnificent will":** Frederick Samuel Dellenbaugh, *A Canyon Voyage: The Narrative of the Second Powell Expedition Down the Green-Colorado River from Wyoming, and the Explorations on Land, in the Years 1871 and 1872* (New York, Putnam, 1908), 73–74.

201 **Powell sang constantly:** Dellenbaugh, *A Canyon Voyage,* 30.

201 **"Imagine a group of rough":** E. O. Beaman, "The Cañon of the Colorado," *Appletons' Journal* 11, no. 265 (April 18, 1874): 483.

202 **drew the double-lined course:** W. L. Rusho, "Francis Bishop's 1871 River Maps," *Utah Historical Quarterly* 37, no. 2 (Spring 1969): 209.

202 **tent of yellow cloth:** E. O. Beaman, "Among the Aztecs," *Anthony's Photographic Bulletin* 3, no. 11 (November 1872): 746.

203 **"infernal howitzer on my back":** Walter Clement (Clem) Powell, "Journal of Walter Clement Powell," *Utah Historical Quarterly* 16–17 (1948–1949): 321.

203 **"great pest to the photographer":** E. O. Beaman, "The Colorado Exploring Expedition," *Anthony's Photographic Bulletin* 3, no. 2 (February 1872): 464.

203 **bring 250 images:** Elizabeth C. Childs, "Time's Profile: John Wesley Powell, Art, and Geology at the Grand Canyon," *American Art* 10, no. 1 (Spring 1996): 12.

205 **a pair of heavy shoes:** Martin J. Anderson, "Artist in the Wilderness: Frederick Dellenbaugh's Grand Canyon Adventure," *The Journal of Arizona History* 2, no. 1 (Spring 1987): 54.

207 **"place for a lunatic-asylum":** Francis Marion Bishop, "Captain Francis Marion Bishop's Journal," *Utah Historical Quarterly* 15 (1947): 216.

207 **their invisible triangles:** Robert W. Olsen, Jr., "The Powell Survey Kanab Base Line," *Utah Historical Quarterly* 37, no. 2 (Spring 1969): 261–68; Richard A. Bartlett, *Great Surveys of the American West* (Norman: University of Oklahoma Press, 1962), 303–05.

208 **"vile, miserable sinners":** Bishop, "Journal," 214.

208 **eventually became a bishop:** Worster, *A River Running West,* 238.

210 **three thousand photographic glass plates:** Wiliam Culp Darrah, "Beaman, Fennemore, Hillers, Dellenbaugh, Johnson and Hattan," *Utah Historical Quarterly* 16-17 (1948–1949): 496.

211 **"We joked him":** Dellenbaugh, *Canyon Voyage,* 237.

CHAPTER 8: FIGHTING THE NATIONAL SURVEYS

212 **thirteen quarto volumes:** John A. Moore, "Zoology of the Pacific Railroad Surveys," *American Zoology* 26, no. 2 (1986): 331.

213 **the year 1867:** Clarence King, *First Annual Report of the United States Geological Survey* (Washington, D.C.: Government Printing Office, 1880), 4.

214 **"a touch of Alcibiades":** Henry Adams, *The Education of Henry Adams* (New York: The Modern Library, 1996), 311.

214 **"brilliant and beaming creature":** Robert Wilson, *The Explorer King: Adventure, Science, and the Great Diamond Hoax—Clarence King in the Old West* (New York: Scribner, 2006), 231.

215 **Would America develop her rich:** Henry Nash Smith; "Clarence King, John Wesley Powell, and the Establishment of the United States Geological Survey," *The Mississippi Valley Historical Review* 34, no. 1 (June 1947): 38.

217 **"I could endure cheerfully":** Mike Foster, "Ferdinand Vandeveer Hayden as Naturalist," *American Zoology* 26, no. 2 (1986): 343.

217 **firmly establishing dinosaur paleontology:** "Leidy, Joseph," *American National Biography Online*, www.anb.org; Leonard Warren, *Joseph Leidy: The Last Man Who Knew Everything* (New Haven, CT: Yale University Press, 1998): 82.

217 **who first discovered Permian rocks:** Mike Foster, "The Permian Controversy of 1858: An Affair of the Heart," *Proceedings of the American Philosophical Society* 133, no. 3 (1989): 370–90.

217 **impatience bordering on rudeness:** Foster, *American National Biography Online*, www.anb.org; Foster, "Permian Controversy," 377; Foster, *Strange Genius*, 351.

219 **"might as well strike out":** Foster, *Strange Genius*, 211.

220 **"efficient route for moving troops":** Bartlett, 337–38.

220 **"an astounding 72,250 square miles":** Ibid., 339–40.

220 **"extended from fifty to sixty":** George M. Wheeler, "Geographical Report, Vol. 1," in *Report upon United States Geographical Surveys West of the One Hundredth Meridian* (Washington, D.C.: Government Printing Office, 1889), 45.

222 **lost the stout case:** Ibid., 165.

222 **three hundred of them broke:** Robin E. Kelsey, "Viewing the Archive: Timothy O'Sullivan's Photographs for the Wheeler Survey, 1871–74," *The Art Bulletin* 85, no. 4 (December 2003): 720, n.3.

222 **"Dishonestly if we can":** Mark Twain, "The Revised Catechism," *New-York Tribune*, September 27, 1871, 6.

223 **four thousand inexpensive weekly magazines:** Debora Rindge, "Science and Art Meet in the Parlor: The Role of Popular Magazine Illustration in the Pictorial Record of the 'Great Surveys,'" in *Survey the Record: North American Scientific Exploration to 1930*, ed. Edward C. Carter, II (Philadelphia: American Philosophical Society, 1999), 181.

224 **Powell could pay $500:** Thurman Wilkins, *Thomas Moran: Artist of the Mountain* (Norman: University of Oklahoma Press, 1998), 108.

224 **"I am troubled to know":** Foster, *Strange Genius*, 254.

224 **"only real foe":** Hayden to Gardner, February 1873, cited in Foster, *Strange Genius*, 253.

225 **"Jackson will knock spots":** Moran to Hayden, January 28, 1873, in Joni Louise Kinsey, "Creating a Sense of Place: Thomas Moran and the Surveying of the American West" (PhD diss., Washington University, 1989), 297.

225 **"I will utterly crush him":** "Geographical and Geological Surveys West of the Mississippi, May 26, 1874," House of Representatives Serial Set, Vol. No. 1626, Session Vol. No. 4, 43rd Congress, 1st Session, House Report 612, 63.

226 **need full-page engravings:** Hurd de Houghton to Powell, March 6, 1873, in Kinsey, 299.

226 **a passel of commissions:** Thomas Moran, *Home-Thoughts, from Afar: Letters of Thomas Moran to Mary Nimmo Moran* (East Hampton, NY: East Hampton Free Library, 1967), 41–42.

227 **commissioners divided up in September:** Worster, *A River Running West*, 274–75.

228 **all but the painter:** Moran, *Home-Thoughts*, 31.

229 **"And yet the force":** J. E. Colburn, "The Colorado Cañon," *New York Times*, September 4, 1873, 2.

229 **"a horde of savages":** "Report of Special Commissioners J. W. Powell and G. W. Ingalls on the Conditions of the Ute Indians of Utah; the Pai-Utes of Utah, Northern Arizona, Southern Nevada, and Southeastern California; the Go-Si Utes of Utah and Nevada; the Northwestern Shoshones of Idaho and Utah; and the Western Shoshones of Nevada . . ." (Washington, D.C.: Government Printing Office, 1874), 23.

230 **"I am constrained to protest":** Worster, *A River Running West*, 285.

230 **"more about the live Indian":** Wallace Stegner, "A Dedication to the Memory of John Wesley Powell, 1834–1902," *Arizona and the West* 4, no. 1 (Spring 1962): 1.

231 **beauty and sublimity:** Ibid., 307–8.

232 **Dante's portrayal of hell:** Clarence Cook, "Art," *Atlantic Monthly* 34, no. 203 (September 1874): 375, 376.

232 **"thousand battles had been fought":** Powell, *Exploration*, 174.

233 **"[W]e do not know":** "Thomas Moran's Paintings," *Congressional Record*, 44th Congress, 1st Session, April 4, 1876, 2185.

234 **"was to precipitate a conflict":** "Geographical and Geological Surveys," 33.

234 **stain the hearings:** Ibid., 64, 71.

235 **"his map is so inaccurate":** Ibid., 51–52.

236 **"its pages were quickly turned":** Stephen J. Pyne, *Grove Karl Gilbert: A Great Engine of Research* (Austin: University of Texas Press, 1980), 59.

237 **a work of adventure:** Powell, *Exploration*, preface.

237 **all turned the project down:** Worster, *A River Running West*, 331.

238 **"even hint at the terrible":** Moran to Powell, December 19, 1874, in Worster, *A River Running West*, 332.

240 **"the bond of affection":** Pyne, *Gilbert*, 72.

240 **"we done middling for greenhorns":** Ibid., 65.

241 **"speak of his justice":** Worster, *A River Running West*, 256.

CHAPTER 9: A RADICAL IDEA

244 **poet Walt Whitman:** This, and details of fair, in Robert W. Rydell, *All the World's a Fair: Visions of Empire at American International Exhibitions, 1876–1916* (Chicago: University of Chicago Press, 1984), 9–37.

244 **West's alien outlines:** "Characteristics of the International Fair," *Atlantic Monthly* 38, no. 228 (October 1876): 497. There's some debate on whether Jack Hillers's photographs also were included on the glass windows. See Rindge, 190, fn.44.

244 **rich display of maps:** Rindge, 190.

244 **pride in his plaster models:** William Henry Jackson and Howard R. Driggs, *The Pioneer Photographer: Rocky Mountain Adventures with a Camera* (Yonkers-on-Hudson, NY: 9 World Book Company, 1929), 273.

245 **"life-size papier-mâché and stuffing":** J. S. Ingram, *The Centennial Exposition Described and Illustrated* (Philadelphia: Hubbard Bros., 1876), 151.

245 **"is a hideous demon":** W. D. Howells, "A Sennight of the Centennial," *Atlantic Monthly* 38, no. 225 (July 1876): 103.

246 **list of Colorado mountains:** Thomas G. Manning, *Government in Science: The U.S. Geological Survey, 1867–1894* (Lexington: University of Kentucky Press, 1967), 37.

246 **package fifteen chromolithographic prints:** Rindge, 190–91.

246 **paleontologist Charles White:** Foster, *Strange Genius,* 283.

247 **Congress had cumulatively appropriated $690,000:** Bartlett, 311.

247 **surveying almost six million acres:** David R. Dean, "Soldiers and Scientists: The Politics of Exploring the American West, 1803–1879" (PhD diss., Arizona State University, August 2006), 366.

247 **Holman's son had joined:** Manning, 37–38.

247 **"a tight squeeze for us":** Powell to Newberry, January 25, 1877, in Worster, *A River Running West,* 343.

247 **King had met Powell:** Wilson, 232.

247 **"I beg of you":** Foster, *Strange Genius,* 293.

248 **"so much of a fraud":** Newberry to Hewitt and Garfield, January 20, 1877. Powell Survey, Letters received, RG 57, National Archives, Washington, D.C.

249 **"most valuable and important collection":** Foster, *Strange Genius,* 286.

249 **claiming to have 1,500 negatives:** Foster, *Strange Genius,* 287.

250 **"desired to devote himself exclusively":** William H. Goetzmann, *Exploration and Empire: The Explorer and the Scientist in the Winning of the American West* (New York: W.W. Norton & Company, 1966), 581–82; Foster, *Strange Genius,* 288.

252 **"All the good public lands":** James B. Power, "Unsold Public Lands: Grave Errors in Recent Statements—Large Opportunities for Agriculture in the Northwest," *New York Tribune,* July 21, 1877, 4.

252 **"part of this 'arid' region":** Ibid.

253 **envisioned himself the successor:** "Long, Stephen Harriman," *American National Biography Online,* www.anb.org.

254 **"wholly unfit for cultivation":** Edwin James, *Account of an Expedition to the Rocky Mountains* (London: Longman, Hurst, Rees, Orme, and Brown, 1823), 24.

254 **"When I was a schoolboy":** Walter Prescott Webb, *The Great Plains* (New York: Grosset & Dunlap, 1973), 152.

255 **flag atop a vertiginous:** "Frémont, John Charles," *American National Biography Online,* www.anb.org.

256 **"almost without limitation":** "Gilpin, William," *American National Biography Online,* www.anb.org.

256 **within an Isothermal Zodiac:** Charles N. Glaab, "Visions of Metropolis: William Gilpin and Theories of City Growth in the American West," *The Wisconsin Magazine of History* 45, no. 1 (Autumn 1961), 24.

257 **"You can lay track":** John Warfield Simpson, *Visions of Paradise: Glimpses of Our Landscape's Legacy* (Berkeley: University of California Press, 1999), 95.

258 **"a gradual increase in moisture":** Ibid., 95.

258 **"Divine task! Immortal mission!":** William Gilpin, *Mission of the North American People, Geographical, Social, and Political* (Philadelphia: J. P. Lippincott & Co., 1873), 124.

259 **"that the day was won":** Joseph Stanley-Brown, "John Wesley Powell: Memorial Address Delivered Before the Literary Society, December 13, 1902," Darrah Papers, Box 2 Folder 7, Mss B-361.

260 **most brazen gamble of his career:** Wallace Stegner, *Beyond the Hundredth Meridian: John Wesley Powell and the Second Opening of the West* (New York: Penguin Books, 1954), 229

260 **"most remarkable books ever written":** Ibid., xxii.

261 **"perennially yield bountiful crops":** J. W. Powell, "Report on the Lands of the Arid Region of the United States," House of Representatives, Ex. Doc. No. 73, 45th Congress, 2nd Session, viii.

262 **arid cultures stood or fell:** W. R. Gardner, "Some Thoughts on Report on the Lands of the Arid Region of the United States by J. W. Powell," *Society & Natural Resources* 1, no. 1 (1988): 88.

264 **"organization now under my charge":** "Surveys of the Territories. Letter from the Acting President of the National Academy of Sciences transmitting a report on the surveys of the Territories," December 3, 1878, House of Representatives, 45th Congress, 3rd Session, Misc. Doc. No. 5, 11.

264 **leading to an unhealthy rivalry:** Ibid., 16.

265 **"The time must soon come":** Ibid., 20.

266 **"attempt to transform a savage":** Ibid., 26.

267 **"renounces all claim or desire":** Worster, *A River Running West*, 364.

267 **"no one episode illustrates":** Stanley-Brown, "John Wesley Powell."

268 **He was a "wretched geologist":** Worster, *A River Running West*, 365.

268 **"is an enemy of mine":** Foster, *Strange Genius*, 299.

270 **"its rugged mineral-seamed mountains":** Henry Nash Smith, "Clarence King, John Wesley Powell, and the Establishment of the United States Geological Survey," 48.

272 **"My blood was stirred:** Ibid., 55.

273 **"Hamlet with Hamlet left [out]":** Ibid., 56.

CHAPTER 10: TAKING OVER WASHINGTON

274 **"remains in an inchoate condition":** Worster, *A River Running West*, 371.

277 **"I congratulate you":** Ibid., 392.

277 **had championed geology:** Edward Orton, "Geological Surveys of Ohio," *The Journal of Geology* 2, no. 5 (July–August 1894): 508.

278 **Powell had lent Garfield:** Darrah, *Powell of the Colorado*, 17.

278 **"the General had again arranged":** Joseph Stanley-Brown, "An Eventful Career," Darrah Papers, Box 2 Folder 7, Mss B-361.

278 **"been far more than just":** Hayden to Powell, March 22, 1881, in Worster, *A River Running West*, 415.

280 **"cool, dry, and ample" air:** "Report of Prof. Simon Newcomb, U.S. Navy," *Reports of Officers of the Navy on Ventilating and Cooling the Executive Mansion During the Illness of President Garfield* (Washington, D.C.: Government Printing Office, 1882), 3–5.

280 **replacing King's decentralized organization:** Preston Cloud, "The Improbable Bureaucracy: The United States Geological Survey, 1879–1979," *Proceedings of the American Philosophical Society* 124, no. 3 (June 30, 1980): 158.

281 **identifying the nation's mineral wealth:** "Report of the Secretary of the Interior," 46th Congress, 3rd Session, House Ex. Doc. 1, Pt. 5, Vol. 2, 389.

281 **growing needs of the iron:** Mary C. Rabbitt, "The United States Geological Survey: 1879–1989," U.S. Geological Survey Circular 1050 (1989), 11.

281 **developing theories of ore formation:** Manning, 70.

281 **King, the man of mountains:** Pyne, *Gilbert*, 114.

282 **1.2 billion acres of land:** Rabbitt, "The United States Geological Survey," 10.

282 **despite a request for $500,000:** R. T. Evans and H. M. Frye, "History of the Topographic Branch (Division)," U.S. Geological Survey Circular 1341 (2009), 6.

283 **"extend the operations":** J. W. Powell, *Fourth Annual Report of the United States Geological Survey to the Secretary for the Interior 1882–'83* (Washington, D.C.: Government Printing Office, 1884), xiii.

283 **"three- or even four-dimensional":** Cloud, 160.

283 **three impressions per plate:** Scott Kirsch, "The Allison Commission and the National Map: Towards a Republic of Knowledge in Late Nineteenth-Century America," *Journal of Historical Geography* 36 (2010): 33.

284 **mapping 600,000 square miles:** Manning, 93.

284 **55,000 quadrangle maps:** Charles G. Groat, "The National Map—A Continuing, Critical Need for the Nation," *Photogrammetric Engineering & Remote Sensing* 69, no. 10 (October 2003): 1089.

284 **"cannot do any scientific work":** U.S. Senate Misc. Doc. 82, 49th Congress, 1st Session, 40.

284 **six-story Hooe Iron Building:** James W. Goode, *Capital Losses: A Cultural History of Washington's Destroyed Buildings* (Washington, D.C.: Smithsonian Books, 2003), 178–79, 338–39.

286 **"a stoic who suffered":** "John Wesley Powell: Proceedings of a Meeting Commemorative of His Distinguished Services, Held in Columbian University Under the Auspice of the Washington Academy of Sciences, February 16, 1903," *Proceedings of the Washington Academy of Sciences* 5 (1903): 129.

286 **"seeing analogies and making comparisons":** Edward Anthony Spitzka, "A Study of the Brain of the Late Major J. W. Powell," *American Anthropologist*, New Series 5, no. 4 (October–December 1903): 642.

286 **"half a dozen minds":** Pyne, *Gilbert*, 127.

287 **USGS collaborated with:** Andrew S. Kelly, "The Political Development of Scientific Capacity in the United States," *Studies in American Political Development* 28 (April 2014), 19.

287 **new divisions at Harvard:** Ibid., 24.

287 **an indoor picnic:** Darrah, *Powell of the Colorado*, 162, 323.

287 **seven-year-old daughter, Bessie:** Pyne, *Gilbert*, 161; Darrah, *Powell of the Colorado*, 282–83.

288 **population rise from 75,000:** Scott Kirsch, "Regions of Government Science: John Wesley Powell in Washington and the American West," *Endeavor* 23, no. 4 (1999): 157.

288 **three thousand gaslights:** Leonard D. White, *The Republican Era: 1869–1901: A Study in Administrative History* (New York: Macmillan, 1958), 3.

288 **"meet two or three times":** Kirsch, "Regions," 157.

289 **"Survey of such magnitude":** Powell to Becker, April 29, 1884, in Worster, *A River Running West*, 429.

290 **to secure greater efficiency:** Sen. Misc. Doc. 82, March 16, 1886, 49th Congress, 1st Session.

290 **combined annual budget:** Kirsch, "Allison Commission," 29.

291 **a federal science doctrine:** Ibid., 32.

292 **"we do not usually tell":** Ibid., 11.

292 **"it did not occur":** Ibid., 18.

293 **"power of improving the minds":** Ibid., 36.

294 **even more informed citizenry:** Ibid., 35.

294 **"ladies" on the payroll:** "Finding Against Hilgard," *New-York Tribune*, August 7, 1885, 2.

294 **without congressional authority:** *Cincinnati Commercial Tribune*, August 13, 1885, 1.

294 **Hayden had been sent:** *The Evening Star*, August 21, 1885, 1.

295 **"these scientific people cannot show":** *New York Herald*, September 18, 1885, 3.

295 **"gang of cheap newspaper men":** Worster, *A River Running West*, 429.

295 **"baseless and absurd":** "The Geological Survey," *New York Tribune*, November 9, 1885, 2.

295 **"abolish the whole survey":** John W. Powell, *On the Organization of Scientific Work of the General Government. Part 2—Additional Statements* (Washington, D.C.: Government Printing Office, 1886), 1014.

296 **"don't wish the Government":** Ibid., 1015.

296 **only the wealthy:** Powell to Allison, February 26, 1886, in Powell, *On the Organization*, 1070–84.

297 **"ambitious scheme of geology":** A. Hunter Dupree, *Science in the Federal Government* (New York: Harper & Row, Publishers, 1957), 215.

297 **"pernicious tendency" of certain bureaus:** *New York Times*, May 3, 1886.

CHAPTER 11: A TOUGH OPPONENT

301 **driving upward of 300,000 people:** K. John Holmes, "Pushing the Climate Frontier," *Nature* 501 (September 18, 2013): 311.

302 **"capable of supporting":** William D. Rowley, *The Bureau of Reclamation: Origins and Growth to 1945*, Vol. 1 (Denver, CO: U.S. Government Printing Office, 2006), 67.

302 **the sale of these tracts:** *Reno Evening Gazette*, October 17, 1888, 3.

303 **"public good presents no demand":** Grover Cleveland, Fourth Annual Message (first term), December 3, 1888, The American Presidency Project, www.presidency.ucsb.edu/ws/?pid=29529.

304 **identified 147 reservoir sites:** Donald J. Pisani, To *Reclaim a Divided West: Water, Law, and Public Policy, 1848-1902* (Albuquerque: University of New Mexico Press, 1992), 163, 164.

304 **would travel to the Dakotas:** Russell R. Elliot, *Servant of Power: A Political Biography of Senator William M. Stewart* (Reno: University of Nevada Press, 1983), 114.

305 **forced the resignation:** Michael W. Bowers, *The Nevada State Constitution* (New York: Oxford University Press, 2011), 17–18.

305 **claimed that "Stewart's Castle":** Kathryn Allamong Jacob, *Capital Elites: High Society in Washington, D.C., after the Civil War* (Washington, D.C.: Smithsonian Institution Press, 1995), 82.

305 **"grew jealous of the attentions":** *The Daily Critic*, June 11, 1890, 1.

305 **"Hold the waters":** "Official Report of the Proceedings and Debates of the First Constitutional Convention of North Dakota, Assembled in the City of Bismarck, July 4–August 17, 1889," (Bismarck, ND: Tribune State Printers, 1889), 412.

306 **"Such monopoly by the speculators":** *The Cheyenne Daily Leader*, July 30, 1889, 1.

306 **to irrigate 200,000 acres:** Pisani, 148.

306 **suspended 134,000 filings and entries:** Ibid., 150.

306 **"The segregation of irrigable lands"**: *Rocky Mountain News,* January 21, 1889.

307 **"generated more venom"**: Wallace Stegner, *Beyond the Hundredth Meridian,* 324.

308 **"Scientists Wage Bitter Warfare"**: *New York Herald,* January 12, 1890, 10.

308 **integrating water rights**: Holmes, "Pushing," 311.

309 **had failed to reckon**: J. W. Powell, "The Lesson of Conemaugh," *The North American Review* 149, no. 393 (August 1889), 154.

310 **"What these people want is"**: Report of the Special Committee of the United States Senate on the Irrigation and Reclamation of Arid Lands. 51st Congress, 1st Session, Sen. Rpt. 928, Pt. 5, 90.

310 **"What we want now"**: Ibid., 95.

311 **By all accounts**: For these and other details about Dutton, see Wallace E. Stegner, "C.E. Dutton—Explorer, Geologist, Nature Writer," *The Scientific Monthly* 45, no. 1 (July 1937), 83.

313 **"has been better spent"**: Report of the Special Committee, Pt. 5, 146.

314 **approach as a "one-sided affair"**: Ibid., 169–70.

314 **"great blunders . . . involving"**: Ibid., 183, 186.

314 **"I would rather be defeated"**: Stewart to M. L. Power, May 29, 1890, in John M. Townley, "Reclamation in Nevada, 1850–1904" (PhD diss., University of Nevada, Reno, 1976), 161, 167.

315 **lest lands and waters fall**: Report of the Special Committee, Pt. 1, 135.

315 **"hydraulic feudal system"**: *Evening Star,* May 28, 1890.

315 **"a mass of humbug"**: *Evening Star,* May 29, 1890.

316 **"drunk with power"**: Worster, *A River Running West,* 502.

316 **"a frequent, almost daily visitor"**: *The Daily Critic,* June 11, 1890, 1.

316 **Noble categorically denied**: "Letter from the Secretary of the Interior," 51st Congress, 1st Session, Senate Ex. Doc. 141, 2–8.

316 **"charged Reagan with falsehood"**: *The Daily Critic,* June 13, 1890.

317 **"almost a criminal act"**: Sundry Civil Appropriations Bill, 51st, 1st Session, Sen. Rpt. 1466, 60.

317 **"Senator, in the first place"**: Ibid., 79.

318 **"self-government by hydrographic basins"**: J. W. Powell, "Institutions for the Arid Lands," *Century Illustrated Magazine* 40, no. 1 (May 1890), 114.

320 **"to the Government: Hands off!"**: Ibid., 113.

320 **"better servants than wild clouds"**: J. W. Powell, "The Irrigable Lands of the Arid Region," *Century Illustrated Magazine* 39, no. 5 (March 1890): 768, 766.

320 **"powers of the National Government"**: Pisani, 164.

322 **"tycoon of many tails"**: *Evening Star,* July 17, 1890.

323 **not return to classifying lands**: Rowley, 66.

324 **"likes strong loyalty"**: Mary C. Rabbitt, *Minerals, Lands, and Geology for the Common Defence and General Welfare. Vol. 2, 1879–1904* (Washington, D.C.: U.S. Government Printing Office, 1980), 213.

325 **"Whatsoever might be bold"**: Clarence E. Dutton, *Tertiary History of the Grand Cañon District* (Washington, D.C.: U.S. Government Printing Office, 1882), 141–42.

CHAPTER 12: LAST STAND

326 **twenty-five-day "grand excursion"**: Clifford M. Nelson, "The Fifth International Geological Congress, 1891," *Episodes* 29, no. 4, 279; W. M. Davis,

Biographical Memoir of John Wesley Powell (Washington, D.C.: The National Academy of Sciences, 1915), 56.

327 **"good humor prevailed.":** K. R. Aalto, "The 'Grand Excursion' of the Fifth International Geological Congress (1891): Celebrating geological exploration of the American West," *Rocky Mountain Geology* 46, no. 1 (Spring 2011), 98.

327 **"We have nothing comparable":** Worster, *A River Running West,* 510.

327 **Powell accepted the Cuvier Prize:** Aalto, 99.

328 **Senate cut the survey's budget:** Manning, 204.

328 **560 state and private banks:** A. Bower Sageser, "Los Angeles Hosts an International Irrigation Congress," *Journal of the West* 4, no. 3 (1965): 411.

329 **"not merely a matter":** William E. Smythe, *The Conquest of Arid America* (New York: The Macmillan Company, 1907), 267.

329 **"but a sterile wilderness":** "The Arid Land," *San Francisco Chronicle,* March 3, 1889, 6.

329 **applauded the choice of venue:** "An Important Gathering," *Los Angeles Times,* July 10, 1893, 4.

329 **delegates gawked at:** Sageser, 421; *Official Report of the International Irrigation Congress, Held at Los Angeles, California* (Los Angeles: Los Angeles Chamber of Commerce, 1893), 5.

331 **Very heated remarks were made:** *Albuquerque Morning Democrat,* October 14, 1893: 1.

331 **"first sensation of the delegates":** *The Irrigation Age* 5, no. 7 (November 1893): 148.

332 **"[T]he powers of nature":** "Annual Address of the President," *Bulletin of the Philosophical Society of Washington* 6 (1884), LII.

333 **ARID AMERICA IS FIGHTING:** *The Irrigation Age* 5, no. 7, 147.

333 **in the best of odor:** "Irrigating Arid Lands," *San Francisco Chronicle,* October 16, 1893, 4.

333 **total under cultivation today:** Worster, *A River Running West,* 530.

334 **"America's version of the Egyptian":** Howard G. Wilshire, Jane E. Nielson, and Richard W. Hazlett, *The American West at Risk: Science, Myths, and Politics of Land Abuse and Recovery* (New York: Oxford University Press, 2008), 231.

334 **never crystallized coherent:** Pisani, 334.

335 **"by sheer force of character":** "Twenty-Third Annual Report of the Director of the United States Geological Survey to the Secretary of the Interior, 1901–2" (Washington, D.C.: U.S. Government Printing Office, 1902), 12.

EPILOGUE

339 **irrigate nearly six million acres:** David Owen, *Where the Water Goes: Life and Death Along the Colorado River* (New York: Riverhead Books, 2017), 6.

339 **Every locality wanted:** Marc Reisner, *Cadillac Desert* (New York: Penguin Books, 1993), 116.

339 **not enough river water for everyone:** John Fleck, "Taking more water from the Colorado River's upper basin," June 23, 2015, http://inkstain.net/fleck/.

340 **a curious omen befell Washington:** H. H. Bennett, "Tons of Dirt from Central Plains Deluged City," *Washington Post,* March 10, 1935, B9; "D.C. Invaded by Dust Storm from Midwest," *Washington Post,* March 22, 1935, 1.

341 **relying too heavily on:** USGS Third Annual Irrigation Survey, see K. John Holmes, "A historical perspective on climate change assessment," *Climactic Change* 129, no. 1–2 (March 2015): 353.

342 **"common practice of public fraud":** C. D. Wilber, *The Great Valleys and Prairies of Nebraska and the Northwest* (Omaha: Daily Republican Print, 1881), 71.

342 **"Irrigation emerged as an individual":** National Research Council, *New Era for Irrigation* (Washington, D.C.: National Academies Press, 1996), 6.

342 **will also take time:** K. John Holmes, "Pushing the Climate Frontier," *Nature* 501 (September 19, 2013), 311.

Index